# The Eighteenth Century in Sikh History

# The Eighteenth Century in Sikh History

## Political Resurgence, Religious and Social Life, and Cultural Articulation

Karamjit K. Malhotra

OXFORD

UNIVERSITY PRESS

# OXFORD
UNIVERSITY PRESS

Oxford University Press is a department of the University of Oxford.
It furthers the University's objective of excellence in research, scholarship,
and education by publishing worldwide. Oxford is a registered trademark of
Oxford University Press in the UK and in certain other countries

Published in India by
Oxford University Press
22 Workspace, 2nd Floor, 1/22 Asaf Ali Road, New Delhi 110002, India

ISBN-13: 978-0-19-946354-1
ISBN-10: 0-19-946354-9

Typeset in ScalaPro 10.5/13
by Tranistics Data Technologies, New Delhi 110 044
Printed in India by Manipal Technologies limited, Manipal

*For my parents*
*Dalip Singh Malhotra and Sheetal Kaur*
*and*
*my late grandmother*
*Satwant Kaur*
*with much affection and gratitude*

# Contents

*List of Figures*                                                    ix
*Preface*                                                             xi
*Acknowledgements*                                                    xiii

Introduction: Scope, Sources, and
Debate about Dates                                                    1

### Part I  Sikh Political Resurgence and Sikh Polity

1. 'Rāj Karegā Khālsā'                                                19
2. The Khalsa Rāj (1765–99)                                           59

### Part II  Religious and Social Life

3. God, Guru, and Gurdwārā                                            101
4. Rites and Ceremonies                                               142
5. Ethical Concerns of the Khalsa                                     170
6. The Sikh Social Order: Composition, Caste,
   and Gender                                                         192

### Part III  Cultural Articulation

7. The Old and New Literary Forms                                     233
8. Painting and Architecture                                          256

Conclusion: Convergence on Sikh Identity                    281


*Appendix: The Goddess in Eighteenth-Century Sikh Literature*    290
*Glossary*                                                       301
*Select Bibliography*                                            313
*Index*                                                          329
*About the Author*                                               342

# Figures

I.1  The Region                                              xvi

1.1  The Mughal Dominions (Early Eighteenth
     Century)                                                31
1.2  The Punjab (Late Eighteenth Century)                    47

8.1  A King Pays Homage to Guru Nanak            Between 256
                                                     and 257
8.2  Disciples of Bal Nath Come to Meet
     Guru Nanak                                  Between 256
                                                     and 257
8.3  Portrait of Tara Singh Gheba                Between 256
                                                     and 257

# Preface

The eighteenth century is remarkable for major political changes in Indian history. In the Mughal province of Lahore (Punjab), it was marked by a political revolution in which first the authority of the Mughal governors and then of Ahmad Shah Abdali was replaced largely by the erstwhile peasants and artisans who had joined the Khalsa order instituted by Guru Gobind Singh. The present study explores the remarkable transformation in the religious, social, and cultural life of the Sikhs at the time, and takes a fresh look at their political struggle and polity.

As it emerges from this book, the eighteenth century served as a bridge between the Sikh tradition of the sixteenth and seventeenth centuries and the later history of Sikhs. Before the end of the period, the 'Sikh' came to be equated with the 'Singh', who dominated not only politically but also numerically and ideologically, constituting thus the mainstream of the Sikh social order. Cumulatively, these developments contributed towards the crystallization of a distinctive Sikh identity.

Scholars located in several disciplines have taken interest in different aspects of Sikh history in the eighteenth century. My conclusions are often different from their views, but I have generally desisted from entering into controversies. I have concentrated on sources of the eighteenth century in order to understand the period on its own terms.

This work is a substantially revised version of my doctoral thesis completed in 2009 under the supervision of Professor Indu Banga, now Professor Emeritus in the Department of History at

Panjab University, Chandigarh. I am grateful to Professor Banga for her continued guidance, meticulous care, and kind support in general. I had the privilege of discussing my work with Professor J.S. Grewal. He allowed me access to his library, and was generous with his time. He was particularly helpful with the use of Persian sources. Unsparing with his criticism, Professor Grewal made me think and rethink about several aspects of the subject. Over all this time he has been a source of inspiration for me.

Over the years I have incurred the debt of several eminent historians, social scientists, scholars of Sikh Studies, and Punjabi and English literature. I am particularly thankful to a number of senior scholars at the institutions and universities at Patiala, Chandigarh, Amritsar, Ludhiana, Delhi, Aligarh, Kolkata, Santiniketan, and Kharagpur in West Bengal, and the UK, USA, and Canada for their appreciation of my efforts. I wish to acknowledge the benefit derived from my interactions with Professor Gurinder Singh Mann, until recently Kapany Professor for Sikh and Punjab Studies, University of California, Santa Barbara. I am indebted to Professor Irfan Habib and Professor Shireen Moosvi of Aligarh Muslim University, Aligarh, for their gracious hospitality and kind interest in my work. My informal discussions at Santiniketan with Professor Mandakranta Bose of the University of British Columbia, Vancouver, were immensely helpful. I would also like to acknowledge the encouragement received from Professor Reeta Grewal of Panjab University and help received from Professor Sheena Pall from time to time.

The maps in this volume were prepared to the specifications of the publishers by S. Mohan Singh, cartographer at the Centre of Advanced Study in Geography at Panjab University. Komal prepared the final manuscript with diligence and care. I am thankful to them.

On the personal front, I wish to thank my family for their moral support and interest.

**Karamjit K. Malhotra**

# Acknowledgements

I gratefully acknowledge the award of Junior Research Fellowship of the Indian Council of Historical Research, New Delhi, for pursing this study.

I am also indebted to a number of other institutions, their keepers, and their staff. In the course of working on this book, I consulted published and unpublished sources in various repositories, libraries, and personal collections. Bhai Kahan Singh Library, Punjabi University, Patiala, where I saw over fifty special collections, is one of the richest repositories for research in Sikh and Punjab history. For help in various ways, I am thankful to its former and present librarians, Dr Davinder Kaur and Dr Saroj Bala; and to Dr Mehar Kaur, who looks after the library of the Department of Punjab Historical Studies at this University. I could access several important sources at Bhai Gurdas Library, Guru Nanak Dev University, Amritsar, for which I am thankful to Dr H.S. Chopra, then the university librarian. I saw rare books and manuscripts at Dr Balbir Singh Sahitya Kendra, Dehradun. I recall the hospitality of its late director, Smt. Mohinder Kaur, with affection. I also got useful materials from the Punjab Languages Department Library, and Central Public Library, at Patiala; Sikh History Research Department Library, Khalsa College, Amritsar; and A.C. Joshi Library, Panjab University, and Dwarka Das Library, both at Chandigarh. I saw some material at Vishveshvaranand Vedic Research Institute, Hoshiarpur, as well. Outside Punjab, I located some unpublished files and rare books at the National Archives of India, New Delhi; made use of the libraries of the Indian Institute of Advanced Study, Shimla, and the Centre of

Advance Study in History at the Aligarh Muslim University, Aligarh; consulted manuscripts at the Asiatic Society and the National Library, both in Kolkata; and also at the Harmandar Sahib and the Khuda Baksh Oriental Public Library, Patna. I recall with gratitude that Dr Imtiaz Ahmad, the then director of the Khuda Baksh Library, was particularly helpful during my stay in Patna.

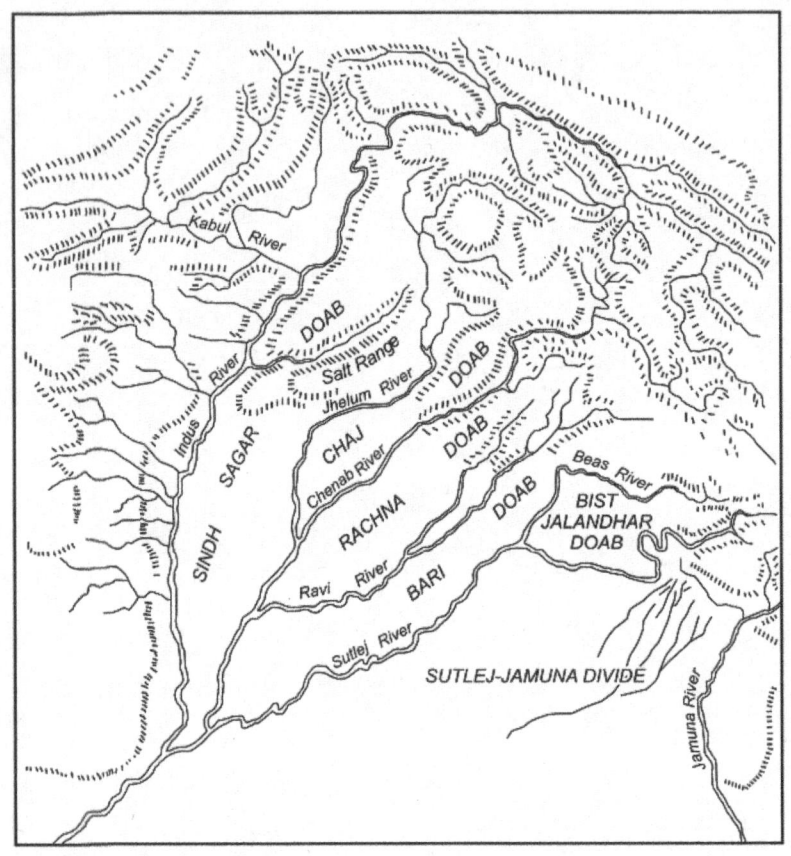

**FIGURE I.1**   The Region
*Source:* Adapted from Map 1, in J.S. Grewal, *The Sikhs of the Punjab, The New Cambridge History of India*, II.3 (New Delhi: Cambridge University Press, 2014).

# Introduction

*Scope, Sources, and Debate about Dates*

The rise of Sikhs into political power during the eighteenth century is regarded as one of the most significant developments in the history of the Punjab region (see Figure I.1). Early British historians looked upon the institution of the Khalsa as the dividing line between the history of the Sikhs as a religious community and the history of the Khalsa as a political entity.[1] The strength of this historiographical tradition is reflected in the works of the twentieth-century Indian historians like N.K. Sinha and Hari Ram Gupta who dwell almost exclusively on the political history of the Sikhs and their government during the eighteenth century.[2] Teja Singh and Ganda Singh talk of the 'religious foundations' of the Sikh Panth under the Sikh Gurus and its 'political foundations' under Banda Singh, leading eventually to the emergence of the Khalsa as a sovereign power.[3]

The recent work on the eighteenth-century Khalsa by Purnima Dhavan is meant to pose a challenge to any simplistic reading of the Khalsa warrior tradition. The author concedes that the ethical and spiritual dimension of the Sikh practice was an important factor in the situation, but asserts that the Khalsa and their allies did not think in terms of a single homogeneous spiritual practice. Furthermore, the demand of political alliances, campaigns, kinship loyalties, and their own circumstances constantly forced the Khalsa to reconcile, interrogate, and, at times, wilfully ignore what it meant to be a Khalsa. Thus, not ideology alone but the empirical realities around also became relevant for the making of the Khalsa warrior tradition. In this context Dhavan uses some contemporary works of Sikh literature to clarify or support her basic hypothesis. Despite the relative novelty of her approach, Dhavan's work remains confined to the political domain.[4]

As a legacy of early British historical writing on Sikhs, the eighteenth-century Sikh polity has been equated with the 'Khalsa Commonwealth' or the 'misaldārī system' on the argument, or with the implication, that Ranjit Singh (1780–1839) put an end to this system and replaced it by a monarchical government. On this assumption, Bhagat Singh makes an elaborate study of Sikh polity.[5] This conceptualization has been questioned by J.S. Grewal in a few seminal essays,[6] and Indu Banga has given a cogent exposition of the late eighteenth-century Sikh polity, extending its scope to political organization, collection, and distribution of land revenue and landed rights, viewing the state of Ranjit Singh largely as a continuum of the period of Sikh rule in the late eighteenth century.[7]

## SCOPE

During the past three or four decades, controversies in Sikh studies have raised issues which touch upon some new dimensions of Sikh history during the eighteenth century, highlighting the importance of themes like Sikh identity, the doctrines of Granth as the Guru (Guru Granth) and Panth as the Guru (Guru Panth), history and status of what is now called the *Dasam Granth*, the Khalsa *rahit* (way of life), and the issues of caste and gender.[8] Some notice has also been taken of Sikh literature and art of the period as well as Sikh ethics. Evidently, these non-political aspects suggest the possibility of an integrated approach to the religious, political, social, and cultural life of Sikhs during the eighteenth century.[9]

The present study covers all the major aspects, which are more or less interrelated, of the history of eighteenth-century Sikhs. The processes of political struggle and state formation were intimately linked with the activities of Guru Gobind Singh on the one hand and social re-formation of the Khalsa on the other. The Sikh rulers and ruling class appeared for the first time in the socio-political order marked by the dominance of the erstwhile lower castes. No hierarchy was upheld in principle and even former outcastes were, in some ways, treated as equals. The issues of caste and gender in the Sikh social order acquired an added importance in the context of the ongoing tension between the norm of equality and the existing realities. The sectarian lines of division were not obliterated, but the Khalsa identity became the predominant Sikh identity by the end of the eighteenth century.

Like their politics, social cohesion among the Khalsa was undertowed by their religious doctrines and institutions. The twin doctrine of Guru Granth and Guru Panth became the basis of the principle of unity and equality among the Khalsa. The sanctity of the *gurdwārā* was enhanced by the presence of the *sangat* (congregation) and the Granth (regarded as the Guru). Gurdwaras associated with the Gurus became the places of Sikh pilgrimage. The Harmandar (also spelt as Harmandir and called Darbār Sāhib and known popularly as the Golden Temple) in Amritsar emerged as the foremost place of Sikh worship and pilgrimage. Distinctly, Sikh ceremonies and rites in which the Brahman had no key role to play began to be evolved, advocated, and adopted. The ethical norms and the norms of Sikh belief and practice were the same for all members of the Khalsa order. The remarkable cultural articulation among the Sikhs from the last decades of the seventeenth century to the last decades of the eighteenth century was related as much to the institution of the Khalsa as to the establishment of Sikh rule. Some old forms of Sikh literature were modified and some new literary forms appeared during the century. Similarly, the interests of the new rulers and the possibilities of patronage from them had a direct bearing on the artistic and architectural activities of the Sikhs during the late eighteenth century.

## SOURCES

The wide scope of this study is matched by the wide range of contemporary sources used for it. Much of the evidence used covers historical and non-historical works in Gurmukhi, Persian, and English. Furthermore, the literary works in Gurmukhi contain very largely the evidence that relates to the social and cultural life of Sikhs during the eighteenth century, unlike the sources in Persian and English, which dwell largely on Sikh political activity and organization. I may emphasize that I have tried to make exhaustive rather than selective use of sources in all the three scripts. To these sources are added some archival, administrative, and legal documents, and the *hukamnāmās* (written orders) of the period. The material objects that throw light on the subject consist mainly of coins, monuments, and paintings.

Of all the forms of evidence on the religious, social, and political life of Sikhs during the eighteenth century, the contemporary works in Gurmukhi are the most comprehensive, but their importance is unequal, depending on their form, subject matter, and date. Much controversy has arisen from the confusion regarding the dates of contemporary sources, and some important misconceptions have emerged as much due to an excessive dependence on the later sources, as to a perfunctory attitude towards Gurmukhi literature. I have tried to make full use of eighteenth-century Sikh literature and take a rounded view of the period. Ample consideration is given to what the sources have to say, analysing each source as a whole for a proper appreciation of its evidence. This evidence is compared with that of the other Gurmukhi works and the works in Persian and English.

The *rahitnāmā* form elaborating the Khalsa way of life appears to be more important than the others in so far as it sets the religious, social, and political goals for the Khalsa. Within this form there can be qualitative and quantitative differences between any two works. The subject matter of a particular source related directly to the eighteenth-century Khalsa is more important for our present purpose. But presentation of the earlier period remains relevant for the eighteenth-century view of Sikhs on their past. The normative statements in the rahitnāmās are complemented and supplemented by empirical evidence from the narratives of the activities of the tenth Guru and the Khalsa, and from the non-Sikh sources, which professedly refer to realities. Extensive use of this evidence has been combined with the seventeenth-century background, taking note of the bearing of Sikh ideology on the political, religious, social, and cultural developments of the eighteenth century. It is axiomatic that the relative reliability of a work and its value for the historian would depend ultimately on the date of its composition.

## DEBATE ABOUT DATES

For the dates of the rahitnāmās we may start with W.H. McLeod whose work on this subject is generally treated as reliable. He looks at his own contribution as consisting of three instalments which are historiographical in import: (a) *The Chaupa Singh Rahit-Nama* (1987), (b) *Sikhs of the Khalsa: A History of the Khalsa Rahit* (2003), and (c) *Prem Sumārag: The Testimony of a Sanatan Sikh* (2006). About *The Chaupa Singh Rahit-Nama* McLeod maintains that this rahitnāmā was the earliest, dating apparently from the middle of the eighteenth century (between 1740 and 1765). The *Prem Sumārag*, for McLeod, initially belonged to the middle years of the nineteenth century. It is 'impossible', says McLeod, to draw adequate conclusions about the four rahitnāmās in verse, two of which are attributed to Nand Lal and one each to Prahilad Rai (or Prahilad Singh/ Prihlad Singh) and Desa Singh. Since the prose rahitnāmā (*Sākhī Rahit Pātisāhī 10 / Sākhī Rahit Kī*), attributed to Nand Lal, is invariably found attached to *The Chaupa Singh Rahit-Nama*, McLeod is inclined to place it in the middle years of the eighteenth century. The other prose rahitnāmā attributed to Daya Singh appears to McLeod to be a work of the early nineteenth century.[10]

Before McLeod's *Sikhs of the Khalsa* was published in 2003, Jeevan Singh Deol took note of a copy of the *Tankhānāmā* of Nand Lal in the Library of Guru Nanak Dev University in Amritsar.[11] This copy was bound with a number of several other works in MS 770, dated 1718–19. Referring to it as a 'dramatic' discovery, Mcleod felt obliged to place the *Tankhānāmā* (called *Nasīhatnāmā* in MS 770) within a few years of Guru Gobind Singh's death. The *Sākhī Rahit Pātisāhī 10* (also spelt as *Pātsāhī* and *Pātshāhī*) and the rahitnāmā attributed to Prahilad Rai or Prahilad Singh were now advanced to the 1730s. The rahitnāmās of Desa Singh and Daya Singh were placed in the late eighteenth or the early nineteenth century, close to 1800. The *Prashan-uttar* (called rahitnāmā by Ganda Singh and Piara Singh Padam) of Bhai Nand Lal was not a typical rahitnāmā for McLeod; it was predominantly a doctrinal statement about the threefold nature or signification of the 'Guru'. The date of its composition given in the text (4 December 1695) was open to doubt, but McLeod was prepared to place it in the time of the tenth Guru, sometime in the late 1690s. McLeod entertained the possibility, albeit remote or slender, of the well-known Bhai Nand Lal Goya being the author of this work. McLeod then goes into some detail of the views of other scholars on the date of composition of the *Prem Sumārag*, and moves from the middle years of the nineteenth century to the middle or later part of the reign of Ranjit Singh.[12]

In his third instalment on this genre, McLeod goes into the question of dating the *Prem Sumārag*. The discovery of a composite manuscript of 1815 induced him to place it 'at least in the early years of the nineteenth century and probably back in the eighteenth century'.[13] Finally, in a subsequent article, he places the *Prem Sumārag* in the late eighteenth century.[14] Thus, whereas several other scholars had placed this rahitnāmā in the early eighteenth century, McLeod moved reluctantly from the mid-nineteenth to the late eighteenth century, looking for the discovery of dated manuscripts.

However, in Gurinder Singh Mann's view, the *Prem Sumārag* 'marked the peak among the rahit documents produced at Anandpur' and it harmonized 'with Sikh religious, social and political aspiration of the rule of the *deg* and *tegh*'. He claims to have examined several manuscripts, including a copy prepared in 1707. He goes on to point out that the reference made by its first editor, Bhai Randhir Singh, to a manuscript of 1701 seen by him acquires enhanced credibility. In any case, Mann places the *Prem Sumārag* squarely within the lifetime of Guru Gobind Singh.[15]

In the past decade some other rahitnāmās too have come to be seen in a different light. On the basis of a close study of the *Nasīhatnāmā* in MS 770, I have suggested that there is nothing in its contents against the assumption that it was written during the time of Guru Gobind Singh.[16] Mann, in fact, is inclined to place it in the late 1690s. A manuscript of the rahitnāmā of Chaupa Singh seen by Mann bears the date 1700. He argues convincingly that the preface and a set of prescriptions that follow constitute the original core, to which the remaining sections were added later. He is emphatic that the preface and the prescriptive part have a 'clear literary integrity, standing as independent unit of text, and the sections that follow have distinct characteristics of their own'. Mann rightly underlines that the importance of the rahitnāmā of Chaupa Singh 'cannot be overstated'.[17]

In this context Mann makes the general statement that whereas other historians tend to ignore the colophons in the extant manuscripts or printed texts, he does not find any reason to be sceptical. McLeod, for instance, does not take the colophons into serious consideration in dating the rahitnāmās. For Mann, 'the rise of these documents at Anandpur makes lot more sense than would any other time during the eighteenth century'. Indeed, colophons, texts, and contexts go together. Mann places the rahitnāmā of Prahilad Singh early in 1697 on the basis of eight extant manuscripts of this work. By implication, it was written in Anandpur (equated with 'Abchal Nagar' or 'the city eternal' of the text). Similarly, he accepts Sammat 1752 (1694) as the year in which Bhai Nand Lal's *Prashan-uttar* was first recorded.[18] In a recent essay, J.S. Grewal has come to the conclusion that no feature in the text of the *Sākhī Rahit* goes against the assumption that it was a work from the lifetime of Guru Gobind Singh. Indeed, it could have been originally composed around 1700.[19]

Turning to the other Sikh literary works of the eighteenth century, it may be noted that there has been general agreement about the dates of only a small number of these: the *B40 Janamsākhī* (1733), the *Bansāvalīnāmā Dasān Pātshāhiān Kā* (1769), the *Mahimā Prakāsh* (1776), the *Gurū Kiān Sākhiān* (1790), and Sukha Singh's *Gurbilās Pātsāhī 10* (1797). It may, however, be mentioned that the manuscripts of the *Bansāvalīnāmā* bear the date 1779 as well as 1769, and that there are references in its text to occurrences later than 1779.[20] In the case of the *Gurū Kiān Sākhiān*, it has been pointed out that 1790 was the date of the manuscript in Bhattakhari, the script used by the Bhatts. It was transliterated into Gurmukhi in 1868, and a copy of this Gurmukhi manuscript was used for editing. Mistakes could occur at all these three stages: once for transliteration and twice for copying. There is no way in which such mistakes can now be corrected because no manuscript of the *Gurū Kiān Sākhiān* is available anymore. Nevertheless, the years 1769 and 1790 remain the generally acceptable dates for the *Bansāvalīnāmā* and the *Gurū Kiān Sākhiān* respectively.[21]

The *Parchiān* of Sewa Das has *sākhīs* (episodes) on all the ten Gurus, but mostly on Guru Gobind Singh. Raijasbir Singh argues that this work was written between 1711 and 1737 and not in 1741, as claimed by Ganda Singh on the basis of a manuscript of that date.[22] Hari Singh, the editor of its text, places it in 1708 on the basis of the date given in the manuscript he used. He points out, however, that the description of Nander on the death of Guru Gobind Singh could not be true for 1708. Kharak Singh and Gurtej Singh, who have translated and edited this work, accept the date 1708, explaining that the description of Nander varies in copies made at different times because Nander was developing as a centre of pilgrimage for the Sikhs. They maintain that the manuscript edited by Hari Singh was completed in October 1708.[23] Gurinder Singh Mann, who has actually seen a manuscript completed in 1709, confirms that the *Parchian* was written soon after the death of Guru Gobind Singh.[24]

Jasbir Singh Sabar, the editor of the *Gian Ratnavali*, refers to eighteen known manuscripts of this work. He is aware of W.H. McLeod's argument that its extant versions could not be the work of Bhai Mani Singh because he is mentioned in the third person in the prologue and the epilogue. Contrary to the suggestion of Surjit Hans that the author of this work was an Udasi, Sabar argues at length that the *Gian Ratnavali* was composed by Bhai Surat Singh, who belonged to the Damdami Taksal founded by Bhai Mani Singh. For the date of the *Gian Ratnavali*, Sabar argues that in all probability it was composed in Amritsar in 1770.[25]

Another work attributed to Bhai Surat Singh is the *Sikhan di Bhagatmala*, also called *Bhagat Ratnavali*. It has been edited by S.S. Padam who places its completion between 1778 and 1783. The original manuscript was destroyed, but the earliest available manuscript was a copy of 1798. The editor says that forty-eight manuscripts of this work are available and twenty-one of them carry dates. The number of sakhis in the manuscripts of the basic tradition is 160. The text consists of 30 pauris (stanzas) of Bhai Gurdas and 160 sakhis, including those related to all the ten Gurus.[26]

The collection of sakhis known as the *Mahima Prakash* (*Vartak*) has been published recently and its editor, Kulwinder Singh Bajwa, discusses its date, ranging from 1741 to the early nineteenth century, in the light of the views of other scholars. He comes to the conclusion that this work was composed in 1773.[27] Discussing the question of its date in some detail in a recent article, J.S. Grewal comes to the conclusion that there seems to be no reason why the *Mahimā Prakāsh (Vārtak)* should not be placed in 1824, the date it carries. It is also clear that this work is based almost entirely on two earlier works: the *Parchiān* of Sewa Das (1708–9), and Sarup Das Bhalla's *Mahimā Prakāsh* (1776).[28]

Another well-known collection of doubtful authenticity, popularly called the *Sau Sākhīs*, carries the title *Gur Ratan Māl* in the texts edited by Piara Singh Padam and Gurbachan Singh Nayyar.[29] The earliest manuscripts used by its editors were inscribed in the late 1830s. However, the date given in the text for the last sākhī is 1734 and for the rest 1724. The author's name is Bhai Sahib Singh. Both the editors point out that there are a number of prophecies that suggest that some of its contents came from a later date. What the editors do not mention, and what has not been observed by any other scholar, is that a large number of episodes in this work bear a clear imprint of the sākhīs in the *Parchiān Sewadās*. This raises the question whether the other sākhīs too were taken from some literary works. The episodes given in the *Sau Sākhīs* are either in prose, or in verse, or in both prose and verse. The sākhī form brings in narrative but the thrust of the work is on the rahit of the Khalsa. It is difficult, however, to be sure about the time of any of the sākhīs in this work. In fact, there is a remarkable indifference to chronology all through.

As regards the *vār* form of literature used for heroic poetry, we find that a number of vārs were written in the time of Guru Gobind Singh, including the *Vār Sri Bhagautī Jī Kī*, popularly known as the *Chandī dī Vār*.[30] The most popular vār of the eighteenth century is the *Ramkalī Vār Pātshāhī Dasven Kī*. Its author, 'Gurdas', refers to his composition as *Vār Bhagautī*. The editor of the *Vārān Bhai Gurdas*, which includes the *Vār Bhagautī*, points out that this work was also known as *Vār Sri Bhagautī Jī Kī Pātshāhī* 10. Furthermore, in some manuscripts there is a *dohrā* (couplet) at the end that mentions 'Gurdas Singh' as its author. A couplet in a copy of the work called the *Sarab Loh Granth*, which was compiled at the court of Guru Gobind Singh, states that Gurdas Singh completed his composition in 1700. The editor goes on to point out, however, that there is a reference in the available texts of this vār to the end of

the twelfth century of the Hijra calendar, which carries the implication that this vār was composed after 1787 (AH 1200). There is
also a reference to the end of the Mughal rule, followed by the
ascendancy of the Khalsa.[31] In his discussion on the Sikh sources
of the time of Guru Gobind Singh, Gurinder Singh Mann regrets
that the dating of 'this important composition is yet to receive the
attention it deserves'.[32]

A clue to this problem is found in the work of Piara Singh
Padam who attributes *Vār Bhagautī* to Bhai Gurdas the second,
who was a poet at Guru Gobind Singh's court. Padam points out
that the first fourteen stanzas of this vār are of six lines each, and
the last six stanzas are of twenty or twenty-eight lines each, written
in a somewhat different style and idiom. He suggests that the first
part represents the original vār of Bhai Gurdas the second, and the
remaining verses were added by an unknown poet probably in the
time of Ranjit Singh.[33] It may be added that in the work edited by
Padam the *Vār Rāmkalī Pātshāhī Dasvīn* consists of twenty stanzas,
unlike the vār in the *Vārān Bhai Gurdas*, which has twenty-eight
stanzas. In any case, the text of the *Vār Bhagautī* is a source both
for the beginning and the end of the eighteenth century.

Beginning with the *Gurbilās* genre narrating the life and exploits
of Guru Gobind Singh in verse, we find that the *Gur Sobhā* has
a special importance for the reference it makes to the vesting of
Guruship in the Khalsa and Gurbāṇī by Guru Gobind Singh a day
before his death. For its date, Akālī Kaur Singh had argued in 1927
that the year *athāvan* (Sammat 1758, AD 1701) in the text should be
read as *athānav* (Sammat 1798, AD 1741) to account for the events
of Guru Gobind Singh's life up to 1708 in its text. The year 1741
remained acceptable till the publication of a new edition of the
*Gur Sobhā* in 1969 in which Ganda Singh as its editor rejected
1741 on the argument that there was no reflection in the text of any
event after the death of Guru Gobind Singh for over three decades.
Ganda Singh refers to a later work that mentions Sammat 1768 (AD
1711) as the year of composition. Henceforth, the year 1711 became
increasingly acceptable.[34]

However, this date did not become quite acceptable to McLeod
for many years, and some important arguments in his own works
were based on the assumption that the *Gur Sobhā* was composed in

the 1740s. In 1984, McLeod refers to this work as 'variously dated 1711 and 1745'.[35] Five years later, he reiterates that its actual date is yet to be finally settled: 'The two contending dates are 1711 and 1745.' He goes on to say that the importance of the work would be greatly enhanced if 1711 was definitely established as the date of its composition. It would then be placed very close to the death of Guru Gobind Singh.[36] In 1997, McLeod sees a strong probability in favour of 1711 as the year of the completion of the *Gur Sobhā*.[37] He concedes finally in 2003 that the claims for 1711 are much stronger.[38]

Arguing further about the date of the *Gur Sobhā*, Gurinder Singh Mann places it closer to the death of Guru Gobind Singh. He maintains that there is 'no supporting evidence' for 1711 in the extant manuscripts. He suggests that Sainapat started his work in 1701 and went on writing till late in 1708. For the years 1701–8, thus, he wrote contemporaneously, and this first-hand account of the events 'may have even been recited before and corrected by the Guru himself'.[39]

In his Introduction to Koer Singh's *Gurbilās Pātshāhī 10*, Fauja Singh places this work in 1751 in accordance with the date recorded by the author.[40] Surjit Hans rejects this date on the basis of its contents, and places it in the early nineteenth century,[41] which has been accepted by a number of historians. Questioning this assumption, Madanjit Kaur argues at length that Koer Singh's work can be safely placed between 1751 and 1762, the two possible interpretations of the statement made by the author himself towards the end of his work. She goes on to refute all the arguments put forth by Hans one by one.[42] Gurtej Singh, who is aware of the position taken by Hans, accepts the year 1751 as the authentic date.[43] Indeed, the contents of Koer Singh's work make better sense in a context earlier than the declaration of Sikh rule in 1765.

The *Gurbilās Pātshāhī 6* published by Punjabi University is based on a copy of 1839, the earliest manuscript available to the editor. It was collated with two later manuscripts. In all the three manuscripts the author of the work is Bhai Bhagat Singh (not Sohan Kavi who is generally associated with this work). The date of its composition given in these manuscripts is 1718, but in their content there are references to the incidents of the early nineteenth century. Because of the variations in the printed texts and available manuscripts, the editor infers that the copyists had interfered with the text. As he says, it is impossible to establish an authentic text.[44]

Finally, we may turn to the *Sri Gur Panth Prakāsh* of Ratan Singh Bhangu, which is primarily a historical work concerned largely with the eighteenth century. All its episodes (sākhīs) are meant to answer the basic question of 'how the Sikhs became a sovereign people'. The text edited by Bhai Vir Singh as the *Prāchīn Panth Prakāsh* mentions Sammat 1898 (AD 1841) as the year of its completion.[45] In a later edition, Balwant Singh Dhillon accepts the date 1841, but points out that Bhangu is talking of correcting or revising two earlier manuscripts. Therefore, the question arises, which two manuscripts?[46] On the basis of several manuscripts of Bhangu's work actually seen, Gurinder Singh Mann has argued in favour of an earlier date, closer to or during the years of Captain Murray's tenure as assistant to the political agent in Ludhiana in the second decade of the nineteenth century.[47]

The whole range of debate about the time at which the major literary works under review were produced suggests three broad phases: (*a*) the last decade of the seventeenth and the first decade of the eighteenth century, marked by literary resurgence; (*b*) the fourth, fifth, and sixth decades of the eighteenth century, as a relatively lean phase of literary articulation; and (*c*) the seventh decade onwards, when there is again a kind of literary resurgence. All the important Gurmukhi works taken up for this study can be placed in one or the other of the following three phases:

## The Early Phase

1. *Prashan-uttar*
2. *Tankhānāmā (Nasīhatnāmā)*
3. Rahitnāmā of Prahilad Singh
4. *Rāmkalī Vār Pātshāhī Dasven Kī* (first fourteen pauṛīs)
5. *Sākhī Rahit Pātisāhī* 10
6. The rahitnāmā associated with Chaupa Singh (preface and the prescriptive part)
7. *Prem Sumārag Granth*
8. *Sri Gur Sobhā*
9. *Parchiān* of Sewa Das

## The Middle Phase

1. *B40 Janamsākhī*
2. The rahitnāmā associated with Chaupa Singh (last three sections, consisting of two narratives with the *tankhā* part in between)
3. Koer Singh's *Gurbilās Pātshāhī 10*

## The Last Phase

1. *Bansāvalīnāmā Dasān Pātshāhiān Kā*
2. *Mahimā Prakāsh*
3. *Giān Ratnāvalī*
4. *Sikhān dī Bhagatmālā*
5. *Rāmkalī Vār Pātshāhī Dasven Kī* (last six pauṛīs)
6. *Gurū Kiān Sākhiān*
7. Sukha Singh's *Gurbilās Pātsāhī 10*
8. Rahitnāmā of Desa Singh
9. Rahitnāmā of Daya Singh
10. *Sri Gur Panth Prakāsh*

It may be added that the early phase covered Guru Gobind Singh's activities, both before and after the institution of the Khalsa. The middle phase was marked by the mounting clash of the Khalsa with the Mughal governors first, and then with Ahmad Shah Abdali. The last phase was marked by a sense of triumph in a situation of relative peace and possibilities of patronage under Sikh rule.

## NOTES AND REFERENCES

1. J.S. Grewal, *Historical Writings on the Sikhs (1784–2011): Western Enterprise and Indian Response* (New Delhi: Manohar, 2012).
2. Narendra Krishna Sinha, *Rise of the Sikh Power* (Calcutta: A. Mukherjee & Co., 1963 [1936]). Hari Ram Gupta, *History of the Sikhs: Evolution of the Sikh Confederacies 1708–69*, vol. 2 (New Delhi: Munshiram Manoharlal, 2014). This work is an enlarged version of the author's doctoral thesis originally published from Calcutta in 1939 as *History of the Sikhs 1739–1768 (Evolution of the Sikh Confederacies)*.

3. Teja Singh and Ganda Singh, *A Short History of the Sikhs* (1465–1765) (Patiala: Punjabi University, 1999 [1950]).

4. Purnima Dhavan, *When Sparrows Became Hawks: The Making of the Sikh Warrior Tradition, 1699–1799* (New York: Oxford University Press, 2014 [2011]).

5. Bhagat Singh, *Sikh Polity in the Eighteenth and Nineteenth Centuries* (New Delhi: Oriental Publishers and Distributors, 1978).

6. J.S. Grewal, *Sikh Ideology, Polity and Social Order: From Guru Nanak to Maharaja Ranjit Singh* (New Delhi: Manohar, 2007 [1996]), pp. 147–82; essays are titled, 'Ahmad Shah of Batala on the Misl'; 'Ganesh Das on the Secular Aspirations of the Khalsa'; 'Eighteenth-Century Sikh Polity'; and '"Patshah of the Panth": Jassa Singh Ahluwalia'.

7. Indu Banga, *Agrarian System of the Sikhs: Late Eighteenth and Early Nineteenth Century* (New Delhi: Manohar, 1978).

8. J.S. Grewal, *Recent Debates in Sikh Studies: An Assessment* (New Delhi: Manohar, 2011).

9. For the widened scope of Sikh studies of the eighteenth century, see Karamjit K. Malhotra, 'Expanding Scope of Sikh Studies on the Eighteenth Century', *Panjab Journal of Sikh Studies* 3 (2013): 33–71.

10. W.H. McLeod, trans. and ed., *The Chaupa Singh Rahit-Nama* (Dunedin, New Zealand: University of Otago Press, 1987), pp. 10–11.

11. Jeevan Singh Deol, 'Eighteenth Century Khalsa Identity: Discourse, Praxis, and Narrative', in *Sikh Religion, Culture, and Ethnicity*, ed. Christopher Shackle, Gurharpal Singh, and Arvind-Pal Singh Mandair (Surrey: Curzon, 2000), pp. 25–46.

12. W.H. McLeod, *Sikhs of the Khalsa: A History of Khalsa Rahit* (New Delhi: Oxford University Press, 2003), pp. 44–6, 65–73, 148–51.

13. W.H. McLeod, trans., *Prem Sumārag: The Testimony of a Sanatan Sikh* (New Delhi: Oxford University Press, 2006), p. 6.

14. W.H. McLeod, 'Reflections on the *Prem Sumārag*', *Journal of Punjab Studies* 14, no. 1 (Spring 2007): 126–32.

15. Gurinder Singh Mann, 'Sources for the Study of Guru Gobind Singh's Life and Times', *Journal of Punjab Studies* (Special Issue on Guru Gobind Singh) 15, nos 1 and 2 (Spring–Fall 2008): 250–1, 297n107.

16. Karamjit K. Malhotra, 'The Earliest Manual on the Sikh Way of Life', in *Five Centuries of Sikh Tradition: Ideology, Society, Politics and Culture*, ed. Reeta Grewal and Sheena Pall (New Delhi: Manohar, 2005), pp. 55–81.

17. Mann, 'Sources for the Study of Guru Gobind Singh's Life and Times': 249–50, 275n97, 276nn101–4.

18. Mann, 'Sources for the Study of Guru Gobind Singh's Life and Times': 249, 275nn97, 99.

19. J.S. Grewal, 'The Singh Way of Life: The *Rahitnāmās*', in *Four Centuries of Sikh Tradition: History, Literature, and Identity* (New Delhi: Oxford University Press, 2011), p. 207.

20. Raijasbir Singh, ed., *Bansāvalīnāmā Dasān Pātshāhiān Kā* (Amritsar: Guru Nanak Dev University, 2001), Introduction, pp. 20–2.

21. Bhai Svarup Singh Kaushish, *Gurū Kiān Sākhiān*, ed. Piara Singh Padam (Amritsar: Singh Brothers, 1999 [1986]), pp. 9–10.

22. Raijasbir Singh, ed., *Guru Amar Das: Srot Pustak* (Amritsar: Guru Nanak Dev University, 1986), pp. 208–11.

23. Kharak Singh and Gurtej Singh, trans and eds, *Episodes from Lives of the Gurus: Parchian Sewadas* (Chandigarh: Institute of Sikh Studies, 1995), pp. 1–8. The Gurmukhi text published by the editors, referring to it as the *Parchiān Sewādās*, has been used in the present study.

24. Mann, 'Sources for the Study of Guru Gobind Singh's Life and Times': 252, 119n278–9.

25. Jasbir Singh Sabar, ed., *Giān Ratnāvalī: Janamsākhī Sri Guru Nanak Dev Jī* (Amritsar: Guru Nanak Dev University, 1993), pp. 5, 46, 50–9, 70–1.

26. S.S. Padam, ed. *Sikhān dī Bhagatmālā* (Amritsar: Singh Brothers, 2013), p. 61. Padam claims that this work is better than the earlier edited works which are discussed in detail. The introductory part covers 202 pages in which the editor gives a comprehensive discussion of all aspects of this work.

27. Kulwinder Singh Bajwa, ed., *Mahimā Prakāsh (Vārtak)* (Amritsar: Singh Brothers, 2004), pp. 13–23.

28. J.S. Grewal, 'The Basic Significance of the *Mahima Prakash (Vārtak)*', in *The Punjab Revisited: Social Order, Economic Life, Cultural Articulation, Politics, and Partition (18th–20th Centuries)*, ed. Karamjit K. Malhotra (Patiala: Punjabi University, 2014), pp. 28–35. Grewal points out that the Bhalla family interests are reflected in the early sākhīs upto Guru Tegh Bahadur, and the Udāsī interests are reflected in the thirty-eight sākhīs of Guru Gobind Singh taken from the *Parchiān*. Thus, the *Vārtak* as a whole presents only a small portion of fresh or significant evidence. Cf. Raijasbir Singh, *Guru Amar Das*, pp. 438–43.

29. Piara Singh Padam, ed., *Parchiān Sau Sākhī* (Amritsar: Singh Brothers, 1997). Also, Gurbachan Singh Nayyar, ed., *Gur Ratan Māl: Sau Sākhī* (Patiala: Punjabi University, 1995).

30. Kala Singh Bedi, ed., *Vār Sri Bhagautī Jī Kī (Chandī dī Vār)* (New Delhi: Punjab Book Store, 1965), pp. 103–43. Padam has pointed out that the correct title of this work is *Vār Durgā Kī*. See Piara Singh Padam, ed., *Punjābī Vārān* (Amritsar: Singh Brothers, 2008), pp. 156–68.

31. Gurdas (Singh), *Rāmkalī Vār Pātshāhī Dasven Kī*, in *Vārān Bhai Gurdas*, ed. Giani Hazara Singh (Amritsar: Khalsa Samachar, 1962 [1911]), pp. 662–76.

32. Mann, 'Sources for the Study of Guru Gobind Singh's Life and Times': 280n129.

33. Piara Singh Padam, *Punjābī Vārān*, pp. 171–7.

34. Sainapat, *Sri Gur Sobhā*, ed. Ganda Singh (Patiala: Punjabi University, 1967). Simultaneously, this view was confirmed by Shamsher Singh Ashok in his introduction to his edited version of the work, Sainapat, *Shri Gur Sobhā* (Amritsar: SGPC, 1967), pp. 3–5.

35. W.H. McLeod, trans. and ed., *Textual Sources for the Study of Sikhism* (Manchester: Manchester University Press, 1984), pp. 11–12.

36. W.H. McLeod, *The Sikhs: History, Religion and Society* (New York: Columbia University Press, 1989), p. 63.

37. Hew [W.H.] McLeod, *Sikhism* (London: Penguin Books, 1997), p. 59.

38. McLeod, *Sikhs of the Khalsa*, p. 60.

39. Mann, 'Sources for the Study of Guru Gobind Singh's Life and Times': 252, 278n115, 117, 118.

40. Koer Singh, *Gurbilās Pātshāhī 10*, ed. Shamsher Singh Ashok (Patiala: Punjabi University, 1968), pp. 2, 295.

41. Surjit Hans, *A Reconstruction of Sikh History from Sikh Literature* (Patiala: Madaan Publications, 2005 [1987]), pp. 247–50.

42. Madanjit Kaur, 'Koer Singh's *Gurbilās Pātshāhī 10*: An Eighteenth Century Sikh Literature', in *Sikhism*, ed. Jasbir Singh Mann and Kharak Singh (Patiala: Punjabi University, 1992), pp. 161–72.

43. Gurtej Singh, 'Compromising the Khalsa Tradition: Koer Singh's *Gurbilās*', in *The Khalsa: Sikh and Non-Sikh Perspectives*, ed. J.S. Grewal (New Delhi: Manohar, 2004), p. 47.

44. Gurmukh Singh, ed., *Gurbilās Pātshāhī 6* (Patiala: Punjabi University, 1997). See also *Gurbilās Chhevīn Pātshāhī* (Patiala: Punjab Languages Department, 1970).

45. Ratan Singh Bhangu, *Prāchīn Panth Prakāsh*, ed. Bhai Vir Singh (New Delhi: Bhai Vir Singh Sadan, 1993), p. 471 and note.

46. Ratan Singh Bhangu, *Sri Gur Panth Prakāsh*, ed. Balwant Singh Dhillon (Amritsar: Singh Brothers, 2004), Introduction [p. xii, letter *chhachhā* in Gurmukhi Script]. Henceforth referred to as *Sri Gur Panth Prakāsh*.

47. Gurinder Singh Mann, paper presented at the Symposium on History and Literature, organized by the Institute of Punjab Studies, Chandigarh, at the 72nd session of the Indian History Congress in Patiala in December 2011 (seen in typescript).

# Part I
# Sikh Political Resurgence and Sikh Polity

# 1 'Rāj Karegā Khālsā'

The history of Sikhs during the eighteenth century is generally seen from the perspective of the decline of the Mughal Empire. Seen from the Sikh viewpoint, however, it becomes the story of their rise to power. Their struggle was a corollary of their conviction that the Khalsa created by the tenth Guru in 1699 was ordained to rule. The idea that 'the Khalsa shall rule' (*rāj karegā Khālsā*) had become current in the lifetime of Guru Gobind Singh. Within two years of his death, the uprising of the Khalsa under the leadership of Banda Singh in 1710 was a 'revolt' from the viewpoint of the Mughal emperor but it was a bid for sovereignty for the Khalsa. The attempt failed but the ideal survived.

Persecuted and suppressed by the Mughal authorities after the execution of Banda Singh in 1716, the Khalsa reorganized themselves slowly but surely to become a threat for the Mughal governors of the province who were still very powerful. The survival of the Khalsa as a political entity was made possible essentially by their ideology and institutions. Their numbers and their striking power began to increase after the invasion of India by Nadir Shah in 1739. His successor, Ahmad Shah Abdali, claimed within a decade all the trans-Indus territories of the Mughal Empire that Emperor Muhammad Shah had formally ceded to Nadir Shah, along with four *mahāl* (the *parganas* of Gujrat, Aurangabad, Pasrur, and Sialkot) in the province of Lahore. In 1752, the Mughal emperor ceded the provinces of Lahore and Multan to Ahmad Shah Abdali, formally marking the transfer of power in the region from the Mughals to the Afghans.

Significantly, by this time, some of the leaders of the Khalsa had begun to issue orders to the local functionaries in certain pockets of territory within the province of Lahore. The Khalsa looked upon the Afghans as their new, and in some ways more powerful, enemy.

The political struggle became more intense after 1752 and culminated in the ouster of the Afghans from the province of Lahore and the formal declaration of Khalsa Rāj in the lifetime of Ahmad Shah Abdali, in 1765. The organizational and institutional practices evolved during the political struggle left a legacy for the Sikh polity of the late eighteenth century in the form of Misals, Rākhī, Gurmatā, and the Dal Khalsa.

## THE SEVENTEENTH-CENTURY BACKGROUND

Sikh confrontation with the Mughal state had begun after the martyrdom of Guru Arjan in 1606. His son and successor, Guru Hargobind (1606–44), took to martial activity and built what is now known as the Akāl Takht (eternal throne), adjacent to the Harmandar in Ramdaspur. He encouraged his followers to adopt soldierly habits. In the time of Jahangir, he was detained in the fort of Gwalior as a political prisoner for some time. During the reign of Shah Jahan, he fought a few battles against the Mughal faujdārs. He was victorious, but he left the province of Lahore and settled at Kiratpur in the principality of the chief of Hindur (later known as Nalagaṛh). Guru Hargobind maintained a considerable number of horses and matchlockmen till his death in 1644.[1]

In this situation of confrontation with the Mughals, cleavage within the Sikh Panth became increasingly conspicuous. The first to leave Guru Hargobind was his uncle Prithi Chand, the elder brother of Guru Arjan. Reluctant to acknowledge even Guru Arjan, he openly declared himself to be the Guru after Guru Arjan's death. Writing contemporaneously, Bhai Gurdas denounces Prithi Chand and his followers, using the derogatory term 'Mīṇās' for them. The second person to put forth rival claims was Guru Hargobind's grandson, Dhir Mal, the elder son of Baba Gurditta who was no longer alive. Dhir Mal did not recognize his younger

brother Har Rai as the Guru, and claimed to be the seventh Guru
at Kartarpur in the Jalandhar Doāb. He received a large piece of
revenue-free land from Shah Jahan. Guru Har Rai went to the
aid of Dara Shukoh against Aurangzeb in 1658. Called to Delhi,
Guru Har Rai sent his son Ram Rai who adopted a compromising
attitude. Guru Har Rai appointed his younger son, Har Krishan,
as the Guru. Ram Rai did not acknowledge him and eventually
established his own centre at Dehradun under the patronage of
Aurangzeb. Guru Hargobind's successors remained dissociated
from the Mughal state.[2]

Aurangzeb called Guru Har Krishan to Delhi, probably on
a representation from Ram Rai. While in Delhi, Guru Har
Krishan died of small pox after announcing that his successor
was his granduncle (Bābā) Tegh Bahadur, the fourth son of Guru
Hargobind, who was living in Bakala, between Kartarpur and
Ramdaspur. Approached by the Sikhs, he accepted the office of
Guruship. His decision could annoy several parties: Ram Rai and
his patron Aurangzeb, Dhir Mal at Kartarpur, and Miharban's son
Harji at Ramdaspur. Guru Tegh Bahadur did not stay at Bakala,
nor at Kiratpur. He founded a new centre at Makhowal in the
hill principality of Kahlur (later known as Bilaspur). He consoli-
dated his hold over the *sangats* of the Gangetic Plain in the late
1660s, and returned to the Punjab when Aurangzeb was taking
repressive measures against non-Muslims and even non-Sunni
Muslims. Questioning the emperor's authority to interfere in
religious matters, the Guru tried to reassure the people. He was
called to Delhi in 1675, tried, and condemned to death. He died as
a martyr to the principle of freedom of conscience.[3] The event had
a profound effect on his son and successor Guru Gobind Singh
and his followers.

Guru Gobind was in his early teens in 1675. For ten years he
prepared himself and his followers for martial activity. The chief of
Kahlur, Bhim Chand, became increasingly anxious that the Guru
should recognize his political authority. But Guru Gobind was not
willing to compromise the autonomy of Makhowal. Tension was
mounting. In 1685, Guru Gobind received an invitation from the
chief of Sirmur (later known as Nahan) to settle in his territory and
the Guru accepted his invitation as a politic measure.[4]

In the Sirmur state Guru Gobind established his headquarters at Paonta, close to the border of Sirmur with the state of Garhwal. There was a background of a protracted feud between the chiefs of Sirmur and Garhwal; Paonta served as a kind of buffer between the two. The martial activity of Guru Gobind at Paonta did not please the Garhwal chief and he advanced against Paonta. Guru Gobind moved out to give him battle at a place called Bhangani. His victory at Bhangani enhanced his reputation in the hills. He had good resources in men, bows and arrows, javelins, swords, maces, and horses. But he had no intention of embroiling himself any further in the affairs of a chief who had tricked him into a difficult situation. Guru Gobind returned to Makhowal in 1689 and founded the town of Anandpur.

Meanwhile, Bhim Chand refused to pay tribute as a vassal of the Mughal emperor. This gesture of defiance obliged the Mughal faujdār of Jammu to send a force against him. The commandant of this force was supported by some loyal Rajput vassals of the Mughal emperor. On Bhim Chand's invitation, Guru Gobind participated in the battle at Nadaun. Soon after the battle, however, Bhim Chand agreed to pay tribute to the Mughal faujdār. Guru Gobind expressed his disapproval of Bhim Chand's submission by plundering a village in his territory, and returned to Anandpur to resume his usual activities.

From 1693 to 1696 three expeditions were sent against Guru Gobind by the Mughal faujdār of Jammu. The first was sent against Anandpur under a young commander who was disheartened to find the Guru ready for battle and left without a fight. Another expedition was sent against him, but its commander was killed on the way by some of the hill chiefs. Guru Gobind did not participate personally in this battle but sent a small contingent of men who died fighting. Yet another Mughal force was sent under a Rajput commandant, Jujhar Singh, who was defeated and killed by the rebel chiefs. Aurangzeb then sent his son, Mu'azzam (later Bahadur Shah), to the Punjab in 1696 to punish the rebel chiefs and their supporters. Guru Gobind, however, remained safe at Anandpur.

## BID FOR SOVEREIGNTY (1699–1716)

The *Bachittar Nātak* composed at Anandpur in 1698, presents a world view in which God is believed to intervene in the affairs of his creation from time to time to establish true worship. The agencies chosen for the purpose make use of physical force to overwhelm the forces of evil. In this work Guru Gobind himself is said to have been ordained by God to spread true faith (*dharam*) among men and to bring them to their sense of duty towards God. He had come to fulfil God's purpose, without personal enmity towards anyone. This composition can be seen as an enunciation and a justification of Guru Gobind's mission. Its primary emphasis is on the justness of his cause and the necessity of espousing it.[5]

Guru Gobind decided to put his plan into operation on a Baisākhī (Vaisakhi, Bisakhi, Visakhi) day. The generally accepted year for this central event of Guru Gobind Singh's life is 1699. The gathering addressed by him at Anandpur was unusually large,[6] and he asked the Sikhs at some stage to offer their lives for the sake of dharam. Offers came one by one and Guru Gobind stopped the demand at five. These five beloved Sikhs (*panj pyāre*), who deliberately decided to dedicate their lives to the cause of righteousness, were initiated all afresh (through *khande kī pahul*).[7] The distinguishing mark of khande kī pahul, as the name suggests, was the use of a *khandā* (double-edged sword) in the preparation of *pahul* (the rejuvenating water, also called *amrit*). The Sikhs who took pahul became 'Singh' and they were asked to keep their *kes* (hair) uncut, and to bear arms. Guru Gobind himself took pahul from the five and became Guru Gobind Singh.[8] As noted earlier, several rahitnāmās were compiled in the lifetime of Guru Gobind Singh. One of these, associated with Bhai Nand Lal, contains the couplet embodying the ideal of sovereign rule (rāj karegā Khālsā).[9]

The increasing number of armed Singhs at Anandpur was seen by Bhim Chand, the chief of Kahlur, as a threat to the integrity of his dominions. He asked Guru Gobind Singh to pay tribute as the token of submission, but the Guru was not prepared to acknowledge his authority. The chief formed an alliance with some other hill chiefs to attack Anandpur. Unable to dislodge the Guru, the allied chiefs approached the Mughal faujdārs. Their combined forces obliged Guru Gobind Singh to cross the River Sutlej into the territory of a friendly chief. The Mughal troops went back. Without their support, the chief of Kahlur was unable to stop Guru Gobind Singh from recovering Anandpur.[10]

Back at Anandpur, Guru Gobind Singh was left free for two years to strengthen his position. The fortifications of Anandpur were improved and the Sikhs were trained in the use of cannon. The Khalsa started visiting Anandpur in larger numbers. Their needs, combined with their new temper, resulted in the 'conquest' of all the villages in the neighbourhood of Anandpur, which greatly alarmed the hill chiefs. They approached their suzerain Aurangzeb for protection as his vassals. An apparently petty and local conflict was transformed into a trial of strength between the Khalsa under the leadership of Guru Gobind Singh and the Mughal state. A long blockade and solemn promises of safety induced the Khalsa to agree to evacuate the fortresses, and Guru Gobind Singh left Anandpur towards the end of 1705 against his own better judgement. He was attacked by the Mughal troops while crossing the stream Sarsa in flood. Another battle was fought at Chamkaur on the day following in which Guru Gobind Singh's two eldest sons died fighting. His two younger sons and the Guru's mother had fallen into the hands of the faujdār of Sarhind. On their refusal to accept Islam, the young boys were executed. Mata Gujri, the Guru's mother, died on the same day. Wazir Khan, the faujdār of Sarhind, attacked a group of the Khalsa at a place called Khidrana (now Muktsar).They died fighting and Wazir Khan returned to Sarhind. This was the last campaign undertaken by a Mughal faujdār against Guru Gobind Singh.[11]

Guru Gobind Singh sent to Aurangzeb a composition called the *Zafarnāma* (epistle of victory) accusing the Mughal authorities of perfidy. The *Zafarnāma* states that the Guru had no quarrel with the Mughal government as such, but he had to defend himself with the force of arms as the last resort in the given situation. Indeed, it was lawful to resort to arms when there was no other way.[12] He was thus appealing to the emperor's sense of moral justice without relinquishing his own inalienable right to defend his claims. Aurangzeb was affected by the moral force and determination reflected in the *Zafarnāmā*. He sent special messengers to conciliate Guru Gobind Singh and he agreed to meet Aurangzeb for negotiations. On his way to the Deccan he heard the news of Aurangzeb's death, and met his successor Bahadur Shah at Agra. The Guru went fully armed; he was received well and given a costly gift. He felt after the meeting that he would go back to Anandpur. But he remained close to the imperial camp for nearly a year, and the issue was still unresolved. For his own reasons Bahadur Shah went on postponing the decision to restore the status quo ante.[13]

Towards the end of September 1708, when the imperial army halted near Nander in the Deccan, Guru Gobind Singh decided not to accompany the royal camp any further. There he met an aggressive renunciate (*bairāgī*), now known as Banda Singh, who took the pahul and adopted the *rahit* of the Khalsa.[14] Guru Gobind Singh commissioned him to lead the Khalsa against their oppressors in the Punjab.[15] A few days later, Guru Gobind Singh was badly wounded by an Afghan connected with either Wazir Khan or an imperial officer. Before the Guru breathed his last on 7 October 1708, he vested Guruship in the Granth Sahib and proclaimed the Khalsa to be a political community.[16]

At this time, Banda Singh was on his way to the Punjab with a small band of the Khalsa, and the orders (*hukamnāmās*) of Guru Gobind Singh addressed to the eminent Khalsa sangats and individuals in different parts of the country, notably the Punjab. Reaching the pargana of Kharkhauda (in Haryana) he dispatched messengers with the Guru's hukamnāmās. There was a good response. Banda Singh attacked the prosperous town of Samana before the end of 1709, and after its conquest appointed Fateh Singh as its *thānādār*. He then moved towards Sadhaura and occupied the town. Marching towards Sarhind, he occupied Chhat and Banur. He was now ready to attack Sarhind, the headquarters of Wazir Khan, the faujdār of the administrative division (*sarkār*) of Sarhind. Wazir Khan came out of the city to give battle near Chappar Chiri. He was killed in the battle and his troops were defeated. The city and the fort of Sarhind were occupied on 24 May

1710. The city was sacked and plundered. Sucha Nand, the leading official of Wazir Khan, who was believed to be hostile to the Guru, was killed and all his property was confiscated. The conquest of Sarhind added immensely to the resources of Banda Singh; he was soon able to occupy nearly the whole territory between Panipat and Ludhiana.[17]

After the conquest of Sarhind, Banda Singh got a coin struck presumably from the mint at Sarhind. In the contemporary context, the act of striking of the coin was a declaration of sovereignty by itself. It bore the following inscription in Persian:

Sikka zad bar har do 'ālam teg-i Nanak wāhib ast,
Fateh Gobind (Singh) Shāh-i Shāhān fazl-i Sachā Sāhib ast.

The coin refers to the victory of Guru Gobind Singh, the king of kings, as the grace of the True Lord, and the coin struck in both the worlds with the aid of the sword of Guru Nanak. The victory of the Khalsa, thus, is the victory of Guru Gobind Singh and the sword that makes it possible is ultimately the ideology of Guru Nanak. The coin struck by the Khalsa claimed universal sovereignty, and derived authority from the Gurus and God.[18]

A seal was prepared for use on orders to be issued. A hukamnāmā of December 1710 bears the impression of the seal with the following inscription in Persian:

Deg-o teg-o fateh-o nusrat bedirang,
Yāft az Nanak Guru Gobind Singh.

Here, the gifts of the cauldron to cook food for the hungry, the sword as the symbol of power and protection, and of unlimited victory are received by Guru Gobind Singh from Guru Nanak. In other words, the sovereignty of the Khalsa is derived from Guru Nanak and Guru Gobind Singh through a line of eight other Gurus. The import of this inscription is the same as that of the inscription on the coin: the authority of the Khalsa is derived from the Gurus. There is no reference to Banda Singh, or any other individual, in this hukamnāmā, and there is a great emphasis on following 'the rahit of the Khalsa'.[19]

Significantly, the Khalsa had occupied Ramdaspur (now known as Amritsar) before the occupation of Sarhind and formed groups (jathās) to paralyse the Mughal administration. A few battles were fought in the Bari Doāb with Bhagwant Rai's fortress on the Ravi as the base of the Khalsa. In the Jalandhar Doāb, a battle was fought near Rahon between the Khalsa and Shams Khan, the faujdār of the Doāb. By October 1710, while the Mughal administration of the province of Lahore had been challenged by the Khalsa, Banda Singh had occupied the Sutlej–Jamuna Divide. The contemporary Mirza Muhammad makes the statement that places like Saharanpur, Buṛia, Sadhaura, Chhat, Ambala, Shahabad, Thanesar, Sarhind, Pail, Ropar, Bahlolpur, Machhiwara, and Ludhiana were occupied by the Khalsa under the leadership of Banda. All the territory from Thanesar to the bank of the Sutlej came under their control. Half of the administrative circle (chaklāh) of Saharanpur was annexed to their dominions. Many villages in the province of the Punjab too came into their hands.[20]

A new administration was set up in the conquered territories. Baj Singh, who had accompanied Banda Singh from Nander, was made the 'governor' of Sarhind, with Ali Singh (who was earlier in the service of Wazir Khan) as his deputy (nāib). Baj Singh's brother, Ram Singh, was given the charge of Thanesar, jointly with Binod Singh, who too had accompanied Banda Singh from Nander. Fateh Singh was confirmed in the governorship of Samana. Banda Singh repaired the fort of Mukhlispur in the hills near Sadhaura and renamed it Lohgaṛh. On a high summit surrounded by craggy rocks and a deep ravine, this relatively inaccessible place served as his headquarters.[21]

It is generally maintained that many large landholders (zamīndārs) were now replaced by peasants as landowners.[22] This equation of zamīndārs with large proprietors or landlords is misleading. The zamīndār in Mughal terminology did not necessarily possess proprietary rights over agricultural land. Zamīndāri rights at any rate were not proprietary rights in land.[23] In the sense of intermediaries for the collection of revenues on behalf of the Mughal authorities, Tiloka and Rama (the ancestors of the rulers of Nabha, Jind, and Patiala) who supported Banda Singh, themselves were zamīndārs.[24] Some other small zamīndārs were retained by the new administration. However, the refractory intermediary zamīndārs were replaced.

The Mughal emperor Bahadur Shah heard of the fall of Sarhind on 30 May when he was near Ajmer. He left the place to march towards the Punjab. He was near Shahabad on 28 November 1710 when he heard the news that 3,000 Sikh horsemen and 2,000 foot soldiers were entrenched on his side of the town and a large number of them had gone to the fort of Sarhind. He marched towards Sadhaura and ordered Muhammad Amin Khan, one of his eminent nobles, to move upon Sarhind by forced marches. Before his arrival, Sarhind was captured by Shams Khan. The emperor reached Sadhaura on 4 December. On the day following, Rustam Dil Khan, the quarter-master general (*bakhshī*) of the Mughal army, who had been ordered to go forward to select a suitable place for the imperial camp, was attacked by the Khalsa with arrows, rockets, and musket balls. However, when the imperial troops under Prince Rafi us-Shan joined Rustam Dil Khan, the Khalsa were outnumbered. After a hard fight till sunset, the Khalsa fell back upon the fort of Lohgaṛh. On 9 December the emperor encamped on the bank of the stream called Som within sight of Lohgaṛh. On 11 December, the imperial troops under the prince reached the foot of the hill and the fort of Lohgaṛh was closely invested by more than 60,000 Mughal troops. After a brave defence, Banda Singh escaped safely into the higher hills.[25]

Sorely disappointed, the emperor remained encamped near Lohgaṛh till 24 March 1711 in the vain hope of news of Banda Singh's capture. Now he ordered that the chief of Nahan, Raja Bhup Prakash, who was regarded as sympathetic to the Khalsa, should be put in the iron cage meant for Banda Singh, taken to Delhi, and imprisoned. The imperial camp moved towards Lahore. On 10 June 1711, the emperor heard the news near Hoshiarpur that the Khalsa under the leadership of Banda Singh had killed the former faujdār of Jalandhar, Shams Khan, in a battle in the Bari Doāb. The Khalsa established their thānās in the parganas of Batala and Kalanaur and crossed the River Ravi to sack Aurangabad and Pasrur. The emperor deputed Muhammad Amin Khan for the suppression of Banda Singh. On 15 June 1711, it was reported to the emperor that Muhammad Amin Khan and Rustam Dil Khan had defeated Banda Singh near Pasrur but he had fled into the hills. On 31 August 1711, it was reported that Rustam Dil Khan had abandoned the campaign without the emperor's orders and gone to Lahore. The emperor ordered that he should be imprisoned and his huge property confiscated. Muhammad Amin Khan was reported to have won a battle against the Khalsa in January 1712. The Khalsa were still in the field when the emperor died on 28 February 1712.

The struggle for succession after Bahadur Shah's death gave the Khalsa an opportunity to re-establish their power. Banda Singh was quick to re-occupy Sadhaura and Lohgaṛh. During the short reign of Jahandar Shah, Muhammad Amin Khan was sent against the Khalsa. The new faujdār of Sarhind, Zainuddin Ahmad, was placed under his command. They kept Sadhaura and Lohgaṛh under siege for several months but without much effect. Muhammad Amin Khan was recalled in December 1712. Jahandar Shah was defeated by Farrukh Siyar in January and killed in February 1713. Abd-us-Samad Khan was now made the governor of Lahore by Farrukh Siyar and ordered to destroy Banda. Abd-us-Samad Khan succeeded in recovering Sadhaura in July 1713 and laid siege to Lohgaṛh. Banda Singh put up strong fortifications for defence but then evacuated the fort early in October to escape into the hills.[26]

The local leaders of the Khalsa put up resistance whenever and wherever they could. In March 1714, the Khalsa of the Kahnuwan pargana under the leadership of Jagat Singh attacked the Afghans of Kiri Pathan and sacked and plundered their fortress. In August 1714, a body of the Khalsa numbering about 7,000 attacked Ropar and fought a battle with the deputy faujdār of Sarhind. They were obliged to retreat. In the beginning of 1715, Banda Singh appeared in the plains from the direction of Jammu and established control over the parganas of Kalanaur and Batala again. The emperor administered a sharp reproof to Abd-us-Samad Khan and sent imperial troops for an effective campaign against the Khalsa. After an engagement with the Mughal troops, Banda Singh took up a defensive position at Gurdas Nangal. In April, Abd-us-Samad laid siege to the place, and the Khalsa put up a strong resistance for more than eight months before they were starved to surrender on 17 December 1715. Farrukh Siyar received the happy news of the capture of Banda and his companions on 22 December when he was celebrating the anniversary of his victory over Jahandar Shah.[27]

Abd-us-Samad Khan entered the city of Lahore with Banda Singh and over 700 of his companions as prisoners. Banda Singh had fetters on his feet, a ring round his neck, and a chain round his back; he was placed in a cage, and chained to it at four points. Two Mughal officers were tied to him on each side on the same elephant. His companions were mounted on donkeys and camels, with paper caps over their heads. A huge crowd of spectators gathered in bazaars and streets and on house tops. Sometime later, the prisoners were escorted to Delhi by Zakariya Khan, the son of Abd-us-Samad Khan, and Qamruddin Khan, the son of Muhammad Amin Khan. The procession reached Delhi towards the end of February 1716.[28] There too, Banda Singh and his companions provided an attractive spectacle for the people.

The execution of the political prisoners began in the first week of March 1716. Two British representatives, John Surman and Edward Stephenson, reported from Delhi to the President of the Fort William Council in Bengal that each day a hundred of them were beheaded, but none 'apostatized from this new formed religion'.[29] On 17 March, Mirza Muhammad saw the corpses of the executed prisoners suspended from trees around the city.[30] Khafi Khan describes the courage of a young prisoner who refused to be saved from the executioner's sword.[31] Seventeen others were executed in the third week of June. More executions followed. At the end, Banda Singh himself was executed in the cruellest possible manner: his eyes were taken out, his hands and feet were cut off, his flesh was torn with red-hot pincers, and his body was hacked to pieces.[32] Banda Singh could nevertheless give a tangible shape to the Khalsa ideal of sovereignty, and this example was never forgotten. The rise of the Khalsa under him and their steadfastness in the face of death have been attributed recently to 'an inspiring ideology' that could also 'compensate for the initial lack of political organization and military apparatus'.[33]

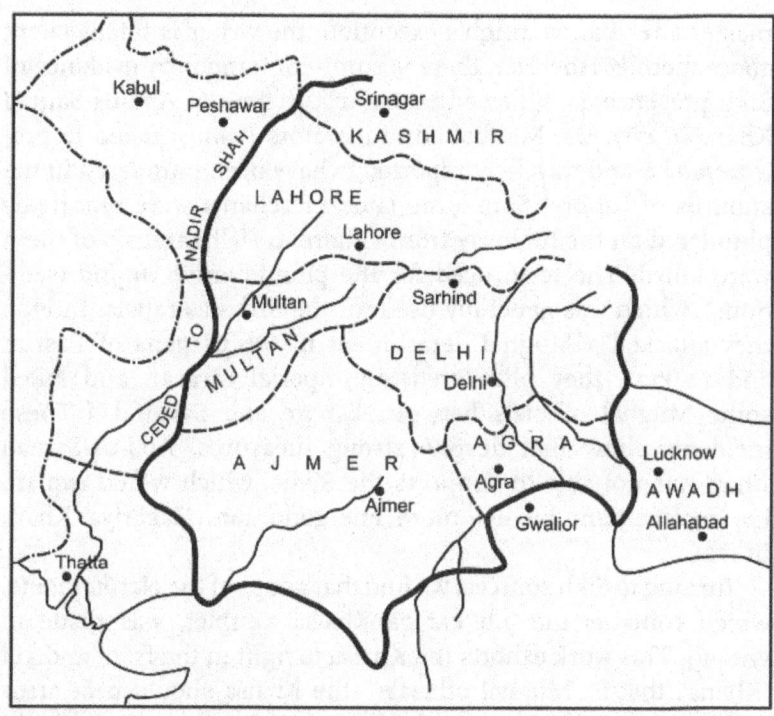

**FIGURE 1.1**   The Mughal Dominions (Early Eighteenth Century)
Source: Adapted from Map 3, in J.S. Grewal, *The Sikhs of the Punjab, The New Cambridge History of India*, II.3 (New Delhi: Cambridge University Press, 2014).

## STRUGGLE AGAINST THE MUGHALS (1716–52)

The contemporary news reports and chronicles provide some information on the 'dark phase' from 1716 to 1739. The anonymous author of the *Asrār-i Samadī*, completed in 1728–9 for Abd-us-Samad Khan as the governor of Multan by his munshī who belonged to Kalanaur, mentions only the last campaign of the Khan against Banda who is referred to as the self-styled leader of the Nanak-Panthis, called Singhs, who kept their kes unshorn. As a panegyrist of Abd-us-Samad Khan, his munshī tends to assume that the Singhs presented no problem to his master after Banda Singh's execution: the writer is totally silent about them.[34] However, there is some contemporary evidence of Sikh presence as outlawed rebels in the time of Abd-us-Samad Khan. In 1717, the Mughal administrators (*'āmils*) failed to protect traders and travellers reported to have been plundered in the suburbs of Lahore. Sometime later, merchants were reportedly plundered on the highway from Lahore to Delhi and six of them were killed. The term used for the plunderers is *mufsid* (seditious), which was generally used for the Sikhs as rebels. In 1721, they attacked a Mughal detachment in the pargana of Pasrur, and in 1726 they plundered an imperial caravan and killed some Mughal officials between Lahore and Sarhind.[35] These incidents show that despite strong measures, Abd-us-Samad Khan was not able to suppress the Sikhs, which would explain his replacement by his more energetic son, Zakariya Khan, in 1726.

Turning to Sikh sources, we find that a copy of the *Nasīhatnāmā*, which contains the 'rāj karegā Khālsā' couplet, was made in 1718–19. This work exhorts the Khalsa to fight in the front and kill 'Khans', that is, Mughal officials—the Khalsa should bear arms and fight every day. There is also the injunction that a Sikh should never submit to the 'Turks'. All this acquires great significance in combination with the evidence of the Mughal sources that indicate that Sikh 'outlaws' remained active in the time of Abd-us-Samad Khan.[36]

Another form of evidence on this phase consists of the hukamnāmās of Mata Sundari and Mata Sahib Devi, the widows of Guru Gobind Singh. Most of the available hukamnāmās were issued from 1717 to 1734. Among a number of interesting matters, there are letters addressed to the sons of Rama, the younger son of Chaudhari Phul. They were all increasing their resources and power by now, especially Ala Singh. Another individual addressed is Bhai Alam Singh who is the leader of a group (*jamā'atdār*). Significantly, they are blessed with *deg*, *teg*, and *fateh*, the three terms used in the inscription on the seal of 1710. This hukamnāmā was written in 1726.[37]

According to Kesar Singh Chhibber, who had lived in Ramdaspur as a young person in the late 1720s, new arrangements were made for the management of the affairs of the Harmandar Sahib in 1727 on the suggestion of Mata Sahib Devi. Kesar Singh Chhibber's father, Gurbakhsh Singh, was made the superintendent (*dārogha*) of the treasury and the cowshed (*gāo-khānā*). Chhibber refers also to the conflict between the Akāl Purkhiā Khalsa and the followers of 'Banda Sahib' over the control of the Harmandar, and the conflict of the Khalsa with the Mughal administration over the control of Ramdaspur.[38]

Ratan Singh Bhangu records that Zakariya Khan had suggested to the emperor that a *jāgīr* could be given to the Khalsa to put them off their guard so that they were settled at one place as an easy target. Subeg Singh was selected to approach the Khalsa with the offer of a jāgīr, a robe of honour, and the title of 'nawab' for their leader. Subeg Singh greeted the Khalsa with '*Vāhegurūjī kī fateh*' and sought to be forgiven (for accepting service with the Mughals). Five Singhs pronounced tankhā (penance) for him and allowed him to make his submission before the *sarbat* (entire) Khalsa. They distributed among themselves the money brought by Subeg Singh, and asked Darbara Singh, presumably their leader, to accept the robe and the title. Darbara Singh said that the Khalsa never wanted 'nawabī': the True Guru had prophesied *pātshāhī* (sovereign rule) for them. The Khalsa could not accept a position of dependence upon someone else. Every Khalsa horseman was to become a sovereign and to establish a seat of authority (*takht*) wherever he occupied some land. There could be no real conciliation between the Khalsa Panth and the 'Turks' (Mughals). Therefore, this robe and title could be given to a Singh who served the Khalsa well. Kapur Singh was seen serving the Khalsa with a large fan. He was asked to put on the robe of honour. Kapur Singh asked in turn that the robe may be sanctified by the touch of the feet of five Singhs and placed over his head. This was done. The revenues of twelve villages close to Ramdaspur were assigned by Zakariya Khan to the Khalsa and they established their camp in Ramdaspur.[39]

Bhangu goes on to say that the number of the Khalsa began to increase. The money received from the revenues was regularly distributed among the Khalsa by Nawab Kapur Singh. Besides bathing in the sacred tank (*amritsar*) early in the morning, they used to hold an assembly (*dīvān*) at the Akāl Bungā. Kapur Singh is reported to have served the Panth with great humility and zeal and taken no decision without consultation. There was a common kitchen, a common treasury, a common storehouse for items of accoutrement, and a common armoury. Their numbers increased so much that it became difficult to maintain a single unit. Nawab Kapur Singh invited the Khalsa to a meeting at the Akāl Bungā. Present among them was Bhai Mani Singh, the granthī of the Harmandar, and Kahan Singh Trehan and Binod Singh Bhalla. Kapur Singh put his proposal before the Sarbat Khalsa that the entire body may be divided into smaller groups (jathās), which was endorsed. Five units (*derās*) were formed, each with its own banner, and five standards were hoisted on the Akāl Bungā: the first jathā of Shahids and Nihangs was placed under Deep Singh and Karam Singh; the second under Karam Singh and Dharam Singh, both Khatris of Amritsar; the third under the Trehan and Bhalla, descendants respectively of Guru Angad and Guru Amar Das; the fourth under Dasaundha Singh, a Gill Jatt of Kot Buddha and the fifth under Bir Singh Ranghretā of outcaste background. The Khalsa thus got some respite and an experience of organization in view of their increasing numbers. The location of the villages given to them increased the importance of Ramdaspur. The Akāl Bungā came into sharper focus as the place where the Khalsa conducted their temporal affairs.

According to Ratan Singh Bhangu, Bhai Mani Singh, a *huzūrī* Sikh of Guru Gobind Singh who was well versed in Gurmat, used to instruct the Sikhs in the Singh way of life. He made proper arrangements for the Harmandar. He used to sit at the Akāl Bungā and pronounce penance for the defaulters. In the 1730s, Bhai Mani Singh agreed to pay rupees 10,000 to the Mughal authorities for holding the Diwali festival in Ramdaspur. The Khalsa were invited to come to Amritsar and to encamp there. Zakariya Khan sent troops under Lakhpat Rai, the dīvān, to ensure peace. He encamped at the nearby Ram Tīrath. The Singhs thought that the Mughal troops had been brought to attack them. Some of them had a quick bath and others returned without bathing. Zakariya Khan's dārogha did not get the stipulated sum, and

Bhai Mani Singh was arrested along with some eminent Singhs. Zakariya Khan demanded money but Bhai Mani Singh said that the Khan could take his life. The qāzīs and mullāhs suggested that Bhai Mani Singh's limbs should be cut off one by one. He was taken to the crossing of the horse-market called nakhās and, at his own suggestion, the executioner began to cut off his limbs. A Sayyid saw this and was frightened to imagine the widespread effect of a curse if uttered by Bhai Mani Singh. He drew his sword and cut off Bhai Mani Singh's head. Reciting the Sukhmaṇī, Bhai Mani Singh felt no pain. The symbol of sikhī (that is, kes) remained intact when his head was cut off as one piece. Bhai Mani Singh is the best known among the Sikh martyrs of the period.

An insight into the psyche of the Khalsa may be had from the account of another martyr of this phase, Bhai Tara Singh. Kesar Singh Chhibber merely mentions his name as if he was well known among the Sikhs.[40] Bhangu narrates his story. A Buttar Jatt of village Van, Tara Singh was a staunch Khalsa of Guru Gobind Singh, ready to fight for a righteous cause and unwilling to submit to the 'Turks'. In his view, armed struggle was necessary for achieving sovereignty. It so happened that Chaudhari Sahib Rai of Naushera used to let his mare feed on the crops of others. Two Singhs asked him to keep his mare tied but he threatened to remove their kes. They retaliated by getting his mare stolen. The proceeds from its sale were used for the langar maintained by Tara Singh. Sahib Rai approached Tara Singh to get hold of the thief. Tara Singh told him that Sahib Rai himself was a thief who stole the crops of others. Sahib Rai went to the Mughal faujdār at Patti and reported that he could not pay revenue to the authorities because Singhs had extorted money from him. The faujdār came to Van to deal with the situation but he was defeated, and his nephew was killed. The faujdār went to Lahore to report to Zakariya Khan who decided upon immediate action. Some of the Singhs suggested that Tara Singh should escape. But Tara Singh told them that he was not afraid of dying. He asked all his companions to leave if they were not prepared to fight unto death. Some of them did leave, but twenty-two Singhs remained with him. We are told that among them were two barbers, one Brahman, one carpenter, two Singhs from Multan and Peshawar, and the rest of them mostly Jatts from the Majha. The governor sent Momin Khan, the faujdār, with 2,200 horsemen, 40 light guns, and 5 elephants. Some Singhs of Lahore came to know of this and informed Tara Singh so that he could escape in time, but he told them that he was determined to fight till he was dead. Momin Khan's guide, who was sympathetic towards the Singhs, informed Tara Singh of the expedition and suggested that he should escape. But he was determined upon martyrdom (*shahīdī*). Eventually, Tara Singh and all his companions died fighting. As presented by Bhangu, Tara Singh never submitted to Mughal authority; he did whatever he thought was right; he defended his position to the point of sacrificing his life with the conviction that the sovereignty of the Khalsa was bound to be established sooner or later.[41] The image of Tara Singh may be seen as an ideal-type created by Ratan Singh Bhangu, but he remains close to the ideal Singh of the *Nasīhatnāmā*, written over a century ago.

Nadir Shah's invasion in 1739 created an opportunity for the Khalsa to increase their resources. They plundered cash, horses, and other goods, believing that the destruction of Mughal prestige and power by the Iranian conqueror was the result of the Guru's prophecy. Nawab Kapur Singh told the Singhs to make the best of this opportunity. Nadir Shah was returning with the fabulous wealth and precious articles plundered from Delhi. He was shorn of some of this plunder by the Singhs on his way from Delhi to Lahore. Nadir Shah asked Zakariya Khan, who had submitted to him, about the home of the plunderers. The Shah was told that they had no home: they remained constantly on the move; they were not afraid of death. Nadir Shah warned Zakariya Khan that he would not be able to suppress such people.[42] The invasion of Nadir Shah brought the Singhs into sharper focus as a serious threat to the governor of Lahore, who now became all the more keen to destroy them.

We can see that the Khalsa believed in their ultimate triumph, and they were prepared to suffer and make sacrifices for their cause. Individuals like Bhai Tara Singh and Bhai Mani Singh became the source of inspiration for others in their life and through their death. In addition to the ideal of 'rāj karegā Khālsā', the tangible legacy of Guru Ram Das, Guru Arjan, and Guru Hargobind respectively in the sacred tank, the Harmandar, and the Akāl Bungā became the symbols of the unity of the Khalsa and the focus of their religious and political life. The idea of the collective authority of the Panth and the complete equality of its members enabled them to organize themselves for effective action in an hour of need.

After Nadir Shah's departure from Lahore in May 1739, Zakariya Khan adopted a policy of systematic persecution of the Sikhs. He occupied Ramdaspur and enlisted the support of both Hindu and Muslim *chaudharīs* in the countryside. Ratan Singh Bhangu narrates the stories of some Sikhs who defied the repressive measures of the local authorities and deliberately courted martyrdom.[43]

A Rajput Muslim of Mandiali, known as Massa Ranghar, was given charge of the Harmandar Sahib in Ramdaspur. He used the premises for his entertainment by professional dancers. The news of this desecration was given by a Sikh to Mehtab Singh, the grandfather of our author, Ratan Singh Bhangu, who was at Jaipur. Mehtab Singh asked him if there was no Sikh in the Punjab to do something about Massa Ranghar. The Sikh replied that most of the Sikhs had left their homes out of fear, like Mehtab Singh himself. This taunt resulted in Mehtab Singh's decision to assassinate Massa Ranghar. He was joined in this mission by Sukha Singh and they reached the shrine disguised as peasants who wanted to pay land revenue to the chaudharī. Mehtab Singh cut off Massa Ranghar's head and both the Singhs rode their horses to escape. Later on, Mehtab Singh was arrested and broken on the wheel.

Ramdaspur was now placed under the direct control of the Mughal administrators. In the face of a strict watch it became difficult for the Singhs to bathe in the sacred tank. One Bota Singh, a Sandhu Jatt of Padhana, used to bathe in the tank at night under cover of darkness and remained concealed in the bushes during the day. He heard someone referring to him as a fake Singh. Cut to the quick by this taunt, Bota Singh decided to reveal himself in his true colours. He started collecting duty on the highway to Lahore and wrote to the governor that he was exercising this authority (as a Khalsa). Zakariya Khan sent a detachment of 100 horsemen to arrest him and Bota Singh died fighting, along with Garja Singh Ranghretā, who had joined this daring enterprise.

Bhangu says that it was reported to Zakariya Khan later on that a Sikh named Taru Singh in the village Poola used to offer food to the Singh outlaws. Bhai Taru Singh was arrested. The Sikhs of Padhana offered to get him released from official custody but Bhai Taru Singh refused the offer, saying that the Gurus had shown him the way to martyrdom for a righteous cause. At Lahore, Bhai Taru Singh was asked to cut off his hair and accept Islam. He insisted that his hair was inseparable from his body. Zakariya Khan ordered that his scalp should be scraped off. Bhai Taru Singh died on 1 July 1745.

It was observed by Anand Ram Mukhlis on 23 August 1746, when he was present in the Punjab, that one year, one month and twenty-three days after Zakariya Khan's death, the peace and prosperity given by the effective rule of Zakariya Khan was destroyed. 'Lawless men, plunderers and adventurers' now peeped out of their holes and 'began to desolate the realm, plundering the cities and villages and ruining families'.[44] These lawless men were chiefly the Khalsa.

Zakariya Khan's elder son and successor, Yahiya Khan confirmed Lakhpat Rai as dīvān. His younger brother, Jaspat Rai, was the faujdār of Eminabad. He attacked a band of Sikhs in the neighbourhood of Eminabad. The Sikhs fought back and a Ranghretā named Nibahu Singh got on to the elephant of Jaspat Rai and cut off his head. The Sikhs then plundered Eminabad. Dīvān Lakhpat Rai vowed vengeance upon the Sikhs. Despite representation from some of the eminent residents of Lahore, the Sikhs living in the city were arrested and executed. A huge army was collected to march against the Sikhs who had taken refuge in the marshes of Kahnuwan in the upper Bari Doāb. Pressed hard, the Sikhs tried to escape into the hills. The main body under the leadership of Sukha Singh fought against the Mughal troops in the Rachna Doāb; many Sikhs died fighting, and some of them were taken prisoner. The remaining Sikhs, about 2,000, crossed the Rivers Ravi, Beas, and Sutlej to take shelter in the Malwa region. Several thousand Sikhs were killed in this sustained campaign and several thousand were taken to Lahore as prisoners and executed. This bloody episode, now known as the 'little carnage' (in contradistinction to the 'great carnage' of 1762), is suggestive of the increased number of the Khalsa by 1746.[45]

By then, Nadir Shah had been murdered, and his eastern dominions replaced by his ablest General Ahmad Shah Abdali, who was also known by the title of the 'Durranī'. Ahmad Shah invaded India in 1747–8. Jassa Singh Ahluwalia, who was associated with Nawab Kapur Singh, led a band of Singhs to Ramdaspur and ousted Salabat Khan, the Mughal officer in charge of the town, to recover it for the Khalsa. On the Baisākhī of 1748, they selected a piece of land near Ramsar to build a small enclosure (*rauṇī*) of mud walls, with watch towers at the four corners and a moat all around, to accommodate about 500 men. Like Ramdaspur, it was called Ram Rauṇī after the name of Guru Ram Das, and even the leaders worked with their hands to construct the fortress.[46]

At the time of the Diwali of 1748, Mir Mannu, the new Mughal governor of Lahore, laid siege to Ram Rauṇī, which lasted for about three months from October to December, and about 200 Sikhs died fighting. Jai Singh Kanhiya, a leading Sikh warrior, decided to go out of Ram Rauṇī and to die fighting. The shouts of 'Sat Srī Akāl' after the collective prayer (*ardās*) were heard by Jassa Singh, generally referred to as Thoka (carpenter), and later known as Ramgaṛhia, who was with the troops of Adina Beg Khan, then the faujdār of Jalandhar Doāb. Jassa Singh decided to join the besieged and sent in a message seeking forgiveness. His request was accepted and he joined the Khalsa with a hundred followers. The news of Ahmad Shah Abdalī's invasion obliged Mir Mannu to raise the siege.

Mir Mannu's dīvān, Kauṛa Mal, favoured the policy of reconciliation with the Khalsa. On Kauṛa Mal's advice, Mir Mannu is said to have given villages worth rupees 1,25,000 a year in jāgīr to the Khalsa. They cleaned the holy tank, which had been filled up in the time of Lakhpat Rai, and celebrated the Diwali of 1749 with great enthusiasm. In 1750, when Mir Mannu sent Dīvān Kauṛa Mal against the rebel Shah Nawaz Khan, the younger son of Zakariya Khan, the dīvān was accompanied by a contingent of Sikhs under Jassa Singh Ahluwalia. Before the Durrani invasion of 1751–2, Mir Mannu allowed Kauṛa Mal to enlist 20,000 Sikhs under the leadership of Sangat Singh and Sukha Singh, both of whom eventually died fighting against the Afghans. For a year and a half, the leaders of the Khalsa cooperated with the Mughal authorities in their own interest and on their own terms.

Later Persian sources, like Sohan Lal Suri's *Umdat ut-Tawārīkh* and Bakht Mal's *Khālsānāma*, refer to the occupation of territories in the Jalandhar, Bari, and Rachna Doabs in the 1750s by the Sikh leaders like Jassa Singh Ahluwalia, Hari Singh, Karoṛa Singh, Jhanda Singh, Jassa Singh Thoka, and Charhat Singh Sukarchakia. It is interesting to note that the seal of Jai Singh Kanhiya on his extant orders (*parwānās*) bears the date 1750. Significantly, on 17 April 1752, one Hukumat Singh was ordering the 'āmils and zamīndārs of Kahnuwan to ensure that there was no interference with the concessions given by the former Mughal rulers to the Mahants of Pindori. The seal of Hukumat Singh, with his name prefixed by 'Akāl Sahāī' and the date 1752, suggests the possibility of similar orders having been issued by a number of Sikh leaders over considerable parts of the Punjab.[47] At any rate, the available evidence leaves no doubt that some of the leaders of the Khalsa were issuing orders to the local officials around 1750, before the provinces of Lahore and Multan were formally ceded by the Mughal emperor to Ahmad Shah Abdali in 1752 (see Figure 1.1).

## TRIUMPH OVER THE AFGHANS (1752–65)

The governorship of Mir Mannu from April 1752 to November 1753 was marked by a sustained campaign against Sikhs, who had begun to exercise authority in pockets of the province. Tahmas Khan, who was a slave of Mir Mannu at this time, recalled later that the Punjab had undergone a radical change on account of the tumult caused by Ahmad Shah Abdali in 1751–2. In the upper Bari Doāb a large number of Sikhs raised disturbance, plundering the population and obstructing the passage of travellers. Pursued by Mir Mannu's commandants, 900 Sikhs went into the fort of Ram

Rauṇī in Ramdaspur. They were besieged. Finally, they came out to give close battle and died fighting. Mir Mannu personally marched to Ramdaspur and encamped there for many days. Among the general measures against the Sikhs, Tahmas Khan mentions special guns prepared for the use of the cavalry, rewards of ten rupees for each Sikh head, and replacement of the mount lost in battle against the Sikhs. In September 1753, Mir Mannu set up his camp outside the city to take prompt action on receiving information from any quarter about the military activity of Sikhs. Tahmas Khan also mentions that the Sikhs who were brought to Mir Mannu as captives were put under the nail-press (*mekhchū*) to die a most painful death. Adina Beg Khan, the faujdār of Jalandhar, sent forty to fifty Sikh prisoners from time to time. They too were executed by crushing them under the nail-press.[48] The later Sikh sources refer to several other ways of torture and execution of even women and children by Mir Mannu.[49] He came to be seen by the Sikhs as their fiercest persecutor. It must be pointed out, however, that this image relates more to his governorship on behalf of Ahmad Shah Abdali than to the tenure as the Mughal governor of Lahore. With their claims to political power, the Sikhs presented the most serious threat to his position.

Hari Ram Gupta refers to the 'rapid rise' of the Sikhs between the death of Mir Mannu in November 1753 and the appointment of the Abdali's son, Taimur Shah, as viceroy of the Afghan territories in India in April 1757.[50] Jassa Singh Thoka rebuilt the fort of Ram Rauṇī which had been demolished by Mir Mannu. It was renamed Ramgarh and Jassa Singh now came to be known as 'Ramgaṛhia'. The Khalsa adopted the Ramgaṛh Fort in Amritsar as the base of their operations. In the early months of 1754, they did not allow the Abdali's faujdār, Qasim Khan, to take charge of Patti. He was forced to take 8,000 of the Sikhs in his service who deserted him after getting matchlocks, bows and arrows, and other war materials and costly gifts.[51] There are other known examples of Sikh activity against the Mughal–Afghan authorities that reflect the increasing resources and power of the Sikhs during this short phase.

Gupta refers to the 'Rākhī system' established by the Sikhs during this phase, which led to 'the final stage of their becoming a political power'. The villagers were to place themselves under the protection of the Khalsa on the promise to pay one-fifth of the produce from the rabī (spring) and kharīf (winter) crops in return for full protection against others. The territories brought under Rākhī, according to Gupta, served as the base for later Sikh principalities. 'Thus, this step supplied them with the idea of raising themselves into territorial chieftains.'[52] It must be pointed out that when Gupta made this observation in the 1930s neither the idea of 'rāj karegā Khālsā' nor the documentary evidence of the parwānās issued by the Sikh leaders was known to historians. A reference has already been made to Hukumat Singh, who had issued an order to the 'āmils and zamīndārs of Kahnuwan in April 1752; he addressed another order to 'the present and future' 'āmils of the pargana in January 1755 to the effect that they should ensure undisturbed continuation of concessions given to the Mahants of Pindori in earlier times.[53] Such orders could be issued only on the assumption that the local administrators would recognize the authority of the individual issuing the order. Thus, what is called Rākhī was simply the continued assertion of political authority over a particular area accompanied by a large reduction in the revenue. The ability of the Sikh leaders to make good their claim to power made them increasingly acceptable to the peasantry. Since no distinction was made on the basis of religion, the Sikh leaders could hope to gain support from the peasantry as a whole.

During the short tenure of Taimur Shah as the governor of Lahore, Wazir Jahan Khan had the strict orders of Ahmad Shah Abdali to suppress the Sikhs. But he succeeded only partially. Two incidents recalled by Tahmas Khan as an eyewitness are indicative of the efforts made by the Afghans to deal with the Sikhs. One day, Jahan Khan was informed that a large army of Sikhs had assembled at Ramdaspur for bathing and they were raising 'disturbance and rebellion'. This referred to the aggressive activity of the Khalsa. At this time, Sardār Ata Khan was engaged in regaining control over another area. Jahan Khan wrote to him to reach Ramdaspur on a particular day. Ata Khan did not reach the place in time and the Sikhs surrounded the Afghan army from all sides. Many of the soldiers got frightened and chose to flee, but the Sikhs did not make way for them, and the fleeing Afghans felt obliged to rejoin the army. Only with the arrival of Ata Khan was the situation saved. The Afghans now pursued the Sikhs to the gate of the town guarded by five Sikhs who died fighting. The Afghan army remained encamped there. Wazir Jahan Khan then marched off 'to gain control of the country and establish his administration'. This appears to be a case of 'regaining' control over territories taken over by Sikhs. The other incident narrated by Tahmas Khan is equally telling. Two Afghan horsemen coming from Sarhind were murdered near Kartarpur, the place of Sodhi Badbhag Singh in the Jalandhar Doāb. Wazir Jahan Khan sent special horsemen (sazāwals) to 'Sodhi Ramdas' (Badbhag Singh) to find the murderers. They treated the Sodhi harshly and he went into hiding. The sazāwals sacked Kartarpur but returned empty-handed. From every side tumult and rebellion began to be raised by Sikhs. Wherever the Afghan army went it came back defeated. Even the environs of Lahore were affected. Thousands of Sikhs attacked the city every night and sacked the quarters outside the city wall. The administration of the country was thrown into disorder.[54]

Significantly, by this time, Adina Beg Khan had been alienated by the Afghans. He defeated them in the Jalandhar Doāb with the support of Sikh leaders. For fear of Wazir Jahan Khan, however, he took refuge in the hills. From there he sent repeated requests to the Maratha commander Raghunath Rao to extend the Maratha dominions up to the Indus, offering to pay rupees 1,00,000 for each day of march and rupees 50,000 for halting. It may be mentioned that by this time the Marathas under the Peshwa had established their control over Delhi and had taken the Mughal emperor under their protection. Responding to Adina Beg Khan's proposition, the Maratha commander, Raghunath Rao, besieged Sarhind early in March 1758. He was soon joined by the Sikhs to plunder Sarhind, where the younger sons of the tenth Guru had been bricked alive. Jahan Khan decided to vacate Lahore. Raghunath Rao reached Lahore on 11 April 1758, but he was not inclined to stay on. The Marathas conferred the title of Nawab on Adina Beg Khan and leased out the province to him for rupess 75,00,000 a year. Adina Beg Khan too did not wish to stay in Lahore. He went to Batala and died in September. The Peshwa then sent Dattaji Sindhia with a strong force to the Punjab. He found that in and around Lahore, Sikhs were predominant and they commanded a vast force. He went back to Delhi.[55]

The Marathas realized rather late that they could not hold the Punjab without Sikh support. When Afghan troops started towards India in October 1759, the Maratha commandants began to retreat. From October 1758 to October 1759, Sikhs had extended the area of their influence and strengthened their control over the territories occupied earlier.

Ahmad Shah Abdali's presence in India but away from the Punjab in 1760 enabled the Sikhs to further consolidate their power. An incident mentioned by Tahmas Khan is interesting in this connection. Rustam Khan Bangash, who had been appointed by Ahmad Shah as the commandant of the four parganas (mahāl) that had been ceded to Nadir Shah, came out of the city of Sialkot to fight with the Sikhs. He had only 150 horse and foot soldiers. Tahmas Khan also joined him. They were both captured. Tahmas Khan was released for a small sum but Rustam Khan had to pay rupees 22,000 as ransom. Tahmas Khan states later that Sa'adat Khan and Sadiq Khan, the Afridi Afghans who had been appointed by Ahmad Shah as commandants of the Jalandhar Doāb in April 1761, were defeated and thrown out like flies out of milk. The Sikhs acquired 'dominance and possession' from the Indus to the Sutlej.[56]

The increasing power of Sikhs obliged Ahmad Shah Abdali to subdue them decisively. He came to Lahore early in 1762 and was informed that the Sikhs were encamped near the village Kup, with their women and children. According to Bhangu, Jassa Singh Ahluwalia and Charhat Singh Sukarchakia were the top leaders at this time. They decided to adopt a defensive strategy, moving towards Barnala, with their baggage, women, and children under their protection. The Afghans pursued the Sikhs from early morning till sunset, killing thousands of them in a single day. As mentioned earlier, the event is called the 'great carnage' (*vaddhā ghallūghārā*) with reference to the 'little carnage' (*chhotā ghallūghārā*) of 1746.[57] Tahmas Khan, who participated in the action, states that 25,000 Sikhs were slain on that day. He nevertheless felt that disorders would arise again and all routes would be closed. The terror of Sikhs was increasing day by day even in the central parts of the province. Soon after Ahmad Shah's departure from Lahore, disorders arose in the entire country.[58]

News reports from Delhi throw further light on the growing power and confidence of the Sikhs after the great carnage. A report of 14 April 1763 refers to the mutual deliberations of the 'Sikh chiefs' and the 'division and distribution of the country among themselves'. They proposed to march beyond the Jamuna into the territories around Saharanpur and other areas. No one dared or had the power to oppose them. They wrote to the Mughal court that the money collected for Ahmad Shah Abdali should be paid to the Khalsa and that in case of delay, they would be obliged to attack Delhi. In August 1763 it was reported by the news writer that the Sikhs had established their control over the Sindh Sagar Doāb, and they would oppose the Abdali on the River Indus if he marched towards the Punjab. Ahmad Shah crossed the Indus after the Sikh chiefs had returned to Ramdaspur for the Dusehra. He was attacked by the Sikhs after he crossed the River Chenab. The Afghan army was routed. The Abdali put his horse into the river to escape. The news report continues that after 'the great battle and the defeat suffered by him there at the hands of the Sikhs, the Shah reached the River Jhelum, and his troops fled hither and thither in disorder'. The Shah exhorted them to stand up but no one listened to him. 'Travelling thirty kurohs in one day-and-night, out of the terror of the Sikhs, they reached Hasan Abdal.' They recrossed the Indus on 25 February 1764.[59]

Already in January 1764, Sarhind had been attacked and occupied by the Khalsa under the leadership of Jassa Singh Ahluwalia. Its Afghan governor, Zain Khan, was shot dead in an attempt to escape. The entire sarkār of Sarhind, worth about rupees 60,00,000 a year, came into the possession of the Sikhs. They dispersed as soon as the battle was over and riding by day and night, each horseman would throw his belt or scabbard, his articles of dress and accoutrement, into successive villages to mark them as his. According to Ratan Singh Bhangu, a Gurmatā had been passed in the presence of Guru Granth Sahib that no one would be dislodged by a stronger individual from a place first occupied; anyone dislodging another would be ejected by the Khalsa.[60]

Ahmad Shah Abdali realized the gravity of the situation and made an all-out effort later in the year to reassert his authority in the Punjab. According to Qazi Nur Muhammad, who accompanied the Afghan forces on this expedition, the Abdali invited Mir Nasir Khan, the Baloch chief of Kalat, to join him in jīhād against the Sikhs. Mir Nasir Khan dropped the idea of going to Mecca for pilgrimage and joined the Shah at Eminabad with 12,000 Baluchis. There was a determined resistance from the Sikhs. The Shah decided to destroy Ramdaspur as he had done several times before. He reached Ramdaspur on 1 December 1764 when there were only a few Sikhs in charge of the Akāl Bungā. Qazi Nur Muhammad says that they were only thirty but 'they did not at all show any fear of being killed nor the dread of death'.[61] Bhangu tells us that their leader was Gurbakhsh Singh Nihang who used to lead the Khalsa standards in battle. Each one of them died fighting as a martyr. They were cremated together and a memorial (*shahīdganj*) in their honour was later built near the Akāl Bungā.[62]

The Abdali marched towards Delhi by slow marches. At Kunjpura on the Jamuna he decided to return. Before he recrossed the Sutlej, the Afghan army was attacked by the Khalsa. Qazi Nur Muhammad gives a detailed account of this campaign. The battle continued for two days, more to inflict losses on the Shah than to win a decisive victory. A similar engagement took place before the Shah crossed the River Beas. After his departure from the Punjab in March 1765, the Sikhs met at Amritsar for the Baisākhī and resolved to take possession of Lahore. It was captured by Gujjar Singh, Lehna Singh, and Sobha Singh. They struck a coin as the formal declaration of Sikh sovereignty. The inscription on this coin was the same as the one on the seal used in the time of Banda Singh:[63]

> Deg-o teg-o fateh-o nusrat bedirang,
> Yāft az Nanak Guru Gobind Singh.

Evidently, the declaration of sovereign rule in 1710 was never forgotten by the Khalsa.[64]

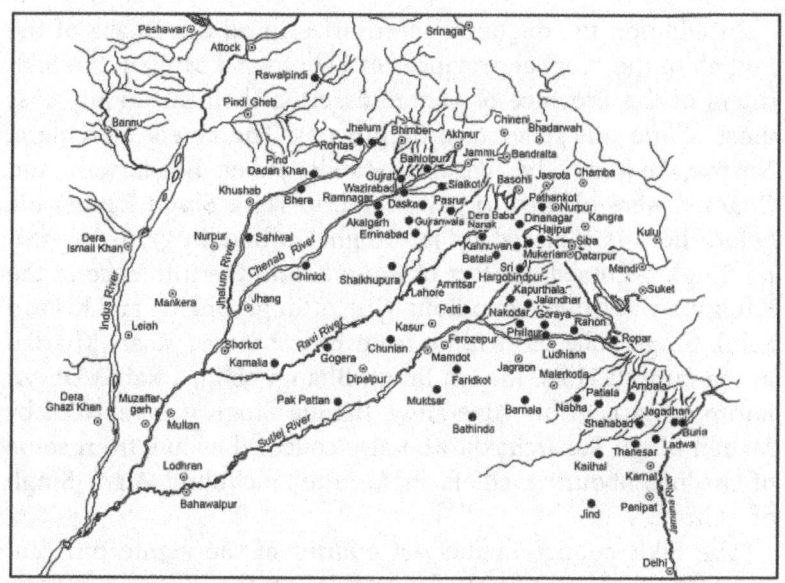

**FIGURE 1.2**   The Punjab (Late Eighteenth Century)
Important Places Associated with the Sikh Chiefs
*Source*: Adapted from Map 4, in J.S. Grewal, *The Sikhs of the Punjab, The New Cambridge History of India*, II.3 (New Delhi: Cambridge University Press, 2014).

## IN THE LATE EIGHTEENTH CENTURY

The primary concern of the Sikh chiefs after the declaration of their sovereignty in 1765 was to consolidate their position and to increase their human and material resources. In this process, there developed tensions among them, sometimes leading to armed conflict. The emergent Sikh rulers of the province of Lahore had still to contend with the non-Sikh chiefs of the Punjab plains as well as the old chiefs of the hills and Ahmad Shah Abdali and his successors. Besides the Mughal emperor and his ministers, the Sikh chiefs of the Sutlej–Jamuna Divide had to face several new powers: the Jat chiefs of Bharatpur, the Afghans of Rohilkhand, the Nawab of Awadh, the Marathas, the East India Company, and the Irish adventurer George Thomas.

In addition to conquering territories in all the Doabs of the Punjab in the Mughal provinces of Lahore and Multan, the Sikh rulers of the province of Lahore asserted their suzerainty over most of the hill states (see Figure 1.2). The chiefs of Kangra, Nurpur, Jaswan, Siba, Basohli, Mandi, Suket, Bhadarwah, and Chamba were obliged to pay tribute to Jassa Singh Ramgarhia before he was replaced by Jai Singh Kanhiya in 1776. In 1783, Jai Singh occupied the fort of Kangra, and the influence of the Kanhiyas was extended to Kulu. Gujjar Singh Bhangi and his son Sahib Singh collected tribute from Bhimbar and Khari Khariali in the Jammu Hills. Jhanda Singh Bhangi obliged Ranjit Dev of Jammu to accept his suzerainty. Jhanda Singh was replaced by Mahan Singh Sukarchakia who also collected tribute from some of the neighbouring chiefs in Jammu, including Alam Singh of Akhnur.[65]

The Sikh politics in the last quarter of the eighteenth century was more remarkable for internal strife than for territorial expansion. Jassa Singh Ramgarhia, Jai Singh Kanhiya, Gujjar Singh Bhangi, and Jhanda Singh Bhangi were fighting among themselves for supremacy in the hills. In 1774, Charhat Singh Sukarchakia and Jai Singh Kanhiya supported Ranjit Dev of Jammu against his son Brij Raj Dev who was supported by Jhanda Singh Bhangi. Both Charhat Singh and Jhanda Singh died during this campaign. Soon afterwards, the Kanhiyas and the Bhangis fought over Pathankot. In 1776, Jassa Singh Ahluwalia and Jai Singh dislodged Jassa Singh Ramgarhia from his territories in the province of Lahore, and he remained in the wilderness till 1785, when Mahan Singh Sukarchakia enabled him to defeat Jai Singh in a battle near Batala. The issue of ascendancy among the Sikh chiefs of the province was undecided when Mahan Singh died in 1791.[66]

After Ahmad Shah Abdali's death in October 1772, his son and successor, Taimur Shah, failed to take any action when Multan was occupied by Jhanda Singh. However, he became active, when the Sikh chiefs began to threaten the trans-Indus Derajat. He reconquered Multan in 1780 and subjugated Bahawalpur and Sind. Before long, he recovered Kashmir and appointed his own governor. After Taimur Shah's death in 1793, his eldest son Shah

Zaman thought of leading an expedition into India in 1794–5 and reached Rohtas. But he had to go back to Kabul because of the trouble created by his half-brother Sultan Mahmud. In 1796–7 Shah Zaman marched up to Lahore. Its Sikh chiefs left the city and the people of Lahore presented to him a *nazrāna* of rupees 1,00,000. Before he could persuade or compel the Sikh chiefs to submit to him, he had to go back again due to the trouble created by Sultan Mahmud. Shah Zaman reoccupied Lahore unopposed in 1798. He wanted the Sikh chiefs to acknowledge his authority. But soon he heard of the invasion of Afghanistan by the ruler of Persia and hurried back to Kabul to be defeated and blinded by Sultan Mahmud. Mahan Singh's son and successor, Ranjit Singh, occupied Lahore in 1799, marking the beginning of his ascendancy among the Sikh chiefs. [67]

In the Sutlej–Jamuna Divide, the Sikh chiefs of Patiala, Nabha, Jind, Malaud, Bhadaur, Kaithal, and Faridkot belonged to the region. The other Sikh chiefs, like those of Ambala, Shahabad, Chilaundi, Kalsia, Thanesar, Chhachhrauli, Ladwa, and Buria belonged originally to the province of Lahore. They were generally more aggressive in politics. In the absence of Emperor Shah Alam, Najibuddaula was the virtual dictator in Delhi till 1770. He had to bear the brunt of the incursions of the Sikh chiefs into the Ganga–Jamuna Doāb. After his death in 1770, his son Zabita Khan succeeded to his estate, but there were two rivals at the Delhi court: Najaf Khan and Abdul Ahad Khan. The Sikh chiefs took advantage of this rivalry and became more active around Delhi and across the Jamuna. In 1776, they plundered Meerut, Sikandara, and Khurja, and advanced up to Aligarh. In 1779, Abdul Ahad Khan formed a plan of attacking Patiala with support from Baghel Singh, Karora Singh, and Desa Singh of Kaithal. Several of the trans-Sutlej Sikh chiefs came to the help of Amar Singh of Patiala, and Abdul Ahad Khan was forced to retreat. [68]

The Maratha Sardār Mahadji Sindhia acquired ascendancy in Delhi in the early 1780s. In the name of the Mughal emperor, he proposed a treaty with the Sikh chiefs but they broke with Mahadji after some time. In 1786, the Marathas helped Patiala against the other Sikh chiefs. In 1787, Ambaji tried to subdue the Sikh chiefs with the support of Baghel Singh and Dulcha Singh but the expedition failed. Mahadji Sindhia could retard the advance of the Sikh chiefs into the Ganga–Jamuna Doāb, but he could not put a stop to their activity.

Contemporary British records bear witness to the activities of the Sikh chiefs beyond the River Jamuna. In 1780, the British advised their ally, the Nawab of Awadh, to seek support of the Rohillas against the Sikhs who were 'committing depredations in Rohilkhand'. In 1785, the irruptions of the Sikhs up to the right bank of the Ganges made it necessary for the East India Company to keep a watchful eye over the western frontier of the British provinces and those of Awadh. In 1787, a body of Sikhs defeated the Maratha troops within a hundred kilometres of Anupshahr and it was thought necessary to send a detachment of the Company's forces towards the British cantonment of Anupshahr to prevent any sudden attack by the Sikhs. In 1790, it was reported that about 10,000 Sikhs plundered some villages on the borders of the Nawab's territories, and two battalions with the requisite artillery were ordered to march to Anupshahr. In early 1791, 30,000 to 40,000 Sikhs plundered a few villages close to the Nawab's territories. The first instance of Sikh aggression against the Nawab of Awadh had been to carry off Lieutenant Colonel Robert Stuart during his morning ride near the cantonment in Anupshahr. The British could secure Stuart's release after nine months, mainly through the good offices of Begam Samru.[69]

In the late 1790s, while the chiefs of the Sutlej–Jamuna Divide were threatened by the rise of George Thomas, the British became more concerned also with the invasions of Shah Zaman. In 1796–7, Shah Zaman's design appeared to be to establish his authority in the Punjab, and not to advance into Hindustan. In 1798, he reportedly wanted to shift his capital from Kabul to Lahore, and was determined this time to march on Delhi. The governor general pressurized Persia to move against Afghanistan so that Shah Zaman felt threatened. The Sikhs in the trans-Sutlej region cut off his supplies, harassed his army, and prepared for action against him. Shah Zaman returned to Kabul. Lieutenant Colonel J. Collins, the British Resident at Fatehgarh (in the Ganga–Jamuna Doāb) who was in contact with many of the Sikh chiefs, received from Ranjit Singh a letter to the effect that it was in the common interest of the British and Ranjit Singh to keep his country safe from Shah Zaman's invasions.[70] Ranjit Singh was becoming conscious of his position among the Sikh chiefs.

## IN RETROSPECT

The political developments covered in this chapter fall into four broad phases. The first phase began with the martial activity of Guru Hargobind in the early seventeenth century and ended with the death of Guru Gobind Singh in 1708. This background to the eighteenth century was first marked by increasing confrontation between the Mughal state and the mainstream Sikhs, reaching its culmination in the execution of Guru Tegh Bahadur in 1675. Guru Gobind Singh's creative response to the new situation culminating in the institution of the Khalsa was more systematic and fundamental. His political activity was accompanied by a supportive literary resurgence for sustained inspiration. The ideal of political ascendancy was deliberately and carefully cultivated and propagated. The followers of Guru Gobind Singh were transformed into a political community that derived its inspiration from religious ideology for pursuing political power. Just before his death, Guru Gobind Singh transferred his authority to the collectivity of the Khalsa, with the Granth Sahib as their guide in all situations. Their operative slogan as well as the goal was 'rāj karegā Khālsā'. The stage was set for a long struggle.

The second phase started soon after the death of Guru Gobind Singh with the establishment of a sovereign state by the Khalsa under Banda Singh in the Sutlej–Jamuna Divide that was maintained for a few years with ups and downs. The Khalsa lost the first round but created an example, which reinforced the aspiration to rule. They suffered persecution and suppression under the Mughal governors, but survived as a political entity. They continued their struggle. Before the transfer of the province of Lahore to the empire of Ahmad Shah Abdali in 1752, they were exercising political control over pockets of territory in the central Punjab.

A new phase started with Ahmad Shah Abdali's invasions of India. The Khalsa were steadily gaining power and resources while Ahmad Shah was preoccupied with apparently more important matters in northern India and Afghanistan. In 1760, when he was trying hard to strike down the Marathas, the Khalsa established their hold over much of the Punjab. In the early 1760s, Ahmad Shah established his suzerainty over the chiefs of the Sutlej–Jamuna Divide, but failed to dislodge the Khalsa from the province of Lahore. Aware of their own power and strength, the Khalsa declared their sovereignty by striking a coin at Lahore. What sustained them in the successful pursuit of the goal of Khalsa Rāj was their ideology and the institutions created on its basis, besides the revival of Ramdaspur as the centre of their religious and political activity.

In the last phase, the character of Sikh politics changed. The Sikh rulers after the declaration of Sikh sovereignty in 1765, generally, were more concerned with the affairs of their territories than with fresh conquests. The new situation was marked as much by internal conflicts among the Sikh chiefs themselves as their campaigns for the expansion of their influence and the desire to increase their resources.

## NOTES AND REFERENCES

1.  For an outline of the activities of Guru Hargobind, see J.S. Grewal, *The Sikhs of the Punjab* (The New Cambridge History of India, II.3) (Cambridge: Cambridge University Press, 2014 [1990]), pp. 62–7. See also Teja Singh and Ganda Singh, *A Short History of the Sikhs (1465–1765)* (Patiala: Punjabi University, 1999 [1950]), pp. 35–46.

2.  For a discussion on these dissident groups, see J.S. Grewal, 'Cleavage in the Panth', in J.S. Grewal, *Sikh Ideology, Polity and Social Order: From Guru Nanak to Maharaja Ranjit Singh* (New Delhi: Manohar, 2007 [1996]), pp. 78–85.

3.  J.S. Grewal, 'In Defence of the Freedom of Conscience', in Grewal, *Sikh Ideology, Polity and Social Order*, pp. 86–91. See also '"Frighten No One and Be Afraid of None": Guru Tegh Bahadur', in J.S. Grewal, *Four Centuries of Sikh Tradition: History, Literature, and Identity* (New Delhi: Oxford University Press, 2011), pp. 136–58. For a biography of the ninth Guru, see Harbans Singh, *Guru Tegh Bahadur* (New Delhi: Sterling Publishers, 1982).

4.  J.S. Grewal and S.S. Bal, *Guru Gobind Singh: A Biographical Study* (Chandigarh: Panjab University, 1987 [1967]). Also, J.S. Grewal, 'Guru Gobind Singh: Life and Mission', *Journal of Punjab Studies* 15, nos 1 and 2 (Spring–Fall 2008): 6–10. This and the next three paragraphs are based on these two works.

5.  For the text of the *Bachittar Nātak*, see *Sri Dasam Granth Sāhib*, ed. Ratan Singh Jaggi and Gursharan Kaur Jaggi (New Delhi: Gobind Sadan, 1999), vol. 1, pp. 104–91. See also J.S. Grewal, '*Bachittar Nātak*: Proclamation of a Mission', in Grewal, *Sikh Ideology, Polity and Social Order*, pp. 92–5. Also, J.S. Grewal, 'Declaration of "Righteous War": The Bachittar Nātak', in Grewal, *Four Centuries of Sikh Tradition*, pp. 161–76.

6.  Sainapat, *Sri Gur Sobhā*, ed. Ganda Singh (Patiala: Punjabi University, 1967), pp. 20–1. Also, Sainapat, *Shri Gur Sobhā*, ed. Shamsher Singh Ashok (Amritsar: Shiromani Gurdwara Prabandhak Committee, 1967), pp. 29–30. The title is spelt slightly differently in these two editions as shown here.

7.  Koer Singh, *Gurbilās Pātshāhī 10*, ed. Shamsher Singh Ashok (Patiala: Punjabi University, 1968), pp. 127–9.

8.  *Rahitnāmā Bhai Daya Singh*, in *Rahitnāme*, ed. Piara Singh Padam (Amritsar: Singh Brothers, 1995), pp. 68–9. See also Ratan Singh Bhangu, *Sri Gur Panth Prakash*, ed. Balwant Singh Dhillon (Amritsar: Singh Brothers, 2004), p. 36.

9.  It needs to be underlined that the 'rāj karegā Khālsā' couplet occurs in the rahitnāmā called the *Nasīhatnāmā* (also called *Tankhānāmā*) included in MS 770, dated 1718–19, which is clearly a copy. For a study of this work, see Karamjit K. Malhotra, 'The Earliest Manual on the Sikh Way of Life', in *Five Centuries of Sikh Tradition: Ideology, Society, Politics and Culture*, ed. Reeta Grewal and Sheena Pall (New Delhi: Manohar, 2005), pp. 55–81.

10. Grewal, 'Guru Gobind Singh: Life and Mission': 17–18.

11. Grewal and Bal, *Guru Gobind Singh*, pp. 135–6, 140–1.

12. For the transliteration and Punjabi translation of the *Zafarnāma*, which is in Persian, see Jaggi and Jaggi, *Dasam Granth*, vol. 5, pp. 676–91.

13. J.S. Grewal, '*Zafarnāma*: Declaration of Moral Victory', and 'Insistence on Justice', in Grewal, *Sikh Ideology, Polity and Social Order*, pp. 96–106. For a detailed analysis see Louis E. Fenech, *The Sikh Zafar-nāmah of Guru Gobind Singh: A Discursive Blade in the Heart of the Mughal Empire* (Oxford: Oxford University Press, 2013).

14. For a contemporary bardic account in Persian of Banda Singh's meeting with the tenth Guru, see Nath Mal, *Amarnāma*, trans. and

ed. Ganda Singh (Amritsar: Sikh History Society, 1953), pp. 18–39. For a later account, see Kesar Singh Chhibber, *Bansāvalīnāmā Dasān Pātshāhiān Kā*, ed. Ratan Singh Jaggi, in *Parkh*, vol. 2 (Chandigarh: Panjab University, 1972), pp. 156–7. See also Karamjit K. Malhotra, 'Banda Singh in Chhibber's *Bansavalinama*: Image, Idea and Reality', *Panjab Journal of Sikh Studies* 2 (2012): 113, 116.

15.   Chhibber, *Bansāvalīnāmā*, pp. 156–7. See also Karamjit K. Malhotra, 'Banda Singh Bahadur in the *Mahima Prakash*', *Journal of Sikh Studies* 36 (2012): 100, 101, 105.

16.   Sainapat, *Sri Gur Sobhā*, ed. Ganda Singh, pp. 123–31. See also J.S. Grewal, '*Gursobhā*—In Praise of Khalsa', in Grewal, *Sikh Ideology, Polity and Social Order*, p. 109. Also, J.S. Grewal, 'The Guru Khalsa: Sainapat's Sri Gur Sobhā', in Grewal, *Four Centuries of Sikh Tradition*, pp. 177–86.

17.   For accounts of Banda Singh's conquests in Persian sources, see J.S. Grewal and Irfan Habib, eds, *Sikh History from Persian Sources: Translations of Major Texts* (New Delhi: Tulika/Indian History Congress, 2001), pp. 108, 116–18, 133–4, 143, 161. The individual sources covered here are: 'Reports from Bahadur Shah's Court 1707–10'; Muhammad Qasim, '*Ibratnāma*; Mirza Muhammad, '*Ibratnāma*; Muhammad Hadi Kamwar Khan, *Tazkiratu's Salātīn Chaghatā*; and Muhammad Shafi 'Warid', *Mir'āt-i Wāridāt*. For a description of the battle of Chappar Chiri, see Ganda Singh, *Life of Banda Singh Bahadur* (Patiala: Punjabi University, 2006 [1935]), pp. 42–5.

18.   For the inscription on the coin, see Surinder Singh, *Sikh Coinage: Symbol of Sikh Sovereignty* (New Delhi: Manohar, 2004), p. 41.

19.   For a facsimile of the hukamnāmā, see Ganda Singh, ed., *Hukamnāme: Gurū Sāhibān, Mātā Sāhibān, Banda Singh Ate Khalsa Ji De* (Patiala: Punjabi University, 1967), pp. 194–5.

It is interesting to note that in sākhī 16 of the *Parchiān Sewādās*, composed in 1708, there is a reference to the seal of Guru Gobind Singh, which he uses in a certain situation. In another situation in sākhī 30, the tenth Guru in a loud voice recites the couplet 'deg teg fateh be-dirang, simrate Guru Nanak fateh Guru Gobind Singh'. It appears that the seal and the words inscribed on it were used by Guru Gobind Singh himself. See Sewadas, *Episodes from Lives of the Gurus: Parchiān Sewādās*, trans. and ed. Kharak Singh and Gurtej Singh (Chandigarh: Institute of Sikh Studies, 1995), pp. 138, 146.

20.   Mirza Muhammad, '*Ibratnāma*, p. 135.

21.   Muhammad Qasim, '*Ibratnāma*, p. 117. See also Teja Singh and Ganda Singh, *A Short History of the Sikhs* (Patiala: Punjabi University, 1999 [1950]), pp. 83–4.

22. Ganda Singh, *Life of Banda Singh Bahadur*, pp. 58–9.

23. For a discussion on the zamīndārī system in Mughal India, see Irfan Habib, *Agrarian System of Mughal India (1566–1707)* (New Delhi: Oxford University Press, 1999 [1963]), pp. 169–229.

24. Bhangu, *Sri Gur Panth Prakāsh*, p. 85. It is interesting to note that even in 1765 Ala Singh refers to himself as 'a zamīndār'. See 'News Reports from Delhi, 1759–65', in J.S. Grewal and Irfan Habib, eds, *Sikh History from Persian Sources: Translations of Major Texts* (New Delhi: Tulika/Indian History Congress, 2001), p. 202.

25. Muhammad Qasim, '*Ibratnāma*, p. 121. For a description of the siege by an eyewitness, see Muhammad Hadi Kamwar Khan, *Tazkiratu's Salātīn Chaghatā*, in J.S. Grewal and Habib, *Sikh History from Persian Sources*, pp. 144–51. The description in the following paragraph also is based on this source.

26. Mirza Muhammad, '*Ibratnāma*, pp. 137–8. Ganda Singh, *Life of Banda Singh Bahadur*, pp. 121–2.

27. For an eyewitness account of the siege of Gurdas Nangal, see Muhammad Qasim, '*Ibratnāma*, pp. 125–6.

28. This description is based on Mirza Muhammad, '*Ibratnāma*, and Kamwar Khan, '*Tazkiratu's Salātīn Chaghatā*, pp. 139, 140, 153.

29. 'The English Report of Banda Bahadur's Arrival as Captive at Delhi', in J.S. Grewal and Habib, *Sikh History from Persian Sources*, p. 127. Also, John Surman and Edward Stephenson, 'Massacre of the Sikhs at Delhi in 1716', in *Early European Accounts of the Sikhs*, ed. Ganda Singh (Calcutta: Indian Studies Past & Present, 1962), pp. 49–52.

30. Mirza Muhammad, '*Ibratnāma*, p. 141.

31. Khafi Khan, *Muntakhabu'l Lubāb*, in J.S. Grewal and Habib, *Sikh History from Persian Sources*, pp. 158–9.

32. Anon., *Asrar-i Samadi*, trans. Janak Singh (Patiala: Punjabi University, 1972), pp.14–15. See also Khafi Khan, *Muntakhabu'l Lubāb*, p. 158.

33. Indu Banga, 'Raj-Khalsa: Ideology and Praxis', *Journal of Punjab Studies* 15, nos 1 and 2 (Spring–Fall, 2008): 36.

34. Anon., *Asrār-i-Samadī*, pp. vii, 6–15, 16–21 et passim.

35. Muzaffar Alam, *The Crisis of Empire in Mughal North India: Awadh and the Punjab, 1707–48* (New Delhi: Oxford University Press, 2013 [1986]), pp. 179–80. Alam's understanding here is based mainly on the chronicles and news reports of the period in Persian.

36. Malhotra, 'The Earliest Manual on the Sikh Way of Life', pp. 55–81.

37. Ganda Singh, *Hukamnāme*, pp. 196–231.

38. Chhibber, *Bansāvalīnāmā*, pp. 182–6. See also Bhangu, *Sri Gur Panth Prakāsh*, pp. 158–65.

39. Bhangu, *Sri Gur Panth Prakāsh*, pp. 204–11, 215–20. This and the following two paragraphs are based on Bhangu's account.
40. Chhibber, *Bansāvalīnāmā*, pp. 164, 196.
41. Bhangu, *Sri Gur Panth Prakāsh*, pp. 183–93.
42. Bhangu, *Sri Gur Panth Prakāsh*, pp. 220–4. The dialogue between Nadir Shah and Zakariya Khan as recorded by Ahmad Shah of Batala in the early nineteenth century went as follows:

> Nadir Shah: Have you got any troublesome characters in the country?
> Zakariya Khan: None, except a group of Hindu *faqīrs*, who assemble twice to bathe in a tank which they regard as a place of pilgrimage.
> Nadir Shah: Where do they live?
> Zakariya Khan: Their homes are in their saddles.
> Nadir Shah: Take care, the day is not distant when these rebels will take possession of your country.

> Quoted in Indu Banga, *Agrarian System of the Sikhs: Late Eighteenth and Early Nineteenth Century* (New Delhi: Manohar, 1978), pp. 13–14 and 14n.

43. Teja Singh and Ganda Singh, *A Short History of the Sikhs*, p. 124. Bhangu, *Sri Gur Panth Prakash*, pp. 227–37, 255–9, 272. The following three paragraphs are based on Bhangu's work.
44. Quoted in Hari Ram Gupta, *History of the Sikhs: Evolution of the Sikh Confederacies (1708–69)*, vol. 2 (New Delhi: Munshiram Manoharlal, 2014 [1939]), pp. 68–70, 363. It may be mentioned that the author of *Tazkirah-i-Anandram Mukhlis* belonged to Lahore. He was serving at Delhi as secretary to the Mughal Wazir Qamruddin Khan.
45. Gupta, *History of the Sikhs*, vol. 2, pp. 73–8. The carnage of 1746 is known as chhotā ghallūghārā and that of 1762 is remembered as the vaddhā ghallūghārā.
46. Teja Singh and Ganda Singh, *A Short History of the Sikhs*, pp. 130–1, 133–7. This and the following two paragraphs are based on this work.
47. For the seal of Jai Singh Kanhiya and orders of Hukumat Singh, see B.N. Goswamy and J.S. Grewal, trans and eds, *The Mughal and Sikh Rulers and the Vaishnavas of Pindori: A Historical Interpretation of 52 Persian Documents* (Simla: Indian Institute of Advanced Study, 2010 [1969]), [hereafter *The Mughal and Sikh Rulers*], documents XVIII, XXIV, XXV, pp. 205–8, 227–9, 231–3. Such documents are known to be in the possession of a large number of religious establishments in different parts of the Punjab.

48. Tahmas Khan, *Qissa-i Tahmas-i Miskin* or *Tahmās Nāma*, in J.S. Grewal and Habib, *Sikh History from Persian Sources* [hereafter *Tahmās Nāma*], pp. 171–2.

49. These women and children are remembered in the Sikh prayer (ardās) recited every day on various occasions by Sikhs all over the world.

50. Gupta, *History of the Sikhs*, vol. 2, pp. 113–17, 124.

51. *Tahmās Nāma*, pp. 173–4. Gupta, *History of the Sikhs*, vol. 2, pp. 121–2.

52. Gupta, *History of the Sikhs*, vol. 2, pp. 126–8. Indu Banga has already pointed out the limitation of Gupta's view. See Banga, *Agrarian System of the Sikhs*, pp. 27–8.

53. *The Mughal and Sikh Rulers*, document XIX, pp. 209–11.

54. *Tahmās Nāma*, pp. 174–7.

55. It may be noted that during the year of Maratha rule in the Punjab there was no mutual trust or cordial cooperation between the Sikhs and the Marathas. Their political interests could not easily be reconciled. For an account of this phase, see Gupta, *History of the Sikhs*, vol. 2, pp. 138–46.

56. *Tahmās Nāma*, pp. 177–81.

57. For an account of the ghallūghārā in the Sikh tradition, see Bhangu, *Sri Gur Panth Prakāsh*, pp. 337–52.

58. *Tahmās Nāma*, pp. 181–3.

59. 'News Reports from Delhi, 1759–65', pp. 190–1, 193–7.

60. For an account of the occupation of Sarhind, see Bhangu, *Sri Gur Panth Prakāsh*, pp. 377–85.

61. Qazi Nur Muhammad, *Jangnāma*, in J.S. Grewal and Habib, *Sikh History from Persian Sources*, pp. 205–7.

62. Bhangu, *Sri Gur Panth Prakāsh*, pp. 386–94.

63. Qazi Nur Muhammad gives a detailed account of this campaign. Nur Muhammad, *Jangnāma*, p. 207. See also Banga, *Agrarian System of the Sikhs*, p. 19.

64. Significantly, ten years later, a coin was struck at Amritsar with the same inscription as on the Sikh coins of 1711 and 1712. For some detail, see Surinder Singh, *Sikh Coinage*, p. 64.

65. Banga, *Agrarian System of the Sikhs*, pp. 41–2.

66. Banga, *Agrarian System of the Sikhs*, pp. 21–2.

67. For detail, Narendra Krishna Sinha, *Rise of the Sikh Power* (Calcutta: A. Mukherjee & Co., 1963 [1936]), pp. 65–74. Hari Ram Gupta, *History of the Sikhs: Sikh Domination of the Mughal Empire (1764–1803)*, vol. 3 (New Delhi: Munshiram Manoharlal, 2009 [1944]), pp. 371–6.

68. See Sinha, *Rise of the Sikh Power*, pp. 76–87, for detail. See also Gupta, *History of the Sikhs*, vol. 3, pp. 65–130.

69. Considerable detail about the trans-Jamuna activities of the Sikhs has been provided by the National Archives of India, New Delhi (NAI), Fort William-India House Correspondence, vol. V, 10 April 1767; vol. IX, November 1780; September 1785; vol. XVI, 23 January 1787; 20 November 1790; 31 January 1791; 1 December 1791. See also Sinha, *Rise of the Sikh Power*, pp. 89–97, and Gupta, *History of the Sikhs*, vol. 3, pp. 196–242.

70. NAI, Foreign/Secret Consultation, 25 January 1797, file no. 6, 31 December 1796 and 25 January 1797; 30 December 1800. See Fort William Correspondence, vol. XVIII. See also Gupta, *History of the Sikhs*, vol. 3, pp. 287–368.

# 2 The Khalsa Rāj (1765–99)

Commenting on the documents of the Vaishnava establishment in Pindori, B.N. Goswamy and J.S. Grewal remark that Sikh documents are more important than the Mughal, not simply because of their number but chiefly because they provide fresh data on Sikh polity and government. Consequently, they are likely 'to impel the historian to look upon the nature of Sikh polity in an altogether new light'.[1] J.S. Grewal has also analysed the early nineteenth-century histories in Persian for their treatment of the eighteenth-century Sikh polity. Using these and other sources, the issues involved are further amplified or clarified by Indu Banga.[2] Their approach is appreciated by Purnima Dhavan, but with qualifications.[3]

The twentieth-century understanding of the late eighteenth-century Sikh polity has been based largely on the early European accounts of Sikhs and the works of Malcolm, Prinsep, and Cunningham. We have analysed this evidence all afresh and added to it the evidence of the early nineteenth-century works of Ratan Singh Bhangu, Ram Sukh Rao, Ahmad Shah of Batala, and Ganesh Das. More crucial is the contemporary evidence of a *hukamnāmā*, news reports, coins, administrative orders, and legal documents of the late eighteenth century, in addition to the archival records of *dharmarth* grants. The general picture that emerges is given at the end on the basis of all these sources.

## SIKH POLITY IN CONTEMPORARY EUROPEAN ACCOUNTS

The growing concern of the East India Company with Sikhs becomes evident in the latter half of the eighteenth century. Robert Orme, the Company's historiographer (1769–1801), made a collection of manuscripts in India which is now in the British Library. A note on the Sikhs written around 1760 refers to the opposition they had put up to Ahmad Shah Durrani, the Mughal emperors, and the governors of Lahore at different times. There was no 'standing Chief' among them, and it was desirable to keep up correspondence with many of them.[4] Some years later, Father Francis Xavier Wendel wrote an account of the Sikhs who strongly affected 'the centre of the empire' of the Grand Mughal and presented a threat to its environs.[5] Colonel Antione Henry Polier, who had personally collected information on Sikhs, expressed his view in 1780 that the rise and progress of the Sikhs could not be attributed so much to their bravery or military knowledge as to the anarchy and confusion that desolated the Mughal Empire after the death of Aurangzeb.[6] Governor General Warren Hastings gathered information systematically from various sources, and it was his well-considered view in December 1784 that Sikhs were a potential 'danger' to the political interests of the East India Company.[7] George Forster ended his considerably long account of the Sikhs with the observation that there was a possibility of Sikhs becoming united under one leader and as a result becoming more formidable than any other Indian power.[8]

The capacity of Sikhs to play a vital role in Indian politics appeared to be connected with their political organization. It is not surprising, therefore, that we find a number of Europeans showing concern with Sikh polity during the late eighteenth century. Father Wendel had observed that the only weakness in Sikh power was that there were 'too many leaders' among the Sikhs. They presented 'only a vast but rough and shapeless body without a head'. There were as many commanders as there were men, and each was independent of the other. They united only when a campaign was to be undertaken, or when they were under attack.[9] Colonel Polier, who was equally hostile towards Sikhs, referred to them as 'a snake with many heads'.[10] The government of Sikhs was 'properly an aristocracy'. No pre-eminence was conceded to an individual, and all the chiefs looked upon themselves 'as perfectly equal in all public concerns'. In the greatest council of the nation, held annually either in Amritsar, Lahore, or some other place, everything was decided by the majority of votes of the members present. This 'Council' or 'Diet' is mistakenly called 'Gurmatā' by Polier (and by all the early British historians of the Sikhs). The subjects of debate were alliances, wars, and the campaigns intended to be undertaken in the ensuing year. The contributions collected in the previous expeditions were distributed in the Council in proportion to the forces of the chiefs who, in turn, had to satisfy their dependants. The forces of the individual chiefs reportedly ranged from mere 15 or 20 horses to 12,000.[11]

Polier goes on to say that the whole force of the Sikhs joined together could number 2,00,000 horsemen, a truly formidable power under one chief. But there were 400 to 500 chiefs who looked upon themselves as independent of each other. They were bound to support one another for defence or aggression but it was not easy to prevail upon them to act in concert. They plundered all they could lay their hands on, except those who were prepared to pay 2 to 5 per cent on the revenue. This was called Rākhī. The chief who collected Rākhī provided protection to the cultivators against all other claimants. Polier noticed that the possessions of the chiefs themselves were exceedingly well-cultivated, populous, and rich. The revenues in general were taken in kind and not in cash (an arrangement that was most favourable to the cultivator). Indeed, few countries were comparable with the territories of Sikh chiefs.[12]

Travelling through the region in 1783, George Forster had something to say about the government of the Sikhs. He talks of general and limited assemblies, and the grand convention called Gurmatā at which the 'army' met to transact the more important affairs of the nation, like the declaration of war or peace, forming alliances, and detaching parties for service. The contributions levied were distributed among the chiefs, proportionately to the number of their troops. They, in turn, satisfied their soldiers. The widely extended dominions of the Sikhs were divided into numerous states, and independent interests were pursued without a regard to general policy. Forster goes on to add that 'the grand assembly' was now rarely summoned; nor had the Sikhs embarked on any united cause. The chiefs in the Punjab hills had agreed to pay a fixed annual tribute to the Sikhs. He refers to the abundance of agrarian production in the Punjab under the Sikh chiefs and also talks of an extensive and valuable commerce maintained in their country.[13]

Writing in 1788, Major James Browne characterized the Sikh government as 'aristocratical, but very irregular and imperfect'. A number of chiefs possessed portions of the country 'either by former right as Zemindars, or by usurpation'. They enjoyed distinct authority in their respective territory, 'uncontrolled by any superior power'. They assembled together on particular occasions 'for the purposes of depredation, or of defence'. In their tumultuous Diet a leader was chosen by majority of votes to command their joint forces during an expedition. His authority was ill obeyed by many other chiefs who thought of themselves 'perfectly his equals', treating him barely as first among equals.[14] Sikhs had become confederated 'for the purpose of conquest', and they called their confederacy '*Khalsa Gee*, or the State, and their grand army *Dull Khalsa Gee*, or the Army of the State'. Browne goes on to comment also on agriculture, trade, and manufactures in Sikh territories.[15]

In short, European interest in the Sikhs was inspired primarily by the fact that they had acquired political power. Contemporary European writers underscored the independence of the numerous Sikh leaders. They united only for attack or defence. These were the two main concerns of the grand assembly of the Sikhs, variously called Council, Diet, or Gurmatā. Their 'confederacy' was called *Khalsa Ji* or 'the State' and their joint forces were called Dal Khalsa or 'the Army of the State'. Two other aspects of the situation are mentioned: the system of Rākhī, and the collection of tribute from the hill chiefs as a token of their subordination to a superior power.

## EARLY NINETEENTH-CENTURY BRITISH HISTORIANS ON SIKH POLITY

In the narrative part of his *Sketch of the Sikhs* (1812), John Malcolm writes that after the death of Banda Singh, Sikhs had no acknowledged general, leader, or prince. 'Each individual followed to the field the Sirdar or chief who, from birth, the possession of property or from valour and experience had become his superior.' These chiefs were of different rank and pretensions. For one reason or another, one chief generally had a lead in their 'national council' or Gurmatā, at which the most powerful was certain of being elected as the leader. This in itself was little calculated to give strength and union. But to unite and to act in one body and on one principle was 'a law of necessity' and 'their sole means of preservation'. Their peculiar usages, the ardent character of their faith, the power of their enemies, and the oppression they had to endure supplied the place of ordinances. Their extraordinary rise to power was due not so much to their boasted constitution as to other causes, combined with the growing weakness and internal contests of their enemies. Whether an oligarchy or a theocracy, the constitution of the Sikhs did not have a single principle that could save it from ruin if vigorously assailed.[16]

The government of the Sikhs could, in theory, be termed 'a theocracy'. The chief maintained his power and authority by professing that he was 'the servant of the Khalsa', that is, the State or the commonwealth. The 'national council' deliberated under the inspiration of an invisible being who watched over the interests of the commonwealth. The forms and actions of the 'national council', which had supreme authority over their confederation, were believed 'to have a mystical meaning'. It was 'their civil and religious duty' to conform to that superior government under which they lived and to follow the rules and laws established by Guru Gobind Singh.[17]

Malcolm looked upon the Akālīs as the leading men in the council held in Amritsar. A class of devotees founded by Guru Gobind Singh, they had defended his institutes against the innovations of Bairagi Banda. They were 'fanatic priests' and 'desperate soldiers'. Malcolm described their distinct appearance. They thought of themselves as 'the defenders' of the Khalsa tradition. In control of the Akāl Bungā, they had 'a great interest in maintaining both the religion and government of the Sikhs' as established by Guru Gobind Singh. Their religious and political influence depended on the continuation of the council in Amritsar. Malcolm describes the proceedings of the assembly (Gurmatā) convened by the Akālīs. But this was not based on what he saw in Amritsar in 1805. A Sikh priest had provided information to him on how such meetings had been held in the past. It is important to point out that Malcolm talks of 'the sole direction of all religious affairs in Amritsar'.[18]

The civil officers to whom the chiefs entrusted their revenue concerns and diplomatic negotiations were generally non-Singhs, the followers of Guru Nanak and not of Guru Gobind Singh; they were educated for peaceful occupations, in which they became adept. The general practice for the collection of the revenue in the Punjab was half of the produce, but the Sikh chiefs never levied the whole of their share. Revenue on sugarcane and perishable crops was collected in cash. The cultivator was treated with indulgence. There was no fixed code for the administration of justice. Minor disputes about property were settled by the village headmen by arbitration, or by the chiefs. The Panchayats played an important role in settling disputes. There was no capital punishment but murder was generally revenged by retaliation. Heavy duties used to be levied upon commercial goods by all the petty chiefs, but the Sikh chiefs had in due course restored the confidence of merchants, and a great part of the shawl trade from Kashmir now flowed through the cities of Lahore, Amritsar, and Patiala to 'Hindustan' (the various cities of Gangetic Plains).[19]

John Malcolm's book on Sikhs was clearly a recognition of the East India Company's increased interest in Sikhs after the extension of its 'protection' to the Sikh chiefs up to the River Sutlej and its treaty with Ranjit Singh in 1809, which recognized him as the sole sovereign on the other side of the Sutlej. The political agents of the governor general, who were to deal with the 'protected' chiefs, kept an eye on the developments across the Sutlej. Some of them collected materials on Sikhs for a better understanding of the changing situation. The materials collected by Captain Murray and Captain Wade were used by Henry T. Prinsep to write a book on the political life of Maharaja Ranjit Singh, preceded by an account of the 'origin of the Sikh power' after the invasion of Nadir Shah and before the death of Ahmad Shah Abdali.[20]

Writing in the early 1830s, Prinsep was the first British historian to give an exposition of the *misaldārī* and the *jāgīrdārī* systems.

Before the Sikhs became undisputed masters of the Punjab, their sardārs or chiefs had been generally followed into the field by relations, friends, and volunteers and not by hired retainers. Most of them looked upon themselves as 'partners and associates' in each enterprise, and they regarded the lands acquired as 'a common property' in which everyone was to have his share according to his contribution to its acquisition. The 'associations' were called misals, implying that they were 'confederacies of equals' under chiefs of their own selection. The sardār was the leader in war and acted as arbiter in peace. He was treated with respect and deference by 'the inferior Sardārs' who, however, had no obligation to obey him beyond what was regarded as of reciprocal benefit or the well-being of the misal.[21]

Prinsep talks about twelve 'principal misals' in the 1760s: the Bhangi, the Ramgaṛhia, the Ghanayya, the Nakkai, the Dallewalia, the Nishanwala, the Faizullapuria, the Karoṛasinghia, the Shahīd and Nihang, the Phulkia and Bhaika, and the Sukarchakia. They were founded at different times and derived their names due to a large variety of reasons. 'Every Misal acted independently, or in concert, as necessity or inclination suggested.' The assembly of the chiefs, called the Sarbat Khalsa, was generally held twice a year on Baisākhī and Diwali in April and October. A 'special council' or Gurmatā was held for discussing expeditions of importance or any matter of more than ordinary moment. When the joint forces of several misals took the field for a predatory enterprise or the collection of rākhā (black mail), the army assumed the designation of 'a Dal of the Khalsa Jī'. Altogether, they could bring about 70,000 horsemen into the field.[22]

When the misals acquired territories, the first duty of the sardārs was to partition out the lands, towns, and villages amongst those who were considered as having made the conquest in common. Every leader (sarkardā) of the smallest party of horse who fought under the standard of the misal demanded a share in proportion to the degree of his contribution to the conquest. The sardari or the chief's portion was divided off first and the remainder was parcelled out as shares (pattīs) of the leaders. These shares were subdivided among 'inferior leaders' according to the number of horses they brought to the field. 'Each took his portion as a co-sharer, and held it in absolute independence.' Thus, when the Sikhs assumed dominion over provinces of Lahore and Sarhind, the country came to be 'ruled by seventy thousand sovereigns'. This state of things could not last long. With the removal of a common enemy and a common danger, internal strife began to besiege the misals.[23]

Prinsep talks of four types of tenures in the territories of Sikh chiefs of the late eighteenth century: *pattīdārī*, misaldārī, *tabadārī*, and jāgīrdārī. Every member of the misal, from a sardār down to a horseman, was a shareholder (*pattīdār*). They all regulated the management of the affairs in their respective shares, treating the cultivators and other people in the area as they liked. Disputes between pattīdārs themselves could be referred to the sarkardā and, if his decision was not satisfactory, to the sardār. The only condition of the tenure was reciprocal aid for mutual protection. However, the pattīdār could not sell his tenure to a stranger, though he could mortgage it or bequeath it to a male relative.[24]

A petty leader who attached himself unconditionally to a misal received land as the reward for his cooperation. He was known as a misaldār, and he was in no kind of dependence on the sardār. He could transfer himself with his possessions to another chief. In other words, the misaldārī tenure gave more freedom than the pattīdārī. The *tabadār* was simply a retainer. Completely subservient to the sardār, he held the tenure at the sardar's will and pleasure. Jāgīrs were given to needy relations, dependents, and soldiers who served well; the holders of jāgīrs were liable to be called upon any time for service with contingents equipped and mounted at their own expense according to the extent of their grant. Both the tabadārī and jāgīrdārī grants were given from the territories of the sardār, and they were far more dependent on him than the other two.[25]

Prinsep also refers to religious and charitable grants made to the Bedis and the Sodhis, or to temples. Such grants were given sometimes to Muslim pīrzādās as well. These grants had 'nothing to distinguish them from what are found all over India'.[26]

Writing after the first Anglo-Sikh War (1845–6), and looking back at the eighteenth century, J.D. Cunningham refers to the coin struck by the Sikh chiefs to proclaim 'their own sway and the prevalence of their faith'. The inscription on the coin was to the effect that Guru Gobind Singh received from Guru Nanak 'grace, power and rapid victory'. Every Sikh was a free and substantive member of the commonwealth, but their means, abilities, and opportunities were varied and unequal. All could not lead, and there were masters as well as servants. The system resolved itself into what Cunningham terms 'theocratic confederate feudalism'.[27]

The system was 'theocratic' in the sense that 'God was their helper and only judge, community of faith or object was their moving principle, and warlike array, devotion to steel of Govind, was their material instrument'. The Sarbat Khalsa, or the whole Sikh people, met in Amritsar at least once a year at the time of Diwali. The assembly of the chiefs, called Gurmatā, sought 'wisdom and unanimity of counsel' from the Guru and the Granth. However, the leaders owed no subjection to one another, and they were imperfectly obeyed by the majority of their followers. The 'feudal' notion was acknowledged as the law and the chiefs partitioned their joint conquests equally among themselves, and divided their respective shares in the same manner among their own leaders of bands who, in turn, subdivided their portions among their own dependents in accordance with the general custom of subinfeudation.

Cunningham further adds that this positive or implicit rule was not applicable to all the Sikh chiefs. Many held lands in which 'the mere withdrawal of a central authority had left them wholly independent of control'. Such individuals could themselves become leaders and acquire new lands for their own use in the name of the Khalsa or commonwealth. In other words, the realities did not conform to any theoretical concept. Cunningham points out that it would indeed be idle 'to call an ever changing state of alliance and dependence by the name of a constitution'. Present in the mind of a Sikh, nevertheless, was a full persuasion of God's grace and deference for 'the mystic Khalsa'.[28]

Cunningham goes on to talk about the 'confederacies' called misals. The term *'misl'* had more than one meaning. In India, it was used for a file of papers or 'anything serried or placed in ranks'. In

Arabic, the word denoted 'alike or equal'. Each Sikh misal obeyed or followed a sardār, simply a chief or leader. But the title was so general that it was applicable to the head of a small band as well as to the commander of a large host of the free and equal 'Singhs'. The confederacies, usually recorded as twelve, did not 'all exist in their full strength at the same time'. One misal could give birth to another. The misals were distinguished by titles derived from the name, village, district, or progenitor of the first or most eminent chief, or from some peculiarity of custom or of leadership. All the misals arose in the Punjab, in the north of the Sutlej, with the exception of the Phulkian, which derived its name from the common ancestor of Ala Singh and other sardārs of the family.[29] From Cunningham's description it seems that different designations were given to them by others, and not assumed by those to whom they were applied.

The nomenclature appeared to Cunningham to be arbitrary. The Nishanias and Shahids scarcely formed misals 'in the conventional meaning of the term'. These two were 'complementary bodies set apart' and honoured by all. The Nakkais never achieved a high power or name. The Dallewalias and the Karoṛasinghias (an offshoot of the Faizullapurias) acquired nearly all their possessions by the capture of Sarhind. Cunningham also refers to a body of men, besides the regular confederacies with their moderate degree of subordination, who 'threw off all subjection to earthly governors' and who peculiarly represented 'the religious element of Sikhism'. These were the Akālīs, the soldiers of God, who claimed for themselves 'a direct institution' by Guru Gobind Singh.[30]

The Akālīs combined warlike activity with the relinquishment of the world. The meek among them were satisfied with the performance of menial offices in gurdwaras but the fierce among them acted as the armed guardians of Amritsar. They took upon themselves 'the authority of censors'. They inspired awe and respect, and sometimes plundered those who were supposed to have injured the commonwealth. They held a position of considerable importance at the Akāl Bungā before Ranjit Singh became supreme. It cost him much time and trouble to suppress them without losing his own reputation with the people.[31]

## EARLY NINETEENTH-CENTURY HISTORICAL WORKS OF NATIVE WRITERS

Ratan Singh Bhangu's *Sri Gur Panth Prakāsh* (Manifestation of the Guru's Panth), written in the second decade of the nineteenth century, is devoted largely to the Khalsa of the eighteenth century. He was concerned primarily with the question of how the Sikhs became sovereign. According to Bhangu, this was actually the question posed in Ludhiana by Captain Murray, the assistant to the British political agent. Bhangu's answer was that the Singhs received sovereign rule (pātshāhī) from the True King. Murray asked, 'Who was the True King?' Bhangu said, 'Nanak.' He was 'the King of Kings' who enabled the sparrows to kill the hawks, and the rabbits to kill the lions.[32] The perfect and the True Guru created the Panth to fight, and every Singh in the saddle became a sovereign ruler (pātshāh).[33] They did not hesitate to fight because rulership could never be acquired without fight and sacrifice of life.[34] Nor could it be accepted from an authority; subjection to earthly authority was not acceptable to them.[35] Bhangu, thus, projects the idea that the Khalsa was instituted to become a sovereign power.

The doctrines of Guru Panth and Guru Granth and resolutions (Gurmatās) of the Khalsa at the Akāl Bungā figure prominently in Bhangu's work. In a crisis—when the Khalsa are not unanimous or clear about what to do—they invoke the authority of the Granth as the True Guru. The words of the Guru act like a sharp sword; whatever is uttered by the Guru comes to pass.[36] Bhai Mani Singh used to sit at the Akāl Bungā and impose penance on the defaulters in rahit. He regarded the sangat as the Guru: there was no difference between the two.[37] The Khalsa used to come to Amritsar at the time of Diwali and Baisākhī, sit in the Harmandar to listen to the Guru's words and to reflect on them, and to hold *dīvān* (general meeting) at the Akāl Bungā to adopt resolutions, and to perform justice to protect the Singhs and destroy their un-Sikh (*asikh*) enemies.[38] It is important to add that in an emergency, Gurmatās were held also at places other than Amritsar.[39]

As mentioned earlier with reference to *Sri Gur Panth Prakāsh*, territories were occupied on the basis of a criterion adopted at the Akāl Bungā: the Singh who occupied a place first of all should not be dislodged. The less powerful occupied small places and eminent sardārs occupied cities and towns. Those who were considerate towards their subjects remained in position but those who took no time to alienate their subjects were soon dislodged. If anyone was dislodged later, the misal intervened on his behalf.[40] This carries the implication that the chiefs of the misals adhered to the Gurmatā, and the misal was the unit for the occupation of territories.

Bhangu's account of the misal of Shiam Singh, who became 'the Sardār of Sardārs', is not without interest. Shiamu or Shamu was the elder son of Mali, a Sandhu Jat of the village Narla. Many people in those days were Sultanis (worshippers of Sultan Sakhi Sarwar). But Shamu went to the establishment (derā) of Mastan Singh who gave him pahul. Mastan Singh himself had received pahul from the five *bhujangīs* who had been initiated by Guru Gobind Singh. He was sent by Guru Gobind Singh with Banda who made him a faujdār. Mastan Singh became a martyr, and Shiam Singh became the head of his derā. He too fought against the 'Turks'. He was a devout Sikh and used to give pahul to all and sundry coming to his derā for this purpose. Incidentally, Bhangu makes an important statement here. Shiam Singh used to share food with 'Hindus' (the persons who belonged to one of the recognized castes of the Hindu social order) and used to give great consideration to the *nich* (who were regarded as outcaste and untouchable in the Hindu social order).[41]

In the 1730s, when Kapur Singh accepted the title of nawab, he gave Shiam Singh the charge of the mortar (*sunehrā*). Many of the Singhs who joined Shiam Singh became sardārs, like Sukha Singh, Karam Singh, and Karora Singh. The first was a Tarkhān, the second a Sarin Khatri, and the third a Sandhu Jat. After Karora Singh's death, Baghel Singh, a Dhaliwal Jat, was given charge of the drum and the standard.[42] The misal came to be known after Karora Singh and not Shiam Singh, Sukha Singh, or Karam Singh.

Bhangu refers to a number of 'misals', or groups. In connection with the 'great carnage' (vaddhā ghallūghārā) of 1762, he mentions the Bhangis, Kanhiyas, Ramgarhias, Nakkais, Nishanchis,

Dallewalias, Kapur-Singhias, Ahluwalias, Sukarchakias, Shiam Singhias, Shahids and Nihangs, Amritsarias, Anandpurias, Ramdasias, Ranghretas, and Masandias, as well as the Bedis, Sodhis, Trehans, and Bhallas. All these are not mentioned as misals but the groups who had taken pahul and constituted the Dal. Apart from the Dal Khalsa, Bhangu refers to the Buddha and the Taruna Dal. The former was constituted by the older misal leaders and the latter by the younger.43 Notwithstanding the importance of the misal, the Buddha and Taruna Dals, and the Dal Khalsa as a whole, Bhangu does not think in terms of a republic. He refers to Jassa Singh Ahluwalia as the son of a poor *kalāl* (distiller) who came to be regarded as the 'Pātshāh of the Panth'.44 In a longish account given by Bhangu, we are told that the great martyr Nihang Gurbakhsh Singh was reborn as Ranjit Singh to become the supreme ruler of the Punjab with the sanction of Guru Gobind Singh.45 The phrase *'hanne hanne pātshāhī'* (sovereignty for every horseman) used by Bhangu is clearly suggestive of a large number of rulers, each one of them exercising independent power in his own territory. The sardār of Ratan Singh Bhangu, who acknowledged no earthly overlord was superior to the Phulkian rajas and maharajas who acknowledged the Mughals and the Afghans (and later the British) as their overlords.

Ram Sukh Rao, the official historian of the state of Kapurthala, projects Jassa Singh Ahluwalia as a sovereign ruler, dwelling on his relations with other Sikh and non-Sikh rulers, his court and camp, his civil administration, and his attitude towards the Harmandar and the descendants of Guru Nanak and Guru Ram Das. The Raja of Kutlehr in the Kangra Hills submitted to Jassa Singh and started paying tribute, retaining the administrative control of his territory.46 Rai Ahmad of Raikot submitted to the Ahluwalia chief who allowed him to retain his territories on the condition of paying annual tribute. Rai Ahmad and his son continued to pay the tribute regularly.47 The two Rajput chiefs, one Hindu and the other Muslim, were clearly subordinate to Jassa Singh.

The position of Sikh chiefs in relation to Jassa Singh, however, is not so clear. In the Jalandhar Doāb, according to the *musāhibs* (courtiers) of Kapurthala, Jassa Singh Ahluwalia had shown kindness to the Singhpurias and entrusted a place like Jalandhar to them. In the time of Jassa Singh's second successor, Fateh Singh, the Singhpuria Buddh Singh was trying to get Hoshiarpur through Ranjit Singh's intervention. According to the courtiers, Hoshiarpur belonged to Jassa Singh. Ranjit Singh also confirmed that Jassa Singh used to have his thānādārs in Hoshiarpur. Nevertheless, Buddh Singh appointed his own thānādār. In the Chaj Doāb, a chief of Sialkot, Natha Singh Shahīd, refers to the time when Jassa Singh plundered the camp of Jahan Khan and gave ten villages to Natha Singh, entrusting to him the charge of the gurdwārā (Ber Sahib) associated with Guru Nanak.[48]

Tara Singh Dallewalia, who was with Jassa Singh at the time of the sacking of Kasur, found a treasure which he was allowed to keep for himself. He purchased horses and employed men to become a sardār. He used to present horses to Jassa Singh to acknowledge that he owed his sardari to him. The Sikh chiefs of Ambala were similarly indebted to Jassa Singh. Karam Singh Nirmalā (Shahabadia) also used to talk about Jassa Singh's kindness to him. The sardār of Mani Majra remained safe from Nihangs and other Singhs by telling them that the place belonged to Jassa Singh. Once during his visit to Mani Majra, Jassa Singh suggested that a fort be built and he himself laid its foundation. The chiefs of Mani Majra were never amiss in paying tribute or performing service expected of them, says Ram Sukh Rao.[49]

Finally, we come to Jassa Singh's relations with the rajas of Nabha, Jind, and Patiala in the Malwa tract. Raja Jaswant Singh of Nabha believed that Jassa Singh Ahluwalia was more considerate towards the rulers of Patiala but he did not allow them to harm the rulers of Nabha in any way. The *vakīls* (representatives) of all the chiefs of Malwa used to stay in Fatehabad, at Jassa Singh's headquarters. Raja Bhag Singh of Jind remembered the kindness shown by Jassa Singh to the chiefs of Jind. Chain Singh, the courtier of Raja Sahib Singh of Patiala, refers to the kindness of Jassa Singh to Raja Ala Singh to whom he had administered pahul, and whom he used to protect against the forces of the Mughals and the aggressive Singhs. In the time of drought or distress, Jassa Singh used to waive the revenue to be paid by the rulers of Patiala (sort of *chahārmīs*, or recipient of a fourth of the revenue, who administered Jassa Singh's territories on his behalf. Elsewhere, Chain Singh says that the rulers of Patiala used to give costly gifts to Jassa Singh, apart from paying revenue and tribute (*māmlā*).[50]

Thus, according to Ram Sukh Rao, Jassa Singh Ahluwalia exercised suzerainty over some Hindu, Muslim, and Sikh chiefs. Only a sovereign ruler could exercise such authority. The sovereign status of Jassa Singh is reflected in his military and civil administration as well. Sahaj Singh is mentioned as an officer in the *khās fauj* (the standing army) of Jassa Singh Ahluwalia; he was paid in jāgīr. Desa Singh is mentioned as a brave warrior from the time of Jassa Singh; he was a sarkardā in his army. There were *jamā'atdār*s as well as sarkardās in his army. Their salaries were paid in cash in six-monthly instalments, and they were provided with horses, weapons, uniforms, tents, and rations by the state. The army consisted of units called derās, which included units of men from the same 'brotherhoods'.[51]

In the court of Jassa Singh Ahluwalia, the dīvān, the bakhshī and all the munshis, vakīls and *musaddī*s used to be present with jackets and sashes worn over their dress. They took their seats in accordance with their rank. For conducting the business of the day, the dīvān and the bakhshī stood respectfully before the sardār and explained each case before getting his signatures on the file. The sardārs of the army, and the courtiers, sat in accordance with their status while others kept standing, ready for service, like the mace-bearers, the proclaimers of the titles of their masters, and other *khidmatgār*s.[52]

For the civil administration, there is a reference to the *kārdār* of Amritsar. Thānādārs were appointed by Jassa Singh Ahluwalia in Bharog and Naraingarh. It seems that they were meant to settle the newly acquired territory. A thānādār was appointed similarly for Butari. The men in the service of Jassa Singh who did not maintain the full quota of horsemen and oppressed people lost their jāgīrs. In the areas where the zamīndārs were refractory, forts were built for maintaining peace and order and collecting the revenues. Both kārdārs and thānādārs were appointed in the territories taken over by Jassa Singh himself after the defeat and death of the Afghan governor of Sarhind.[53]

It is interesting to note that Jai Singh Sodhi of Anandpur was prepared to serve Jassa Singh as a jāgīrdār. Perhaps more important is the fact that Jassa Singh protected the Sodhis of Kartarpur (descendants of Dhir Mal) against Ahmad Shah Abdali, and on their request he persuaded the Singh sardārs and the Akālīs to readmit the Sodhis into the Sikh social order, and to eat with them.[54] Thus, the descendants of Dhir Mal did not remain an excommunicated category.

Jassa Singh Ahluwalia was authorized by the Khalsa to manage all the affairs of the Darbār Sāhib complex, including the Akāl Bungā, the seat of the Akālīs. He appointed Bhai Des Raj as the superintendent (dārogha) who, among other things, kept accounts of income and expenditure. Jassa Singh spent rupees 14,00,000 on the reconstruction of the Harmandar and the Akāl Bungā, besides contributing some materials required for construction.[55] It may be added that the responsibility for the management and improvement of the whole complex in various ways was later assumed by Maharaja Ranjit Singh on behalf of the Sikh Panth.

Two major writers in Persian, who wrote at the behest of the British, have taken notice of elements that have direct bearing on Sikh polity of the late eighteenth century. Ahmad Shah of Batala was the first writer in Persian to talk of misals. In fact, he gives an account of the Sikh misals before taking up the political career of Ranjit Singh, who belonged to the Sukarchakia misal. Thus, in a way, the misal was the most important unit for Ahmad Shah, both for the political activity of the Sikhs and their polity. He makes no comment on the term 'misal', taking it for granted that his contemporaries were familiar with it. However, he makes it clear that the misal was a group or an association. He states that there were more than four or five hundred sardārs among the Sikhs but only a few groups were pre-eminent for their armies, followers, and territories. The most important misals for his purpose were the Bhangi, Faizullapuria, Nakkai, Kanhiya, Ramgaṛhia, Ahluwalia, and Sukarchakia. A misal was normally headed by a single chief, and it acted as a unit for the purpose of war and conquest. But a misal could also have branches, each with a separate army and administration.[56]

According to Ahmad Shah, the association of Singhs with the leader of a misal was voluntary. Succession to leadership was not determined by kinship in all cases, particularly before territorial occupation. Territories were occupied largely on the misal basis. If more than one misal made a joint conquest, the conquered territory was divided between them sooner than later. The character of the misal changed after territorial occupation. In the second quarter of the eighteenth century, the aim of the Singhs had been to paralyze the Mughal administration, but after the middle of the century, it was to occupy territories and to establish their own administration. The qualities of leadership became all the more important. The more reputed leaders came to have larger following and this eminence enabled them to get larger shares in the conquered territories. This did not mean, however, that the power of the chief increased in relation to the sardārs who joined him in the conquest and got a separate share in the conquered territory.[57]

The chief of a misal exercised minimal control over his former associates who now exercised independent power in their own respective territory. Their obligation, according to Ahmad Shah, was limited to active cooperation in situations that called for armed action. Within their territory they were independent for all practical purposes. In a very real sense, thus, the former associates became autonomous rulers of their respective territories. The principle of hereditary succession confirmed their autonomous status. With the application of the hereditary principle for succession, the qualitative difference between the successors of the former chief and the former associate was obliterated almost completely. Before the end of the eighteenth century, there were no chiefs and associates but only chiefs who claimed independent status in their external relations as well as their internal administration.[58]

Ganesh Das, a hereditary *qānūngo* (registrar) of Gujrat, gives primacy to the political ambition of the Khalsa in his account of the Sikh struggle for independence. The Sikhs did not give up their claim to independence despite persistent measures of repression and persecution. Ganesh Das takes notice of Amritsar as the place of congregation for the Khalsa and the presence of the Akālīs there. The Khalsa looked upon the use of arms as their religious duty. Ganesh Das does not give much importance to Gurmatā or the misal. He uses the term 'bādshāh' for Jassa Singh Ahluwalia and Hari Singh Bhangi. Every sardār acted as an autonomous ruler, and strictly in accordance with his interest and good sense.[59]

For Ganesh Das there was no qualitative difference between the position of Sikh chiefs of the late eighteenth century and Ranjit Singh. They were all alike in the way they exercised political power. Ranjit Singh's administration differed from that of his Sikh predecessors only in degree and not in kind. Ganesh Das does notice a few modifications made by Ranjit Singh, but in its main outline, his administration was not essentially different from that of the Sikh rulers of the late eighteenth century.[60]

Ganesh Das takes notice of another aspect of the Khalsa Rāj. For him, cities and towns were an index of trade and manufactures. He talks of de-urbanization during the time of political turmoil in the Punjab and the process of re-urbanization after the establishment of Sikh rule. The city of Lahore had become totally deserted, he says, during the invasions of Ahmad Shah Abdali and the upsurge of the Khalsa known as the Singhs. The twelve localities outside the city wall were razed to the ground, and only a few mansions survived in the nine localities inside the walls. However, when the chiefs of the Khalsa came into possession of the city, they paid attention to its rehabilitation and encouraged people of various places to settle down here. A new impetus was given to its further development when this capital city fell into the hands of Ranjit Singh.[61]

Chak Ramdas or Chak Guru was a place with the tank called amritsar. In its midst the Harmandar was constructed. The population of this town began to increase and a rich settlement came into existence around the tank. The *bungās* (residences) of the Akālīs and the sardārs were constructed all around, and many a man of consequence founded a *katṛā* (closed locality), generally named after the name of the founder. The city came to be called Amritsar as the most important centre of pilgrimage for the Sikhs. Ganesh Das says: 'Today there is no other city in the whole of the Punjab which is as large as Amritsar.'[62]

The home town of Ganesh Das himself, Gujrat in the Chaj Doāb, had suffered the ravages of time. But Sardār Gujjar Singh repopulated the town, giving encouragement and satisfaction to the people who came from all places. The city of Sialkot in the neighbouring Rachna Doāb, where the ancestors of Ganesh Das had first settled in the time of the Lodhis, was sacked by the Khalsa during the reign of Ahmad Shah Abdali, and its mansions were razed to the ground, its houses were deserted, and its population was dispersed. After sometime, however, Jiwan Singh, Sahib Singh, Natha Singh Shahīd, and Mohar Singh Atariwala occupied the city and divided it amongst themselves, covering each locality, lane, and shop. 'They brought back the dispersed people to rehabilitate the town.'[63]

The population of Wazirabad dwindled in the beginning of Sikh rule but it was repopulated by Sardār Gurbakhsh Singh Waraich and his son Jodh Singh, and it became 'a flourishing place again'.[64] Rawalpindi in the Sindh Sagar Doāb was originally a small village. It became a large town under the administration of Sardār Milkha Singh, who cared for the well-being of its inhabitants, traders, and merchants, so that people from all places settled here.[65] In the Bist Jalandhar Doāb, Jalandhar was still a small city 'like many others' says Ganesh Das.[66]

## CONTEMPORARY EVIDENCE OF A HUKAMNĀMĀ, NEWS REPORTS, COINS, OFFICIAL ORDERS, ARCHIVAL SOURCES, AND LEGAL DOCUMENTS

A hukamnāmā of 12 April 1759, addressed to the Sikhs of Pattan by the Khalsa Ji of Sat Srī Akāl Purkh, asks for a contribution of rupees 125 towards the funds for the (reconstruction of) Sri Harmandar Ji, in addition to the usual offers of *dasvandh*, *chalīhā*, *kār*, *bhet*, and ardās due to the Guru. This hukamnāmā bears the impression of a seal with the Gurmukhi inscription Akāl Sāhāi, Khalsa Jī. In the text of the hukamnāmā, the 'Khalsa Jī' is called the 'Guru Khalsa'. This is an explicit reference to the doctrine that the Khalsa Panth was the Guru. The hukamnāmā is issued on the authority of the Khalsa as the Guru from Amritsar on the occasion of Baisākhī, when the entire Khalsa used to meet there.[67] The doctrine of Guru Khalsa (Guru Panth) is the basis for the collective authority of the Khalsa to be exercised from the Akāl Bungā in Amritsar.

The news reports of the early 1760s leave no doubt about the importance of Amritsar as the rallying centre of the Khalsa. The report of 13 March 1763 mentioned the arrival of Jassa Singh Ahluwalia, Jassa Singh Ramgarhia, and other Sikh chiefs in Chak Guru (Amritsar) for the purpose of *ashnān* (bathe) at the time of Baisākhī and for 'mutual deliberation and consultation and distribution of the country among themselves'. On 14 April they were encamped at Chak Guru in large numbers and they proposed to raid the territories around Saharanpur. They had written to Shujauddaula of Awadh and Najibuddaula, respectively the ally and the plenipotentiary of the Afghan king, that the Khalsa had expelled Ahmad Shah from the province of Lahore and they should be paid the money promised to Ahmad Shah. In case of delay in payment, Sikh forces could raid the capital and they 'should not be held to blame for this'.[68]

In the report of 9 July 1763, Jassa Singh and others are stated to have gone to Chak Guru for Gurmatā. All the other chiefs, including Gujjar Singh and Charhat Singh, would come there to hold mutual consultation. 'Whatever is decided after mutual consultation will be acted upon.'[69] According to the report of 11 October 1763, 'the Sikh army' was moving towards Amritsar for the ashnān of Dusehra and Kattakī (Diwali). The Sikh chiefs met again in Amritsar early in March 1764 and, after mutual consultation, decided to encounter Ahmad Shah after he had crossed the River Chenab. They moved their forces towards the Chenab in two or three divisions to give battle to Ahmad Shah. As noted in Chapter 1, the news of Abdali's defeat in a 'great battle' is mentioned in the report of 4 April 1764. The Sikh chiefs then repaired to Amritsar at the time of Holi (*holkā*).[70]

The report of 8 March 1765 is interesting for a distinction that Ala Singh of Patiala saw between himself and the Sikh chiefs of the province of Lahore. Jassa Singh and other Sikh chiefs had sent a message to Ala Singh not to make any settlement with Ahmad Shah Abdali, and assured him of their support if he was besieged. Ala Singh replied: 'I am a *zamīndār*. I first make a settlement; thereafter, I am helpless. You can confront the Shah on equal terms.'[71] Like many other chiefs who were native to the Sutlej–Jamuna Divide, Ala Singh had risen to power within the framework of the Mughal administration, acknowledging the authority of the Mughal emperors. Ala Singh remained subordinate to the Mughal emperor first and then to Ahmad Shah Abdali, but the Sikh chiefs of the Mughal province of Lahore claimed a sovereign status for themselves.

A practice well known over a large part of the contemporary world was to strike a coin as declaration of sovereignty. James Browne refers to a coin struck by Jassa Singh Kalāl (Ahluwalia) in 1758 after expelling the Afghan governor from Lahore. Jassa Singh is said to have ventured to strike rupees at the mint of Lahore in his own name 'by the grace of God'. These coins have become a subject of controversy. Browne himself says that the Diet of the Sikh chiefs later decided to call in all these rupees and to strike new ones in the name of Guru Nanak and Guru Gobind Singh. The Persian inscription on the new coins stated: 'Gooroo Gobind Singh, received from Nanack the *Daig*, the Sword and rapid Victory'. Browne underlines that the Sikhs alone claimed independence out of the many powers raised at the cost of the Mughal Empire. 'They will not suffer the name of his Majesty Shah Alum to appear upon their coin; but have substituted that of their Gooroo; and instead of the year of the King's reign, and of the Hegira, which is the established date on all the coins throughout the empire, they use the era of *Bickermajeet*, called the *Sumbut*.'[72] Browne leaves no doubt that the Sikhs struck coins to declare their sovereign status.

Hans Herrli, for whom the main source of the study of Sikh coinage was Sikh coins, deliberately omits the coins issued by the states of Patiala, Nabha, Jind, and Kaithal on the argument that their coins were a part of the Durrani coinage, and not 'Sikh' coins. The inscription on their coins acknowledges the sovereignty of Ahmad Shah Abdali. It reads:

Hukm shud az qādir-i bechūn b'Ahmad Pādshāh,
Sikka zan bar sīm-o zar az auj-i māhī ta b'māh.

'The command came from the Powerful One to Ahmad the emperor: "To strike coins on silver and gold from the height of Fishes to the Moon".'

This inscription appeared on the coins of Amar Singh and Sahib Singh, the rulers of Patiala, with their respective symbols on them during the late eighteenth century. The same inscription is said to have appeared on the coins of Nabha, Jind, Kaithal, and Malerkotla. Modifications in this practice were made only from the early nineteenth century onwards, particularly after the fall of the Lahore state in 1849, and during the twentieth century.[73]

By contrast, the inscriptions on the coins struck in Lahore, Amritsar, and Multan during the late eighteenth century declared the sovereign status of the Sikh chiefs. It may be recalled that the coins struck in Lahore for general circulation from 1765 onwards bore the following inscription with slight variations:

Deg-o-teg-o fateh nusrat bedirang,
Yāft az Nanak Guru Gobind Singh.

'Guru Gobind Singh received from (Guru) Nanak (as gifts) the cooking pot, the sword and instantaneous victory.'

The source of power and authority here is Guru Nanak, an authority which he passed on to Guru Gobind Singh and to the Khalsa. The coins struck in Multan from 1772 to 1779 bear the same inscription. Coins began to be struck in Amritsar from 1775 onwards with the following inscription with slight variations:

Sikka zad bar har do 'ālam tegh-i Nanak wāhib ast,
Fateh-i Gobind Singh Shāh-i Shāhān fazl-i Sachā Sāhib ast.

'Coin struck throughout the two worlds by the grace of the True One. The sword of Nanak is the bestower of victory on Gobind, King of Kings.'

Here, again, the triumph of Guru Gobind Singh is due to the grace of God, and Guru Nanak is the source of authority. Neither of the two inscriptions acknowledges any earthly suzerain as the source of authority. On the reverse of the Amritsar coins from 1775 to 1795 is mentioned Akāl Bungā, the symbol of temporal authority for the Khalsa.[74]

A number of published official orders of the late eighteenth century throw further light on the position of the individual chief. The orders issued by Jai Singh (Kanhiya), Hukumat Singh, Sahib Singh, Amar Singh, Harbakhsh Singh, and Gurbakhsh Singh (actually Sada Kaur) bear seal impressions. The seals of Jai Singh, Hukumat Singh, and Sahib Singh carry the years 1750,

1752, and 1772 respectively in all their orders, indicating the time when each chief had begun to claim authority. There are no titles with their names: they are simply and starkly 'Jai Singh', 'Hukumat Singh', and 'Sahib Singh'. The only other words are 'Akāl Sāhāi' (God the supporter). We may infer that the individual chief recognized God alone as the source of his power and authority. In the text of the orders, the chief himself is referred to as 'Khalsa Jī' or 'Khalsa Jio'. In a posthumous reference to Jai Singh he is 'Sardār' Jai Singh and he is also called 'Singh Sahib'. There is hardly any doubt that every one of the chiefs was his own authority in the administration of the territory under his control. After the death of Jai Singh, Sada Kaur used the name of her deceased husband, Gurbakhsh Singh, both before and after 1800.[75]

The dated orders cover the years from 1752 to 1800, except the orders of Sada Kaur (of 1807, 1808, and 1809). In the documents of the late eighteenth century, the word used for the order is simply *parwāngī* (order), or *parwāngī-i khās* (special order). In the orders of Sada Kaur (in the name of Gurbakhsh Singh, of course) the epithets *hukam-i āli* and *hukam-i wālā*, both meaning the exalted order, are used in 1808 and 1809. The orders are addressed primarily to the administrators of specific units (*'āmilān*). The officials in general are called *ahlkārān*. The other addressees are the officials in charge of ferries (*guzarbāns*), headmen (*panchas*), and zamīndārs. The format of the documents is very simple but there is an essential similarity with the official orders of Mughal times. There is one addition though: the place at which the order was issued is often mentioned, indicating that the Sikh chiefs were frequently on tour in their territories.

All these documents relate to state patronage. The recipients in almost all cases are the Mahants of the Vaishnava establishment in Pindori named after Bhagwan Jī, and his first successor Narain Jī, who had first received a grant of revenue-free land from the Mughal emperor Jahangir. The successors of Bhagwan Jī received grants from other rulers later. Hukumat Singh orders the present and future 'āmils and zamīndārs of the town of Kahnuwan on 17 April 1752 to ensure that the market and the land held by the Mahants of Sri Pindori of Bhagwan-Narain Jī from the olden days of the emperors remained in their possession. The order of 17 January 1755, addressed to the present and future 'āmils of the pargana of Kahnuwan, mentions eighteen *ghumāons* of land in Kahnuwan proper that had been received from the emperors by way of dharmarth by (the establishment of) Sri Bhagwan Narain Jī in Pindori. Hukumat Singh orders that this land should remain revenue-free in accordance with the former custom, and none should be allowed to interfere with it. Gaura Singh's orders of 22 March 1761 and 5 April 1768 also confirm this position in Kahnuwan. Indeed, the grants of revenue-free lands of Mughal times appear to have been confirmed by Sikh chiefs as a matter of principle.[76]

A number of villages find mention in these documents in connection with the revenue-free grants of land. In an order of Jai Singh, one-fourth each of Sayyidana and Saidar, Maharajpura, Jattowal, 'and other villages' are exempt from revenue (*wāguzār*). Twenty-four ghumāons of an orchard with a well figure in the order of Amar Singh as offering (bhet) for 'Mahant Sahib Kesho Das Jī'. The village Salhupura is mentioned as an old grant in the order of Harbakhsh Singh. In the orders of Sada Kaur, two ghumāons of land in Kalijpur village in the *ilāqah* of Bianpur are mentioned as a former grant of the late Singh Sahib, Sardār Jai Singh. Ten ploughs of land in Talibpur find mention in another order as an old grant in favour of the Mahants of Pindori Jio. It may be added that Jai Singh exempted from transit duty the grains ferried across the Beas from the revenue-free villages of the Mahants. An order of Sada Kaur shows that apart from revenue, lands granted were exempt from all customary cesses, obligations, and forced labour (*begār*).[77]

The term generally used for charitable grants is dharmarth. The Mughal term *āima* appears in two documents. The term used in Sahib Singh's order is simply *punn* (charity). In two documents, the term 'jāgīr' is synonymous with dharmarth. Thus, familiarity with the jāgīrdārī system is reflected in these orders of 1788 and 1800.[78]

Respect for the grantees and their establishment is also reflected in the use of the following terms: for example Sri Pindori Jio, Sri Pindori Bhagwan-Narain Jī, Tarn Taran-i Do Jahan Mahant Sahib

Jio, Sri Mahant Sahib Uttam Surup Mahant Kesho Das Jio, Sri Mahant Sahib Pindori Jī. There are two grantees other than the Mahants of Pindori. Misar Mohan Lal is the recipient of a grant in one document for looking after 'the *sādhs* of Bhai Deva Singh Jio'. In another document, 'Baba Sahib Badbhag Singh Jio' is the recipient of half of the village Lahri Gosain, while the other half is given to the Mahant of Pindori. As in the order of Jai Singh, the principle that there should be 'no discrimination' on the basis of the difference of faith is stated clearly: 'Through the grace of the True Guru, there is no discrimination in the faith of Khalsa Jio.' The grantees are expected to pray for the patron. In the order of Amar Singh on 19 October 1789 blessings (*āshīrbād*) for his long life and prosperity is explicitly mentioned. The term used in an order of Sada Kaur is prayer (*du'ā*).[79] Gaining goodwill of the grantees and their followers was one way of seeking legitimacy for the new rule.

Only one Sikh document from the Jakhbar collection has been published. It bears the seal impression 'Akāl Sāhāi Bhag Singh'. There is no date, but it was probably issued between 1765 and 1809. The dīvān of Bhag Singh is ordered to ensure that no tax was imposed on the goods purchased by the Jogis of Jakhbar from the shopkeepers of Sujanpur. As reported by them to the chief, they had paid no such tax in the past. Bhag Singh goes on to add that they belonged to a religious establishment, with Jogī Subuddh Nāth as its Mahant, and that there should be no interference with the sanctuary of the Nāths.[80]

The other Sikh documents of the Jakhbar collection have not been published. Also known to be in existence are Sikh documents of the Vaishnava establishment of Dhianpur in the upper Bari Doāb, and of several other establishments of the Punjab. Therefore, the evidence presented here on state patronage in the late eighteenth century is only a small part of the relevant evidence on this subject. In other words, the position of the few Sikh chiefs who figure here was not exceptional. As a matter of policy, all Sikh chiefs of the period confirmed old grants and gave fresh grants of their own. In this respect the pattern of state patronage under Sikh rule is very much similar to the one under the Mughals, marking a strong institutional continuity.

Indeed, a number of files in the National Archives of India, New Delhi, confirm the existence of official orders of this kind on a large scale. A large number of archival documents refer to *sanads* in the possession of the grantees. Put together, such documents leave the impression of patronage of Sikh, Hindu, and Muslim individuals and institutions by Sikh chiefs in their territories spread all over the region.

The first striking feature of these records is the large number of Sikh chiefs whose dated orders are referred to as sanads.[81] This number is more than ninety. All the best known Sikh chiefs of the first generation are among the donors: Jassa Singh Ahluwalia, Charhat Singh, Jai Singh Kanhiya, Hari Singh, Jassa Singh Ramgarhia, Hakikat Singh Kanhiya, and Gujjar Singh. It may be added that all the three Sikh chiefs who occupied Lahore in 1765 figure in these documents: Gujjar Singh, Lehna Singh, and Sobha Singh. Six well-known chiefs of the second generation who figure are Bhag Singh Ahluwalia, Mahan Singh Sukarchakia, Sada Kaur (as the widow of Gurbaksh Singh Kanhiya), Jhanda Singh, Ganda Singh, Jaimal Singh, and Sahib Singh Gujratia. There are twenty-six other chiefs whose names are rather familiar, like Bagh Singh Hallowalia, Nar Singh Chamiariwala, Natha Singh Shahīd, Tara Singh Pathankotia, Bagh Singh Muraliwala, and Bhai Lal Singh of Kaithal.[82] There are more than forty chiefs whose names are less familiar, like Bhag Singh Kalalwala, Dharam Singh Kadarabadia, Fateh Singh Kanhiya, Hukumat Singh Ahluwalia, Mehtab Singh Ramgarhia, and Tara Singh Chainpuria.[83] The only important chief of the third generation figuring in these records is Ranjit Singh. All the donors were not men, with at least five women among the donors. Apart from Sada Kaur, they are Kishan Kaur (wife of Charhat Singh), Maee Kurmon (the Nakkai mother-in-law of Ranjit Singh), the Rani of Sardār Bhag Singh, and the widow of Sardār Dal Singh.

For the earliest known grant given by a Sikh chief, there is a reference to an order of Charhat Singh dated 1750, as that of Jai Singh Kanhiya. The first grant given by Jassa Singh Ahluwalia comes from 1752, and the first available grant of Hari Singh is of 1753. It is important to note that at least fifty grants were given by the Sikh chiefs before the formal declaration of their sovereignty in 1765. It is no less significant that the number of grants began to increase after 1765. The total number of recorded grants given by the Sikh chiefs by 1800 was not less than 500. We have seen already that the old grants were confirmed almost as a routine. Understandably, the early grants were mostly of this category. Fresh grants were given increasingly after 1765. This pattern reflects the sequence and size of the territories occupied as well as the political status of the chiefs. These documents possess a special importance not only for Sikh polity but also for the political process through which the Sikhs re-established their rule.

As noticed earlier, recipients of grants from Sikh chiefs were Sikhs, Hindus, and Muslims. Sikh institutions and individuals received the largest proportion of grants. Foremost amongst the institutions was the Darbār Sāhib in Amritsar, followed by the Akāl Bungā and the other bungās. Grants were given to several categories of persons connected with these institutions: head-granthīs, granthīs, *rāgīs*, *rabābīs*, *dhādhīs*, painters, and lighters of lamps, besides Akālīs and others. The keepers of gurdwaras receiving grants were often called the *dharmsāliās*. It may be added that grants were given to several other gurdwaras associated with the Sikh Gurus. Prominent among these were the Manji Sahib Guru Nanak in pargana Sheikhupura, Dera Guru Nanak in Tarn Taran, Dera Sahib Guru Ram Das in Lahore, place of Guru Hargobind in Wadali in pargana Amritsar, Kotha-Guru-ka in the village Valla, associated with Guru Tegh Bahadur, and the shahīdganj in Lahore. Moreover, grants were given to the gurdwaras in Khara Bhai Mangat, Harappa (Multan), Gujranwala and Sialkot in Rachna Doāb, Nurmahal in Jalandhar Doāb, and Chamiari and Saurian in the upper Bari Doāb. Grants were also given for the construction of new gurdwaras in the late eighteenth century. Most of these institutions were associated with Gurus and martyrs. Fairs attracting people from the locality and the region were held at several of these places.

Next in importance to Sikh institutions were the descendants of the Sikh Gurus, especially the Bedis and the Sodhis, the descendants respectively of Guru Nanak and Guru Ram Das. The Bhalla descendants of Guru Amar Das figure among the grantees but not the Trehan descendants of Guru Angad, at least not explicitly.

Another category of Sikh grantees were the ascetic Nirmalās who received patronage for propagating the Sikh faith. The religious identity of the renunciate Udāsīs is not clear but they were prominent among the recipients of grants, notably the establishments of Bhai Pheru, Bhai Santokh Das, and Pritam Das.[84] Granthīs of samādhs, as that of Charhat Singh, too received revenue grants.

In the last quarter of the eighteenth century, two categories of Sikh grantees need special mention. A grant was given to the granthīs who were in charge of the recension known as Bhai Banno Biṛ in the village called Khara Bhai Mangat.[85] The other category of Sikh grantees not yet noticed by any historian is the Hukamnāmiā.[86] Presumably they were the individuals who had in their possession the hukamnāmās of Guru Gobind Singh, asking his Sikhs to extend patronage to the holders of these documents.

Among the non-Sikh recipients of charitable grants figure the Thakurdwaras of the Vaishnavas, the Devidwaras of the Shaktas, the Brahmans in general, and family priests (purohits) in particular. Then there are bairāgīs and the general category of sādhs. It is interesting to find that Dadu Panthis are specifically mentioned among the grantees. A large number of mosques and khānqahs (actually, mausoleums of the Sūfī pīrs) too received grants from Sikh rulers. Muslim individuals who received grants are Shaikhzādās, Pīrzādās, and Sayyids, apart from the general category of fakirs. There is a reference also to a grant for the maintenance of a chhabīl (place for providing free drinking water) as an act of charity or public welfare.

Finally, a remarkable continuity from Mughal times is evident in the administration of justice. The office of the qāzī in Batala continued to function throughout the period of Sikh rule. In the Bhandari collection of legal documents there are at least eight that emphatically demonstrate that the qāzī continued to perform his usual functions in the town at the time of Jai Singh Kanhiya and Sada Kaur. These documents cover the years from 1784 to 1807, and five of these have seal impressions.[87] Qazi Muhammadi was holding the office in 1786 and 1793. His seal bears the date 1773, the year of his appointment. In 1798, 1802, and 1807, however, Qazi Mir Muhammad was in position. His seal bears the date 1795, the year in which he replaced Qazi Muhammadi in the time of Sada

Kaur. Qazi Muhammadi chose to call himself 'servant of the Holy sharī'at' and Qazi Mir Muhammad was 'servant of the law of the Rasul of Allah, the Most High'. They both administered justice in accordance with Islamic law, like their predecessors in Mughal and Afghan times.

Two of these documents are sale deeds (*bai'nāmās*), five are deeds of mortgage (*girvīnāmās*), and one is a kind of affidavit (sanad). The properties sold or mortgaged range from small shops to three-storeyed havelīs, with the amount of mortgage or sale ranging from rupees 18 to rupees 2,950.

The parties to the transactions in these documents varied: the wife of an oil-presser and her son as one and a Duggal Khatri as the other party; a Bhandari Khatri and an Awal Khatri; a Berara Khatri and a Muslim vegetable-seller; the widow of a Bhandari Khatri and a Bania; a Berara Khatri and a Muslim dyer; the wife of a goldsmith, together with a male collateral, and a Kalia Brahman; and the widow of a Hamdani Sayyid, and Rai Anand Singh Bhandari. The sanad made by Nanak Bakhsh, a Nayyar Khatri of Bulharwal, in the presence of Qazi Muhammadi is attested by about ninety persons, mostly Khatris, but including at least one goldsmith and a Shaikh out of the eighteen deciphered names. It also bears the seal impressions of Muhammad Shah, Sevak Ram, and one undated seal with 'Akāl Sahāī'. A seal impression with 'Srī Akāl Sahāī' of Sammat 1822 appears to be a later confirmation. Nanak Bakhsh had lost the girvīnāmā of a havelī he had taken on mortgage and he made this statement to obviate dispute.

## IN RETROSPECT

Looking back at the late eighteenth-century European accounts of Sikhs, we find that the writers raise some of the basic issues of Sikh polity. They assume that there was a central authority among Sikhs called Khalsa Jī, or the confederacy of all the Singhs, which is equated with the State. They constitute the national assembly, called Council or Diet, and also called Gurmatā, that meets in Amritsar once or twice a year to discuss matters of common interest related broadly to three things: matters of defence, organization of campaigns against their enemies, opponents or rivals, and distribution of spoils among themselves. In theory, all the members of the Council were equal, but actually leaders with larger numbers of followers were more influential. All decisions were taken apparently by the majority of votes. A leader was chosen to lead all others in a specific campaign. The combined forces of the leaders were called the Dal Khalsa, or the army of the State. The chosen leader became the first among equals for a specific campaign. The number of leaders was pretty large and each claimed to be independent of the others. This polity as a whole appeared to be a sort of aristocracy.

The leaders came from different backgrounds. The basic difference was between those who increased their power and resources as zamīndārs of the Mughal Empire (mostly in the Delhi province) and those who refused to acknowledge Mughal authority and increased their power and resources as 'rebels' (mostly in the province of Lahore). Two other dimensions of Sikh polity mentioned by late eighteenth-century European writers are tribute and Rākhī. The former was collected from chiefs and the latter from cultivators. What was promised in return was protection against other rulers, or other claimants to the revenue. As a part of their interest in the human and material resources of the Sikhs, the contemporary European writers talk about the prosperous state of agriculture and trade in the territories of the Sikh chiefs.

Among the British historians of the Sikhs, John Malcolm differs from his predecessors in looking at the government of the Sikhs as 'a theocracy'. What he means is that the chief ruled on behalf of the Khalsa, as a servant of the Sikh commonwealth. The 'national council' of the Sikhs functioned on the assumption that they were guided by God in the right direction. The Akālīs, who were in control of the Akāl Bungā and had a great stake in the Council, thought of themselves as the guardians of the tradition established by Guru Gobind Singh. However, they did not interfere in the affairs of the chiefs within their territories. They had sole direction of 'religious affairs' and 'religious ceremonies' in Amritsar.

Prinsep was the first British historian to talk of Sikh misals. Unlike Ahmad Shah of Batala, he talks of twelve misals and refers to them as confederacies. Thus, whereas late eighteenth-century

European writers had looked at the Sikh commonwealth as a confederacy, Prinsep looks at the misal itself as a confederacy. Each misal had a sardār and inferior sardārs but the latter were not subordinate to the former. Each misal had the discretion to act independently or in concert. The territories conquered by a misal were divided first into the share of the chief and the share of others. The latter was divided further among the leaders (sarkardās), and the share of each sarkardā was subdivided among the 'inferior leaders'. Each took his portion as a co-sharer (pattīdār) and held it in absolute independence. In other words, the sarkardās and 'inferior leaders' were as autonomous as the sardār in the internal matters of their respective shares. Indeed, Prinsep talks of 70,000 'sovereigns' in the territories under Sikh rule.

Prinsep sees the misaldārī tenure as different from pattīdārī. A petty leader who unconditionally associated himself with a misal was known as a misaldār or the holder of a misal. In other words, a misaldār commanded a small unit called a misal. The use of the term 'misal' for the confederacy under a sardār, therefore, is illogical, arbitrary and misleading. In any case, the misaldār was rewarded for his cooperation. He was in no way subordinate to the sardār and he could transfer himself with his possessions to another sardār. At the same time, the sardār could have retainers who were totally subservient to him. They were called tabadārs. Prinsep distinguishes them from jāgīrdārs, the holders of jāgīrs, who were called upon any time for service with a stipulated number of horsemen.

Cunningham coined the well-known phrase 'theocratic confederate feudalism' for the Sikh system of government and administration. It was 'theocratic' because the moving principle of the Sikhs was their faith in God, and their only instrument was the sword. The Sarbat Khalsa sought wisdom and unanimity from the Guru and the Granth. Cunningham was sceptical about the validity of the misal as a clear or meaningful concept but he accepted the existence of confederacies, which made the system 'confederate'. It was feudal because the conquered territories were divided and subdivided for various purposes, in a chain of interdependence.

The picture that seems to emerge from this discussion is that of a dynamic process through which the Sikh system of government and administration evolved. The Rākhī, the misal, the Gurmatā, and the Dal Khalsa appear to be related more to the process of acquisition of power in pursuit of the goal of sovereign rule rather than to the institutionalization of government and administration. More important for institutionalization were the exercise of political power by individuals as rulers, the suzerain–vassal relationship, the jāgīrdārī system, and state patronage in terms of dharmarth grants to individuals and institutions. All these aspects of the Khalsa Rāj assimilated it to the Mughal system. In other words, the political revolution of the eighteenth century did not lead to a novel form of government and administration. The ideal of sovereignty was upheld by all the important Sikh chiefs of the former Mughal province of Lahore. The doctrine of Guru Panth, with its inbuilt equality and collective authority, was not institutionalized, though individual Sikh chiefs ruled in the name of the Khalsa. The Akālīs performed a limited role as guardians of the Khalsa way of life, a role that did not include government or administration. The ideals of justice and moderation in the exercise of power were recognized, but their operation was left to the discretion and conscience of the individual ruler.

Focusing on the ideological underpinnings of the political process, Ratan Singh Bhangu confirms that 'the sword of Nanak' was relevant for the rise of Sikh power, and he confirms the idea of 'rāj karegā Khālsā' by asserting that Guru Gobind Singh created the Khalsa as a sovereign entity. Bhangu gives considerable importance to the doctrines of Guru Granth and Guru Panth, the authority of the Akāl Bungā, and the resolutions (Gurmatās) of the Khalsa for the establishment of Sikh rule. He sees the relevance of the Gurmatā for even the occupation of territories and emphasizes the sanctity of Gurmatās. Bhangu's use of the phrase 'hanne hanne pātshāhī', or 'hanne hanne mīr (rulership)' suggests very strongly that he saw no contradiction between the exercise of political power by an individual and the sovereign status of the Khalsa. In other words, the only conceivable form of political organization for him was monarchical.

It is in this context that Ram Sukh Rao projects Jassa Singh Ahluwalia as a sovereign ruler in his relations with other powers and in his management of the civil and military affairs of his own territory. In addition, he looked after the management of the affairs of the Akāl Bungā, the Harmandar Sahib, and the other places in the same complex on behalf of the Khalsa Panth.

For the first time the term 'misl' is used in connection with Sikh politics and polity of the eighteenth century by Ahmad Shah of Batala who treats the misal as an important unit. There were more than four or five hundred sardārs among the Khalsa but preeminent for their armies were a few groups. In other words, all the Singh sardārs were not covered by these groups. Ahmad Shah talks only of the groups that arose in the provinces of Lahore and Multan before 1765. Each group conquered territories in common and divided them among the members of the group. Thus, territorial occupation formed an important stage in the evolution of the group. Another important stage was succession to territory on hereditary basis. Consequently, before the end of the eighteenth century, all the members of a group became rulers of equal rank, albeit with varying resources, like those chiefs who had not joined any group.

Ganesh Das gives almost exclusive importance to Singh sardārs, both big and small, as individuals and ascribes no role to a group. He refers to a *tappādār*, a *nāzim*, a *sūbedār*, and thānādārs appointed by Sardār Gujjar Singh, and to a jāgīrdār appointed by Sardār Mahan Singh. Ganesh Das looks upon every sardār as an autonomous ruler and refers to both Jassa Singh Ahluwalia and Hari Singh Bhangi as bādshāh. There is no difference, thus, in Ranjit Singh's position before and after 1800 in so far as sovereign control over his territories was concerned. Ganesh Das adds a new dimension to our understanding of the state of economy by bringing in the revival of trade and manufacturing in the process of re-urbanization in the territories of Sikh chiefs.

The hukamnāmā of 1759 provides the crucial information that the entire body of the Khalsa as a collective entity derived its authority from the doctrine of Guru Khalsa or Guru Panth. The hukamnāmā resembles the hukamnāmās of the Gurus in asking a Sikh sangat to send cash, and it resembles the orders of the contemporary Sikh chiefs in bearing the seal impression with 'Akāl Sahāī', indicating the assumption of divine sanction for the authority of the Guru Khalsa.

The highest seat of temporal authority for the Khalsa was the Akāl Bungā in Amritsar. Contemporary news reports in Persian make it clear that Sikh leaders held their meetings at the Akāl Bungā in the early 1760s on the occasions of Baisākhī, Dusehra, Diwali, and Holi for consultations among themselves, to take decisions on military campaigns to be undertaken, and on the distribution of conquered territory. The resolutions passed were morally binding for implementation. No single chief was authorized to speak to other powers on behalf of the Khalsa. The news reports also make it clear that Ala Singh called himself a zamīndār. In other words, he did not claim to be sovereign but looked upon Jassa Singh and other Sikh leaders as standing on equal footing with Ahmad Shah Abdali who claimed to derive his authority from God.

In fact, Sikh coins of the late eighteenth century clarify the issue of sovereignty. The very fact of striking the coin at Lahore in 1765 was a declaration of Sikh sovereignty, the goal of 'rāj karegā Khālsā' actually becoming 'khālsā Rāj'. The inscription on the coin is the same as on the seal of 1710 used by Banda Singh, carrying the import that victory, as well as deg and teg, is the gift received from Guru Nanak by (the Khalsa through) Guru Gobind Singh. This coin remained current for a decade as the only Sikh coin minted at Lahore, Amritsar, and Multan. In 1775, a new inscription was used on the coins struck at Amritsar. Significantly, this inscription was the one used initially on the coins issued in 1710, 1711, and 1712 by Banda Singh. It acknowledged the efficacy of 'the sword of Nanak' and attributed the victory of (the Khalsa of) Guru Gobind Singh to the grace of God. No earthly sovereign is recognized in any of the two inscriptions. The coins current in some of the Sikh states of the Sutlej–Jamuna Divide, notably Patiala, the most powerful state in the region, acknowledge the authority of Ahmad Shah Abdali. The chiefs who acknowledged Abdali's authority were supposed to pay tribute to him in return for protection against other rulers. These chiefs retained the government and administration of their territories as de facto rulers. In the former Mughal province of Lahore, the coins declared the sovereignty of the Khalsa. The position of the individual chief, however, was not clear.

The orders issued by Sikh chiefs of the late eighteenth century throw some light on their position. In the first place, such orders had begun to be issued as early as 1750, if not earlier. The seal used on these orders acknowledges the support of God (Akal). The chief is referred to as 'Khalsa Jī' or 'Khalsa Jio' and, later, as 'Sardār' or 'Singh Sahib'. There is no change in the format after 1765. These orders relate to state patronage in the form of charitable grants (dharmarth). The general character of patronage by the Sikh chiefs is exactly the same as in the Mughal times. The Sikh ruler exercised power in his own name, recognizing the authority of God alone. The formal declaration of the sovereignty of the Khalsa, thus, confirmed the sovereign position already assumed by the Sikh chief.

Archival sources relate largely to dharmarth grants, confirmed or issued all afresh, in favour of Sikh, Hindu, and Muslim institutions and individuals, conforming to the broad pattern established in Mughal times. There are also references to jāgīrs given by Sikh chiefs to individuals who served them personally or along with a number of horsemen. Individual horsemen too were given jāgīrs directly by Sikh chiefs. There is hardly any doubt that the jāgīrdārī system was re-established by the Sikh chiefs broadly on the lines laid down by the Mughals. A certain degree of continuity in the administration of justice is evident from the legal documents executed in the court of the qāzī in Batala during the late eighteenth century.

Thus, a complex picture of Sikh polity emerges from our reading of all the sources. It seems that the inscription on the coin which declared the sovereignty of the Khalsa also enabled the individual chief to assume a sovereign status in his internal administration and his political relations with other rulers, whether Sikh or non-Sikh. Formally there was no central authority. A broad similarity of administrative practices under the Khalsa Rāj may be accounted for largely in terms of continuity of Mughal practices in the sphere of justice, revenue administration, jāgīrs, and charitable grants. The Sikh rulers extended state patronage to all religious communities but the individuals and institutions in mainstream Sikhism received a larger share. The institutional practices evolved in the course of the political struggle (Gurmatā, misal, Dal Khalsa, and Rākhī) played an effective role only in the case of Sikh leaders in the region to the north of the Sutlej. The chiefs of the Sutlej–Jamuna Divide came up within the framework of Mughal administration, and introduced no major change. Significantly, while the Sikh chiefs of the Delhi province ruled in the name of their Mughal or Afghan overlords, those of the provinces of Lahore and Multan acknowledged no earthly superior. Thus, there was a qualitative difference between Ala Singh of Patiala and Jassa Singh Ahluwalia of Kapurthala, though both of them were known to be devout Sikhs.

## NOTES AND REFERENCES

1.  B.N. Goswamy and J.S Grewal, trans and eds, *The Mughal and Sikh Rulers and the Vaishnavas of Pindori: A Historical Interpretation of 52 Persian Documents* (Simla: Indian Institute of Advanced Study, 2010 [1969]) [hereafter *The Mughal and Sikh Rulers*], pp. 29–30.

2.  Respectively J.S. Grewal, 'Ahmad Shah of Batala on the Misl', and 'Ganesh Das on Secular Aspirations of the Khalsa', in *Sikh Ideology, Polity and Social Order: From Guru Nanak to Maharaja Ranjit Singh* (New Delhi: Manohar, 2007 [1996]), pp. 147–61. Indu Banga's, *Agrarian System of the Sikhs: Late Eighteenth and Early Nineteenth Century* (New Delhi: Manohar, 1978) discusses the structure and functioning of Sikh polity. For the bearing of Khalsa ideology on Sikh rule, see her 'Raj Khalsa: Ideology and Praxis', *Journal of Punjab Studies* 15, nos 1 and 2 (Spring–Fall 2008): 33–63.

3.  However, Dhavan does not discuss Sikh polity in any detail. In fact, she continues to use the stereotypes of '12 misals', misaldār, and misaldārī throughout her work. Purnima Dhavan, *When Sparrows Became Hawks: The Making of the Sikh Warrior Tradition, 1699–1799* (New York: Oxford University Press, 2014 [2011]), pp. 97–8 et passim.

4.  'Of the Seikh's or Sikhan, c. 1760', in *"Sicques, Tigers or Thieves": Eyewitness Accounts of the Sikhs (1609–1809)*, ed. Amandeep Singh Madra and Parmjit Singh (New York: Palgrave Macmillan, 2004), p. 60.

5.  'Wendel's History of the Jats, Pathans, and Sikhs, 1768', in Madra and Parmjit Singh, *"Sicques, Tigers or Thieves"*, p. 12.

6.  'The Writings of Colonel Polier on the Sikhs, 1776–1802', in Madra and Parmjit Singh, *"Sicques, Tigers or Thieves"*, pp. 77–9.

7.  'Warren Hastings Memorandum on the Threat of the Sikhs, 1784', in Madra and Parmjit Singh, *"Sicques, Tigers or Thieves"*, p. 64.

8. George Forster had travelled through the northern parts of India; his journal, written in the early 1780s, was published in two volumes in 1798 as *A Journey from Bengal to England through the Northern Part of India, Kashmire, Afghanistan, and Persia, and into Russia by the Caspian-Sea* (Patiala: Punjab Languages Department, 1970 [1798]), vol. 1, pp. 339–40.

9. 'Wendel's History of the Jats, Pathans, and Sikhs, 1768', pp. 21–2.

10. 'Antoine Louis Henri Polier, Extract of a Letter from Major Polier at Delhi to Colonel Ironside at Belgram, dated May 22, 1776', in Madra and Parmjit Singh, *"Sicques, Tigers or Thieves"*, p. 72.

11. Colonel A.L.H. Polier, 'An Account of the Sikhs', in *Early European Accounts of the Sikhs*, ed. Ganda Singh (Calcutta: Indian Studies, Past & Present, 1962), p. 61.

12. Polier, 'An Account of the Sikhs', pp. 61–2.

13. Forster, *A Journey from Bengal to England*, vol. 1, pp. 330–8.

14. Major James Browne, *History of the Origin and Progress of the Sikhs* [1788], in Ganda Singh, *Early European Accounts of the Sikhs*, pp. 14–15.

15. Browne, *History of the Origin and Progress of the Sikhs*, pp. 16–17.

16. John Malcolm, *Sketch of the Sikhs* (New Delhi: Asian Educational Services, 1986 [1812]), pp. 89–91.

17. Malcolm, *Sketch of the Sikhs*, pp. 114–15.

18. Malcolm, *Sketch of the Sikhs*, pp. 116–23 and note 122.

19. Malcolm, *Sketch of the Sikhs*, pp. 125–8.

20. Henry T. Prinsep, *Origin of the Sikh Power in the Punjab and Political Life of Maharaja Ranjit Singh with an Account of the Religion, Laws and Customs of the Sikhs* (Patiala: Punjab Languages Department, 1970 [1834]).

21. Prinsep, *Origin of the Sikh Power*, p. 23.

22. Prinsep, *Origin of the Sikh Power*, pp. 23–6.

23. Prinsep, *Origin of the Sikh Power*, pp. 26, 29.

24. Prinsep, *Origin of the Sikh Power*, pp. 27–8.

25. Prinsep, *Origin of the Sikh Power*, pp. 28–9.

26. Prinsep, *Origin of the Sikh Power*, p. 29.

27. Joseph Davey Cunningham, *History of the Sikhs: From the Origin of the Nation to the Battles of the Sutlej* (New Delhi: Rupa & Co, 2003 [1849]), pp. 103–4. Purnima Dhavan attributes the concept of 'theocratic confederate feudalism' to N.K. Sinha. See her *When Sparrows Became Hawks*, p. 20.

28. Cunningham, *History of the Sikhs*, pp. 104–5.

29. Cunningham, *History of the Sikhs*, pp. 106–7n.

30. Cunningham, *History of the Sikhs*, pp. 107–10.

31. Cunningham, *History of the Sikhs*, p. 110.
32. Ratan Singh Bhangu, *Sri Gur Panth Prakash*, ed. Balwant Singh Dhillon (Amritsar: Singh Brothers, 2004), p. 7.
33. Bhangu, *Sri Gur Panth Prakāsh*, pp. 30–3, 194, 196.
34. Bhangu, *Sri Gur Panth Prakāsh*, p. 134.
35. Bhangu, *Sri Gur Panth Prakāsh*, p. 207.
36. Bhangu, *Sri Gur Panth Prakāsh*, pp. 361–2, 381–2 et passim.
37. Bhangu, *Sri Gur Panth Prakāsh*, p. 216.
38. Bhangu, *Sri Gur Panth Prakāsh*, p. 311.
39. Bhangu, *Sri Gur Panth Prakāsh*, pp. 377, 379.
40. Bhangu, *Sri Gur Panth Prakāsh*, pp. 372–3.
41. Bhangu, *Sri Gur Panth Prakāsh*, pp. 404–5.
42. Bhangu, *Sri Gur Panth Prakāsh*, pp. 204–11.
43. Bhangu, *Sri Gur Panth Prakāsh*, pp. 337–49, 385.
44. Bhangu, *Sri Gur Panth Prakāsh*, pp. 211–12.
45. Bhangu, *Sri Gur Panth Prakāsh*, pp. 386–94.
46. Ram Sukh Rao, *Sri Fateh Singh Partap Prabhakar: A History of the Early Nineteenth Century Panjab*, ed. Joginder Kaur (Patiala: Published by the editor, 1980), text, p. 64; Introduction, pp. 21, 24, 27, 40–1, 61 et passim.
47. Rao, *Sri Fateh Singh Partap Prabhakar*, p. 209.
48. Rao, *Sri Fateh Singh Partap Prabhakar*, pp. 172–3, 207.
49. Rao, *Sri Fateh Singh Partap Prabhakar*, pp. 219–20, 223, 224.
50. Rao, *Sri Fateh Singh Partap Prabhakar*, pp. 169, 171, 184, 211–12.
51. Rao, *Sri Fateh Singh Partap Prabhakar*, pp. 154, 166, 311–12.
52. Rao, *Sri Fateh Singh Partap Prabhakar*, pp. 306–7.
53. Rao, *Sri Fateh Singh Partap Prabhakar*, pp. 196–7, 214–15, 385, 387, 414–15, 448, 518–19.
54. Rao, *Sri Fateh Singh Partap Prabhakar*, pp. 177–9, 204.
55. Rao, *Sri Fateh Singh Partap Prabhakar*, pp. 67–9.
56. J.S. Grewal, 'Ahmad Shah of Batala on the Misl', pp. 147–9.
57. J.S. Grewal, 'Ahmad Shah of Batala on the Misl', pp. 149–51.
58. J.S. Grewal, 'Ahmad Shah of Batala on the Misl', pp. 151–3.
59. J.S. Grewal, 'Ganesh Das on Secular Aspirations of the Khalsa', pp. 154–7.
60. J.S. Grewal, 'Ganesh Das on Secular Aspirations of the Khalsa', pp. 158–9.
61. J.S. Grewal and Indu Banga, trans and eds, *Early Nineteenth Century Panjab: From Ganesh Das's Chār Bāgh-i Panjab* (Amritsar: Guru Nanak Dev University, 1975), pp. 115–16.
62. J.S. Grewal and Banga, *From Ganesh Das's Chār Bāgh-i Panjab*, pp. 132–3.

63. J.S. Grewal and Banga, *From Ganesh Das's Chār Bāgh-i Panjab*, pp. 58, 83–4.

64. J.S. Grewal and Banga, *From Ganesh Das's Chār Bāgh-i Panjab*, p. 93.

65. J.S. Grewal and Banga, *From Ganesh Das's Chār Bāgh-i Panjab*, pp. 30, 42.

66. J.S. Grewal and Banga, *From Ganesh Das's Chār Bāgh-i Panjab*, p. 42.

67. Ganda Singh, ed., *Hukamnāme: Gurū Sāhibān, Mātā Sāhibān, Banda Singh Ate Khalsa Ji De* (Patiala: Punjabi University, 1967), pp. 232–3.

68. 'News Reports from Delhi, 1759–65', in *Sikh History from Persian Sources: Translations of Major Texts*, ed. J.S. Grewal and Irfan Habib (New Delhi: Tulika/Indian History Congress, 2001), p. 190–1.

69. 'News Reports from Delhi, 1759–65', p. 192.

70. 'News Reports from Delhi, 1759–65', pp. 193–7.

71. 'News Reports from Delhi, 1759–65', pp. 200–2.

72. Browne, *History of the Origin and Progress of the Sikhs*, pp. 15–17 and notes 8 and 41. Cf. Hari Ram Gupta, *History of the Sikhs 1739–1768 (Evolution of the Sikh Confederacies)* (Calcutta: S.N. Sarkar, 1939), vol. 2, pp. 173–8.

73. Hans Herrli, *The Coins of the Sikhs* (New Delhi: Munshiram Manoharlal, 2004 [1993]), pp. xi and note 2, 218–20, 225.

74. Herrli, *The Coins of the Sikhs*, pp. 19–21, 28–30, 43–53, 162–75, 192–4. It may be pointed out that there are slight variations in the inscription given here.

75. *The Mughal and Sikh Rulers*, documents XVIII–XXXIV, pp. 206–69.

76. *The Mughal and Sikh Rulers*, documents XVIII–XXI, pp. 206–18.

77. *The Mughal and Sikh Rulers*, documents XXIV, XXVII, XXVIII, XXXII, XXXIII, pp. 227–9, 239–45, 259–65.

78. *The Mughal and Sikh Rulers*, documents XXV, XXX, pp. 231–3, 251–4.

79. *The Mughal and Sikh Rulers*, documents XXII, XXIV, XXVII, XXIX, XXX, pp. 219–21, 227–29, 239–41, 247–54.

80. B.N. Goswamy and J.S Grewal, trans and eds, *The Mughals and the Jogis of Jakhbar: Some Madad-i-Ma'ash and Other Documents* (Simla: Indian Institute of Advanced Study, 1967), document XVII, pp. 189–90, 192n1.

81. Unpublished British Records at the National Archives of India, New Delhi (NAI).

82. NAI, Foreign/Political Proceedings. The names of twenty other familiar chiefs are: Amar Singh Bagga, Amar Singh Kingra, Arbel Singh, Baghel Singh, Dharam Singh Amritsaria, Divan Singh Ramgaṛhia, Gulab Singh, Gurbax Singh Doda, Jodh Singh Ramgaṛhia, Jodh Singh Wazirabadia, Karam Singh, Karam Singh Cheena, Mali Singh Ramgaṛhia, Milkha Singh, Nidhan Singh, Ran Singh Nakkai, Sudh

Singh Doda, Tara Singh, Tara Singh Kathgaṛhia, and Tara Singh Ramgaṛhia.

83. NAI, Foreign/Political Proceedings. The other thirty-six Sikh chiefs are: Anokh Singh, Bhag Singh, Bhag Singh Chiniot, Bir Singh, Buddh Singh, Chaṛhat Singh, Chhujja Singh, Dal Singh, Dal Singh Kalalwala, Dasaundha Singh, Dhanna Singh Kalalwala, Dharam Singh Kalalwala, Didar Singh, Ditt Singh, Fateh Singh Shahīd, Gurmukh Singh, Hari Singh Dallewalia, Heera Singh, Jodh Singh, Jodh Singh Saurianwala, Majja Singh, Mal Singh Saurianwala, Mehtab Singh, Mohar Singh Shahīd, Mansa Singh Goraya, Nar Singh Daskewala, Nidhan Singh Randhawa, Punjab Singh Khundewala, Raja Bhag Singh of Jind, Raja Singh, Sher Singh, Sobha Singh, Sobha Singh Dodea, and Surjan Singh.

84. The other Udāsī centres mentioned in the archival records are: Akhaṛās of Ghummand Das, Mela Ram, and Mast Ram at Talwandi, and of Gurdial at Kapurthala.

85. NAI, Foreign/Political Proceedings, 7 January 1853, no. 222. It is an interesting coincidence that Jeevan Deol mentions a recension of the *Banno Biṛ* prepared in 1776. See Chapter 8, note 14.

86. NAI, Foreign/Political Proceedings, 10 June 1853, no. 218.

87. J.S. Grewal, *In the By-Lanes of History: Some Persian Documents from a Punjab Town* (Simla: Indian Institute of Advanced Study, 1975), documents XIII–XVII, XXXII and 'Abstract of Additional Documents', pp. 56–8, 65–6, 187–217, 297–301, 330.

# Part II
# Religious and Social Life

# 3    God, Guru, and Gurdwārā

Turning from the political to the religious life of Sikhs during the eighteenth century, we notice that their conception of God and Guruship and the institution of *dharamsāl* provide the essential links between the pre-Khalsa Sikhs and the Khalsa. In the compositions of the Sikh Gurus, there is a great emphasis on the unity of God and his attributes. These compositions remained the most important source for the conception of God in the eighteenth century. Belief in the unity of Guruship got reinforced with the significant difference that Guruship after Guru Gobind Singh came to be vested in the *shabad-bāṇī* embodied in Granth Sahib as a part of divine revelation, and in the collective body of the Sikhs as *Gur-sangat*.

In this context, there was heightened emphasis on both the Granth and the Panth as the Guru in the eighteenth century. The dharamsāl as the centre of congregational worship (*sangat*) and community meal (langar) became more important as the locus of Guru Granth and Guru Panth. Significantly, the term '*gurdwārā*' began to replace dharamsāl before the end of the eighteenth century. The gurdwaras associated with the Gurus and Sikh martyrs became the places of Sikh pilgrimage. The Harmandar in Amritsar emerged as the premier Sikh institution.

Different forms of Sikh literature are the major sources for this discussion of significant developments during the eighteenth century. Understandably, non-Sikh observers had more interest in the politics of the Khalsa than in their religion, but they did notice the most conspicuous beliefs and practices of the Khalsa. Even though

inadequate, this evidence in Persian and English presents the outsiders' view of Sikh religious life, thus acquiring a significance of
its own. The Sikh and non-Sikh sources, together, throw light on
the evolving doctrinal and empirical situation and its links with
the earlier period.

## CONCEPTION OF GOD

In his *Gur Sobhā*, Sainapat refers to God as Parm Purkh, Kartar—
He is one. Vishnu, Brahma, Mahadev, and Chandi are his creation. Another epithet used for God is Akāl Purkh, underlining
his eternal existence. He was in the beginning, in all cosmic ages,
and he alone shall be in the end. His light is there all the time in
everything and in everyone. He is called Gobind, Parbrahm, and
Parmesar. His names are many but he is one. He is referred to as
*Vāhegurū*. The unity of God is emphasized through *ek* (one) and *ek
onkār* (one eternal God). He is the only true creator and sustainer
of the universe. His power is expressed through his *hukam* (order)
and his kindness through his *kirpā* (blessing). He is the only one
who does everything, is manifest everywhere in all the four directions, and there is no one else. His limits cannot be known and
he cannot be adequately praised. There is great emphasis on the
unity, power, and grace of God.[1]

In Bhai Nand Lal's *Tankhānāmā* (also called *Nasīhatnāmā*), the
epithets used for God are Har, Jagdish, Gobind, Vāhegurū, Khalik
(*khaliq*), and Akal. The epithets Vāhegurū and Akal are characteristically Sikh while the others come from the Shaiva, Vaishnava,
and Islamic traditions. However, all these epithets occur in the
Guru Granth Sahib.[2] In *Prem Sumārag*, the most important epithet for God is Akāl Purkh, the Immortal Being. He is also the
Primal Being (*Parm Purkh*). He is present everywhere, and all
that happens is due to his order (*amr*, hukam).[3] The *Sākhī Rahit*
emphasizes that Akāl Purkh or Vāhegurū is the true Guru. One's
life should be in harmony with his will (hukam).[4]

In the *Rāmkalī Vār Pātshāhī Dasven Kī*, God is *Onkār* (one),
*Ād-purkh* (primal being), *Anbhai* (fearless), *Gurū* (preceptor), *Sat-
nām* (true name), *Abnāsī* (indestructible), *Aghnāsī* (destroyer of sins),
*Sarab-biāpī* (omnipresent), *Alep* (detached), *Nirankār* (formless),

*nirvair* (devoid of enmity), *dukh-dalan* and *dukh-bhanjan* (destroyer of sorrow), *puran* (perfect), *parmesar* (Supreme God), *patit-pāwan* (remover of sins), *dānā* (all wise), *bīnā* (all seeing), *bakhshind* (for-giver), *bhai-bhanjan* and *bhai-nāshan* (destroyer of fear), *mukand* (bestower of liberation), *jogī*, *sanjogī* (leads to union), *rakhwālā* (pro-tector), *rahīm* (merciful), *pātshāh* (king), *sadā hajūr* (ever present), and *sachchā sāhib* (True Lord). All these and many other epithets come from Gurbāṇī, including the compositions of Guru Gobind Singh. It is important to underline that Bhai Gurdas Singh's con-ception of God is characteristically Sikh. God is the only object of worship for him.[5]

It is equally important to note that the eighteenth-century Sikh works underline the exclusive worship of God. In the rahitnāmā of Bhai Prahilad Singh too there is an emphasis on the exclusive wor-ship of the Supreme Being. He who worships any deity other than Akāl Purkh wanders through birth after birth and never attains peace. He who worships idols of stones remains subject to death and rebirth. He who believes in *maṛhī*, grave, or an idol of stone, is not a Sikh of the Guru. The *mantar* of 'Sri Vāhegurū' covers all kinds of recitations; it is the beginning and the end.[6]

In the *Tankhānāmā* it is recommended that, before eating *kaṛāh parsād* (*prasād*) or food (in the langar or elsewhere), a Sikh should utter Vāhegurū.[7] The author of the *Prem Sumārag* says that the only giver of gifts is Akāl Purkh: one should not look towards any-one else. One should concentrate one's mind on the feet of Sri Akāl Purkh and shun the Brahman. Also to be shunned are devi, *devtā*, *butt*, *maṭh*, *maṛhī*, *tīrath*, *barat*, *pūjā-archā*, mantar, *jantar*, *pīr*, *pursh*, *tarpan*, *gāyatrī*, and *sandhyā*. A Sikh should think that Sri Akāl Purkh is always present with him. Detached from the world, he should remain attached to the Creator.[8] According to Koer Singh, Sikhs should take refuge in God and no one else.[9] Bhai Desa Singh recommends that a Sikh should lodge Vāhegurū in his heart and utter Vāhegurū.[10] Daya Singh in his rahitnāmā uses only two epithets for God: Akāl Purkh and Vāhegurū.[11]

However, several Sikh writers of the eighteenth-century talk of the Goddess: the author of the rahitnāmā associated with Chaupa Singh (narrative part), Koer Singh, Kesar Singh Chhibber, Sarup Das Bhalla, and Sukha Singh. In the rahitnāmā associated with

Chaupa Singh, the Supreme Deity mentioned everywhere is either Vāhgurū (Vāhegurū) or Akāl Purkh, the Formless One who is a pure spirit beyond the three qualities (*guṇ*). He is the Perfect Being (Param Purkh), and the Sikh believes only in him.[12] Similarly, God for Koer Singh is the Primal Being, the creator of everything, omnipresent, and transcendent.[13] For Chhibber, God (Prabh) has no limits and he quotes the *Akāl Ustat* for God's attributes.[14] Sarup Das Bhalla uses epithets for God that underline his unity: Parmātmā, Parmesar, Pūran Brahm, Sachā Sāhib, Allah, Maulā, Ilāhī, Khudā. He is both absolute (*nirguṇ*) and with attributes (*sargun*). Some of the attributes mentioned by Bhalla are Alakh, Niranjan, and Nirankar. At the end of most of the *sākhīs* he uses a refrain in which he prays to Sri Vāhegurū.[15] For Sukha Singh, too, God is the Primal Being who is present everywhere and in everything; he is Akal, the creator of gods, men, and demons, Krishan (Krishna) and Bishan (Vishnu), and the whole universe.[16] In the works of these writers, the devi, whether a supreme deity or a creation of God, does not replace Akāl Purkh; she performs a limited role, and she does not figure in the rahit of the Khalsa in any way.[17]

## GRANTH AS THE GURU

In Sainapat's *Gur Sobhā*, it is stated that a day before the death of Guru Gobind Singh, the Singhs asked him about his successor. They were told that besides the Khalsa, the eternal shabad-bāṇī shall be the true Guru.[18] Significantly, in the rahitnāmā known as the *Prashan-uttar*, which was composed by Bhai Nand Lal in 1695, Guru Gobind Singh states that a Sikh who wishes to see the Guru would have his *darshan* in the Granth as the form of the Guru.[19] In this context, an explicit statement is made in the *Rahitnāmā* of Prahilad Singh: 'All the Sikhs are instructed to regard the Granth as the Guru.'[20]

It is, therefore, not surprising that in the *Sākhī Rahit*, shabad is equated with the bāṇī, and the verse of Guru Ram Das, 'bāṇī is the Guru and the Guru is bāṇī', is quoted.[21] The *Prem Sumārag* refers to shabad-bāṇī as the Guru. 'He who wishes to hear the Guru should read the shabad.'[22] Finally, it may be noted that in *Parchiān*

*Sewādās*, completed in Nander in 1709, the title used for the Sikh scripture is 'Guru Granth'.[23] Thus, in the evidence from as early as the days of Guru Gobind Singh we have a clear equation of shabad with bāṇī, of shabad-bāṇī with the Granth, and of the Granth with the Guru. That the doctrine of Guru Granth was well recognized throughout the eighteenth century is confirmed by the texts of the second half of the century, like Koer Singh's *Gurbilās*, Kesar Singh Chhibber's *Bansāvalīnāmā*, Sarup Das Bhalla's *Mahimā Prakāsh*, and Sukha Singh's *Gurbilās*.[24]

Contrary to W.H. McLeod's suggestion,[25] the origins of the doctrine of Guru Granth can be traced to the earlier Sikh tradition. The equation of God with the Guru, the indispensability of the Guru for liberation, and identification of the Guru with the shabad are emphasized in the compositions of Guru Nanak himself. In the eyes of his successors, the divinely inspired compositions of Guru Nanak are equated with the shabad. The compositions of his successors also came to represent the Shabad-Guru. Thus, when Guru Arjan compiled the Granth, the ground was prepared for the equation of bāṇī with the Granth. The equation of shabad with the Guru was well entrenched before Guru Gobind Singh made the declaration.[26]

In his later works also McLeod maintains that the *Gur Sobhā* recognizes only the doctrine of Guru Panth.[27] It is true that Sainapat talks of shabad-bāṇī, and not the Granth, but the term 'shabad-bāṇī' was used for the Granth. McLeod also thinks that the rahitnāmā associated with Chaupa Singh stops short of declaring the Granth to be the Guru.[28] But this rahitnāmā does use the term 'Granth Sahib'; in fact, there is the explicit injunction in a few places that the Guru's Sikh 'should regard Granth Sahib Ji as the Guru'. It refers also to 'Guru Granth Sahib'.[29] McLeod's translation of the rahitnāmā of Desa Singh actually uses the phrase Guru Granth.[30] The text of the rahitnāmā given by Piara Singh Padam, which was surely seen by McLeod, clearly states that, 'between the Guru and the Granth there is no difference'.[31] Similarly, the text of the rahitnāmā of Daya Singh in this collection explicitly enjoins that the Granth should be regarded as the Guru.[32]

An important insight into the crystallization of the doctrine of Guru Granth is provided by Koer Singh's *Gurbilās* in which

one of the charges against the Masands is that they did not pay
due respect to the Granth and regarded themselves as the Guru's
equal. Guru Gobind Singh then instructed the Sikhs to regard
'Guru Granth' as God. Placing five paisās and a coconut before
the Granth, he is reported to have said: 'Whoever wishes to speak
to the Guru should read the Granth, and gain peace; there is no
equal.' Koer Singh reiterates that an essential part of the rahit
of the Sikh is firm faith in Guru Granth, with no regard for any
other scripture.[33]

Kesar Singh Chhibber's evidence is even more telling. He states
that the Sikhs had requested Guru Gobind Singh in 1698 to com-
bine the two Granths into one volume, but the Guru made it clear
that the 'Ādi Granth' was the Guru and the other Granth (later
known as the *Dasam Granth*) was 'our sport' (*khed*). Therefore, the
two should remain separate. Chhibber reports that when the time
of Guru Gobind Singh's departure from this world came close, the
Sikhs asked him with joined hands, 'what would happen to your
sangat?', and the Guru responded with the words, 'The Granth is
the Guru and take refuge in Akal.' Chhibber suggests on his own
that the two Granths being brothers should be regarded as the
Guru. Yet, Chhibber's reference to the 'Ādi Granth' as 'the Tikkā'
(the heir apparent) carries the implication that the 'Ādi Granth'
was to be regarded as far more authoritative. Finally, in his own
times, that is the late 1760s, Chhibber unequivocally says: 'Today
the Granth Sahib is our Guru.' We may be sure that here 'Granth
Sahib' in the singular is the 'Ādi Granth'; a true Sikh of the Guru
is only he who regards the injunctions of the Granth as true. He
who follows the Guru's instructions becomes a member of the
Guru's House.[34]

Sarup Das Bhalla relates that, when the Sikhs of Guru Gobind
Singh asked him about his successor, he declared that the ten
physical forms of the Guru had come to an end. 'In my place now
regard the Granth Sahib as the Guru. He who wishes to speak to
me should read the "Ādi Granth Sahib". This is the way to converse
with me.' Soon afterwards, the Guru expired and his body was
cremated. Henceforth, 'Granth Ji became the Guru in place of Sri
Guru Ji Sahib'.[35] Bhai Desa Singh recommends that a Sikh of the
Guru should see no difference between the Guru and the Granth.[36]

On the whole, Sikh literature of the eighteenth century leaves the impression that the doctrine of Guru Granth had become well established much before the end of the eighteenth century. The 'Granth' was equated with the 'Ādi Granth'. Kesar Singh Chhibber is the only Sikh writer of the eighteenth century to mention the Book of the Tenth King (*Dasven Pātshāh kā Granth*) as close in status to the 'Ādi Granth'. But even he is not making a factual statement. Some modern historians of the Sikhs, who are inclined to think that both the 'Ādi Granth' and the *Dasam Granth* had come to be regarded as the Guru by the beginning of the nineteenth century, if not earlier, are clearly mistaken.[37] A crucial importance is attached by these historians to John Malcolm's statement in his *Sketch of the Sikhs* (1812) that the Book of the Tenth King (Dasven Pātshāh kā Granth) was as holy as the Ādi Granth in the eyes of Sikhs. Even when Malcolm noticed that verses from both the Granths were recited at the time of preparing the water for initiation (*pahul*) and were read every morning and evening,[38] his assumption of parity between the two Granths is based on what a Sikh had told him. Malcolm himself does not equate the Dasven Pātshāh kā Granth with the Guru anywhere in his *Sketch*.

## PANTH AS THE GURU

Sainapat explicitly says that a day before his death Guru Gobind Singh declared that Guruship henceforth was vested in the Khalsa. Concerned only with the Khalsa, he bestowed his robe (*jāmā*) on the Khalsa: 'The Khalsa is my form and I am close to the Khalsa. In the Khalsa I abide from the beginning till the end.'[39] This equation between the Guru and the Khalsa became the basis of the doctrine of Guru Panth.

It has been argued by McLeod, however, that the doctrine of Guru Panth arose from the need for maintaining the Panth's cohesion after Guru Gobind Singh. It assumed a position of primacy within the Panth during the middle years of the eighteenth century, finding a practical expression in the institution of the Gurmatā. After the establishment of Sikh rule in the last quarter of the century, the Gurmatā came to be regarded as a positive hindrance. Corporate decisions could hardly be welcomed by Ranjit

Singh in his effort to bring all other leaders under his own control; he eventually imposed a ban upon all but strictly religious assemblies.[40] In his recent writings, however, McLeod concedes the presence of the doctrine of Guru Panth in the early rahitnāmās, and admits that, the *Gur Sobhā* certainly recognizes the doctrine of Guru Panth.[41]

In fact, the ground began to be prepared fairly early for the impersonal doctrine of Guru Panth in place of personal Guruship. Guru Nanak's decision to install Guru Angad in his place during his lifetime involved the idea of interchangeability between the position of the Guru and that of the Sikh. In the compositions of Guru Ram Das there is an explicit statement: 'The Guru is Sikh and the Sikh is Guru.'[42] In the vārs of Bhai Gurdas, the idea that the Guru is in the sangat gave a peculiar sanctity to the collective body of the Sikhs.[43]

With this background, it is significant that in the rahitnāmā known as the *Prashan-uttar*, one of the three forms of the Guru is the Sikh who remains absorbed in Gurbāṇī and has daily darshan of the Guru. Some of the other qualities of the Sikh are then mentioned to emphasize that such a Sikh was the veritable form of the Guru.[44] The *Sākhī Rahit* underlines the exclusive importance of the Khalsa for the Sikh of the Guru. A similar importance is given to five Sikhs.[45] The statement attributed to the tenth Guru in the rahitnāmā of Prahilad Singh is quite emphatic: 'Regard the Khalsa as the Guru, a manifestation of the Guru's body. The Sikh who wants to meet me should search for me in the Khalsa.'[46] A similar statement occurs in the *Prem Sumārag*: 'The Sikh who wishes to have the Guru's darshan should go to the place where five or more Sikhs are gathered; he should go there and have their darshan with reverence and faith. In this way the Sikh would have the Guru's darshan.'[47] In the rahitnāmā associated with Chaupa Singh, a reference is made to the last days of Guru Gobind Singh when he says: 'The Sarbat Sangat is my Khalsa, and the Khalsa is the Guru.'[48] In Desa Singh's rahitnāmā, the phrase 'Guru Sarup Khalsa' is used for the injunction that a Singh should perform services for the Khalsa whose sight (darshan) destroys all sins. In another injunction, the Singhs are told to have love for one another and to remove all feeling of enmity; no Singh should attack another

Singh; he should regard the Khalsa as the Guru.[49] Bhai Daya Singh maintains in his rahitnāmā that the Panth was made manifest in accordance with the order of Srī Akāl Purkh, and that the Sikhs should regard the Panth and the Granth as the Guru.[50]

That this idea became well-entrenched is evident also from Koer Singh's *Gurbilās* in which we find Guru Gobind Singh proclaiming that a Sikh could have his darshan in the Panth by regarding the Khalsa as the Guru. It is emphasized further that a Sikh should perform services for the Khalsa with total dedication, and look upon them as his parents as well as his Guru. The Guru had made the Panth like himself; all sins vanished by seeing the wonderful Panth of Akal as an equal (*ṣānī*) of the Guru himself.[51] It is extremely important to note that in the hukamnāmā of April 1759 referred to in Chapter 2, the issuing authority is mentioned as the 'Khalsa Jī under the protection of Akal'. The scribe refers to the Khalsa of 'Sat Srī Akāl Purkh Jī' as 'Guru-Khalsa'.[52] While writing about the last days of Guru Gobind Singh, when he was asked about his successor, Chhibber too mentions that a part of his answer was that 'the Guru is Khalsa, Khalsa is the Guru'.[53] Even when Bhalla does not explicitly equate the Khalsa with the Guru, he refers to the Khalsa as sovereign even without any territorial possessions.[54] Sukha Singh equates the sangat with the Guru and suggests that the Guru is always present in the Khalsa sangat. When the five Singhs administered *amrit* to Guru Gobind Singh, there was no longer any difference between the Guru and the Sikhs. For Sukha Singh, the sangat and the Guru stand equated.[55]

As regards the relative standing of the Panth and the Granth, it is significant that the Khalsa sought guidance from Guru Granth. Ratan Singh Bhangu describes a situation in which the issue before the Khalsa was whether or not to attack Kasur, the stronghold of the Pathans who had abducted the wife of a helpless Brahman. Finally, it was decided to seek guidance from Guru Granth Sahib. The *vāk* (order) taken from the Granth was interpreted as favouring an attack. The town of Kasur was sacked and the Brahman's wife was restored to him.[56] Bhangu gives greater importance to Guru Panth and Gurmatās than any other Sikh writer, yet looks upon the authority of Guru Granth Sahib as superior. It was open to the Khalsa to interpret the Granth and to take collective decisions that were authoritative but the authority of which did not transcend that of Guru Granth Sahib.[57] The twin doctrine of Guru Panth and Guru Granth, thus, became the two sides of the same coin.

## DHARAMSĀL AS THE CENTRE OF CONGREGATION AND COMMENSALITY

The dharamsāl as the place where Sikhs gathered for worship symbolized the Sikh faith as its most visible institution. Significantly, the term 'dharamsāl' occurs in Gurbāṇī. J.S. Grewal suggests that though used often as a metaphor by Guru Nanak, Guru Amar Das, and Guru Arjan, the term 'dharamsāl' came to be used also for a working institution that was the locus of sādh-sangat, or the congregation of Sikhs. Referring to the use of the term *gurduār* (Guru's door) by Guru Nanak, Guru Angad, Guru Amar Das, Guru Arjan, and Bhai Gurdas, Grewal suggests that the central dharamsāl where the Guru was personally present came to be equated with 'Gurdwārā'.[58] Furthermore, Bhai Gurdas seems to use the word gurdwārā literally for the place where the Guru was personally present, but he refers far more frequently to the dharamsāl as the place where the Sikhs came together for worship. In his vārs the term 'sādh-sangat' is used synonymously with dharamsāl. The spiritual and the socio-cultural aspects of the life of Sikhs get enmeshed here: Sikhs meet in the dharamsāl; they serve the Guru; wash the feet of others; serve them water and wave the fan; grind corn for the langar; play musical instruments; write *pothīs* of Gurbāṇī; bring offerings from what they have honestly earned; and they learn to live in accordance with God's will.[59] Undoubtedly, the dharamsāl is central to the life of the Sikhs.

Writing in the middle of the seventeenth century, the author of the *Dabistān-i Mazāhib* notices ardās as a common feature of Sikh religious worship in the dharamsāl.[60] In fact, Sikhs believed that the collective prayer of the sangat was more efficacious than that of any individual. The Janamsākhīs depict the centrality of the dharamsāl in the life of Sikhs. The importance of the dharamsāl was epitomized in the martyrdom of Guru Tegh Bahadur, which, according to Sainapat, was undertaken deliberately to protect the dharamsāl. This was the reason why Aurangzeb ordered the demolition of 'Sikh temples' in his zeal to suppress the movement.[61]

The hukamnāmās of Guru Hargobind, Baba Gurditta, Guru Har Krishan, Guru Tegh Bahadur, Mata Gujri, Guru Gobind Singh, Banda Singh, Mata Sundari, and Mata Sahib Devi, which cover the period from the 1630s to the 1730s, provide some insights into the institution of the dharamsāl. These hukamnāmās are addressed to the Sikh sangats of the east in places like Patna, Alamganj, Bina, Benares, Mungher, and Dhaka, and to Sikh sangats in the Punjab in places like Pakpattan and Naushehra Pannuan. The Sikhs are instructed to remember God and the Guru, and also to go to the dharamsāl every day for *kīrtan* and *Āratī Sohilā* and to celebrate Gurpurabs. It is most likely that a hukamnāmā was read out to the sangat in the dharamsāl and it was treated with veneration and preserved as a sacred object. The offerings made by Sikhs in cash and kind were probably collected in the dharamsāl and sent to the Gurus through the Masands before the institution of Khalsa, and after their removal, through specially authorized individuals or the postal agents called *mewaṛās*. The dharamsāls came to be controlled and managed mostly by the Khalsa who were no longer only the 'Guru's Khalsa' or 'my Khalsa', but 'Vāhegurūjī kā Khalsa' or the 'Khalsa of Akāl Purkh'. The local sangats functioned largely through the dharamsāl for resolving disputes and undertaking welfare work. The institution of dharamsāl provided the link between the former Sikh sangats and the new Khalsa sangats of the early eighteenth century.[62]

Apparently, the dharamsāl was the place where pahul was administered. After the institution of Khalsa, when the initiated Singhs returned to Delhi to tell the sangat gathered in the dharamsāl what had happened in Anandpur, the Sikhs present there are said to have accepted the Guru's decision by taking pahul from five Singhs.[63]

In the rahitnāmās of the eighteenth century, the dharamsāl figures as the most important institution of Sikhs. Daily visits to the dharamsāl are prescribed in *The Chaupa Singh Rahit-Nama*. It mentions that after his morning prayers at home, a Sikh should go to the dharamsāl and join the sādh-sangat. He should take some offering with him according to his means: flowers, fruit, grain, or cash. Similarly, in the afternoon, if possible, and in the evening without fail, he should go to the dharamsāl to sit in the congregation of Sikhs. He should perform *kathā-kīrtan* or listen to it. Going to the sādh-sangat is as important as the faith in Gurbāṇī and the external symbols of kes, kirpān (sword), and *kachh* (short breeches). When a Sikh of the Guru returns after business in the country or abroad, he should go to the dharamsāl first and then go home. Not necessarily but preferably, he should pray in the dharamsāl before setting out on such business. Sitting among Sikhs in the presence of the Granth Sahib in the dharamsāl, a Sikh of the Guru should not feel proud of his personal merit, wealth, or youth. There is no greater source of merit than joining the sādh-sangat. To build a dharamsāl was the foremost duty of Sikhs. 'Wherever there are five, seven, ten or a hundred Sikh homes in a habitation, they must build a place of the Guru, a dharamsāl.'[64]

A suitable person was needed to look after the dharamsāl and to manage its affairs on behalf of the local community. A Sikh of the Guru in charge of 'the Guru's place' should be kind in disposition, and not irritable or greedy. Called *dharamsāliā* (keeper of the dharamsāl), he should prefer to remain celibate; a person of moral integrity (*jatī, satī*), he should have the qualities of patience, detachment, kindness, and restraint. He himself should observe the rahit. He should be mentally alert and physically clean. He should serve others and share food with them. He should overlook the faults of others, have genuine sympathy for them, and look to the welfare of others (*parsuārth*). He should ensure that anything belonging to a visitor from outside was not stolen or misplaced. Local Sikhs should be considerate towards such a dharamsāliā. On all occasions of some importance, an ardās should be performed. The Guru's house is meant for the poor Sikhs of the Guru who are in need of help, and who are devout and who observe the rahit. There should be no women's quarters in the dharamsāl. At another place, the term 'pujārī' (one who performs religious services) is used in the context of the dharamsāl. The pujārī should not misappropriate or misuse any part of the offerings that come in the name of the Guru. Such an act results in destruction of intelligence and wisdom (*buddh*). A pujārī should not be proud, ignorant, or dishonest. He should not be lustful or prone to anger, a slanderer, or a haughty person. Nor should he allow himself to be called 'bhaī' or 'mahant'.[65] Bhai Desa Singh reiterates that a Singh should never think of appropriating anything from the dharamsāl. Even as a pujārī, he should never take much from the offerings. He should take only what he needs for subsistence. He should never use the offerings for his wife or son; he should use these for the open kitchen.[66]

The *Tankhānāmā* at the beginning of the eighteenth century and the rahitnāmā of Bhai Daya Singh towards its end empha-size the importance of the way in which the sacred food should be prepared for distribution in the dharamsāl. The Sikh who prepared karāh parsād is expected to be meticulous. All the three ingredients (flour, sugar, and ghee) should be taken in equal quan-tities. The spot where parsād is to be prepared should be swept and plastered; the utensils to be used should be scrubbed and washed; the person to prepare the parsād should bathe and recite 'Vāhegurū, Vāhegurū' all the time; a new pitcher should be used for fresh water; when the parsād is ready, it should be placed on a four-legged low table and praises of God are to be sung. Prepared in this manner the karāh parsād becomes the source of grace.[67] The Sikh who distributes parsād must cover his head. It is stated further in the *Tankhānāmā* that if he distributes karāh parsād unequally among the Sikhs with the idea of saving it for himself he remains in sorrow for ever.[68] In the rahitnāmā of Bhai Daya Singh, the three items for the karāh parsād come from three dif-ferent sources: sugar from Vishnu, flour from Mahadev, and ghee from Brahma. It is emphasized that if equal quantities of all these three items called *tribhāg* are not used for preparing karāh parsād it would not reach the Guru.[69] The rahitnāmā of Bhai Desa Singh recommends that while preparing karāh parsād one should recite Guru Nanak's *Japujī* and Guru Gobind Singh's *Jāp*.[70]

In the rahitnāmā of Desa Singh, great emphasis is laid on the importance of the way in which food for the community meal (langar) is to be prepared. Apart from the detail of procedure and items required, it is emphasized that no article of leather should be brought into the kitchen, nor should a dog, a Muslim, or a Chandāl enter the cooking area. A Singh who strictly follows the injunctions (*rahitvant*) is expected to know how to prepare the langar and to ensure its equal distribution (*sam-vartārā*). No meat should be cooked in the langar, and no alcoholic drink should be used. They who cut their hair or who are outcaste are not to be allowed to cook food; nor are they who use bhang (cannabis sativa) or tobacco for intoxication. Ardās is to be performed before distributing the langar. Every item of food should be placed in a clean utensil and offered to the Gurus as *bhog*, with their form lodged in the heart, or it should be offered to the Granth as the Guru. Everyone should sit on the floor to eat, with no distinction made between one another. The food should be distributed among men, women, and children. This is the right way to prepare and serve the langar, says Bhai Desa Singh.[71]

There is great emphasis on congregational worship in eighteenth-century Sikh literature. Sainapat refers to the dharamsāl as the place where the shabad is sung. The sangat or the collective body of local Sikhs meets in the dharamsāl. References to congregational worship are quite frequent. God's praises are sung in the true congregation (*sat-sangat*); this boon comes through good fortune. Sikhs are enjoined to appropriate true association (*satsang*). A Sikh should join the sangat with love in his heart. There is no peace without the sangat. In the true congregation one meets the Sikhs (*sants*) and suffers no sorrow (*dukh*). All one's desires are fulfilled through ardās in the congregation.[72] In the *Tankhānāmā*, the Sikh who does not go to satsang in the morning is a great defaulter. He who goes to satsang but whose mind wanders away from the shabad finds no honourable place in this world, or the next. He who does not invite a poor Sikh to sit with him is a great defaulter. He who talks without an understanding of the shabad gains nothing. He who does not bow his head after the kīrtan fails to meet God. There is hardly any doubt that karāh parsād was distributed at the end of congregational worship or performance of kīrtan and kathā in the dharamsāl.[73] In *The Chaupa Singh Rahit-Nama*, a Sikh who does not go to a congregation (dīvān) of Sikhs for hearing (kīrtan) is humiliated in the end. He who goes to the sangat and looks at women with evil intention also suffers humiliation in the end.[74] It may be added that in the last chapter of his *Gurbilās*, Koer Singh refers to the *Rahirās* and the distribution of bhog in the Sikh congregation in Nander in which Guru Gobind Singh himself participated. Koer Singh quotes the well-known words of Guru Ram Das that congregational worship is an essential part of the daily routine of a Sikh. Koer Singh goes on to mention the presence of rabābīs and *dhādīs* in the sangat.[75]

There are clear indications that individual worship complemented congregational worship for the Khalsa. In the *Sākhī Rahit* it is recommended that a Sikh should rise in the last quarter of the night, bathe, and read or recite the *Japujī* and the *Jāp*. At midday he should wash his hands and feet and read the *Japujī* and the *Jāp*. In the evening, about an hour before sunset, he should read the *So-Dar* and the *Rahirās*. He should love the shabad throughout the day: 'Bāṇī is Guru, and Guru is Bāṇī.'[76] Bhai Daya Singh also recommends that a Sikh should go to the gurdwārā and pray before undertaking anything important. He should not go to the sangat empty-handed and should participate in the kīrtan.[77]

The *Prem Sumārag* has four sets of instructions for the daily life of a Khalsa Sikh. The first relates to early morning worship: to wake up in the last quarter of the night, to bathe with fresh or warm water from head to foot, or to wash hands and feet and face if for any reason enough water was not available or one was ill, and to recite the *Japujī*, the *Jāp*, and the *Ānand* five times. If there is any worldly business, one should recite the '*charan kamal*' *Ārati* and offer ardās and then proceed. If there is no such hurry, one should read Gurbāṇī from the Pothī-Granth as much as possible. After this, he should attend to his work with his heart in the bāṇī-shabad. At midday, he should wash his hands and feet all afresh and read both the *Japujī* and the *Jāp*. If this were not possible, he should concentrate on Akāl Purkh and recite the '*pākī nāi pāk*' stanza, and utter seven times, 'Sri Vāhegurū Akāl Purkh Jī, I have taken refuge with you' and recite the first *Savvayyā* of Guru Gobind Singh. This is as meritorious as the recitation of the *Japujī* and the *Jāp*. Two gharīs before sunset, a Khalsa should read the *So-Dar* and the *Rahirās*. At the time of bhog, he should bow his head after reading the *Japujī* and the *Jāp*. He should make a personal prayer, submitting to God's will and taking refuge with him.[78]

In the rahitnāmā of Bhai Prahilad Singh, it is prescribed that the Sikh should sing the Guru's song every morning. In the forenoon he should eat nothing before reciting the *Japujī* and the *Jāp*, and every evening he should recite the *Rahirās* before eating his meal. He should memorize the bāṇī selected from both the Granths, and he should regularly recite the *So-Dar* and the *Sohilā* at the end of the first quarter of the night.[79] According to the *B40 Janamsākhī*, three things were essential for the Panth: *nām* (meditation on God), *dān* (selfless charity), and *isnān* (a bath, for moral as well as physical purity). The daily life of the Sikh began with bathing and reading of the Pothī before eating anything, participating in the kīrtan at night, and reciting the *Ārati Sohilā* before going to sleep.[80] In *The Chaupa Singh Rahit-Nama* it is recommended that a Sikh of the Guru must bathe early in the morning with cold water and recite the *Japujī* five times and any other bāṇī that he knows by heart. Before going to the dharamsāl he should offer prayer. He who performs no ardās before an important undertaking receives no honour in the divine court. In the evening he should recite the *Rahirās* and the *So-Dar* at his place, or join the sādh-sangat. He who sticks to one's dharam and sings the bāṇī of the Guru attains liberation. A Sikh of the Guru is also expected to contribute the tenth part of his income (dasvandh) and to maintain a separate box (*golak*) for this purpose.[81]

In the *Gur Sobhā*, the purifying nām is equated with the Gurbāṇī sung with love and devotion. The poet prays that he may meditate on the Name, which is more helpful than kith and kin and all other earthly goods. There is a whole Savvayyā to this effect with the refrain, 'Nām Gobind Gobind kaho'. On the whole, the term 'nām' is equated with God and the name of God, but much more so with shabad-bāṇī. The word shabad is used in the context of *bhagtī* (loving devotion), but generally equated with Gurbāṇī. Thus, recitation of God's name and reading of Gurbāṇī were integral to the daily life of a Sikh.[82]

The Sikh mode of worship to the exclusion of every other form of worship is emphasized in several of these works. According to the *Prem Sumārag*, the Khalsa of Srī Akāl Purkh should believe in no other Guru (than the ten Gurus) and should not worship anywhere except where there is the light of the shabad.[83] In *The*

*Chaupa Singh Rahit-Nama* too, the most important belief shared
by all Sikhs is belief in the shabad of the Guru, his bāṇī. Since a
Sikh of the Guru is not to believe in any Guru (other than Guru
Nanak and his successors), or to pray for anything to anyone other
than the Guru, he should read the bāṇī of the Guru and reflect on
it. A Sikh of the Guru should not read or hear any bāṇī, shabad,
or sākhī other than that of the Guru. He who sings anything other
than the Guru's shabad goes to the realm of death (*jam* or Yama).
One should talk only about the Guru and his bāṇī, commit the
bāṇī to memory, and disseminate shabad-bāṇī.[84]

Evidently, the Sikh form of worship as it figures in contemporary Sikh literature excludes virtually all other forms known to be
current during the eighteenth century. The *Sākhī Rahit* underlines
that the Sikh of the Guru worships through the shabad alone. He
does not go to a sepulchre (*maṛhī-masāṇī*) and he does not listen to
a pādhā, a mian, or a mahant. He listens only to Gurmat. He who
observes the rahit lives in peace in this world and the next.[85] Daya
Singh emphasizes that the Khalsa should not follow any belief or
practice of another panth. Like the author of the *Prem Sumārag*, he
uses a number of terms symbolic of the Brahmanical and popular
religious practices to be avoided. In addition, a Singh should not
drink water from the hands of a *kanpātā* jogī, and should avoid the
worshippers of Sakhī Sarvar and the followers of fakirs. He should
not trust a Jaini, a Mauni, or a 'Turk'.[86]

Exclusive validity of the dispensation of Guru Nanak and his
successors in the Kaliyuga is explicitly stated. In the *Sākhī Rahit*,
the dispensation of Guru Nanak and his successors is meant to
replace all earlier or contemporary dispensations.[87] The *Prem
Sumārag* underscores that in addition to the traditional three
gunas, 'the fourth quality' of *sahaj-jog* was meant for the Kaliyuga.
The panths of Hindus and the *mlechh* would deviate from their
dharam and the whole world would become oblivious of all social
norms in matrimonial and sexual matters. Dharam would fly away
like a bird. The '*parm mārg*' created through God's grace would
save the Sikhs, the Khalsa of Srī Akāl Purkh.[88] In the *Gur Sobhā*
too, nām and shabad alone are the means of liberation in the
Kaliyuga. Just as in the earlier Sikh tradition liberation-in-life is
the supreme purpose of life, so it is for the Khalsa. If anything,

the social commitment of the Khalsa, whose duty is to bear arms, to fight, and if necessary, to die fighting in the field of battle for the sake of dharam, is more pronounced.[89] The emphasis on the Sikh mode of worship and liberation-in-life as the goal of life is an important legacy of early Sikh tradition for eighteenth-century Sikhs.

## EMERGENCE OF AMRITSAR AS THE PREMIER CENTRE OF SIKH PILGRIMAGE

The places associated with the Gurus became the places of Sikh pilgrimage in the eighteenth century. According to Koer Singh, Guru Gobind Singh declared *muktsar*, the pool (*dhāb*) where forty Singhs had died fighting and earned the title of *mukte* (the redeemed ones), to be a great place of pilgrimage (*tīrath*), equal in fact to Amritsar.[90] Some other places also acquired importance in the eyes of the Sikhs in the latter part of the century. Sukha Singh refers to the Khalsa sangat of Sodhis in Anandpur where the people lived under the protection of seven standards (*dhujā*). The most important of all these was Sri Kesgarh. Sukha Singh composed his *Gurbilās* there. He highlights the importance of 'Abchalnagar Nanderِ' (literally, the city eternal) where the tenth Guru could be seen in the sangat. According to Sukha Singh, the Darbar in Abchalnagar was constructed at the spot where Guru Gobind Singh had passed on to the other world. By visiting this place a Sikh became pure like a base metal touched by the philosopher's stone. At this door of the Guru, Sikhs and sadhs received four gifts: *budh, bibek, suridhī,* and *siddhī* (intellect, wisdom, prosperity, and spiritual powers). Praises of God were sung there day and night and Ārati was performed. Sukha Singh goes on to add that some of the Khalsa left Abchalnagar to perform services at the Harmandar in Sri Patna. He makes it a point to mention that he too had visited the darbār in Patna before coming to Anandpur. Thus, Sukha Singh refers to the sanctity of the three most important places associated with Guru Gobind Singh: Anandpur, Nanderِ, and Patna.[91] Daya Singh recommends pilgrimage to Abchalnagar (Nanderِ). A Singh who goes to Jagannath should offer rupees 25 as penance when he comes to the Takht in Abchalnagar, and seek initiation (amrit) all afresh. Daya Singh also says that there can be no *sikhī* without having the sight of Kesgarh and Sri Anandpur Sahib.[92]

By the end of the eighteenth century, a number of places in the Punjab associated with the Gurus and martyrs had become the site of gurdwaras supported largely by Sikh rulers. Early British revenue records provide information on several of these.[93] Sarup Das Bhalla refers to the memorials (*dehurā*) raised for the younger sons of Guru Gobind Singh, Mata Sahib Devi, and Mata Sundari.[94] Bhalla does not say so but such memorials were visited by Sikhs for acquiring merit. Bhai Daya Singh refers to the Akālī (or Nihang) as the ideal Sikh whose life was marked by the remembrance of Akal. He goes to Amritsar on the occasion of Baisākhī and Diwali, to Anandpur on the occasion of Hola, and to Abchalnagar for the redemption of his family.[95]

Chhibber provides a clue to the emergence of Ramdaspur as the central dharamsāl and the most important centre of pilgrimage in the early eighteenth century. Mata Sahib Devi decided that the general gatherings at the time of Baisākhī and Diwali should be held not in Delhi but in Ramdaspur. For this purpose, Guru Gobind Singh's maternal uncle Kirpal Singh was sent to Ramdaspur in 1727 to regularize the affairs of the Darbār Sāhib. He consulted the panchas of the town who represented the Khatris, Brahmans, Bhabhras (Jain traders), and peasant proprietors, besides masons and carpenters, among others. They welcomed the idea of holding biannual gatherings of the Khalsa in Ramdaspur. Kirpal Singh selected four persons for different functions. The task of collecting custom was entrusted to Sahaj Singh Trehan; matters related to the affairs of the neighbouring villages were the responsibility of the Brahman Dianat Rai; the accredited messenger (mewaṛā) Man Singh was appointed as the *ardāsiā*; Kesar Singh's father, Gurbakhsh Singh Chhibber, was made the *dārogha* of the cowshed and given charge of the treasury and workshop (*kārkhānā*). Four masons were employed to work every day for construction and maintenance. The offerings that came to the Darbar were sent to the shop of Shiam Bhabhra who kept a regular account of the quantities received. Chhibber goes on to add that the community kitchen was kept open for sādhs, sants, fakirs, and strangers. Daily subsistence was fixed for the blind, the lame, the old, and needy Sikhs. This help was extended to old Sikh women (*Sikhṇīs*) as well. Those who worked for the establishment were paid on a monthly basis. The amount left unutilized was sent to Delhi through a pay order (*hundī*). Kahan Singh Kalāl was given the task of getting the hundi prepared in Lahore and taking it to Delhi. Chhibber also refers to the contest between the Khalsa and the followers of Banda (Bandaīs) over the control of 'the Guru's place and the Guru's town'. It culminated in an armed fight between them over the offerings received at the time of Baisākhī and Diwali. Eventually, the Khalsa became supreme in Ramdaspur. The importance of Ramdaspur for the Khalsa made it important for the Mughals who tried to control it.[96]

Throughout the eighteenth century, the Harmandar and the Akāl Bungā together remained the rallying centre of the Khalsa, where they gathered on Baisākhī and Diwali to deliberate upon common issues of defence and conquest. The hukamnāmā of 1759 refers to the Harmandar being reconstructed (after it was destroyed by Ahmad Shah Abdali in 1757 when Baba Deep Singh and other Sikhs had become martyrs in its defence).[97] In April 1762, the Harmandar was blown up with gunpowder by Ahmad Shah Abdali, the bungās built around the sacred tank were destroyed, and the tank itself was filled up with the debris of the demolished buildings.[98] As mentioned earlier, it was on this occasion that a small number of Sikhs had died fighting in defence of the Harmandar and were cremated together at a spot near the Akāl Bungā where a martyrs' memorial (shahīdganj) was later constructed.[99] Significantly, Bhangu refers to the sacred space as 'the door of the Guru' (*gurdwārā*): 'It was sacred, like the land of Kurukshetra; by dying at this gurdwārā as a true Sikh one acquired the merit of a thousand lives.'[100] By the 1760s, the Harmandar was well established as by far the most important gurdwārā of the Sikhs.

The importance of the Harmandar together with the Akāl Bungā as the loci of the collective decisions of the Khalsa, continued to grow, adding to the sanctity of these institutions. Bhangu refers to Gurmatās adopted by the Khalsa at the Akāl Bungā from time to time, especially on the occasions of Baisākhī and Diwali.[101] It was during the 1760s that the Khalsa passed a Gurmatā in favour of occupying the entire sarkār of Sarhind to which a reference has been made earlier.[102]

By 1770, the Khalsa Sardārs were in control of the two institutions. They took interest in the development of the place and many of them built residences (bungās) around the Harmandar. Their joint efforts went into the reconstruction of the tank, the Harmandar, the connecting bridge, and the entrance (Darshanī Deoṛhī) in the 1770s. The construction of other bungās around the tank was completed during the next decade. Much of the construction work was supervised by Des Raj who had been appointed by Jassa Singh Ahluwalia. Significantly, the granthī, Gopal Das of the Udāsī order, was replaced by a granthī named Chanchal Singh.[103]

According to Ram Sukh Rao, when Jassa Singh Ahluwalia came to know that the whole place had been leased by Ahmad Shah Abdali to Sahib Rai of Naushera, he paid up the whole amount that was due and allotted pieces of land to the sardārs for utilization. He himself constructed a *katṛā* behind the Akāl Bungā and named it 'Guru ka Katṛā' (later known as Guru Bazaar), allocating its income for the maintenance of the Darbār Sāhib. Jassa Singh also appointed mutasaddīs, ardāsiās, granthīs, and pujārīs for the Harmandar, the Akāl Bungā, and other places. Jassa Singh used to send money for the construction work. Once, when accounts were taken, Bhai Des Raj reported that rupees 14,00,000 had been spent by the Ahluwalia Sardār, in addition to the materials he contributed towards construction. Fateh Singh Ahluwalia was given pahul as a young man at the Akāl Bungā by Sadhu Singh who was granted a village, and money was distributed among the poor. The third storey of the Akāl Bungā was constructed by the Ahluwalia chief by way of dasvandh for the Harmandar. Apart from offering gold to the Harmandar, villages were granted to the granthī.[104] Archival evidence shows that other Sikh rulers and jāgīrdārs too made offerings to the Harmandar in different ways.[105]

The increasing importance of the Harmandar and its sanctity during the eighteenth century is reflected in the observations of the contemporary writers. Kesar Singh Chhibber refers to '*sri amritsar*' as the supreme place of Sikh worship.[106] Sarup Das Bhalla praises 'sri amritsar' as the Guru's door to liberation. By seeing this place all sorrows vanished through God's grace; by bathing in the sarovar all sins were washed through the grace of the destroyer of sins; by bowing at this place came peace; loving devotion to God was lodged in the heart in 'sri amritsar'. In a whole sākhī in praise of 'sri amritsar', thousands of Gursikhs are stated to bathe in the sarovar, reciting Gurbāṇī; 'sri amritsar' is said to have been created by the Guru for the redemption of the world. God is believed to reside in the Harmandar. For Bhalla, this place is unique in all the three worlds.[107] Daya Singh says that not to bathe in the tank of nectar (amritsar) was to remain impure.[108]

With the emergence of Ramdaspur as the spiritual and political centre of the Khalsa, a new kind of literature began to be produced. Kavi Sant Das, in his *Ustat Sri Amritsar Jī Kī* written around 1777, asserts that there was no place comparable to the sacred tank (amritsar) in the Kaliyuga; it was the supreme tīrath of all the four cosmic ages (*yugas*). Anyone who showed disrespect to amritsar was cursed and never came again to this place.[109] Kavi Kankan praises the town of Ramdaspur and the contemporary rulers. The people in Ramdaspur lived in peace; there was no poverty or fear of the Raja; they were affluent and enjoyed all comforts. Ramdaspur was supreme among all the places of pilgrimage.[110] Writing his *Ustat Sri Amritsar Jī Kī* towards the end of the eighteenth century, Kavi Saunda says that no other pool of water in all the three worlds was like amritsar; in the midst of the pool was the beautiful Harmandar, the house of Ram. No one had been able to calculate the cost of its construction. The Pathan who showed disrespect to it received a mark on his face as the symbol of ignominy (the reference presumably is to the cancer of the nose suffered by Ahmad Shah Abdali). The power of the Afghans began to decline and Mir Mannu and Adina Beg Khan had been deprived of everything in the world. The Khalsa attained rulership by bathing in the sacred tank. The poet goes on to say that the Khalsa came to Ramdaspur and bowed their head before the Harmandar; sitting in their bungās, they sang the praises of God. All men and women in the town (*nagrī*) of Guru Ram Das lived in peace.[111]

## SIKH RELIGIOUS LIFE IN PERSIAN AND ENGLISH SOURCES

Significantly, the Khalsa of Guru Gobind Singh figure far more prominently in the Persian chronicles and the Persian news reports of the eighteenth century than the Sikhs of his predecessors. In the latter half of the century, the Khalsa also begin to figure in the writings of European observers and in the Fort William Correspondence. These Persian and English sources provide significant insights into the Sikh faith and institutions as well as the ideological underpinnings of the political process during the eighteenth century. Generally, these writers dwell on the different aspects of the Sikh faith that they considered significant or interesting.

For Sujan Rai Bhandari, the essence of Sikh worship was the reading of Gurbāṇī and the singing of Gurbāṇī using musical instruments. The faith that Sikhs had in their Guru was seldom seen in other religious groups. 'If a person arrives at midnight and takes the name of Baba Nanak, though he be a stranger and unknown person, even a thief, robber, or a person of evil conduct, they treat him as a brother and friend and serve him in a manner proper to his needs.'[112] Mirza Muhammad, who was an eyewitness to the entry of Banda Singh and his companions in Delhi as prisoners, testifies to the deep faith and equanimity of the Sikhs who kept singing and reciting 'melodious verses' (from Gurbāṇī).[113] Rai Chaturman Saksena, who completed his *Chahār Gulshan* in 1759–60, thought of Guru Nanak as a Vaishnava who worshipped Ram, but the contemporary 'Nanak-Panthīs' were opposed to the Veda. Their separate faith is said to have emerged from the innovations of Guru Nanak's spiritual successors.[114] Qazi Nur Muhammad, who accompanied Ahmad Shah Abdali in his campaign against the Sikhs in 1764–5, is explicit that the Sikhs followed a separate path from that of the Hindus; they had 'a distinct religion of their own'.[115]

Commenting on the steadfast devotion of the Sikhs for the Guru, Ghulam Ali Khan states that if the 'pīr' of the Sikhs asked them to cut off their heads they would do it immediately on getting a hint of the order.[116] According to the author of the *Tashrīḥu'l Aqwām*, the essence of Sikh worship was the reading of the verses of their Guru, which they recited and sang with music; they did not believe in anyone except their master whose bāṇī they worshipped.[117]

Turning to the European observers of the last quarter of the eighteenth century, we find that Charles Wilkins witnessed the Sikh worship in Patna, which he was told was performed five times daily. It consisted of the reading of Granth Sahib and the singing of shabads to the accompaniment of a small drum and two or three cymbals. The congregation joined in chorus and then they stood up for a long prayer. This was followed by distribution of karah prepared with flour and sugar mixed with clarified butter. In his conversations with two of the Sikhs present, Wilkins learnt that apart from Granth Sahib in Punjabi and in Gurmukhi script, there was another Granth held in almost as much esteem, and it was composed in a language similar to Hindi.[118] The reference presumably is to the Granth known as the Book of the Tenth Guru.

According to George Forster, Guru Nanak, the founder of the 'Sikh Nation', had forbidden the worship of images. The only object that they admitted into their place of worship was the Granth. Their prayer was addressed to one God. Forster observed that there were many essential differences between the religious code of the Hindus and that of the Sikhs. At the same time, however, there were strong features of similarity in their ground-work. The essential deviation from the Hindu system appeared to be the mode of initiation, which removed the barriers of caste and occupation.[119] In James Browne's account, the Sikh system appears to bear the same kind of relation to the Hindu religion as the Protestant did to the Romish, 'retaining all the essential principles, but being abridged of most of its ceremonies, as well as of the subordinate objects of veneration'. Browne thinks that in the beginning, Sikhs formed merely a speculating, quiet, and inoffensive sect, but persecution by the Mughal state transformed them into a political community. The union of religion and politics by Guru Gobind Singh made the movement popular.[120]

John Griffiths refers to Guru Nanak's claim of 'a divine revelation', and looks upon this claim as a way of divesting the Guru of obedience to all human authority. The tenets of Guru Nanak were collected in a book known as 'Granth Jī'. It was kept at a place called Amritsar where Sikhs assembled in hundreds of thousands twice a year, in April and October. From their belief in the worship of one Supreme God, it could be safely inferred that they possessed many of the good qualities of humanity.[121] In his *History of the Reign of Shah Aulum,* William Francklin refers to the Granth as the scripture of the Sikhs. Embodied in this book was a system of religion composed from 'the speculative and contemplative theories' of the Islamic conception of the divine. Guru Nanak delivered this system to his followers as of divine origin. The harmless and inoffensive devotees of Guru Nanak and his successors were transformed into a political community by the aggressive actions of the officers of Aurangzeb who put Guru Tegh Bahadur to death. The Sikhs continued to gain numerous converts.[122]

The growing importance of amritsar in Ramdaspur as the focal point of the religious life of Sikhs was noticed by a number of contemporaries. According to Muhammad Qasim Lahauri, who wrote his *'Ibratnāma* in 1723, 'lakh upon lakh of Sikhs gathered on the Baisākhī day for bathing at a big tank known as amritsar in Chak Guru'.[123] Tahmas Khan refers to the large gathering of Sikhs for bathing at Chak Guru (Ramdaspur) in 1757.[124] According to a contemporary news report of 1763, reconstruction of the shrine after it had been demolished by Ahmad Shah Abdali a year earlier, was still going on at the time of Diwali in 1763 when large number of Sikhs were reported to have assembled in Ramdaspur. It was also reported that Afghans wearing conical caps (*kulāh*) were working there as labourers.[125] When Ahmad Shah Abdali decided to destroy the Harmandar once again, he found, to his surprise, that some Sikhs had stayed back for its defence. 'They did not at all show any fear of being killed nor dread of death', records Qazi Nur Muhammad and all thirty Singhs died fighting.[126]

In the news reports from Delhi during the years 1759–65, there are references of Sikhs coming to the tank of amritsar in Chak Guru for the purpose of bathing at the time of Baisākhī, Dusehra, Diwali, and Holi. At the time of the Baisākhī of 1763, Sikh chiefs were reported to be encamped by the side of the tank at Chak Guru in large numbers so that the moment they were free from the ceremonies of bathing (ashnān), they could raid the territories across the Jamuna. In August 1763, Sikh chiefs reportedly met at Chak Guru 'for mutual deliberation and consultation' and resolved to establish their control in the Jalandhar Doāb. When they received news of Jahan Khan's march against Charhat Singh, they decided to go to his support in October 1763. They had assembled at the Chak Guru for the ashnān of Dusehra and Diwali (Kattakī). After meeting at Chak Guru in April 1764, the chiefs marched to the Jhelum River to establish their posts (thānās) at various places. In November 1764, they assembled at Chak Guru for ashnān and then dispersed in several directions to establish their control.[127] The news reports also refer to the '*karāh Guru*' as a collection made from the territories overrun by them.[128]

We may now take up John Malcolm's *Sketch of the Sikhs*, which pays great attention to the religion of the Sikhs, making use of verses from the Ādi Granth, the *Dasam Granth*, the vārs of Bhai Gurdas, and the *Rāmkalī Vār* of Gurdas (Singh) in English translation. In his own words, Malcolm gives 'a short and hasty sketch' of the 'history, customs, and religion' of Sikhs.[129] His 'account of the Sikh religion is more detailed than that of his predecessors', but his 'conceptualization of Sikh beliefs and practices is not clear'.[130] It became the basis of much of the later historical writings by Western and Indian writers. Therefore, Malcolm's view of the religious beliefs and practices of the Sikhs may be taken up in some detail.

The religion of the Sikhs for Malcolm was interesting and important, but it was also difficult to understand. It appeared to present a kind of paradox to him. Guru Nanak's creed was 'grounded on the most sublime truths', but it was blended with Hindu mythology and Islamic fables. In an effort to explain this, Malcolm suggests that Guru Nanak's purpose was not to destroy but to reform the religion of his 'tribe', and to reconcile the two jarring faiths to his doctrine. He called upon the Hindus to abandon the worship of idols and return to the original worship of one God; he called upon Muslims to abstain from cow slaughter and persecution of Hindus. He had all praise for God but he did not condemn polytheism. Malcolm concludes that Guru Nanak could be considered 'more in the light of a reformer than of a subverter of the Hindu religion'.[131]

Malcolm believed that Guru Nanak learnt many of the maxims from the mendicants of the Sūfī sect. Kabir was 'a professed Sūfī' and Guru Nanak refers to him constantly, admiring his writings. Kabir inculcated the doctrine of equality of human beings in relation to God. Guru Nanak emphasized the importance of toleration and he disliked war. His life, like his doctrine, was peaceable. He adopted the habits of sanyāsīs and other holy mendicants, and he conformed to their customs. His 'extraordinary austerities' are praised by his followers.[132] The Sikhs who adhered to Guru Nanak's tenets were hardly to be distinguished from 'the great mass of Hindu population'. The first successors of Guru Nanak appeared to have taught 'exactly the same doctrine' as their leader. In his decision to take up arms, Guru Hargobind is said to be justified 'even by the usage of the Hindus'.[133]

It was reserved for Guru Gobind Singh to give 'a new character' to the religion of his followers. He did not make any material change in the tenets of Guru Nanak, but he established institutions and usages that separated his followers from other Hindus. With one blow, he abolished all the invidious distinctions of caste. He called upon his followers to devote themselves to arms to free themselves from the oppressive government of the time. His religious doctrine was meant to be popular, and it promised equality. Every Khalsa Singh was equal, with a like title to the good things of this world and the blessings of a future life. Despite his 'veneration' for Durga Bhavani, the Goddess of courage, it was impossible to reconcile Guru Gobind Singh's religion and usages with Hindu beliefs. The tenth Guru proceeded at once to subvert the foundation of the whole system. 'Wherever the religion of Guru Govind prevails, the institutions of Brahma must fall.' The universal admission of proselytes, the abolition of caste distinctions, the eating of all kinds of flesh, except beef, the form of worship, and the general devotion of all Singhs to arms were altogether irreconcilable with Hindu mythology. The Sikh religion now became popular with the more numerous lower orders.[134]

Malcolm states that for Sikh writers, especially Bhai Gurdas, Hinduism and Islam had degenerated and stood opposed to each other. Guru Nanak was sent by God to restore the true worship of God among both Hindus and Muslims and to found a new path and a new dispensation. The Sikh writers talk of Guru Nanak's meeting with God who commissioned him to start a new panth for the whole of mankind. Therefore, Malcolm surmises that Sikhs entertained the idea of 'divine origin of their faith'. Malcolm questions the originality of Guru Nanak's message, and maintains that Guru Nanak borrowed indifferently from the Qur'ān and the Shāstras and his example was followed by his successors.[135]

Malcolm, admittedly, was not personally acquainted with the mode of worship introduced by Guru Nanak for the adoration of God as the Supreme Being. The dharamsāl as the place of Sikh worship was generally a plain building, without any images. On every solemn occasion, verses from the Ādi Granth were read or recited. These verses were all in praise of the deity, religion, and virtue, and against impiety and immorality. Guru Nanak's *So-Dar* in Malcolm's view 'displays the supremacy of the true God, and the inferiority of all the Devtas, and other created beings, to the universal Creator'. He draws the inference that Guru Nanak grounded his religion entirely on 'a principle of pure deism' (monotheism).[136]

Taking a superficial view of the developments after Guru Nanak, Malcolm says that the followers of Guru Nanak began to pay adoration to his name, which was at variance with his teachings. They clothed him in all the attributes of a saint, and considered him a selected instrument of God to make the true faith known to fallen men. They gave him divine honours, performed pilgrimage to his sepulchre, and referred to him in their prayers as their saviour and mediator. Malcolm notices that Kartarpur (Dera Baba Nanak) continued as a place of religious resort and worship. A small piece of Guru Nanak's garment was exhibited to pilgrims as a sacred relic in the dharamsāl in Kartarpur.[137]

Whereas Guru Nanak was considered to be the author of the Sikh religion, Guru Gobind Singh was revered as the founder of the worldly greatness and political independence of Sikhs. They retained all their veneration for Guru Nanak but they deemed Guru Gobind Singh to be 'equally exalted'. Guru Gobind Singh was the tenth and the last acknowledged religious ruler of the Sikhs.[138] He told the Khalsa surrounding his deathbed that he had delivered the Khalsa over to Immortal God. They were asked to read the Granth and to follow its tenets. Guru Gobind Singh assured them of his aid and protection. From his dying words the Sikhs believed that they had been placed under the peculiar care of God.[139] Malcolm is clear about the end of personal Guruship with Guru Gobind Singh but he makes no explicit reference to the vesting of Guruship in the Granth or the Panth.

Malcolm goes on to say that Guru Gobind Singh in his *Bachittar Nātak* gives an account of his divinely sanctioned mission. Through the means of religious enthusiasm, he transformed his followers into 'a warlike race'. His principal religious institution was pahul or initiation of the double-edged sword. The 'Sikhs' who became 'Singhs' began to wear their hair long, put on a blue dress, and devote themselves to arms for the defence of the commonwealth of the Khalsa. The ceremony of initiation and the essential rahit is then described. One of the injunctions of this rahit was to go to Amritsar to pay devotions to the Khalsa. Guru Gobind Singh ordered the principal persons among the newly initiated Singhs to initiate him exactly as he had initiated them. Later on, at the point of death, the Guru is said to have exclaimed: 'Wherever five Sikhs are assembled, there I also shall be present.' Martyrdom for the faith, in what he calls the 'Dasamā Pādshāh Kā Granth', is the road to honour in this world, and eternal happiness in the future.[140]

As noticed earlier, Malcolm refers frequently to the Ādi Granth and the Dasamā Pādshāh Kā Granth in his *Sketch of the Sikhs*. The former Granth was compiled by Guru Arjan and the latter by Guru Gobind Singh; the former came to be known as the Ādi or the first Granth to be distinguished from the latter. The Ādi Granth contained the compositions of the Sikh Gurus up to Guru Tegh Bahadur and thirteen other persons. Malcolm refers to the language and script of the two Granths, their major thrust, and their use for worship.[141] The authorship of the 'Dasamā Pādshāh Kā Granth' is attributed by Malcolm to Guru Gobind Singh. It was not limited to religious subjects. But on the authority of a Sikh informant. Malcolm states that it was as much revered among the Sikhs as the Ādi Granth; both the Granths were said to be placed in the 'national council' when it passed important resolutions. However, when the chiefs deliberated and aimed at unanimity, they invoked the sacred Granth and swore by 'our scripture'.[142] It is almost certain that 'Granth' and 'scripture' refer here to the Ādi Granth. But, as noted earlier, Malcolm does not refer specifically to Guruship being vested in the Granth.

## IN RETROSPECT

Together, Sikh and non-Sikh sources reflect an evolving under-standing of a dynamic situation. Notwithstanding the occasional differences of detail between Sikh sources, there is a broad con-sensus about the essential elements in the religious life of Sikhs during the eighteenth century.

The rahitnāmās lay down what the Khalsa should believe and practise as their faith. In addition to the belief in ten Gurus, Guru Granth, and Guru Panth, great stress is laid on the unity of God. A number of epithets, besides Vāhegurū and Akāl Purkh, are used for him. He alone should be the object of worship. A Khalsa should observe a daily regimen of individual and congregational worship. At home early in the morning, after bathing and before eating, he should recite the *Japujī* and the *Jāp*. In the evening he must recite the *So-Dar* and the *Rahirās*, and before going to sleep he should recite the *Sohilā*. This is the necessary minimum. He should read the bāṇī of the Guru and reflect on it. In this con-nection, two compositions of the tenth Guru, the *Akāl Ustat* and the *Chandī dī Vār*, are also mentioned. A Khalsa should go to the dharamsāl in the morning and listen to kīrtan, participate in the ardās and receive karāh parsād. He should conduct himself well in relation to men and women present in the sangat (also called dīvān). He should make offerings to the Guru (Granth Sahib). The way in which karāh parsād was to be prepared and distributed is spelt out, indicating the importance given to it.

The ideal of religious life of the Khalsa is embodied in 'nām, dān, isnān', combining devotion and charity with purity. The Khalsa were required to take pahul, keep the kes unshorn, adopt the name 'Singh', bear arms, wear kachh, keep the kanghā, use the salutation of 'Vāhegurūjī kā Khālsā, Vāhegurūjī kī fateh', go for pilgrimage to places associated with the Gurus, like Amritsar, Anandpur, Patna, and Nander, and to celebrate Gurpurabs or important occasions in the lives of the Gurus.

Equally significant are the proscriptions for the Khalsa. Rahitnāmās rule out the worship of a maṛhī, a grave, an idol of stone, a god, a goddess, or a pīr. The Khalsa should shun the worshippers of Sakhī Sarvar and the followers of fakirs; the only medium of worship for the Khalsa was shabad, and not tarpan, gāyatrī, and sandhyā. The Khalsa were also enjoined to shun tobacco in any form and never to eat halāl meat.

In other works of Sikh literature of eighteenth century, the unity of God is underlined, the doctrines of Guru Granth and Guru Panth are upheld, and the unity of the ten Gurus is emphasized or taken for granted. In some of the works of the latter part of the eighteenth century, however, it is stated that Guru Gobind Singh invoked or worshipped the Goddess for instituting the Khalsa. Evidently, her role is limited and she is not the Supreme Deity to be worshipped. A few works tend to assimilate Guru Nanak with the earlier incarnations of Vishnu, but Guru Nanak is generally regarded as the incarnation of Raja Janak, which signifies his equal interest in spiritual and temporal matters. Kesar Singh Chhibber tended to Brahmanize the Sikh tradition but even he mentions all the most important injunctions of the Khalsa rahit. A few works refer to the dress of the Khalsa. Some of the works refer to the construction of memorials (dehurā) at places associated with the Gurus and Sikh martyrs. On the whole, the common ground between the rahitnāmās and the other works is far larger than their differences.

Persian writers capture some of the essential features. According to their writings, Sikhs were monotheists who worshipped the Supreme God. They did not worship idols. The reading of Gurbāṇī and singing of the hymns of Granth Sahib are mentioned as the essence of Sikh worship. The 'Sikhs of the Khalsa' did not cut their hair; they wore a chain of iron in place of the sacred thread. They visited Amritsar at the time of Baisākhī and Diwali in large numbers for bathing. They were separate from the Hindus and opposed to the Vedas. Their salutation was 'Vāhegurūjī kī fateh'. They were also hostile to *hukkā* smokers.

The European writers are relatively more comprehensive. They refer to the dharamsāl as the centre of Sikh worship, which consisted of the reading of the Granth, singing of hymns, performance of ardās, and distribution of karāh parsād. The end of personal Guruship with Guru Gobind Singh is alluded to. The mode of initiation into the Khalsa removed all barriers of caste and occupation. The Khalsa kept unshorn hair, bore iron bracelets, wore a blue dress, and carried arms. Their salutation was 'Vāhegurūjī kā Khālsā, Vāhegurūjī kī fateh'. They never used tobacco. They visited Amritsar twice a year in large numbers. Choirs assembled at the Harmandar, where the Granth was installed, chanted hymns from three in the morning till late at night. Women, too, bathed in the tank. Another place of religious resort was Kartarpur (Dera Baba Nanak), where a piece of Guru Nanak's garment was shown as a sacred relic.

In short, if eighteenth-century Sikh literature provides in a sense the Sikh view of the religious life of the Sikhs, the accounts of the non-Sikh contemporaries are significant for what they considered worth recording on the basis of their personal observation or information received from their contemporaries. Significantly, much that is stated in Persian and European sources confirms the normative statements in the rahitnāmās. Many of the religious beliefs and practices recommended for the Khalsa in the rahitnāmās figure in other Sikh literature. Both Persian and European writers mention the basic features. In spite of some differences in contemporary accounts, the degree of consensus is pretty large. Understandably, Sikh sources provide much more information than non-Sikh sources.

Though extremely important in themselves, the doctrinal and institutional developments of the eighteenth century must be seen in relation to their roots in the earlier period of Sikh history. The idea of Shabad-Guru goes back to the compositions of Guru Nanak, and we can see the shabad becoming equated with Gurbāṇī in the compositions of his successors. The Pothī (Granth) compiled by Guru Arjan was copied during the seventeenth century as a sacred scripture for Sikh communities in different parts of the country and its importance began to increase in the eyes of Sikhs. Guru Tegh Bahadur added his own compositions to the corpus and Guru Gobind Singh prepared an authenticated recension. Before his death, he declared the Granth to be the Guru, and the idea became increasingly acceptable to the Khalsa.

Copies of the Granth began to be made in larger numbers for the local Sikh communities. Significantly, belief in the ten Gurus from Guru Nanak to Guru Gobind Singh and in Guruship of the Granth became the foremost tenets of the Khalsa during the eighteenth century.

The doctrine of Guru Panth can also be traced to the decision of Guru Nanak to install one of the disciples as the Guru in his lifetime. In the compositions of his successors, great importance is given to the Sikh, so much so that the Sikh is equated with the Guru by Guru Ram Das. The Sikh congregation acquired even greater importance: God was believed to be present in the sangat. Much before the institution of the Khalsa, the Sikh sangat came to be equated with the Guru. The position of the former masands was given to local Khalsa sangats by Guru Gobind Singh, and before his death, he declared the collective body of the Khalsa to be his successor. Thus, the Granth and the Khalsa represented two sides of the coin of authority for the Khalsa. The doctrine of Guru Panth developed simultaneously with the doctrine of Guru Granth. During the period of political struggle, the doctrine of Guru Panth acquired great importance as the operative principle of organization. However, it was not institutionalized, and it did not remain operative in the government and administration of the Khalsa rulers. At any rate, the equality built into the doctrine was not translated into any democratic forms. Therefore, it did not acquire the same kind of importance in the social and cultural life of the Khalsa as the doctrine of Guru Granth.

The first dharamsāl was established by Guru Nanak for congregational worship and community meal. The institution multiplied with the increasing number of Sikhs under his successors, and acquired great importance as the centre of Sikh religious life. The maintenance and control of the dharamsāls was entrusted to individuals authorized by the Guru. As the representatives of the Guru, Masands became increasingly important. When the Masands were finally removed by Guru Gobind Singh, management and control of the dharamsāl became the responsibility of the local Khalsa sangat. With the growing importance of the doctrines of Guru Granth and Guru Panth, the dharamsāl became all the more important because the Granth was installed in the dharamsāl and the sangat was present there. It is not surprising, therefore, that the term 'gurdwārā' began to be used for the institution of dharamsāl. As the abode or door of the Guru, the sacred space acquired greater importance during the eighteenth century.

From the very beginning, special sanctity was attached to the dharamsāl where the Guru was present. Therefore, the dharamsāls in Kartarpur, Khadur, Goindval, Ramdaspur, Kiratpur, and Anandpur had great importance in the eyes of contemporary Sikhs. In the eighteenth century, the Khalsa took control of the Harmandar Sahib in Ramdaspur and revived the institution of Akāl Bungā as the focal point of a political community. The importance of Ramdaspur began to increase in the context of the political struggle of the Khalsa. As their rallying centre, it may be said to have played a more important role than any individual leader. Before the end of the eighteenth century, the town of Ramdaspur became the city of Amritsar with the sacred tank, the Harmandar and the Akāl Bungā, together, making it the premier place of Sikh pilgrimage. It may be added that gurdwaras were constructed at most other places associated with the Sikh Gurus and martyrs. The places associated with Guru Gobind Singh—Anandpur, Patna, Nander, and Damdama (Talwandi Sabo)—acquired special importance for Sikhs.

Lastly, whereas Sikh writers emphasize doctrinal and ideological continuities with early Sikh tradition, non-Sikh works generally look upon the creation of the Khalsa and its aftermath as a departure from the Sikh past. Seen as a whole, contemporary evidence clearly points not only to continuities since the sixteenth century, but also to a deliberate departure from the prevalent systems of belief and concomitant practices in north India, with implications for Sikh rites and ceremonies as well.

## NOTES AND REFERENCES

1.  Sainapat, *Shri Gur Sobhā*, ed. Shamsher Singh Ashok (Amritsar: Shiromani Gurdwara Prabandhak Committee, 1967), pp. 10–13, 33, 35, 38–40, 49–50, 95, 119 et passim.

2.  Karamjit K. Malhotra, 'Earliest Manual on the Sikh Way of Life', in *Five Centuries of Sikh Tradition: Ideology, Society, Politics and Culture*, ed. Reeta Grewal and Sheena Pall (New Delhi: Manohar, 2005), pp. 55–81.

3. Randhir Singh, ed., *Prem Sumārag Granth Arthāt Khalsai Jīvan Jāch* (*Pātshāhī Dasvīn*) (Jalandhar: New Book Company, 1965 [1953]), pp. 1–6, 9.

4. *Sākhī Rahit Pātisāhī 10*, in *The Chaupa Singh Rahit-Nama*, trans. and ed. W.H. McLeod (Dunedin, New Zealand: University of Otago Press, 1987) [hereafter *Sākhī Rahit Pātisāhī 10*], pp. 133–8. The whole rahitnāmā is so short that there may not be much point giving specific reference to each statement.

5. Gurdas (Singh), *Rāmkalī Vār*, in *Vārān Bhai Gurdas*, ed. Giani Hazara Singh (Amritsar: Khalsa Samachar, 1962 [1911]), vār 41, pp. 664–6.

6. *Rahitnāmā Bhai Prahilad Singh*, in *Rahitnāme*, ed. Piara Singh Padam (Amritsar: Singh Brothers, 1995), pp. 65, 66, 67.

7. Malhotra, 'Earliest Manual on the Sikh Way of Life', p. 68.

8. Randhir Singh, *Prem Sumārag Granth*, pp. 8–9.

9. Koer Singh, *Gurbilās Pātshāhī 10*, ed. Shamsher Singh Ashok (Patiala: Punjabi University, 1968), p. 130.

10. *Rahitnāmā Bhai Desa Singh*, in Piara Singh Padam, *Rahitnāme*, p. 128.

11. *Rahitnāmā Bhai Daya Singh*, in Piara Singh Padam, *Rahitnāme*, pp. 68–72.

12. McLeod, *The Chaupa Singh Rahit-Nama*, pp. 57, 60, 79, 86, 92, 98, 130.

13. Koer Singh, *Gurbilās Pātshāhī 10*, pp. 17–18.

14. Kesar Singh Chhibber, *Bansāvalīnāmā Dasān Pātshāhiān Kā*, in *Parkh*, vol. 2, ed. Ratan Singh Jaggi (Chandigarh: Panjab University, 1972), p. 2.

15. Sarup Das Bhalla, *Guru Nanak Mahimā Arthāt Mahimā Prakāsh*, ed. Shamsher Singh Ashok and Gobind Singh Lamba (Patiala: Punjab Languages Department, 1970), part I, pp. 13, 63, 204, 332, 345, 346; Sarup Das Bhalla, *Mahimā Prakāsh*, ed. Gobind Singh Lamba and Khazan Singh (Patiala: Punjab Languages Department, 1971), part II, pp. 8, 419, 645.

16. Bhai Sukha Singh, *Gurbilās Pātsāhī 10*, ed. Gursharan Kaur Jaggi (Patiala: Punjab Languages Department, 1989), pp. 1–2, 71, 76, 177.

17. See Appendix for some detail.

18. Sainapat, *Shri Gur Sobhā*, p. 132.

19. *Rahit Nāmā*, in *Bhai Nand Lal Granthāvalī*, ed. Ganda Singh (Malacca [Malaysia]: Sant Sohan Singh, 1968), p. 192.

20. *Rahitnāmā Bhai Prahilad Singh*, p. 67.

21. *Sākhī Rahit Pātisāhī 10*, pp. 133–7.

22. Randhir Singh, *Prem Sumārag Granth*, pp. 6, 18.

23. Sewadas, *Episodes from Lives of the Gurus: Parchian Sewādās*, trans. and ed. Kharak Singh and Gurtej Singh (Chandigarh: Institute of Sikh Studies, 1995), p. 128.

24. For a discussion, see Ganda Singh, *Guru Gobind Singh's Death at Nanded: An Examination of Succession Theories* (Patiala: Punjabi University, 2008 [1972]), pp. 23, 26–7, 29.

25. In his early work, W.H. McLeod suggested that Guru Gobind Singh's declaration may be a retrospective interpretation of a tradition which owes its origin not to an actual pronouncement of the Guru but to an insistent need for maintaining the Panth's cohesion during the later period; that the corporate aspect of the doctrine possessed greater importance during the eighteenth century; and that it lapsed later to concede an undisputed primacy to the scriptural Guru when the doctrine of the Guru Panth made way for the ascending doctrine of Guru Granth. See his *The Evolution of the Sikh Community* (Delhi: Oxford University Press, 1975), pp. 45, 50, 56, 58.

26. See J.S. Grewal, 'The Doctrines of Guru Panth and Guru Granth', in J.S. Grewal, *Sikh Ideology, Polity and Social Order: From Guru Nanak to Maharaja Ranjit Singh* (New Delhi: Manohar, 2007 [1996]), pp. 223–8.

27. W.H. McLeod, *Sikhs of the Khalsa: A History of Khalsa Rahit* (New Delhi: Oxford University Press, 2003), pp. 233–4. Also, W.H. McLeod, *Discovering the Sikhs: Autobiography of a Historian* (Delhi: Permanent Black, 2004), pp. 147–8.

28. McLeod, *Sikhs of the Khalsa*, p. 234.

29. McLeod, *The Chaupa Singh Rahit-Nama*, pp. 60, 74–6, 100.

30. McLeod, *Sikhs of the Khalsa*, pp. 234, 306. In his discussion of Guru Granth and Guru Panth, however, McLeod says that Desa Singh is 'doubtful and favours the qualifications of the Granth'. In the translation of this rahitnāmā, on p. 306 of McLeod's work, however, the term 'Guru Granth' is used.

31. *Rahitnāmā Bhai Desa Singh*, p. 135.

32. *Rahitnāmā Bhai Daya Singh*, p. 71.

33. Koer Singh, *Gurbilās Pātshāhi 10*, pp. 130, 283–4, 287.

34. Chhibber, *Bansāvalīnāmā*, pp. 136, 163–4, 198, 215, 221–2.

35. Bhalla, *Mahimā Prakāsh*, part II, p. 892.

36. *Rahitnāmā Bhai Desa Singh*, p. 135.

37. How this mistaken assumption got perpetuated among scholars located in the West is illustrated here. McLeod, for example, approvingly quotes John Malcolm's statement on the procedure followed in the general assembly of the Khalsa (Sarbat Khalsa) in adopting

resolutions (Gurmatās), when the Ādi Granth and the *Dasam Granth* were reportedly placed before the chiefs and principal leaders and they all bent their heads before these scriptures. McLeod then refers to the *Dasam Granth* as the 'second scripture' of the Sikhs and discusses it as 'the first of their supplementary scriptures'. See, McLeod, *The Evolution of the Sikh Community*, pp. 48–9, 59, 79–81. Referring to Malcolm as quoted by McLeod, Cole remarks that the assembly present acknowledged the Guruship of both the Ādi Granth and the *Dasam Granth* as the scripture. See W. Owen Cole, *The Guru in Sikhism* (London: Darton, Longman & Todd, 1982), p. 81. In a later work, McLeod reiterates that during the eighteenth century, the same respect was given to the *Dasam Granth* as to the Ādi Granth. Both were regarded as 'the visibly present Guru'. See *The Sikhs: History, Religion, and Society* (New York: Columbia University Press, 1989), p. 89. Concurring with McLeod, Oberoi clearly brackets the Ādi Granth and the *Dasam Granth* as the Sikh scriptures that were purportedly treated at par by the 'Sanatan Sikhs' following the older Khalsa conventions. See Harjot Oberoi, *The Construction of Religious Boundaries: Culture, Identity and Diversity in the Sikh Tradition* (Delhi: Oxford University Press, 1994), pp. 90, 93, 201. Subsequently, Jakobsh also states that the Sikhs held the *Dasam Granth* at par with the Ādi Granth and she refers to the authority of John Malcolm. Doris R. Jakobsh, *Relocating Gender in Sikh History: Transformation, Meaning and Identity* (New Delhi: Oxford University Press, 2003), p. 45.

38. John Malcolm, *Sketch of the Sikhs* (New Delhi: Asian Educational Services, 1986 [1812]), pp. 173, 182–3, 185. For a detailed notice of Malcolm's treatment of Sikh religion, see the section 'Sikh Religious Life in Persian and English Sources' of this Chapter.
39. Sainapat, *Shri Gur Sobhā*, p. 132.
40. McLeod, *The Evolution of the Sikh Community*, pp. 17, 45–50.
41. McLeod, *Sikhs of the Khalsa*, pp. 233–4. Also see his *Discovering the Sikhs*, p. 148.
42. J.S. Grewal, *A Study of Guru Granth Sahib: Doctrine, Social Content, History, Structure and Status* (Amritsar: Singh Brothers, 2009), p. 146.
43. Grewal, 'The Doctrines of Guru Panth and Guru Granth', p. 225.
44. *Rahit Nāmā*, pp. 192–4.
45. *Sākhī Rahit Pātisāhī* 10, pp. 133, 135.
46. *Rahitnāmā Bhai Prahilad Singh*, p. 66.
47. Randhir Singh, *Prem Sumārag Granth*, p. 18.

48. McLeod, *The Chaupa Singh Rahit-Nama*, pp. 98, 123. In another situation, two *hazūrī* Sikhs attribute to the tenth Guru the statement that he is present in the Sarbat (collectivity), the Khalsa is his body, and that the Khalsa is the Guru.

49. *Rahitnāmā Bhai Desa Singh*, pp. 129–30.

50. *Rahitnāmā Bhai Daya Singh*, p. 71.

51. Koer Singh, *Gurbilās Pātshāhī* 10, pp. 138–9.

52. Ganda Singh, ed., *Hukamnāme: Gurū Sāhibān, Mata Sāhibān, Banda Singh Ate Khalsa Jī De* (Patiala: Punjabi University, 1967), pp. 232–3. This hukamnāmā is addressed to the Sikhs of Pattan. For a discussion of the evidence of the hukamnāmās, see the next section.

53. Chhibber, *Bansāvalīnāmā*, pp. 163–4.

54. Bhalla, *Mahimā Prakāsh*, part II, p. 828.

55. Bhai Sukha Singh, *Gurbilās Pātshāhī* 10, pp. 45, 178, 451.

56. Ratan Singh Bhangu, *Sri Gur Panth Prakāsh*, ed. Balwant Singh Dhillon (Amritsar: Singh Brothers, 2004), pp. 385–91.

57. Bhangu, *Sri Gur Panth Prakāsh*, pp. 311, 377, 379, 380, 399.

58. J.S. Grewal, 'The Gurdwara', in *Religious Movements and Institutions in Medieval India* (History of Indian Science, Philosophy and Culture in Indian Civilization, vol. 7, part 2), ed. J.S. Grewal (New Delhi: Oxford University Press, 2006), pp. 533–47.

59. Bhai Gurdas, *Vārān Bhai Gurdas*, vār VI, pauṛīs 12, 13, 17; vār XX, pauṛī 6; vār XXXIV, pauṛīs 16, 17; vār XXXX, pauṛī 11.

60. 'Mobad', *Dabistān-i Mazāhib*, in *Sikh History from Persian Sources: Translations of Major Texts*, ed. J.S. Grewal and Irfan Habib (New Delhi: Tulika/Indian History Congress, 2001), p. 76.

61. Respectively J.S. Grewal, 'The Gurdwara', pp. 537–8; *Ahkām-i 'Ālamgīrī* (1703–7), in J.S. Grewal and Habib, *Sikh History from Persian Sources*, p. 97.

62. For the text of the hukamnāmās, see Ganda Singh, *Hukamnāme*.

63. Sainapat, *Shri Guru Sobhā*, pp. 42–3.

64. McLeod, *The Chaupa Singh Rahit-Nama*, pp. 57–8, 70, 76–7.

65. McLeod, *The Chaupa Singh Rahit-Nama*, pp. 61, 65–6, 76–7.

66. *Rahitnāmā Bhai Desa Singh*, p. 132.

67. See Malhotra, 'The Earliest Manual on the Sikh Way of Life', pp. 68, 73.

68. *Tankhānāmā*, in Ganda Singh, *Bhai Nand Lal Granthāvalī*, pp. 195, 198.

69. *Rahitnāmā Bhai Daya Singh*, p. 68.

70. *Rahitnāmā Bhai Desa Singh*, p. 135.

71. *Rahitnāmā Bhai Desa Singh*, pp. 133–5.

72. Sainapat, *Shri Gur Sobhā*, pp. 10–11, 35–7, 42–3, 46, 98, 101, 104.
73. *Tankhānāmā*, in Ganda Singh, Bhai Nand Lal pp. 195–9.
74. McLeod, *The Chaupa Singh Rahit-Nama*, pp. 57, 58, 62, 66.
75. Koer Singh, *Gurbilās Pātshāhī* 10, pp. 277, 285.
76. *Sākhī Rahit Pātisāhī* 10, pp. 135, 136, 137.
77. *Rahitnāmā Bhai Daya Singh*, p. 69.
78. Randhir Singh, *Prem Sumārag Granth*, pp. 5–7.
79. *Rahitnāmā Bhai Prahilad Singh*, pp. 65–7.
80. W.H. McLeod trans. and ed., *The B40 Janam-Sākhī* (Amritsar: Guru Nanak Dev University, 1980), pp. 110nn471, 113, 143.
81. McLeod, *The Chaupa Singh Rahit-Nama*, pp. 57, 58, 60, 63.
82. Sainapat, *Shri Gur Sobhā*, pp. 36–9, 48–9, 71, 130–4.
83. Randhir Singh, *Prem Sumārag Granth*, pp. 1–8, 18.
84. McLeod, *The Chaupa Singh Rahit-Nama*, pp. 57, 58, 66, 74, 92.
85. *Sākhī Rahit Pātisāhī* 10, p. 133.
86. *Rahitnāmā Bhai Daya Singh*, pp. 69–74. Daya Singh reinforces that a Singh should avoid the Brahman as a religious functionary as also his gods, goddesses, ritual practices, and modes of worship (pūjā, archā, mantar, tarpan, gāyatrī, sandhyā, barat, and ekādasī barat) as well as *gor*, maṭh, maṛhī, pīr, and purkh.
87. *Sākhī Rahit Pātisāhī* 10, pp. 133–8.
88. Randhir Singh, *Prem Sumārag Granth*, pp. 149–50.
89. Sainapat, *Shri Gur Sobhā*, pp. 10, 13, 64, 90, 94, 144, 147, 149. Sainapat talks of liberation (*gat, khalāsī*) and the liberated person becoming pure (*khālas*).
90. Koer Singh, *Gurbilās Pātshāhī* 10, p. 128. This place is now known as Muktsar.
91. Sukha Singh, *Gurbilās Pātsāhī* 10, pp. 3, 444–7.
92. *Rahitnāmā Bhai Daya Singh*, pp. 71–2.
93. For detail, see Chapter 2, pp. 85.
94. Bhalla, *Mahimā Prakāsh*, part II, pp. 877–8.
95. *Rahitnāmā Bhai Daya Singh*, pp. 74–5.
96. Chhibber, *Bansāvalīnāmā*, pp. 182–6.
97. Ganda Singh, *Hukamnāme*, pp. 232–3.
98. Ganda Singh, *Ahmad Shah Durrani: Father of Modern Afghanistan* (Bombay: Asia Publishing House, 1959), p. 282.
99. Bhangu, *Sri Gur Panth Prakāsh*, pp. 386–94.
100. Bhangu, *Sri Gur Panth Prakāsh*, p. 305.
101. Bhangu, *Sri Gur Panth Prakāsh*, p. 311.
102. Bhangu, *Sri Gur Panth Prakāsh*, pp. 360–5.
103. Madanjit Kaur, *The Golden Temple: Past and Present* (Amritsar: Guru Nanak Dev University, 1983), pp. 49–52, 142–4, 178–82.

104. Ram Sukh Rao, *Ram Sukh Rao's Sri Fateh Singh Partap Prabhākar: A History of Early Nineteenth Century Punjab*, ed. Joginder Kaur (Patiala: Published by the Editor, 1980), pp. 66–9.

105. For detail, NAI, Foreign/Political Proceedings, 10 June 1853, no. 217. It is interesting to note that the Bhangi chiefs Hari Singh, Jhanda Singh, and Ganda Singh appear to have been the earliest to give land grants to the Harmandar.

106. Chhibber, *Bansāvalīnāmā*, p. 198.

107. Bhalla, *Mahimā Prakāsh*, part II, pp. 293, 320–4.

108. *Rahitnāmā Bhai Daya Singh*, p. 72.

109. For a discussion of this poetical work on Amritsar, Kavi Sant Das Chhibber, *Ustat Sri Amritsar Jī Kī* (c. 1777), in Sarwan Singh, 'Amritsar in Medieval Punjabi Literature: An Historical Analysis' (PhD diss., Guru Nanak Dev University, Amritsar, 1994), pp. 173–95.

110. Kankan Kavi, *Das Gur Kathā*, in Sarwan Singh, 'Amritsar in Medieval Punjabi Literature', pp. 196–211.

111. Kavi Saundha, *Ustat Sri Amritsar Jī Kī*, in Sarwan Singh, 'Amritsar in Medieval Punjabi Literature', pp. 212–29.

112. Sujan Rai Bhandari, *Khulāṣatu't Tawārīkh*, in J.S. Grewal and Habib, *Sikh History from Persian Sources*, p. 92.

113. Mirza Muhammad, *'Ibratnāma*, in J.S. Grewal and Habib, *Sikh History from Persian Sources*, p. 140.

114. Rai Chaturman Saksena, *Chahār Gulshan*, in J.S. Grewal and Habib, in *Sikh History from Persian Sources*, p. 164.

115. Qazi Nur Muhammad, *Jangnāma*, in J.S. Grewal and Habib, *Sikh History from Persian Sources*, p. 209.

116. Ghulam Ali Khan, *'Imādu's Sa'ādat*, in J.S. Grewal and Habib, *Sikh History from Persian Sources*, p. 213.

117. James Skinner, *Tashrīḥu'l Aqwām*, in J.S. Grewal and Habib, *Sikh History from Persian Sources*, pp. 217–18.

118. Charles Wilkins, 'The Sikhs and their College at Patna', in Ganda Singh, ed., *Early European Accounts of the Sikhs* (Calcutta: Indian Studies, Past & Present, 1962), pp. 71–5.

119. Forster, *A Journey from Bengal to England*, vol. 1, pp. 293–5, 307–8.

120. Major James Browne, *History of the Origin and Progress of the Sikhs*, in Ganda Singh, *Early European Accounts of the Sikhs*, pp. 13–19.

121. John Griffiths, 'A Memorandum on the Punjab and Kandhar', in Ganda Singh, *Early European Accounts of the Sikhs*, pp. 90–3.

122. William Francklin, 'The Sikhs and Their Country', in Ganda Singh, *Early European Accounts of the Sikhs*, pp. 97–8.

123. Muhammad Qasim, '*Ibratnāma*, in J.S. Grewal and Habib, *Sikh History from Persian Sources*, p. 118.

124. Tahmas Khan, *Qissa-i Tahmas-i Miskin* or *Tahmās Nāma*, in J.S. Grewal and Habib, *Sikh History from Persian Sources*, p. 174.

125. 'News Reports from Delhi, 1759–65', in J.S. Grewal and Habib, *Sikh History from Persian Sources*, p. 194.

126. Qazi Nur Muhammad, *Jangnāma*, pp. 206–7.

127. 'News Reports from Delhi, 1759–65', pp. 191, 193, 199.

128. 'News Reports from Delhi, 1759–65', pp. 190–1, 193, 194, 196.

129. Malcolm, *Sketch of the Sikhs*, p. 3.

130. J.S. Grewal, *Historical Writings on the Sikhs (1784–2011): Western Enterprise and Indian Response* (New Delhi: Manohar, 2012), p. 78.

131. Malcolm, *Sketch of the Sikhs*, pp. 144–8.

132. Malcolm, *Sketch of the Sikhs*, pp. 145–6.

133. Malcolm, *Sketch of the Sikhs*, p. 148.

134. Malcolm, *Sketch of the Sikhs*, pp. 148–51.

135. Malcolm, *Sketch of the Sikhs*, pp. 152–67.

136. Malcolm, *Sketch of the Sikhs*, pp. 168–71.

137. Malcolm, *Sketch of the Sikhs*, pp. 21–2, 172.

138. Malcolm, *Sketch of the Sikhs*, pp. 75–6.

139. Malcolm, *Sketch of the Sikhs*, p. 196.

140. Malcolm, *Sketch of the Sikhs*, pp. 174–90.

141. Malcolm, *Sketch of the Sikhs*, pp. 31 and notes 51–2, 169, 173, 182, 187–8.

142. Malcolm, *Sketch of the Sikhs*, pp. 51–2, 120–2.

# 4  Rites and Ceremonies

There is evidence in the Sikh scripture that the system of Sikh beliefs and practices was accompanied by new rites.[1] As may be expected, a priori, Sikh literature provides the maximum information on the ideal norms and actual practices in the eighteenth century. Professing to provide empirical information, non-Sikh sources affirm much of what Sikh sources say about the rites and ceremonies of eighteenth-century Sikhs. While the Persian works are relevant for the early period, the European accounts are relevant for the latter part of the century. All these sources have been analysed to discuss the rites and ceremonies recommended for Sikhs and actually practised by the Khalsa during the eighteenth century. This literature has been studied in four unequal phases with an eye on continuity and change: (a) the pre-Khalsa background; (b) the early eighteenth century; (c) the middle decades; and (d) the late eighteenth century.

## THE PRE-KHALSA BACKGROUND

Guru Nanak and his successors underscored the futility of existing Brahmanical rites and rituals and recommended alternative practices.[2] The first Guru, for example, discards the notion of pollution (sūtak) associated with child birth.[3] He underscores that the notion of pollution from menstruation, and birth and death, is an illusion. In his *Japujī*, he rejects ritualistic bathing, purification, and charities.[4] He underlines the futility of the sacred thread worn customarily at the initiation ceremony of the males of the three upper castes as a symbol of distinction between higher and lower castes. However, it had no bearing on the conduct of those who were entitled to wear it.[5] Guru Nanak's song of joy (*Sohilā*) is relevant for both wedding and death (as leading to union with God).[6] The *Alāhṇiāṅ* of Guru Nanak were meant to be sung in place of the traditional mourning songs.[7] He ridicules the performance of *shrāddh* to feed the dead ancestors, or the practice of offering rice balls (*pind*) to the dead through the mediacy of Brahmans. The popular practice of floating lamps in water as a part of obituary rites is regarded by Guru Nanak as meaningless.[8]

The *Ānand* composed by Guru Amar Das, celebrating the experience of joy in liberation, began to be sung or recited on major occasions like birth, marriage, and death, as well as on all important occasions in a Sikh's life.[9] Guru Ram Das says that this true song of joy is to be sung in the true house where truth is meditated upon. Guru Arjan invites Sikhs to listen to the *Ānand* so that all their wishes are fulfilled.[10] It is also likely that this composition was sung to celebrate the birth of his son Hargobind. Guru Gobind Singh included it among the five compositions to be recited at the time of initiation into the Khalsa order.[11]

The third Guru disapproves of satī upheld by Brahmans and practised by the upper castes; he also denounces the practice of female infanticide prevalent among them.[12] The *Sadd* composed by Baba Sunder[13] refers to Guru Amar Das enjoining the Sikhs to perform kīrtan or sing God's praises after his death in place of the traditional kīryā and *pind-pattal*.[14] In other words, the Guru's last wish was that no Brahmanical rites should be performed after his death.

Guru Ram Das's compositions, called 'Ghoṛiāṅ' and 'Lāvāṅ', become significant in view of the importance of the institution of marriage in Sikhism, which enjoins Sikhs to be householders. The first of these compositions was meant to replace the folk songs sung by women before and at the time of the bridegroom mounting the mare (*ghoṛī*) for departure with the wedding party.[15] The composition called the *Lāvāṅ* came to be recited at the time of the four rounds (*lāvāṅ*) taken by the bridegroom followed by the bride, which eventually became the core of the Sikh wedding ceremony.[16] Incidentally, the number of rounds in the marriage performed by Brahmans was seven.

Thus, several of the existing rites and ceremonies, whether popular or Brahmanical, were modified or discarded in favour of new practices that can be regarded as 'Sikh'. The priest or pandit, the kingpin of the Brahmanical system, does not seem to have a recognized role to play in these procedures.[17]

Though there is no explicit statement in Guru Granth Sahib about the place of collective supplication (ardās) in connection with the rites of passage, it is likely that no ceremony could be considered complete without this essential feature of the Sikh mode of worship. A stanza in Guru Arjan's *Sukhmaṇī* now serves as a prelude to the formal ardās. References to supplication occur frequently in Gurbāṇī. Guru Nanak lays emphasis on ardās with a feeling of complete surrender. Guru Angad enjoins that it should be made standing. Guru Arjan underlines that it should be made with folded hands.[18] It is not surprising, therefore, that a mid-seventeenth-century non-Sikh source like the *Dabistān-i Mazāhib* comments on the distinctiveness of the 'custom' of praying 'together' among the followers of Guru Nanak.[19] Another contemporary, Bhai Gurdas, testifies that a Sikh's daily religious routine (*nit-kīryā*) ended with the prayer followed by the sharing of parsād by all.[20] The practice of praying collectively and partaking of parsād at the end was apparently well established by the turn of the seventeenth century. It may be recalled that the *Nasīhatnāmā* (*Tankhānāmā*) attaches great importance to the correct method of preparing the karāh parsād.[21]

When Guru Gobind Singh instituted the Khalsa and introduced the initiation of the double-edged sword (khande kī pahul), another method of initiation was already current among Sikhs. The term often used for this is *charan-amrit*. The question, however, is whether like 'most religious sects' in India, Sikhs also followed the ritual of initiation in which 'the toe of a Guru was dipped into water' and 'then given to the new initiate to drink'.[22] Bhai Kahan Singh of Nabha suggests that 'during the pontificate of the nine Gurus an initiate was given the charan-amrit to drink which was called *charan-pahul* or *pag-pahul*', but he does not explain it further.[23] Since the phrase 'dust of the feet' (*charan-dhūṛ*) occurs frequently in the *Vārs* of Bhai Gurdas, one may ask: the dust of whose feet was used for initiation?

Bhai Gurdas seems to be referring to 'the dust of the feet of the Sikhs of the Guru'.[24] The compositions of Guru Ram Das and Guru Arjan in particular dwell on the sanctity of the dust of the feet of the men of God (interchangeable, among others, with the Sikh, Sādh, Sant, and Har-jan), which is said to be more efficacious than pilgrimage to all the sacred places.[25] It is unlikely that given their stress on humility in these compositions the Gurus would approve of an initiate taking the water touched by their toe. This assumption is supported by the centrality of congregational worship in Sikh religious practice, and the importance of sādh-sangat in the compositions of all the Gurus.[26] Even the mode of initiation described in the *Dabistān*,[27] though a variant on Bhai Gurdas, does underline that it could not possibly be the Guru's toe. In all probability, it was the 'dust of the feet' of Sikhs, that is, those who had advanced on the path of the Guru, which was used for preparing charan-amrit for initiation.

The substance of Sikh rites and ceremonies appears to be in place by the beginning of the eighteenth century,[28] which was reinforced and amplified by the rahitnāmās and the Gurbilās literature, and corroborated in some important respects by the Persian and English sources.

## THE EARLY EIGHTEENTH CENTURY

The longer rahitnāmās of the period dwell on the rites of initiation, birth, marriage, and death. In the context of the institution of the Khalsa, however, the new rite of initiation appeared to be central to the interrelated injunctions of Guru Gobind Singh. This is particularly evident in the works now placed by some scholars in his lifetime.

In the rahit part of *The Chaupa Singh Rahit-Nama*, the author says that a Sikh of the Guru must take pahul of the double-edged sword. The Sikh who administers pahul should follow the mode established by the Guru. Five palmfuls of pahul should be drunk by the initiate, and it should be sprinkled five times on his head and eyes. The initiated Sikh should exclaim, 'Vāhegurūjī kā Khālsā, Vāhegurūjī kī fateh'. He should then be given the sacred formula (*mantar*) of the true name (*satnām*) and instructed in the Sikh way of life. The Sikh who administers pahul should be one who himself observes the rahit and who is free from lust, anger, pride, and ignorance; he should not be an idler. He should be intellectually wide awake and without a physical or moral defect.[29]

The positive and negative injunctions for the Khalsa were the obverse and reverse of the new situation. The pahul is closely linked with keeping the hair (kes) unshorn. The initiated Sikh is called Kesdhārī. A Sikh should never keep unshorn hair without taking pahul. The sanctity of the kes is emphasized in various ways and it serves as an alternative to the sacred thread and the sacred mark. The kes is mentioned among the five most important positive injunctions along with the kachh and kirpān, while the remaining two are bāṇī and sādh-sangat. The sword as 'Sri Sahib' is to be held in reverence, in fact is to be worshipped, as it was done by the Guru himself. Among the negative injunctions mentioned in this rahitnāmā is one that instructs not to have any association with the dissenting groups (Mīṇās, Dhir Mallias, and Ram Raiyās), besides the Masands and Masandias. A Sikh should never kill an infant daughter and have no association with those who kill their daughters. He should not smoke or inhale tobacco. The three most important injunctions of the rahit are against female infanticide, tonsure (*bhaddan*), and the use of tobacco. It may be noted that service of Sikhs is recommended for those who aspire to become leaders (sardārs).[30]

The *Prem Sumārag*, which we regard as one of the earliest rahitnāmās, lays great stress on initiation into the order of the Khalsa. The essential feature of initiation is khande kī pahul, which should be sweetened before it is administered to the volunteer. He should put on a kachh, and bear five arms. The minimum number of the Khalsa present at the time of initiation should be five, and five stanzas (pauṛīs) of the *Ānand* should be recited. An ardās is specified: 'This Sikh has come to Sri Guru Akāl Purkh and the Khalsa for refuge. He may be given the gift of the faith of the Khalsa of Srī Akāl Purkh. His mind may remain steady and all his wishes may be fulfilled.' The Sikhs of the Khalsa pray for him: 'May Guru Baba Akāl Purkh fulfil his wishes.' The whole procedure is described in detail. The administering of pahul is followed by some general instructions with regard to the beliefs and ethics of the Khalsa.[31]

A married woman could take pahul from a pious Sikh (Gurmukh). 'She should have education in Gurmukhi, read and love shabad-bāṇī.' The initiated Sikh women (Sikhṇīs) should associate with one another and reflect on the shabad. A widow could also take pahul. However, no saffron (*kesar*), which is associated with married women, should be sprinkled in her case; she should wear an iron ring on her finger, and observe restraint and chastity. It is explicitly stated that the injunctions given in the first two chapters of the rahitnāmā are meant for both men and women.[32]

Sainapat does not describe the ceremony of initiation at the time of the institution of the Khalsa but he does refer to 'khande kī pahul' and underlines its importance. The persons initiated adopt the epithet 'Singh', bear arms, and exclaim 'Vāhegurūjī kī fateh'. Sainapat is emphatic about the excommunication of the 'five reprobate groups'. The sanctity of kes is emphasized.[33] Guru Gobind Singh says in the *Parchiān Sewādās* that the sangat would be transformed by handling the sword (*bhagautī*). He declares that his Sikhs would not remain without kes and without weapons (*shastar*). All the Sikhs of the Guru kept unshorn hair and arms in obedience to his declaration.[34]

The hukamnāmās bear witness to the fact that Guru Gobind Singh removed the Masands and instructed his Khalsa not to have any association with them and their followers. Sikhs are asked to take pahul. The epithet 'Singh' appears frequently in the hukamnāmās of the early eighteenth century. The Khalsa are asked to come to Anandpur fully armed. In a hukamnāmā of Guru Gobind Singh issued to the sangat of Benares, the Sikhs are referred to as 'Vāhegurūjī dā Khālsā' (instead of the earlier 'Guru's Khalsa' or 'my Khalsa'). A hukamnāmā of Banda Singh, dated 12 December 1710, refers to 'Srī Akāl Purkhjī kā Khalsa', a phrase that appears frequently later in the hukamnāmās of Mata Sundari and Mata Sahib Devi; it also refers to five weapons and 'the rahit of the Khalsa'.[35]

In the *Amarnāma*, Guru Gobind Singh is emphatic that Sikhs should take amrit to become 'Singhs'. Taking of amrit is helpful against the enemy and also at the end of one's life. They should eat food in the langar with all others and ensure that no one remained hungry. They should not kill an animal in the Muslim fashion.

They should pay no heed to what Brahmans say. There was no point in performing Brahmanical rites (*kīryā karam*).[36]

Persian sources of the early eighteenth century contain no detail of the Sikh rite of initiation or the rites of passage, but they do contain a few references with a close bearing on initiation and rahit. A report from the court of Emperor Bahadur Shah, dated 24 May 1710, refers to the dismissal of the Masands by Guru Gobind Singh by one stroke of the pen to establish the Khalsa. 'It was settled by him that the Sikhs of the Khalsa would not cut the hair of the head, moustaches and beard and would be known as the Sikhs of the Khalsa.' The report goes on to add that a great disturbance occurred among the community of the Khatris over the new injunctions, due to which marriages between the two groups were given up. Actual fighting took place in Ramdaspur in pargana Patti.[37] Writing in 1728–9, the author of the *Asrār-i Samadī* refers to the followers of Banda as 'Singhs' who wore unshorn hair; he refers also to deg and teg respectively for the langar and the sword.[38]

Turning to the rites related to birth, *The Chaupa Singh Rahit-Nama* recommends that on the birth of a male child the father should give him the water in which the feet of five Sikhs have been washed to drink as pahul. If the child was to be brought up as Kesdhārī, that is, with his hair unshorn, he should be given khande kī pahul. His name should be chosen from Granth Sahib. Then he should be bathed with curd.[39]

For the author of the *Prem Sumārag*, however, the ceremonies connected with the birth of a child start with conception. The features to figure in these ceremonies are pahul for the mother, and the constant sight of weapons like the double-edged sword (khandā), bow, arrow, and sword. If a son is born, he should first be made to bow to arms and the Granth-Pothī, and the first feeding (*guṛhtī*) given to him should be touched by khandā. An ardās should be performed. Sanctified food (parsād) should be distributed among the Khalsa and among the kith and kin on the same day. Other ceremonies for the son include pahul administered to him by five Sikhs, piercing of his ears for rings made of gold or silver, keeping his kes intact, naming him with the suffix 'Singh', and feeding Sikh men and women present on the occasion.

Significantly, the same ceremonies are recommended on the birth of a daughter, with appropriate variation in detail. The daughter should also be administered pahul and she should be named with the suffix 'devi'. Her nose and her ears should be pierced.[40]

Regarding marriage, there is only one sentence in the work attributed to Chaupa Singh (who was himself a Brahman), which recommends that a Sikh of the Guru should employ a Brahman at the wedding ceremony. It is not clear, however, whether the Brahman in this situation is a Sikh who could perform a Sikh ceremony, or a priest who is supposed to perform the wedding ceremony according to Brahmanical rites. The evidence of this rahitnāmā on other rituals makes it almost certain that the Brahman in question is a Sikh.[41]

The author of the *Prem Sumārag* is more explicit as well as comprehensive. He recommends that a betrothal ceremony should precede marriage by one and a half months. The bride should pray to Srī Akāl Purkh for a happy union; she should not invoke the blessing of any god or goddess. The wedding ceremony should be performed in the last quarter of the night. The bridegroom should put on arms while riding for the wedding to the bride's home. The wedding ceremony should be performed by a Sikh of the Khalsa of Srī Akāl Purkh. He should ask both the bride and the bridegroom for their consent to marry each other, and also for the consent of their elders. Fire, like Sri Bhagautī Jī and Sri Khalsa Jī, was to be lighted as a witness to the wedlock. An ardās should be made to Sri Guru Akāl Purkh for the happy and pious life of the married couple. They should go round the fire clockwise, and each time a stanza of the *Lāvān* should be recited and some ghee thrown into the fire. After all the four rounds, khande kī pahul should be administered to the couple. Five pauṛīs of the *Ānand* should be sung and then karāh parsād should be distributed. The couple should make supplication only to Sri Vāhegurū Akāl Purkh and should not worship any god or goddess; they should not resort to any *jantar* (magical device) or mantar (magical formula).[42]

The rites and ceremonies related to death too have some variations of detail due perhaps to the background and purposes of the writers. According to the prescriptive portion of the work associated with Chaupa Singh, there should be no mourning on the death of a

Sikh. No tonsure should be performed. The Guru's shabad should
be sung when the dead body is taken away for cremation. Parsād
should be distributed among the persons present. Granth Sahib
should be installed in the home for a complete reading. Its exposition (*kathā*) and kīrtan should be performed for eleven, thirteen,
fifteen, or seventeen days of the *bhog-pāṭh*, according to the means
of the family of the deceased. The practice of customary charity
is recommended. There is emphatic rejection of traditional offerings to the dead, as also of fasts, pilgrimages, modes of worship,
mantars, sandhyā, and ritual offering of water (*tarpan*). In fact, a
Sikh should have no recourse to a Brahman who is without kes.
Nor should a Sikh of the Guru perform any ceremony by putting
a thread (*dhāgā*) over his body, or a mark on his forehead. Chaupa
Singh's suggestion that ashes of the deceased should be taken to
the Ganga for immersion might have been inspired by his own
Brahmanical background.[43]

According to the *Prem Sumārag*, there should be no beating of
the breasts by women on the death of a Sikh; all men and women
present should sing the *Alāhṇiān*. The men should not remove
their turbans. A new pair of kachh should be put on the body of
the deceased after it has been washed. After dressing it, a sword
should be placed on its right. There should be no wailing: the will
of God should be accepted without any sign of grief. The widow
should adopt simplicity and restraint, think of the deceased as ever
present with her, and read the Pothī of shabad-bāṇī.[44]

Significantly, the essential procedure in all situations, with
appropriate variation in detail, is the same for men and women,
for the young and the old, for the married and the unmarried,
for mothers and childless widows. There should be no mourning.
Unlike *The Chaupa Singh Rahit-Nama*, the *Prem Sumārag* recommends that the ashes of the Khalsa could be consigned to a nearby
stream or buried in the earth. For condolence, there should be no
association with Masands and their followers, and with those who
practise tonsure. All the three had turned away from the Guru. On
death anniversary, all kinds of food should be served to the hungry
and the Khalsa, and kīrtan should be performed.[45]

Sainapat refers only to the cremation of Guru Gobind Singh.[46]
An interesting insight into the desirable practice related to death

is provided by the *Amarnāma*. Guru Gobind Singh was informed of the death of a Singh on the cot, and the other Singhs wanted to know what was to be done. They were told not to worry; the life of this Sikh was marked by humility, and his thoughts were on the Guru at the time of his death; he had certainly gone to heaven. They should offer ardās and consign the body to the river. There was no need to call a Brahman, or to wait for the parents of the deceased. The Sikhs consigned the body to the river, uttering 'Vāhegurū'. A similar episode is mentioned in this work in connection with a Sikh of Guru Arjan.[47]

Mirza Muhammad, writing in Persian around 1715, refers generally to new customs introduced by Guru Gobind Singh for the Sikhs of the Khalsa.[48] According to Muhammad Qasim Lahauri, another near contemporary, Guru Gobind Singh's followers assembled after his death from all sides and 'proceeding with their own prescribed rituals, cremated his body with due ceremony'.[49]

## THE MIDDLE DECADES

For the middle decades of the eighteenth century, when the Khalsa were occupied with a life and death struggle against the Mughals and the Afghans, the number of Sikh sources is relatively small. The two available works—the narratives and the tankhā portion of *The Chaupa Singh Rahit-Nama* and Koer Singh's *Gurbilās*—refer mainly to initiation and matters related to death, which appeared to be especially relevant in the situation.

In the narrative of the rahitnāmā, we find for the first time a description of what Guru Gobind Singh did for administering *kesān dī pahul* (initiation of the kes). Chaupa Singh was asked to bring a bowl of water, to stir it with a knife, and to recite five of the *Savvayyās* of Guru Gobind Singh. Dīvān Sahib Chand requested that some sugar bubbles (*patāshās*) may be mixed with the water to make it tasteful and Dharam Chand was asked to bring the patāshās. When the pahul was ready, Chaupa Singh took the bowl in his hand and stood before the Guru. Taking five palmfuls of water, the Guru sprinkled it five times over Chaupa Singh's eyes and five times over his head. Guru Gobind Singh then recited the famous Savvayyā of the *Chandī Charitra*, which starts with 'deh

Sivā bar mohe ihae', and ends with prayer for death on the field of battle. With his own hands he gave pahul to Chaupa Singh who was asked to exclaim 'Vāhegurūjī kā Khālsā, Vāhegurūjī kī fateh'. Four other Sikhs, named Dhanna Singh, Hari Singh, Mewa Singh, and Jodh Singh requested for pahul. Thus, on the first day, five Sikhs were made Kesdhārī. For the future, five Sikhs were to be present at the time of administering pahul. The persons initiated were to add the epithet 'Singh' to their name and to keep arms. On the second day, thirty-five Sikhs were initiated and on the third day, sixty. The Guru underlined that the kes were the distinctive mark of a Singh. Distribution of karāh parsād is mentioned as an integral part of the ceremony. Hukamnāmās were issued to the Sikhs that they should not recognize the authority of the Masands. Among the many things that armed Kesdhārī Singhs were to do was to fight and establish their rule. For this purpose the Goddess was invoked. A lot of space is given to this episode in the narrative. Nevertheless, the distinctiveness of the new panth from Hindus and Muslims is underscored.[50]

The third section of the rahitnāmā dealing with penance emphasizes the sanctity of the kes, beard, and turban, the importance of ardās and karāh parsād, and the obligation of saluting with 'Vāhegurūjī kā Khalsa' and responding with 'Vāhegurūjī kī fateh'. It is in this part of the rahitnāmā that initiation of women by pahul of the double-edged sword is prohibited. Association with the five excommunicated groups and with the killers of infant daughters is emphatically prohibited. In the fourth section (second narrative), the kes is mentioned as the mark of the Kesdhārī Singh, the seal of the Guru.[51]

Significantly, *The Chaupa Singh Rahit-Nama* brackets the Kesdhārīs with Sahajdhārīs in several ways. The daily personal and congregational worship is the same for both. The Sahajdhārīs too keep the beard uncut, discard tonsure, and shun tobacco. However, they seem to have the discretion to keep or discard the sacred thread. For funerary rites they also arrange bhog-paṭh, kīrtan, ardās, and distribution of karāh parsād. They believe in no guru other than the ten Gurus from Guru Nanak to Guru Gobind Singh. They subscribe to doctrines of Guru Granth and Guru Panth. For initiation, a Sahajdhārī takes charan-pahul, which is prepared by reciting five pauṛīs of the *Japujī* and five pauṛīs of the *Ānand* when patāshās are mixed with water in which the lactern (*manjī*) of Guru Granth Sahib has been washed.[52] Through these observances, the Sahajdhārī becomes a 'Khalsa' but not a 'Singh'. For the European writers of the late eighteenth century, however, the 'Sahajdhārī' would become a blanket term for all non-Singhs, called the Khulāsā (Khalāsā) Sikhs.[53]

Koer Singh gives a different version of the ceremony of initiation performed by Guru Gobind Singh at the time of instituting the Khalsa. The Guru poured clear water into a vessel of iron and started reciting mantars. Kirpa Ram informed Mata Jī (the Guru's mother) that the Guru was going to institute the Khalsa Panth and for this purpose he was preparing the pahul for initiation. She came and put patāshās into the bowl. Having prepared the amrit, the Guru made an ardās. Then he administered amrit to five Sikhs: Daya Singh, a Sobti Khatri of Lahore; Nihchal Singh (Mohkam Chand), a Chhīpa of Dwarka; Sahib Singh, a Nāī of Bidar; Dharam Singh, a Jāt of Hastinapur; and Himmat Singh, a Jhīvar of Jagannath. The first instruction given to the five on this occasion was not to associate with those who cut their hair and killed their infant daughters, or with the Mīṇās, the Masands and the 'Turks'. The initiate should discard every other form of worship and take refuge in the Wielder of the Sword. He should bear arms, keep his kes unshorn, wear kachh, and keep a dagger (*kard*). He should keep a kanghā to comb his kes twice a day.[54]

Koer Singh mentions that just before Guru Gobind Singh's death, Mata Sahib Devi expressed her wish to burn herself on his funeral pyre. The Guru told her that this was not to be done. The implication is quite clear: the practice of satī was forbidden. Furthermore, before the funeral pyre prepared for Guru Gobind Singh was lighted by a Brahman Singh, Guru Gobind Singh is said to have disappeared, but he was seen by an Udāsī who was asked to tell the Khalsa not to mourn but to observe the Khalsa rahit.[55]

## THE LATE EIGHTEENTH CENTURY

With a noticeable increase in the number of the Khalsa in the late eighteenth century, it is not surprising that both Sikh and

European sources are concerned mainly with the initiation rite as the means of induction into the Khalsa order.

Kesar Singh Chhibber's account of the procedure adopted by Guru Gobind Singh for administering pahul to Sikhs for instituting the Khalsa is broadly similar to that given in the narrative of *The Chaupa Singh Rahit-Nama.* The two appear to represent the same tradition. The initiates are instructed to keep their kes unshorn. The kes are to replace the sacred thread and the sacred mark as a distinct marker of the identity of the third community (*tīsar panth*). One important implication of the sanctity of the kes is that no rite connected with tonsure was to be performed. The emphatic injunction in support of kes is matched by the strong injunction against tobacco. Kesdhārī Singhs should bear arms and wear blue dress. They should not associate with the Mīṇās, Dhir Mallias, and Ram Raiyās, nor with the Masands. The other category of people with whom the Khalsa should not associate were those who killed their infant daughters.[56]

Sarup Das Bhalla refers to initiation of the double-edged sword in connection with the institution of the Khalsa. Five Sikhs were given pahul by Guru Gobind Singh. The rest of the Sikhs were told to take pahul from them. The Khalsa were required to keep their hair uncut and wear blue dress. They were to add the epithet 'Singh' to their names. Guru Gobind Singh adopted the same appearance as that of the Khalsa. The attitude of the Khalsa towards the sacred thread is indicated by the statement that one of the panj pyāre, Daya Singh, removed his sacred thread to tie the sword of Guru Gobind Singh. It is explicitly stated later that the sacred thread and the sacred mark had no meaning in comparison with the True Name. The Guru tells his followers that the Khalsa should not be compelled either to remove or to wear the sacred thread.[57] This too suggests the irrelevance of the sacred thread for any cherished belief or practice of the Khalsa.

Significantly, and unlike several other Sikh works of the eighteenth century, the *Gurū Kiān Sākhiān* makes no reference to the Goddess. The account of the khande kī pahul in this work is the most comprehensive. Even the phrase '*panch kakār*' (for the five 'K's) is used, though instead of kes the kakār recommended is '*keskī*' (a small turban worn under the large one). Even so, the kes are there by implication. As a prelude to the institution of the Khalsa, the Masands were punished and turned out, and offerings (dasvandh, chalīhā, and *mannat*) began to be sent directly to Anandpur. As instructed by Guru Gobind Singh, a day before Baisākhī, Dīvan Mani Ram put up five tents, and Bhai Chaupa Rai brought five goats. In each tent one goat was tied. After kīrtan of the *Āsā dī Vār* and kathā of a shabad by Bhai Mani Ram on the Baisākhī day, Guru Gobind Singh called for a head five times. Those who responded in turn to this call were Bhai Daya Singh, a Sobti Khatri of Sialkot; Mohkam Chand, a Chhīpa of Dwarka; Sahib Chand, a Nāī of Bidar; Dharam Chand, a Jāt of Hastinapur; and Himmat Chand, a Mehra (water carrier) Sikh of Jagannath. They were taken into the tents one by one, and asked to slaughter the goat. Then they were dressed afresh with the 5Ks, and the Guru adopted the same form. They all came out. Guru Gobind Singh declared the five Sikhs to be the 'panj pyāre' (the five beloved) as they had passed the test and become *marjīvaṛe* (who were ready to lay down their life for the Guru). The description of the way in which khande kī pahul was prepared and administered is equally graphic, and the injunctions for rahit are rather detailed. Nothing important is left out.[58]

Writing at the end of the century, Sukha Singh dramatically depicts the context in which pahul was prepared for instituting the Khalsa. He refers to the call for volunteers in Kesgaṛh to sacrifice their head for the Guru. After the third call, a follower (*sevak*) stood up. He was taken into a tent, given a sword, and asked to slaughter a male goat with one stroke. Blood flowed from the tent. With the dripping sword in his hand Guru Gobind Singh asked for another head. Another follower stood up after the third call. He too was taken into the tent and asked to slaughter a goat. There was murmuring among the Sikhs who thought that this was the evil effect of invoking the Goddess (Bhavani). The Guru eventually came out of the tent with the panj pyāre. He began to prepare the pahul with fresh water into which Mata jī put patāshās. The pahul was meant to rekindle the dead spirit. When it was ready, the Guru made an ardās and gave this amrit to the panj pyāre, asking them to exclaim 'Vāhegurū'. They were instructed to discard the false thread in favour of the sword, and not to associate with the Mīṇās,

Dhir Mallias, Ram Raiyās, and the Masandias. Sukha Singh says that the fifth category, apparently those who shaved their head, was not concealed from anyone. Guru Gobind Singh declared then that apart from the Wielder of the Sword (God), there was no object of worship. In this way he created the third community (tīsar panth), distinct from and superior to Hindus and Muslims. At the time of his own jagg pavīt (sacred thread ceremony), the young Guru Gobind is said to have told the Brahmans that the Wielder of the Sword had given him the sword as his sacred thread and he would give this protective shield to the Khalsa.[59]

The rahitnāmā of Desa Singh gives primacy to initiation through the double-edged sword to be administered by five Singhs. The initiate is required to carry arms and wear turban and also have a comb (kanghā) and a dagger on his person. He should not make ardās without weapons (shastar), and karāh parsād should be touched by the kard (dagger) before it is distributed equally among all. As in other rahitnāmās, the novitiate in this work is required to shun the reprobate groups, which included the killers of daughters. It may be recalled that the writer dwells at some length on the proper method of preparing the karāh parsād and the langar.[60]

Bhai Daya Singh requests Guru Gobind Singh to issue a rahitnāmā to serve as the source of liberation. Guru Gobind Singh says that the mantar of *'ek onkār satnām'* was given by Shakti (through Guru Nanak); the jantar of Vāhegurū was given by Mohan (Krishna); the *tantar* of *amar-jal* was provided by Varun; sweet was provided by Indra; the vessel of iron was provided by Yamraj; the knife of iron was provided by Kāl; the kes were given by Chandi; the kachh was given by Hanuman; the four *padāraths* (dharma, *artha, kāma,* and *moksha*) accruing from the khande kī pahul were provided by Vishnu; fine flour (*maidā*) was provided by Mahadev; and ghee was given by Brahma for the karāh parsād. These divinities were subordinate to Akāl Purkh and, therefore, subservient to Guru Gobind Singh. Daya Singh adds that the path of liberation (*muktī*) was provided by the *Japujī*; the *Ānand* was given by Guru Amar Das for peace; and the *Chaupaī* and the *Savvayyās* were added by Guru Gobind Singh.[61]

The actual ceremony of initiation is then spelt out in the rahitnāmā. Anyone from the four varnas could take amrit. By taking amrit even the lowest of the low would attain liberation. The person to whom pahul is given should wear kachh, bind his hair in a knot, and tie a turban. He should stand up with an unsheathed sword in hand. The water of amritsar (the sacred tank in Ramdaspur) should be used for preparing amrit. First of all, the whole of the *Japujī* should be recited, followed by the *Chaupaī*, five *Savvayyās*, and five pauṛīs of the *Ānand*, while the kard was used for stirring the water to prepare amrit. A Singh should then take the permission of the assembly (Sarbat) and take the bowl in his hands to let the new entrant drink from it. He should place that kard in his turban. The person who takes pahul should place his right hand over the left to drink it; he should then exclaim, 'Vāhegurūjī kā Khālsā , Vāhegurūjī kī fateh'. In this way he should drink five palmfuls of amrit, and it should be sprinkled over his eyes and head. He should be given the *gur-mantar* of satnām and a new name. He should make an offering of a rupee and a quarter. Then ardās should be performed and the karāh parsād eaten by all together. It is specified that for preparing the karāh parsād on the occasion of administering amrit, jaggery should not be used in place of sugar. Daya Singh emphasizes that those who administer amrit should be devout Sikhs and men of exceptional qualities, because it was first administered by the Guru as the incarnation of Akāl Purkh.[62]

Among the European writers of the last quarter of the century who took note of the initiation ceremony, Charles Wilkins states that if a person showed a sincere inclination to renounce his former beliefs to any five or more Sikhs, he was asked to bring a small quantity of patāshās which were dissolved in pure water; this water was sprinkled on his body and into his eyes, and one of the devout Sikhs instructed him to observe the chief canons of their faith for the rest of his life. Wilkins goes on to add that they were prepared to initiate him into the Sikh faith. In other words, the Sikh faith was open to everyone.[63]

Other contemporary observers—Colonel A.L.H. Polier, George Forster, James Browne, and John Griffiths—refer to the rite of initiation on the basis of what they had heard from Sikhs or non-Sikhs, and their statements collectively contain a number of features: the initiation extended to all classes and creeds, keeping unshorn hair and beard, bearing arms, wearing an iron bracelet on one arm, presence of five or more Sikhs on the occasion, exclamation of 'Vāhegurūjī kā Khālsā, Vāhegurūjī kī fateh', instructions regarding religious, moral, and political duties, and prohibition of the use of tobacco. The intention of the ceremony was to abolish distinctions of caste, and its result was a distinct identity of the Khalsa.[64]

John Malcolm's statement on pahul as the principal institution of the Khalsa is rather elaborate. Guru Gobind Singh admitted converts from all tribes and classes, including Muslims. All those who subscribed to his tenets were at the same level; the Brahman who entered the fold had no higher claim to eminence than the Shudra who swept his house. It was the object of the Guru to make all Sikhs equal. The initiated person added to his name the epithet 'Singh', which till then was assumed only by Rajputs. The Singhs were required to devote themselves to arms, to have steel about them in some shape, to wear a blue dress, to allow their hair to grow, and to exclaim 'Vāhegurūjī kā Khālsā, Vāhegurūjī kī fateh' on meeting one another. The blue dress was still worn by the Akālīs. Malcolm thinks that perhaps Guru Gobind Singh's idea was to separate his followers from all other classes of India by their appearance as much as by their religion.[65]

The way in which Guru Gobind Singh first initiated his followers was described to Malcolm by a Sikh and it is very close to the descriptions in Sikh literature. Guru Gobind Singh had initiated five persons in the first place and they were instructed how to initiate others. 'The convert is told that he must allow his hair to grow, he must clothe himself from head to foot in blue clothes, and he is then presented with five weapons: a sword, a firelock, a bow and arrow and a pike.' Sugar and water were put into a cup and stirred round with a weapon; the first chapter of the Ādi Granth and the first chapter of the 'Dasamā Pādshāh kā Granth' were read, and those who performed the initiation exclaimed, 'Vāhegurūjī kā Khālsā, Vāhegurūjī kī fateh'. After exclaiming this five times, the water prepared for initiation was drunk by the proselyte. A sweet drink prepared in a similar manner was sprinkled over his head and beard. After these ceremonies he was told to abandon all intercourse with five categories of people: the Mīṇās and Dhir Mallias, the Masandias, the followers of Ram Rai, those who killed their infant daughters, and the bhaddanīs who ritually shaved their head and beard. The initiate was instructed to sacrifice his life and property for the cause of the Khalsa, and share with others whatever he received from God. He was directed to read both the Granths every morning and evening.[66]

Writing around the same time, Captain Matthews recorded that 'a Sikh wishing to become a Singh' could go to the Akālīs in Amritsar and give proof of his determination to discard his former beliefs. With his own hands the proselyte then broke his sacred thread (*zunnār*), 'the small thread, or cord, worn across the shoulders by most of the Hindoo sects'. After the performance of certain ceremonies, he was given to drink a sherbat made of sugar and water by an Akālī. After the initiation, he never shaved his beard, nor cut his hair. He became 'heterodox' for the Hindus who considered him as an apostate. He was allowed to eat whatever food he liked except beef.[67]

The sources of the late eighteenth century do not say much about other rites and ceremonies. For marriage, Bhai Desa Singh recommends that it should be endogamous but he does not refer to any rite.[68] Bhai Daya Singh gives preference to a Khalsa Singh for the marriage of a daughter and lays down that 'marriage should not be performed without the *Ānand*' (being recited at the end).[69]

For the ceremonies related to death, Sarup Das Bhalla simply refers to the cremation of Guru Gobind Singh's body. With an implicit reference to the *Sadd* of Baba Sunder, Sarup Das underlines that no Brahmanical rite was to be performed. In fact, Guru Nanak himself is said to have told his followers that no Brahmanical rites were to be performed after his death.[70] According to Sukha Singh, Guru Gobind Singh told his followers that his end was ordained by God and, therefore, it was a matter of rejoicing for him. He instructed that none should wail and cry after him; they should sing the praises of God and perform kathā for forty days, and the lowest of the low should not be debarred from it. All varieties of food was to be prepared and distributed among all the four castes without any distinction. The Khalsa should celebrate the event and organize *chaukī-shabad* or kīrtan by turns.[71] In the *Gurū Kiān Sākhiān*, Sarup Singh refers to the exclamation of 'Vāhegurūjī kā Khālsā, Vāhegurūjī kī fateh' by

Guru Gobind Singh as his last farewell to the Khalsa. His body was washed and dressed, and weapons were placed by its side. After the cremation, the *Sohilā* was recited, ardās was performed, and karāh parsād was distributed.[72]

Only two European observers comment on the practices related to death. Forster notices that the widow was expressly forbidden to destroy herself at the death of her husband, and allowed to renew the ceremonies of marriage. However, adherence to the old practice was strong among the Hindus who had converted to the Sikh faith. Many of their women were seen ascending the funeral pyre; others could not be induced to enter the connubial state for a second time.[73] Captain Matthews states that after cremation, the ashes were thrown into a river. He also refers to the existence of small structures over the spots where some important men had been cremated.[74]

## IN RETROSPECT

When we look back at contemporary evidence for the three phases we have examined, we find that the middle decades, coinciding with the most intense phase of political struggle of the Sikhs, figure only in two sources, which refer to the rites of initiation and death. Though the amount of information from the late eighteenth century or the period of Sikh rule is far larger, it too relates mostly to initiatory and funerary rites. These are also the rites on which Persian and European sources provide information. The rite in connection with birth finds mention in the first phase, in which the Sikh sources cover the ceremony of marriage along with the rites related to initiation and death. However, there is no description of how pahul was prepared and administered on the day of the institution of the Khalsa. Such narratives begin to appear in the middle decades. For the period as a whole, maximum importance is given to initiatory rites, followed at a distance by funerary rites and the ceremony of marriage. There is no uniformity in the rites and ceremonies recommended or described in our sources, but there is a large degree of consensus, and a basic agreement on essentials. Consequently, continuity is more remarkable than change for the eighteenth century as a whole.

Differences of detail notwithstanding, Sikh and non-Sikh sources convey an overwhelming sense of (*a*) the distinctiveness of the path of Guru Nanak, including a distinctive way of life; (*b*) endeavour of the successive Gurus to evolve the rites and ceremonies commensurate with his message; (*c*) emphatic affirmation and dissemination of Sikh rites of passage after the institution of the Khalsa; (*d*) new rites and ceremonies being sufficiently well-entrenched by the eighteenth century; and (*e*) their coexistence with local variations and the previous practices of the group that a Sikh came from. The variations in detail in the contemporary sources arose from the degree of familiarity with the scripture as well as from personal predilections and existential situations of the writers or their informants. It is nevertheless possible to elicit the norms and gather an impression of Sikhs consciously acting on these. There is a sufficiently clear idea of what was rejected, what was instituted—both positively and negatively—and what was adapted. Despite internal variations, the evolving 'Sikh' rites and ceremonies are clearly conceived as non-Brahmanical.

Since the Gurus themselves and the substantial segment of their followers came from within the fold of the Brahmanical system, there was a greater focus on the repudiation of Brahmanical practices in the course of creating alternative rites and ceremonies. There is an emphatic rejection in Guru Granth Sahib of ritual bathing, shaving, purification, charities, fasting, mourning, and pacification of the dead, besides the practice of satī. Disapproval of the sacred thread as the visible symbol of one's ritual status and implicit superiority occurs frequently in the Granth and the later sources. There is a virtual rejection of the mediacy of the professional priests. The framework of the Shāstras is emphatically replaced by that provided by the Sikh scripture. The Pandit and the Pādhā are bracketed with the Mian and the Mahant: their teaching (*mat*) is rejected in favour of Gurmat. The initiate is instructed to learn the Gurmukhi script, read the Granth for himself or herself and reflect on the message of the Gurus. A crisp statement of the Guru in the *Sākhī Rahit* sums up the position: 'All the kīryā-karam of my Panth have been performed by Satguru Akāl Purkh.'[75]

By the beginning of the eighteenth century, specific compositions of the Granth were in use for different stages in a Sikh's life:

the *Ānand* for birth; the *Ānand, Sohilā, Ghoṛiāṅ,* and the *Lāvāṅ* for the ceremonies related to marriage; and the *Japujī, Alāhṇiāṅ, Ānand,* and the *Sadd* for death. Performed in the presence of fellow Sikhs, these ceremonies commenced and ended with collective prayer (ardās). Every ceremony ended with the partaking of the kaṛāh parsād prepared and distributed in a prescribed manner. This was often followed by the common meal (langar), which too was required to be cooked and served in a particular manner. Incidentally, the use of a fire-pit in place of Guru Granth for the wedding ceremony does not make the ceremony Brahmanical. The essential detail was much different.

A person from any caste or creed could be initiated into the Sikh fold by drinking amrit and by agreeing to abide by the injunctions of the Gurus. The available evidence suggests that before the institution of the Khalsa the initiate probably drank the water touched by the toe of the devout Sikhs (rather than that of the Guru). It was called charan-amrit or charan-pahul. It is not unlikely that at places, and as an alternative to the charan-amrit and khande kī pahul, the dipping of a foot of the manjī (lectern) of Guru Granth Sahib in water came into use for the initiation of a Sahajdhārī Sikh, but no Brahmanical rite was recommended for him.

At any rate, the initiation rite introduced by Guru Gobind Singh was meant to replace charan-amrit. The core of the new rite was the stirring of the water with a khandā (double-edged sword) while reciting compositions from Guru Granth Sahib and the *Dasam Granth.* There is broad agreement in the sources over the preparation of the sweetened amrit, and the procedure of administering it, which required, among others things, the presence of five devout Sikhs. Our sources are quite consistent also with regard to the attendant obligations of the initiate regarding beliefs, practices, bearing of arms, and change of name and appearance. The sanctity of the unshorn hair (kes) figures in a big way in the initiation rite and in the life of the Sikh thereafter. This was the obverse of the injunction against having any social relations with those who practised ritual shaving of the head (*bhaddan*) on different occasions. The instructions for the initiate are clear also with regard to the shunning of the reprobate groups who had turned away from the Gurus.

The emphasis in these injunctions on ostracizing the perpe-trators of female infanticide is striking. Our sources mention the disapproval of the practice of satī as well and point to it being relatively less prevalent among Sikhs. It is more than likely in this context that khande ki pahul remained open to women. The statement in the *Prem Sumārag* is significant that khande kī pahul should be given to female infants to be named, girls to be mar-ried, expectant mothers, and even to widows who could remarry in certain circumstances. The attendant detail and obligations are spelt out in each case. The assertion in *The Chaupa Singh Rahit-Nama* against giving khande kī pahul to women can be attributed perhaps to Brahmanical prejudices of the Chhibbers.

Finally, the khandā emerges as an essential constituent of the rites of passage during the eighteenth century. It figures in the ceremonies related to birth, marriage, and death. It sanctified the kaṛāh parsād, and it was required to be worn at the time of making ardās. Although the other arms also figure in these rites, the sword is assigned a place next in importance to the khandā in the ceremonies related to initiation, birth, marriage, and death. Fire is considered sacred, but it is one of the three witnesses to the wedlock, the other two being the sword (Sri Bhagautī Jī) and the community of believers (Sri Khalsa Jī). Water too is an essential constituent of Sikh rites of passage. Proscription regarding diet (not to eat beef and meat prepared in the Muslim fashion) figure in the instructions to the initiate. The initiation through pahul entailing new name, appearance, obligations, social relations, and attitudes had the potential of uplifting the recipient both psycho-logically and socially. It is hardly surprising that before the end of the eighteenth century, the 'Singh' identity had emerged as the dominant one among the followers of the Gurus. A new emphasis on community identity as well as solidarity, irrespective of caste and gender, and a new set of values were built into the Sikh rites and ceremonies.

Even if it is assumed that the ideal put forth by the Gurus was not easily realizable, there is, on the whole, a considerable cor-respondence between the normative injunctions and empirical statements in Sikh and non-Sikh sources of the eighteenth cen-tury. All this leaves a strong impression that without the legacy of the eighteenth century, the Singh Sabha advocacy of uniform Sikh rites and rituals (Rahit Maryādā) would have been unthinkable. In fact, there is a remarkable correspondence between the norms advocated in eighteenth-century Sikh literature and the distinctly Sikh ceremonies advocated and adopted by the leaders of the Singh Sabha movement in the early twentieth century.

## NOTES AND REFERENCES

1. The term 'rite' is used for a social custom or ceremony generally associated with the passage from one important stage to another in someone's life like birth, initiation, marriage, and death. It is also used for the procedure of an individual's entry into a new socio-religious order. Labelled collectively as 'rites of passage', such ceremonies are intended to exert ideological and educative influences over the individual going through these and to help him assimilate the appropriate ideas, norms, and values characteristic of the group he belongs to. His duties, obligations, and privileges, as well as social relations within and outside the community are influenced by the rites he formally goes through. See for example, *A Dictionary of Sociology*, ed. G. Duncan Mitchell (London: Routledge, 1977 [1968]), pp. 98, 146–8.

2. See J.S. Grewal, *A Study of Guru Granth Sahib: Doctrine, Social Content, History, Structure and Status* (Amritsar: Singh Brothers, 2009), pp. 50–7, 67–8, 134–57, for example.

3. See *Shabdārth Sri Guru Granth Sahib Ji*, 4 vols (Amritsar: Shiromani Gurdwara Prabandhak Committee [standard pagination]), pp. 471–3.

4. *Shabdārth*, pp. 1–4, 6.

5. For example, *Shabdārth*, p. 471. Also, Grewal, *A Study of Guru Granth Sahib*, pp. 38–9.

6. *Sohilā* is used for a group of three compositions of Guru Nanak, and one each of Guru Ram Das and Guru Arjan which are recited at night as part of daily worship (*nit-nem*). These compositions are also recited at a Sikh's death, because while praising God, they use similes that lay stress on the worldly existence being transitory, death being inevitable, and the ultimate goal of human life being union with God. See *Shabdārth*, pp. 12–13. Also Ratan Singh Jaggi, *Guru Granth Vishavkosh*, 2 parts (Patiala: Punjabi University, 2002), part I, pp. 241–2.

7. The traditional mourning songs (*alāhṇiān* or dirge) were sung in unison by women led by professional female mourners from

amongst the Nāis, or Mirāsīs. Making use of this poetical form, Guru Nanak composed five *Alāhṇiān*, which generate a feeling of detachment from worldly possessions and relations, and inspire Sikhs to turn towards God without being despondent or afraid of death. It is emphasized that only death, which results in union with God, is praiseworthy. Guru Amar Das also composed four *Alāhṇiān* with a similar import. *Shabdārth*, pp. 578–82. Also, R.S. Jaggi, *Guru Granth Vishavkosh*, part I, pp. 78–9.

8. R.S. Jaggi, *Guru Granth Vishavkosh*, part II, p. 218. See also Grewal, *A Study of Guru Granth Sahib*, p. 41; Raj Bali Pandey, *Hindu Samskaras: Socio-Religious Study of the Hindu Sacraments* (Delhi: Motilal Banarsidass, 1969), pp. 261, 265–6. 'Pind' denotes the ball of rice offered to the dead, and 'pattal' apparently stands for the lamp floating on a reed mat, supposedly to facilitate the dead person's 'progress through the utter darkness that enshrouds the road to the city of Yama'.

9. In the long and lyrical composition called the *Ānand*, Guru Amar Das advises Sikhs to strive to realize God, because the state of bliss (ānand) or liberation through union with God is the ultimate goal of human life. While expounding on the nature of bliss, the Guru uses the metaphor of the seeker encountering several kinds of obstacles and overcoming these with the True Guru's guidance and God's grace. See *Shabdārth*, pp. 917–22.

Guru Amar Das is believed to have composed the *Ānand* on the occasion of the birth of a grandson. The first five and the last pauṛīs of this composition of forty pauṛīs are sung on all important occasions. See also R.S. Jaggi, *Guru Granth Vishavkosh*, part I, pp. 39–40, 99–102. See also Grewal, *A Study of Guru Granth Sahib*, pp. 239–47.

10. Grewal, *A Study of Guru Granth Sahib*, p. 242.

11. R.S. Jaggi, *Guru Granth Vishavkosh*, part I, pp. 99–102. A shortened form of the *Ānand* is also included in the compositions to be used for daily worship (nit-nem).

12. Grewal, *A Study of Guru Granth Sahib*, pp. 144–5.

13. Baba Sunder is believed to be a great-grandson of Guru Amar Das whose last message to the Sikhs and the family is contained in this short composition, which literally means a call or a cry. R.S. Jaggi, *Guru Granth Vishavkosh*, part I, pp. 141, 212.

14. The term 'kīryā' or *kriyā* is used for the Brahmanical pacificatory ceremonies performed on the tenth or the thirteenth day after death.

15. Metaphorically, the bridegroom in this composition of Guru Ram Das denotes the devotee, the mare his body, the bridle his self-control, the whip his love of God, and his wedding-party the sādh-sangat,

which, together, move in the direction of union with God. *Shabdārth*, pp. 575–6, 772–4. See also R.S. Jaggi, *Guru Granth Vishavkosh*, part I, p. 463.

16. Using the metaphor of an ideal married life, the *Lāvān* dwells on the soul's yearning for, and union with, God. Here, the Guru seems to advise the newly married couple to spiritualize their married life. See *Shabdārth*, p. 774. See also R.S. Jaggi, *Guru Granth Vishavkosh*, part II, p. 463. Incidentally, even Sodhi Harji, a great grandson of Guru Ram Das and leader of the dissenting Mīṇās, composed four lāvāns on the pattern of Guru Ram Das's compositions.

17. Grewal, *A Study of Guru Granth Sahib*, pp. 228–9.

18. Grewal, *A Study of Guru Granth Sahib*, pp. 119–22. Also R.S. Jaggi, *Guru Granth Vishavkosh*, part I, p. 75. In its present form ardās is believed to have crystallized sometime during the latter part of the eighteenth century. For its discussion in historical perspective, see J.S. Grewal and Indu Banga, 'The Sikh Prayer (Ardās)', *Panjab Journal of Sikh Studies* 1 (2011): 9–23.

19. 'Mobad', *Dabistān-i Mazāhib*, in *Sikh History from Persian Sources: Translations of Major Texts*, ed. J.S. Grewal and Irfan Habib (New Delhi: Tulika/Indian History Congress, 2001) , p. 78.

20. Bhai Gurdas, *Vārān Bhai Gurdas*, ed. Giani Hazara Singh (Amritsar: Khalsa Samachar, 1962 [1911]), vār VI, pauṛī 3; vār XX, pauṛī 10, where Bhai Gurdas uses the word "mahāparsād' for the sanctified food distributed in a Sikh place of worship.

21. Refer to Chapter 3 for some detail on the preparation and distribution of kaṛāh parsād.

22. For example, Harjot Oberoi, *The Construction of Religious Boundaries: Culture, Identity and Diversity in Sikh Tradition* (New Delhi: Oxford University Press, 1994), p. 61. Jodh Singh tends to support this assumption on the basis of his reading of Bhai Gurdas. See Jodh Singh, trans. and ed., *Vārān Bhāī Gurdās: Text, Transliteration and Translation* (Patiala: Vision and Venture, 1998), vol. 2, vār XXII, pauṛī 14. Jodh Singh translates the last two lines as: 'The *Gurmukhs* have quaffed the dust of the feet of Guru like *amrit*. The tale is also ineffable.' Elsewhere in this work, however, he refers to the Gurmukh taking the holy water touched by the feet of his companions. See, vol. 1, vār I, pauṛī 3.

23. Bhai Kahan Singh Nabha, *Gurshabad Ratnākar Mahān Kosh* (Patiala: Punjab Languages Department, 1999 [1930]), p. 457.

24. Bhai Gurdas, *Vārān Bhai Gurdas*, vār I, pauṛī 3; ār I, pauṛī 23; vār VI, pauṛī 17; vār XXII, pauṛī 14. For a discussion of the importance of the

dust of the feet of the men of piety in the medieval Indian religious traditions, see R.S. Jaggi, *Guru Granth Vishavkosh*, part I, pp. 471–2.

25. *Shabdārth*, respectively pp. 828 and 1263, for example.

26. For several such expressions, see Grewal, *A Study of Guru Granth Sahib*, pp. 111–19.

27. The practice is reported in this mid-seventeenth-century work: 'When they make anyone a Sikh, they wash his feet and pass on the water to the [other] Sikhs so that all may drink of it, and this they regard as a curative.' See 'Mobad', *Dabistān*, pp. 77–8, 84n65.

28. Cf. Oberoi, *Construction of Religious Boundaries*, pp. 61–7. Oberoi maintains that prior to the Khalsa transformation, Sikhs possessed only a fluid identity, and did not think of a distinct set of life-cycle rituals. The Khalsa introduced new rites related to birth, initiation, and death, which gave an individual a new and bounded identity to demarcate the Khalsa from the rest of the 'civil society'. Oberoi's presentation of these rites in a few paragraphs is based on *The Chaupa Singh Rahit-Nama* which he places between 1750 and 1765.

29. W.H. McLeod, trans. and ed., *The Chaupa Singh Rahit-Nama* (Dunedin, New Zealand: University of Otago Press, 1987), pp. 68, 72–3.

30. McLeod, *The Chaupa Singh Rahit-Nama*, pp. 57–9, 63–5, 67–9, 72, 77.

31. Randhir Singh, ed., *Prem Sumārag Granth arthāt Khalsai Jīvan Jāch (Pātshāhī Dasvīn)* (Jalandhar: New Book Company, 1965 [1953]), pp. 15–20.

32. Randhir Singh, *Prem Sumārag Granth*, pp. 20–1.

33. Sainapat, *Shri Gur Sobhā*, ed. Shamsher Singh Ashok (Amritsar: Shiromani Gurdwara Prabandhak Committee, 1967), pp. 32–4, 42–4.

34. Sewadas, *Episodes from Lives of the Gurus: Parchiān Sewādās*, trans. and ed. Kharak Singh and Gurtej Singh (Chandigarh: Institute of Sikh Studies, 1995), p. 139.

35. Ganda Singh, ed., *Hukamnāme: Gurū Sāhibān, Mata Sāhibān, Banda Singh Ate Khalsa Jī De* (Patiala: Punjabi University, 1967), pp. 152–3, 160–5, 168–73, 175–7, 179, 181, 182–91, 194–7, 202–11, 214–17, 222–3. Also Ajit Singh Baagha, *Banur Had Orders* (Delhi: Ranjit Printers & Publishers, nd), pp. 54–5.

36. Nath Mal, *Amarnāma*, trans. and ed. Ganda Singh (Amritsar: Sikh History Society, 1953), pp. 36–9.

37. 'Reports from Bahadur Shah's Court, 1707–10', in J.S. Grewal and Habib, *Sikh History from Persian Sources*, pp. 107–8.

38. (Anon.) *Asrār-i Samadī*, trans. Janak Singh (Patiala: Punjabi University, 1972), pp. 8–9.

39. McLeod, *The Chaupa Singh Rahit-Nama*, p. 65.

40. J.S. Grewal, 'The *Prem Sumārag*: A Sant Khalsa Vision of the Sikh Panth', *The Sikhs: Ideology, Institutions and Identity* (New Delhi: Oxford University Press, 2009), p. 169. For detail, see Randhir Singh, *Prem Sumārag Granth*, pp. 22–6.

41. McLeod, *The Chaupa Singh Rahit-Nama*, p. 72.

42. Randhir Singh, *Prem Sumārag Granth*, pp. 27–38.

43. McLeod, *The Chaupa Singh Rahit-Nama*, pp. 60, 62, 63, 65, 70, 72, 76.

44. Randhir Singh, *Prem Sumārag Granth*, pp. 79–82.

45. Randhir Singh, *Prem Sumārag Granth*, pp. 83–93.

46. Sainapat, *Sri Gur Sobhā*, ed. Ganda Singh (Patiala: Punjabi University, 1967), p. 131.

47. Nath Mal, *Amarnāma*, pp. 27–36.

48. Mirza Muhammad, '*Ibratnāma*, in J.S. Grewal and Habib, *Sikh History from Persian Sources*, pp. 132–3.

49. Muhammad Qasim, '*Ibratnāma*, in J.S. Grewal and Habib, *Sikh History from Persian Sources*, p. 115.

50. McLeod, *The Chaupa Singh Rahit-Nama*, pp. 82–92. For a discussion of the episode of the Goddess, see Appendix.

51. McLeod, *The Chaupa Singh Rahit-Nama*, pp. 100–4, 107, 109, 111–15, 121.

52. McLeod, *The Chaupa Singh Rahit-Nama*, pp. 57–60, 62–4, 74–6, 98, 100, 107, 123. It must, however, be pointed out that there is very little information about the charan-pahul or the Sahajdhārīs in the literature of the period.

53. For a discussion of the Khulāsā (Khalāsā) Sikhs refer to Chapter 6.

54. Koer Singh, *Gurbilās Pātshāhī 10*, ed. Shamsher Singh Ashok (Patiala: Punjabi University, 1968), pp. 128–30.

55. Koer Singh, *Gurbilās Pātshāhī 10*, pp. 286–7, 288–9.

56. Kesar Singh Chhibber, *Bansāvalīnāmā Dasān Pātshāhiān Kā*, in *Parkh*, vol. 2, ed. Ratan Singh Jaggi (Chandigarh: Panjab University, 1972), pp. 125–33.

57. Sarup Das Bhalla, *Mahimā Prakāsh*, ed. Gobind Singh Lamba and Khazan Singh (Patiala: Punjab Languages Department, 1971), part II, pp. 805, 825–9, 831.

58. Bhai Svarup Singh Kaushish, *Gurū Kiān Sākhiān*, ed. Piara Singh Padam (Amritsar: Singh Brothers, 1999 [1986]), pp. 120–5.

59. Bhai Sukha Singh, *Gurbilās Pātsāhi 10*, ed. Gursharan Kaur Jaggi (Patiala: Punjab Languages Department, 1989), pp. 171–85.

60. *Rahitnāmā Bhai Desa Singh*, in *Rahitnāme*, ed. Piara Singh Padam (Amritsar: Singh Brothers, 1995), pp. 128–35.

61. *Rahitnāmā Bhai Daya Singh*, in Piara Singh Padam, *Rahitnāme*, p. 68.
62. *Rahitnāmā Bhai Daya Singh*, pp. 68–9.
63. Charles Wilkins, 'The Sikhs and Their College at Patna', in Ganda Singh, ed., *Early European Accounts of the Sikhs* (Calcutta: Indian Studies, Past & Present, 1962), pp. 74–5.
64. Colonel A.L.H. Polier, 'An Account of the Sikhs', in Ganda Singh, *Early European Accounts of the Sikhs*, p. 63; Major James Browne, *History of the Origin and Progress of the Sikhs*, in Ganda Singh, *Early European Accounts of the Sikhs*, pp. 18–19; and John Griffiths, 'A Memorandum on the Panjab and Kandhar', in Ganda Singh, *Early European Accounts of the Sikhs*, p. 92. See also George Forster, *A Journey from Bengal to England through the Northern Part of India, Kashmire, Afghanistan, and Persia, and into Russia by the Caspian-Sea*, 2 vols (Patiala: Punjab Languages Department, 1970 [1798]), vol. 1, pp. 307–9.
65. John Malcolm, *Sketch of the Sikhs* (New Delhi: Asian Educational Services, 1986 [1812]), pp. 45–8, 50–1, 74, 116–17, 137–8, 148–9, 151.
66. Malcolm, *Sketch of the Sikhs*, pp. 180–5.
67. [Captain Matthews], An Officer of the Bengal Army, 'A Tour to Lahore in 1808', in *The Panjab Past and Present* (Patiala: Punjabi University, 1967), vol. 1, part I–II, p. 112.
68. *Rahitnāmā Bhai Desa Singh*, pp. 129–30.
69. *Rahitnāmā Bhai Daya Singh*, pp. 73–4.
70. Bhalla, *Mahimā Prakāsh*, part I, pp. 345–6.
71. Sukha Singh, *Gurbilās Pātsāhī 10*, pp. 436, 439, 441.
72. Kaushish, *Gurū Kiān Sākhiān*, p. 202. It may be added that Sukha Singh refers merely to the funeral pyre. *Gurbilās Pātshāhī 10*, pp. 441–2.
73. Forster, *A Journey from Bengal to England*, vol. 1, pp. 308–9.
74. [Captain Matthews], 'A Tour to Lahore in 1808', p. 117.
75. *Sākhī Rahit Pātisāhī 10*, in *The Chaupa Singh Rahit-Nama*, trans. and ed. W.H. McLeod (Dunedin, New Zealand: University of Otago Press, 1987), p. 135.

# 5 Ethical Concerns of the Khalsa

The rahitnāmā as a literary genre appeared in the eighteenth century. Though the scope of the rahitnāmā as the Khalsa 'way of life' is not confined to ethics, it is deeply concerned with ethical conduct and values. But this was not something new to the Sikh tradition. Guru Nanak had enunciated that true conduct (*sach āchār*) was above everything else, even the realization of truth. Indeed, good conduct was indispensable for liberation as the supreme goal of life. Nevertheless, the importance of the eighteenth century has been recognized by scholars who have taken interest in and written on Sikh ethics.[1] In this chapter we will analyse the literary works of the period in search of the ethical values and conduct cherished by the Khalsa, both in theory and praxis.

It may be pointed out that ethics are not treated as a theme in any literary work. The injunctions, both positive and negative, are mixed up and scattered in every work. As it may be expected, the number of injunctions in the rahitnāmās is the largest, and by definition, they are normative. Next in importance are the works broadly placed in the category of *Gurbilās*, which contain empirical statements reflecting ethics as well as the norms. Works in Persian and English have the least evidence on ethics but the statements are empirical. Therefore, in a way, all the three categories of literary works have their own importance. Significantly, there is a large degree of consensus in these works, both about the norms and the practices, with no glaring contradictions on the most important ones. The injunctions, on the whole, are quite comprehensive, relating to the personal, domestic, and occupational life of a Khalsa, his relations with other Sikhs, and with non-Sikhs in terms of both friendliness and hostility.

## RAHITNĀMĀS

We may start with the rahitnāmās in their broad chronological order.[2] In one of the earliest and also the longest works, the *Prem Sumārag*, the essence of the whole *rahit* for its author is not to hurt anyone. A Khalsa Singh should speak sweetly to all and he should not indulge in meaningless talk. He should continue to work as long as he can. He should keep one-tenth of his earnings to be spent in the name of Akāl Purkh. He should have a separate room (*kothā*) for whatever is to be offered as mannat and ardās. Out of these savings he should spend on a Sikh, a sadhu, a poor person, and a needy person. His kothā is a treasury of the Guru and he should give clothes and food to sants and Sikhs of Akāl Purkh. He should help other needy persons with money and tell them to maintain a similar treasury in the name of the Guru. If a Khalsa takes money from the Guru's treasury to follow an honest occupation and earns profit, he should either return the money or keep it as the Guru's treasury.[3]

A Sikh (used interchangeably with Singh and the Khalsa) should honour his promise. He should observe restraint and contentment (*sīl, santokh*). It was obligatory for a Sikh to observe fasting, but fasting of the sensory organs. His eyes should not look at another's wife or property; his tongue should not utter falsehood or slander, or seek pleasure in food; his ears should not listen to slander; his hands should not touch another's wife or property; his feet should not move for doing an evil deed; he should not have sexual intercourse with any woman other than his wife; and his nostrils should not indulge in sweet smells. A Sikh should not indulge in sensual pleasures of any kind. This is the kind of fasting that a Khalsa should observe. Sexual pleasure is ultimately the source of sorrow. The term 'bikhia' (*vishaya*) refers to everything pursued for pleasure and comfort, resulting in sorrow and suffering. Too much food is a source of trouble.[4]

These ethical principles are reiterated elsewhere. A Khalsa should not indulge in tall talk nor speak untruth for his own gain; he should avoid backbiting, love of another woman, betraying trust, theft, illicit sexual relations, appropriation of another's property, miserliness, greed, unnecessary violence, pride, lust, anger, attachment, and longing for things that are not available.[5]

The author of the *Prem Sumārag* lays great emphasis on eating together and sharing food with others. When the food is ready, the Khalsa should sit at one place on a fine sheet (*satranjī* or *loī*) or some other cloth, and eat food in their proper dress. They should not bother about the constraints of *chaukā* (the spot plastered with cow dung, with square drawn on it to keep impurities out for eating food alone). Food is pure through God's grace. When food is served the Khalsa should think of the Guru and pray that he may send some hungry person or a Sikh of the Khalsa to share food. If anyone comes, they should feel happy and regard it as the Guru's grace. They should offer food to him in a respectful manner. If no one comes, they should keep one meal separately for a visitor, whether a Khalsa, a Hindu, a Muslim, or just a hungry person. This food is accepted in the divine court. If food is insufficient because of visitors who have come on their own, it should be shared equally by all. This is the source of increase in one's means. The host should eat after others have eaten. There was no prohibition on eating food with all well-disposed persons, whether Hindus or Muslims.[6]

While eating, a Khalsa should remember God and should not smile or laugh. He should utter 'Vāhegurūjī' with every morsel. He should not allow any particle of food to drop to the ground, nor leave it in the plate. If he can afford it by the Guru's grace, he should eat meat every day at least in a small quantity. He should never miss it. God is pleased with its flavour, and it becomes *mahāparsād*; whosoever eats it becomes pure. Even during travel, or in another country, a Khalsa should follow his usual practice; he should eat good healthy food. For drinking water, a pitcher full of water should be kept in a cool place, at a level higher than the ground. The traditional illusions about what should be and should not be eaten are to be discarded. All food is pure. Elsewhere, the author mentions the items of food and fruit to be eaten ideally at different times of the day. A Khalsa should fix the times for eating food, and eat at the fixed time. A Khalsa should not appease his hunger completely. Any vegetable that suits the body can be eaten. For eating meat, the preference should be for an animal killed by his own weapon.[7]

A Khalsa should not use any intoxicant. If he does, then he should use opium of the best quality but no more in quantity than a large mung bean, mixed with spices. For drinking *post* (poppy husk boiled in water), he should use only two and a half poppy pods. If a Khalsa eats bhang it should be mixed with spices and should not exceed two and a half *māsā* (about a milligramme). He who uses alcoholic drinks would go to hell. However, alcohol could be used if prescribed as a medicine. The use of intoxicants is prohibited because it makes the user lazy and indifferent to both God and the affairs of the world. Addiction to intoxicants leads to evil deeds.[8]

The *Prem Sumārag* refers to other domestic matters as well. It is recommended that as far as possible, a Khalsa should sleep in a cot with a piece of cloth fixed over four sticks (*chhappar-khat*) to protect the body from dew. He should not sleep naked. The kitchen, the sitting room (*dīvān-khānā*), and the stable (*tabelā*) should be kept separate from the other rooms in a place of residence. There should be a well in the house. The items of dress, perfume, and ornaments to be used by men and women are also mentioned.[9]

The author goes on to talk about the occupations to be pursued by the Khalsa and the disposal of their earnings. First of all, whatever they do should be in accordance with dharam so that the Guru may increase their resources. The Khalsa are prohibited from taking service or sitting in a shop. Working in one's own home is recommended. However, the product manufactured at home could be sold in the market. A Khalsa should not be irregular in the pursuit of his work. The most preferable occupation for the Khalsa is trade, especially in horses. Next to trade in horses is cultivation of land. If a Khalsa does take up service, it should be soldiering. He should be content with his monthly salary and serve his employer sincerely; he should fight bravely and never indulge in plunder. The Khalsa should divide what they earn into five parts. One-tenth, one-twentieth, or one-fortieth of the earnings should be kept for the Guru. A similar share should be given to mother and father. Then, a share should be separated for the

Khalsa and their food. This is followed by a share for a person's own dress, food, and fragrance. The rest should be saved to be spent on happy occasions, or in a situation of distress.[10]

In connection with the union between husband and wife, the *Prem Sumārag* recommends that the man should have a neat and clean room for sitting and sleeping. He should keep his body clean, use fragrance, and think of Srī Akāl Purkh all the time. The woman should also use fragrance. She should also rub her body with fragrant mixture of gram flower and oil every fourth or eighth day and wash her hair with condiments. She should use fragrant oil for the hair and wear perfumed clothes. She should wear a garland of flowers and put on ornaments for adornment. She should think of Srī Akāl Purkh all the time. She should never be lazy about bathing. A woman should bathe three days after menstruation, and adorn herself. The man and woman should have intercourse in the middle of the second quarter of the night, both thinking of God. For fourteen days they should have intercourse once every night and then wait for menstruation. The man who has intercourse with his wife every day, and not just for the first fourteen days of the cycle, is not a human being but a beast.[11]

The moral obligation of the Khalsa to help one another is underlined in the *Prem Sumārag*. They should stick together through thick and thin, and love one another. If one of them is in danger, the others should be prepared to lay down their lives for him. In such situations Guru Baba Srī Akāl Purkh is always there to support them. About this there could be no doubt whatever, says the author.[12]

In fact, there is considerable emphasis on proper conduct in interpersonal relations. A Khalsa should not smile or laugh too much and he should not speak evil about others. He should think before uttering any word. He should respond to queries of others and not speak to them pointlessly. Sitting in a gathering, he should show respect to others. He should be the first to utter the salutation. He should treat others with love. He should meet better persons than himself. He should sit with other people only so long as it concerns his purposes. If he is dependent on another person, he should work according to the latter's requirement. During the day, he should sit with his family for two to four and a half hours, and similarly during the night. He should meet other people in the customary manner, but inwardly he should keep his mind centred on the Guru's teaching (*updes*).[13]

The relations recommended with others arise from the Sikh ideal of *par-upkār* or the welfare of humanity at large. The Khalsa should not do evil or cause sorrow to anyone. A Khalsa should share his food with the hungry, as noted earlier, and he should give clothes to the naked and the needy. If he thinks that he can be of any help to another person he should regard it as the grace of the Guru and brook no delay. He should leave his own work and use the opportunity for doing something good for others. This is the way to please the Guru. He should satisfy others in any way he can. He should remain indifferent to praise and blame, and should treat the enemy as a friend. Only an untruth spoken for the good of someone else is justified. A Khalsa should help others but not as a favour. Since whatever happens in mundane affairs is in accordance with the will of God, a Khalsa should not feel happy or sorry over the outcome but he should continue with his effort. He should not laugh at others; it ends in misery, because the person at whom he laughs actually acts as ordained by God. Whatever good or bad anyone does is in accordance with the divine order. Therefore, a Khalsa should keep his own end in view. However, in the contemporary context of the eighteenth century, the author does not forget to recommend norms in situations of hostility.[14] This is where the opponents and enemies of the Khalsa figure more or less prominently.

In the rahitnāmā associated with Chaupa Singh the individual's personal conduct, sexual behaviour, and culinary matters are also important. The first appears to be related to some ethical principles, the second to the ideal of married life, and the third to cleanliness and health. A Sikh of the Guru should earn honestly (*dharam dī kirt*). An honest occupation is a gift from God. A Sikh should work according to this principle so long as he is physically capable of doing so. A Sikh of the Guru should speak sweetly. He should never hurt the feelings of another person. He should not resort to abusive language: sweet words bring honour, harsh language brings discredit. He should not blame others (for his own failures). He should perform good deeds selflessly so that he receives the nectar of life. He should never do things half-heartedly or without dedication. True dedication is always voluntary. A deed done under compulsion has no merit. A Sikh should not steal, gamble, or have illicit sexual relations. They who do such things are crushed like sesame seeds (in the oil press). A Sikh should not indulge in slander. There is a cure for everything else but not for slandering.[15]

A Sikh of the Guru should get married. He should not lust for another's wife, nor have sexual relations with any woman other than his wife. He should not have sexual intercourse with his wife during the first or the last quarter of the night. The middling two quarters are more appropriate for this purpose. Getting up early in the morning, he must bathe with cold or hot water. The preference for marrying a Sikh's daughter to a Sikh is implied in an incident in which a poor Sikh requested Guru Gobind Singh for help in the marriage of his daughter. The Guru asked him to whom he was going to give his daughter in marriage and he replied, 'to a Sikh'. The Guru then told his treasurer, Dharam Chand, to ensure that the marriage was well performed. All the expenses of the wedding were paid from the Guru's treasury.[16] This incident carries the implication that the Sikhs should help a needy Sikh in the performance of his daughter's wedding, and that she should preferably be married to a Sikh.

A Sikh should not eat alone. In the name of the Guru he should invite someone else to share his food. In support of this, the well-known line of Guru Nanak is quoted to the effect that he who works hard and gives something to others out of his earning may recognize the right path.[17] The well-known phrase *band* (*vand*) *khānā* (sharing food) is also mentioned at another place in connection with the instruction that a Sikh who has plenty of food, should not eat alone but share with other Sikhs.[18] A Sikh should not eat food without first making an offering (*bhet*). He should not boast about his charity and distribution of food on a festive occasion in the name of the Guru so that he does not become small and trivial.[19] A Sikh who receives food must know whether or not it is lawfully earned, and whether or not it comes from a right place. A Sikh who receives food from a fellow Sikh should regard it as nectar (*amrit*).[20] A devout Sikh should not eat at an improper place.

In support of this injunction, a familiar verse of Guru Nanak is quoted, which refers to those who perform prayers (*namāz*) and yet eat human flesh, who put on sacred thread and yet wield the knife to slaughter animals.[21] A Sikh of the Guru should wash his hands and feet and rinse his mouth before he enters the kitchen to sit for eating food. He should eat food with due respect and he should not speak. While eating, he should not stand up on the arrival of another person. He should utter Vāhegurū before putting a morsel of food in his mouth. A Sikh of the Guru should eat with restraint, not eating to the full. Such food is nectar, the food of gods. What is eaten more than the need is like poison, comparable to animal feed. Overeating is a source of suffering. A Sikh should not give to another person the leavings of his meal. For preparing food, a Sikh should use firewood and not cattle dung cakes. If there is not enough of firewood, he should use at least one stick.[22]

At the end of the part on rahit there are some statements that relate to honest living, good conduct, truthful and sweet speech, service of others, especially of Sikhs, use of sweet tongue, regard for fellow-Sikhs, service of parents, sharing food with others, thinking good of others, remaining content with daily food, and not using any intoxicant. It is emphasized that no other relationship is preferable to the tie between a Sikh and a Sikh.[23]

According to this rahitnāmā, a Sikh of the Guru should never turn away from Sikhs, and should serve other Sikhs with dedication, with disregard to expense. On meeting a needy Sikh, a Sikh should wash his clothes and hair, and offer food to him. This is pleasing to the Guru. A true Sikh should save one-tenth of his profits to be spent in the name of the Guru and for his Sikhs. A Sikh who holds a good position should remember the Sikhs as well as the Guru. Worldly goods are not trustworthy. A Sikh should offer the first fruit and grain to a Sikh, and eat it only afterwards. It is the duty (dharam) of a local Sikh sangat to receive Sikh visitors with affection and respect and meet their needs. Interestingly, the author, who was himself a Brahman, underlines that the service performed for a Brahman Sikh should be double (*dūnī*) the service performed for another Sikh. The reward of such a service is also double. When a Brahman becomes a Sikh, the prestige of sikhī also increases because the Brahman is the teacher of the world. It is significant to note that the son of a prostitute is to be treated in the same manner as the other Sikhs. His birth does not make him necessarily evil. It is not inevitable that he would do undesirable deeds or oblige others to do so. Any person becoming a Sikh of the Guru becomes pure.[24]

In this rahitnāmā, the essence of learning is par-upkār or working for the good of others. A phrase from the bāṇī of Guru Nanak is appropriately quoted: 'The essence of knowledge is service of others' (Vidyā vichārī tān par-upkārī). A Sikh should never hesitate to perform a good deed in the interest of others. He should regard the mouth of a poor person as the Guru's *golak*. In other words, the merit of giving food to the poor is equal to the merit of making offerings to the Guru.[25]

There is a general injunction that a Sikh should show the right path to a person who has gone astray. A Sikh should cultivate kindness towards all (Sarbat). However, he should avoid misplaced kindness. He should not keep evil company (*kusangat*). He should not take water from a Muslim (*tattā*) to drink. Nor should he drink water from a container made from leather. Furthermore, he should place no trust in the oath of a Musalman, or share a sleeping place with him, or sit and eat with him as he is an enemy of *dharam-karam*, the sacred thread, and the cow. As the Guru says, a mlechh should be killed in a battle. The Sikh of the Guru should have no sexual intercourse with a Muslim woman. It is also undesirable for a Sikh to take the side of a person who does not observe rahit (*kurahatiā*) or who is a non-believer (*dharhiā*); nor should he blame an innocent person. A Sikh should not have any dealings with a stranger before knowing him well. Finally, a Sikh of the Guru should not associate with five categories of people: the Mīṇās, the Ram Raiyās, the Dhir Mallias, the Masands, and the Masandias. All these five were related to the Gurus but they were also their slanderers. These people are like the thorns of a tree that also bears flowers and fruit.[26]

The *Nasīhatnāmā* underscores the importance of good deeds in largely similar terms. A Sikh is expected not to indulge in backbiting, slandering, gambling, or stealing. He is not expected to appropriate anything that does not belong to him. He is expected to be generous and charitable, especially towards the Sikhs who come as guests. He is expected to keep a promise he makes. He should not use snuff (*nasvār*), or eat with his head uncovered, or distribute parsād without covering his head. Above all, he is expected to avoid the naked state in all situations, including during baths and the sexual act. This last injunction is clearly intended to be a curb on sensuality. A Sikh is expected to observe strict fidelity to his wife. He must not visit a prostitute and he should not develop liaison with another woman. A Sikh is instructed not to look with lustful eyes on women present in the sangat.

These injunctions are reinforced when addressed specifically to the Khalsa. A Khalsa should not indulge in slander; he should practise charity; curb sensual pleasures; avoid misdeeds; discard all false sense of honour, that is, pride; flee from a female stranger; not have an eye on things which do not belong to him; never harm a created being because the creator of all beings is offended if anyone of them is harmed; protect the poor; and recite the Name and remain attached to it and the Gurbani. Finally, he should stick to his dharam even at the cost of his life.

Then, there are injunctions in the *Nasīhatnāmā* with a direct bearing on the contemporary political situation. The Khalsa should be in the front to fight; they should kill 'Khans'; destroy the enemy; attack their opponents; ride horses; be ready all the time to fight; bear arms; and kill 'Turks', showing no respect for their authority. Since 'Turks' were the enemy, a Sikh was not expected to take meat from a 'Turk' for eating. Moreover, a Sikh should not touch iron with his feet, because iron had great sanctity in the form of weapons.[27]

Then there are the familiar proscriptions in the *Sākhī Rahit*. The injunction against the use of tobacco is reiterated in very strong terms. To smoke or to snuff tobacco is like eating beef. To look at the daughter or sister of another person with lust is a great sin. A Sikh of the Guru should never steal another's property. He should not slander others. The Guru's word is clear on this point: every disease can be treated for cure but there is no cure for the slanderer.

It is underlined in the *Sākhī Rahit* that nothing is more important than living in accordance with dharam: its essence is to feed the hungry and to clothe the naked; and to serve Sikhs as brothers in faith. Guru Gobind Singh has emphasized that nothing else is as meritorious as feeding a fellow Sikh (Gurbhāī). All increase in one's wealth and merit is due to the service of Gurbhāis. To serve the Gurbhāī is to serve the Guru. To turn away from the Gurbhāī is to turn away from the Guru. This is the Guru's own word and must be accepted as true. He who accepts it attains happiness, and he who does not would be drowned in suffering. This great emphasis on the service of the Gurbhāī is further reinforced in the *Sākhī Rahit*. Sri Krishan ji told his friend Udhe (Udhav) that fasting on *ekādasī* (eleventh day of the bright moon) earns the merit of feeding a lakh of Brahmans; even a lakh of cows given in charity does not equal the merit of fasting. A Sikh of the Guru who feeds his Gurbhāī with love earns four-fold the merit of fasting on ekādasī. This is because a Gurbhāī is like the Guru. He who treats the Gurbhāī in this manner attains liberation.[28]

The rahitnāmā of Bhai Prahilad Singh, though very brief, contains the ethical injunctions that underline the essential concerns of the other rahitnāmās. He who serves the Guru and his Sikhs, and who disregards demons and gods, is a form of Akāl Purkh; the Khalsa is the manifest body of God. The Guru is pleased with the Sikh who cooks food and offers it to another Sikh. A Sikh should not have any dealings with the Mīnās, the Masandias, and those who cut off the hair of their heads, or kill their infant daughters. The whole life is wasted if a Sikh takes food from the hands of the killer of an infant daughter. A Sikh who inhales snuff goes to hell.[29]

In the rahitnāmā of Bhai Daya Singh, the injunctions with regard to the individual Sikh, his relations with fellow Sikhs and with others are found mixed together even in single statements. Not to associate with the Masandias, the Dhir Mallias, the Ram Raiyās, and those who cut off the hair of their heads is given as the first injunction of the rahit, which is followed by the service of Singhs. A Singh should not speak falsehood, nor look at another woman with lust; he should discard anger, pride, attachment, backbiting, unnecessary violence, and untruth. He should do no evil to others, nor should he hurt their feelings; he should speak sweetly. He should earn his living honestly and he should be indifferent to both joy and sorrow. He should share his food with others and do whatever he can for them, for this is the way to please the Guru. He should recognize the divine *hukam* and entertain no pride; with the exterior of the lion he should behave like a cow. He should not sleep or speak too much. He should earn his living honestly and serve the Sikhs; the Guru is the bestower of all gifts. To attain liberation in life, a Sikh should refrain from five things: appropriating another's wealth (*par-dhan*), associating with other women (*par istrī*), slandering others (*par-nindā*), gambling on dice, and drinking liquor.[30]

Using several metaphors for items of the rahit, the author states that a Singh should wear the kachh of calm disposition and right mode. He should not wear a loin cloth or a dhotī, but wear a kachh made from five or two and half yards of cloth. Ears and the nose should not be pierced. A Sikh of the Guru should not put collyrium in the eyes, nor should he inhale snuff. He who bathes in a naked state goes to hell. A Sikh should not sleep naked. He who kills his infant daughter, or gives his daughter to a person who cuts off the hair of his head, or gambles, or drinks liquor, or eats meat from a 'Turk', or goes to a prostitute, goes to hell. A Singh should have nothing to do with a person who associates with a 'Turk'. A Sikh should not curse another Sikh, nor should he bow to anyone other than the Sikhs who have received the gift of the form of the Guru. Such a Singh obtains everything. Most of these injunctions are reiterated with slight variations or difference of emphases in the remaining portion of the rahitnāmā.[31]

In the rahitnāmā of Bhai Desa Singh, the injunction against slander and misappropriation appears as a part of the original core of the rahit enunciated by Guru Gobind Singh. It is followed by the injunction on charity according to one's capacity. A Singh should regard lust, anger, pride, and greed as his enemies. About his occupation, it is generally stated that he should do nothing that involves an infringement of rahit. The three occupations recommended are agriculture, trade, and crafts, but a Singh could take up other occupations according to his inclination. It is interesting to note that the term used for occupation is 'service' (*tehal*). A Singh should pursue his occupation in all earnestness and never think of theft or robbery. He should not go to a prostitute, should not gamble, and should not smoke tobacco. Nor should he use charas, ganja, and tobacco in any form. There was no bar on eating opium if it was no more than a *rattī*, and no bar on using bhang if it was no more than a *māsā*. Taking in a larger quantity, an intoxicant is certainly harmful. The only meat he should eat is mutton, for which a he-goat is to be slaughtered by one stroke (*jhatkā*) of the sword. He should never wear a cap. A Singh should avoid five evils: association with another woman, gambling, untruth, stealing, and liquor. He should never become so engrossed in his family that he forgets the Guru and God. He should never discard humility and never keep evil company; there is no comfort in the company of evil men. If a Singh becomes rich and prosperous, he should regard this as a gift from the Guru. A Singh should never take pride in his position, deeming it to be his own achievement; he should always remain subject to the Guru's teaching. If he uses food cooked by someone else, he should never forget to purify it with his dagger (kard). When he distributes food he should do it evenly, not giving more to one and less to another. He should never become a false witness, or take bribe for giving justice. For eating food, a Singh should wash his hands; he should never eat alone. He should share his food with as many Singhs as possible. When a Singh goes out to meet the call of nature, he should take a full water pot with him; he should put away his weapons while he is sitting to relieve himself.[32]

It is interesting to note that writing in the period of Sikh rule, Bhai Desa Singh recommends that a Singh should inspire members of all the four varnas to become Singhs. Perhaps, the author is thinking of non-Singhs within the fold of Sikhism. In any case, he states that there are many *panth*s in the world; none of them should be slandered because all the panths are God's *dhām* (place, abode); they remember God's name in their own way.[33]

For relations with other Singhs, this rahitnāmā recommends that if a Singh has to take service, he should take service with a Singh as to serve him is as meritorious as serving the Guru. A Singh should love other Singhs and never bear enmity towards them. A Singh should never strike another Singh with a weapon; he should fear the wrath of the Guru-Khalsa. A Singh should shun a person who has taken pahul but does evil things and infringes the rahit. There were many kinds of Khalsa but it was necessary to identify those Singhs who lived in accordance with the rahit. The author is emphatic about the importance of rahit for the Singh. Only he who follows the rahit is a true Sikh of the Guru.[34]

## GURBILĀS LITERATURE

Sainapat emphasizes that a Khalsa should cultivate kindness and righteousness, and discard all greed. The Khalsa of Vāhegurū should not use the hukkā, nor should they cut the hair of the head or beard. A Sikh should never commit evil deeds or be oblivious of God. A Khalsa should not be deceitful. He who discards pride and takes refuge with sants, acquires a pure body. Sainapat refers to penance (tankhā) for an ethical failure. A slanderer of the Sikhs of the Khalsa is bound for hell. Sainapat does not identify the slanderers but he does emphasize that there are five categories of people with whom the Sikhs of the Guru should not associate; they should neither see the face of those who cut off the hair of their heads, nor go to them for mourning or other such occasions. These are the categories of people who have not joined the fold of the Khalsa. Instead of associating with them, a Sikh of the Guru should love the Khalsa sangat.[35]

Koer Singh refers to the injunction against gambling, going to a prostitute, and entertaining greed of any kind. The Khalsa should feed the hungry. Guru Gobind Singh introduced the practice of inter-dining among the Khalsa, irrespective of their background in terms of Shudar, Vaish, Khatri, and Brahman. This carries the implication that the Khalsa were not to observe the formalities of chaukā based on the distinctions of caste. The Khalsa should not have any sexual relations with a Muslim woman, nor should they trust the 'Turks'. They who do not heed this injunction suffer in the end. Before his death Guru Gobind Singh is said to have underlined that the Khalsa should not have any illicit sexual relations, nor should they have any association with a 'Turk'. Guru Gobind Singh recites the hymn of Guru Arjan, in which the liberated Sikh gets rid of lust, anger, greed, and attachment. Koer Singh talks of ethical norms in connection with the rahit proclaimed by the tenth Guru at the time of instituting the Khalsa. Apart from the injunction against association with those who cut their hair and those who killed their infant daughters, the Khalsa were to shun the Mīṇās, the Masands, and the 'Turks'. Above all, the Khalsa should sacrifice their life for the cause of the Guru.[36]

For Kesar Singh Chhibber too Sikh beliefs and right conduct are intertwined. The essence of rahit is not to do an evil deed. A Sikh of the Guru should perform service for the devout Sikhs. Chhibber refers to an incident in which a Sikh preserves his faith and is not tempted by a prostitute, even though he loses the chance to become rich. A Sikh woman should never think of any man other than her husband. A Sikh too should love his wife and never dream of another woman. He should not be engrossed in *māyā*; he should discard *haumai* and attachment. One of the charges against the Masands was that they molested Sikh girls by force or deceit. They also oppressed Sikhs. By implication, the Sikhs of the Guru should not do such things. A Sikh of the Guru had nothing to do with Muslims and should not allow them to enter his home. It is emphasized that he should not go to prostitutes, use tobacco, gamble, or steal, nor have illicit sexual relations.[37]

Chhibber appreciates the Sikh warrior's death on the field of battle; such a martyr goes to heaven. He lays great emphasis on charity. In order to underline the obligation of dasvandh, he suggests that the ideal thing to do is to give one-fourth of one's profits or earnest earnings in charity. In support of this he quotes Granth Sahib to the effect that every gift comes from God. He who gives charity in the name of God receives two-fold to ten-fold of the amount given in charity in his future birth as a human being. A Sikh of the Guru should never be lured by māyā and he should share with other Sikhs whatever he receives through the Guru's grace. A Sikh should be careful about the food he eats. Good food produces good qualities and bad food is injurious to life and intelligence. Going to a prostitute is an evil.[38]

For Chhibber, the relationship between Sikhs is as sacrosanct as the relation with kith and kin. If a Sikh becomes a Raja, a musaddī, a *sāh* (merchant), or a chaudharī, he should help Sikhs in every situation. All defaults of a Sikh are forgiven if he is a functionary in a government and helps Sikhs in the court. A Sikh musaddī should try his best to help Sikhs. Four injunctions of the rahit are obligatory even for such a musaddī: not to smoke, not to observe bhaddan, not to kill an infant daughter, and not to associate with the five reprobate groups—the Masands or Masandias, the Dhir Mallias, the Ram Raiyās, and the Mīṇās. If a Sikh falters in any of these injunctions, he should seek forgiveness of the Sikhs, and they should not hesitate to forgive him. A Sikh should have great regard for a fellow Sikh (Gurbhāī); to deceive a Sikh amounts to turning away from the Guru. A Sikh should love Sikhs and perform service for devout Sikhs.[39]

Chhibber gives explicit support to the varna ideal. Sikhs have a common faith but not caste obligations. He suggests, however, that if a Sikh wishes to enter into matrimonial relation with a devotee of the Guru irrespective of his caste background, he should waste no time, but he should request the sangat for forgiveness afterwards. Chhibber's Brahmanical predilections come to the surface when he suggests that a Brahman Sikh should be honoured more than the others.[40]

Furthermore, Chhibber quotes a verse of Guru Nanak that a Sikh, or even a Hindu, should stick to his dharam, to emphasize that a Sikh should not learn a language of the mlechh, like Arabic, Turkish, or Persian. He should never think of taking the side of 'Turks' in any way. It is stated in Granth Sahib and the Gita that one should stick to one's own dharam even if another's dharam is better. He deviates from his own dharam if he learns the language of the mlechh and appreciates the Qur'ān and the *Kateb* (Semitic books) or he who sides with the 'Turks'. Chhibber goes on to add that a Sikh should discard association with the mlechh and the Chandāl. A Sikh of the Guru who does not discard evil association is bound to see his life wasted. Invoking the authority of Guru Gobind Singh, Chhibber lays great emphasis on destroying the 'Turks'.[41]

Sukha Singh makes only a few statements that have a bearing on ethics, and these too appear in connection with the rahit pronounced at the time of instituting the Khalsa. A Sikh of the Guru should not associate with five categories of people: the Mīṇās, the Masandias, the Dhir Mallias, and the Ram Raiyās; the fifth category is not mentioned because it was believed to be known to everyone. This was a strict injunction of Guru Gobind Singh. It is also said that a Sikh should not associate with the mlechh. Conversely, a Sikh should serve the sants; this was the secret of everlasting rule.

A Sikh of the Guru should bow at the feet of the Khalsa. No one else among gods and human beings had the same status as the Khalsa. Immersed in divine light, they had become superior to gods.[42]

## PERSIAN AND ENGLISH WORKS

Understandably, non-Sikh writers did not empathize with the Khalsa sufficiently to grasp, let alone appreciate, the ethical norms emphasized in Sikh literature. For this reason, what non-Sikh observers notice or find worth mentioning becomes particularly meaningful.

Qazi Nur Muhammad makes the following significant observation on the ethical practices of the Kesdhārī Singhs:

Leaving aside their [mode of] war, hear you of another aspect that distinguishes them among warriors. At no time do they kill one who is not a man (*namard*). Nor would they obstruct the passage of a fugitive. They do not plunder the wealth and ornaments of a woman, be she a well-to-do lady or a maid-servant. There is no adultery among the Sikhs, nor are these people given to thieving. Whether a woman is young or old they tell her, '*Budhiya*, go and occupy a corner'. The word '*Budhiya*' in the Hindi language means 'old woman'. No thief is to be found among these Sikhs, nor is house-breaker [present] among them. They do not approve of adulterers and house-breakers.

In Qazi Nur Muhammad's view, these traits distinguished Sikhs from the other people of Hindustan.[43]

The early European writers too do not say much about Sikh ethics, though their comments have a bearing on what was considered desirable. John Surman and Edward Stephenson point to the steadfast devotion, remarkable patience, and acceptance of God's will with reference to the Sikhs who were being beheaded in Delhi in March 1716 (before Banda Singh was executed).[44] James Browne finds the Khalsa's abstinence from tobacco rather remarkable, especially when its use was common among other Indians. However, they used spirits and bhang to the extent of intoxication.[45] Polier, Francklin, and Malcolm comment on the abstinence of Sikhs from tobacco and their indulgence in intoxicants in terms similar to those of Browne.[46] Polier observes that even when Sikhs plundered and burnt towns and villages (during their incursions across the Jamuna), they seldom killed in cold blood, or made slaves.[47] Malcolm also comments on the value of courage and the belief that martyrdom for the faith was the shortest and the most certain road to honour in this world and eternal happiness in the future. He underlines their spirit of equality as the vital principle of the Khalsa.[48]

It may be relevant to add that giving a brief description of the Sikhs as a community, James Skinner reiterates in his *Tashrīhu'l-Aqwām* that they avoided the smoking-pipe, and they did not eat beef but they ate the meat of wild pig and other animals and birds, and they consumed liquor. The meat of an animal slaughtered in the Muslim manner (halāl) was distasteful and forbidden to them; they ate jhatkā meat, that is, the meat of an animal slaughtered by single stroke of the sword.[49]

## IN RETROSPECT

The most comprehensive statement on the ethical concerns of the Khalsa comes from the two largest rahitnāmās: the *Prem Sumārag* and *The Chaupa Singh Rahit-Nama* which lay down individual, communitarian, and social obligations. There are recommendations on culinary and domestic matters, relations of a Sikh with other Sikhs, and the relations of Sikhs with all others. To take up social responsibility with a deep sense of commitment is the foremost obligation. Not to hurt the feelings of a fellow human being is the basic principle. However, exceptions are made on the bases of religious beliefs and practices, and political concerns. No association with certain socio-religious groups and hostility towards the rulers and their supporters are strongly emphasized. For the rest, the principle of par-upkār, or welfare of others, is all inclusive. On the whole, the emphasis is on honest living, good conduct, truthful and soft speech, and service of others. Use of all intoxicants is prohibited in most works, and those who allow the use of some intoxicants, insist on moderation. No other relationship is preferable to the relationship of the Sikh faith.

The short rahitnāmās do not have much to say directly about ethics but what they actually say becomes important because it is a part of the essential rahit for the authors. Any kind of mis-appropriation, stealing, and gambling are prohibited. Backbiting and slandering are denounced. Sensuality in general and sexual indulgence in particular is to be kept under restraint. Illicit sexual relations are condemned. The essence of dharam is to serve the hungry and the naked. The Khalsa should protect the poor. Great regard, consideration, and concern for fellow Sikhs are empha-sized. At the opposite end are the 'Turks' to whom no respect is to be shown and who are to be killed in the field of battle.

The rahitnāmās of the time of Sikh rule indicate a few new concerns. For example, a Singh should encourage members of all the four varnas to become Singhs: what is new here is not 'four varnas', but the encouragement to be given. Yet, the catholicity built into the Sikh scripture is not lost sight of. All panths, other than the Khalsa, should be seen as adoring God in their own way. Significantly, the two later rahitnāmās generally reiterate what we find in the early rahitnāmās.

Gurbilās literature lays stress on regard for fellow Sikhs. The relationship of faith is as important as the concern for kinship, if not more. The Khalsa should stick to their dharam even at the cost of life. The Khalsa from all the four varnas should eat together. A Khalsa should share his food with others. They should have no friendship or connection with Muslims. They should never come near a Muslim woman, just as they should not go to a prostitute, or have illicit sexual relations with any woman.

Persian and European sources do not say much about the eth-ics of Sikhs. The war ethics of the Khalsa include no attack on a fugitive or a non-combatant, and no molestation of women. They never made slaves. The Khalsa did not use tobacco in any form. However, they are said to have used intoxicants like liquor, opium, and bhang. They avoided halāl, and ate jhatkā meat.

Finally, the ethical norms figuring in Sikh literature are sup-ported often with verses from Guru Granth Sahib, thus bridging the eighteenth century with the earlier period. While reinforcing the essential features of the Sikh way of life, the institution of the Khalsa supplemented and complemented the existing norms. A bearing of the contemporary political situation is also evident in the formulations given by Sikh writers and corroborated occasionally by non-Sikh observers. Together, Sikh and non-Sikh sources of the eighteenth century underscore the conscious creation of a social order with serious ethical concerns.

## NOTES AND REFERENCES

1. For a discussion on Sikh ethics from religious and philosophical perspectives, see Avtar Singh, *Ethics of the Sikhs* (Patiala: Punjabi University, 1996 [1970]); Surinder Singh Kohli, *Sikh Ethics* (New Delhi: Munshiram Manoharlal, 1975); Nripinder Singh, *The Sikh Moral Tradition: Ethical Perceptions of the Sikhs in the Late Nineteenth/ Early Twentieth Century* (Columbia, Missouri: South Asia Publications, 1990). For a critical review of these works see Karamjit K. Malhotra, 'On the Study of Sikh Ethics', *Panjab Journal of Sikh Studies* 1 (2011): 70–81.

2. For the recent understanding on the dates of the rahitnāmās, see 'Introduction' of this book.

3. Randhir Singh, ed., *Prem Sumārag Granth arthāt Khalsai Jīvan Jāch* (*Pātshāhī Dasvīn*) (Jalandhar: New Book Company, 1965 [1953]), pp. 8–11.

4. Randhir Singh, *Prem Sumārag Granth*, pp. 14, 17–18.

5. Randhir Singh, *Prem Sumārag Granth*, pp. 19–20.

6. Randhir Singh, *Prem Sumārag Granth*, pp. 61–3.

7. Randhir Singh, *Prem Sumārag Granth*, pp. 62–5, 69, 76.

8. Randhir Singh, *Prem Sumārag Granth*, p. 67.

9. Randhir Singh, *Prem Sumārag Granth*, pp. 70–2.

10. Randhir Singh, *Prem Sumārag Granth*, pp. 73–4.

11. Randhir Singh, *Prem Sumārag Granth*, pp. 74–6.

12. Randhir Singh, *Prem Sumārag Granth*, p. 12.

13. Randhir Singh, *Prem Sumārag Granth*, pp. 76–8.

14. Randhir Singh, *Prem Sumārag Granth*, pp. 8, 9, 17–18, 19–20. Among other things, and in the contemporary context, association of any kind with a Muslim male or female is strictly forbidden.

15. W.H. McLeod, trans. and ed., *The Chaupa Singh Rahit-Nama* (Dunedin, New Zealand: University of Otago Press, 1987), pp. 57, 59, 62, 64–5, 69, 71–2, 74, 77–8, 103–4.

16. McLeod, *The Chaupa Singh Rahit-Nama*, pp. 58, 60, 63, 64, 66.

17. McLeod, *The Chaupa Singh Rahit-Nama*, p. 57.

18. McLeod, *The Chaupa Singh Rahit-Nama*, p. 65.

19. McLeod, *The Chaupa Singh Rahit-Nama*, p. 63.

20. McLeod, *The Chaupa Singh Rahit-Nama*, pp. 61, 66.

21. McLeod, *The Chaupa Singh Rahit-Nama*, p. 61.

22. McLeod, *The Chaupa Singh Rahit-Nama*, pp. 59, 63, 67, 71, 72.

23. McLeod, *The Chaupa Singh Rahit-Nama*, pp. 77–8.

24. McLeod, *The Chaupa Singh Rahit-Nama*, pp. 60, 62, 66, 68–9, 70–1.

25. McLeod, *The Chaupa Singh Rahit-Nama*, pp. 68, 71–2, 74, 78.

26. McLeod, *The Chaupa Singh Rahit-Nama*, pp. 59, 67, 72, 78.

27. Karamjit K. Malhotra, 'Earliest Manual on the Sikh Way of Life', in *Five Centuries of Sikh Tradition: Ideology, Society, Politics and Culture*, ed. Reeta Grewal and Sheena Pall (New Delhi: Manohar, 2005), pp. 66–71. The three paragraphs on the *Nasīhatnāmā* are based on this discussion.

28. *Sākhī Rahit Pātisāhī 10*, in McLeod, *The Chaupa Singh Rahit-Nama*, pp. 133–5, 137.

29. *Rahitnāmā Bhai Prahilad Singh*, in *Rahitnāme*, ed. Piara Singh Padam (Amritsar: Singh Brothers, 1995), pp. 65–7.

30. *Rahitnāmā Bhai Daya Singh*, in Piara Singh Padam, *Rahitnāme*, p. 69.

31. *Rahitnāmā Bhai Daya Singh*, pp. 70–4.

32. *Rahitnāmā Bhai Desa Singh*, in Piara Singh Padam, *Rahitnāme*, pp. 126–35.

33. *Rahitnāmā Bhai Desa Singh*, p. 131.

34. *Rahitnāmā Bhai Desa Singh*, pp. 129, 130, 132, 133.

35. Sainapat, *Shri Gur Sobhā*, ed. Shamsher Singh Ashok (Amritsar: Shiromani Gurdwara Prabandhak Committee, 1967), pp. 31, 33, 37–41.

36. Koer Singh, *Gurbilās Pātshāhī 10*, ed. Shamsher Singh Ashok (Patiala: Punjabi University, 1968), pp. 129–30, 132, 136, 282–3, 287–8.

37. Kesar Singh Chhibber, *Bansāvalīnāmā Dasān Pātshāhiān Kā*, in *Parkh*, vol. 2, ed. Ratan Singh Jaggi (Chandigarh: Panjab University, 1972), pp. 118, 120, 127, 129, 132–4.

38. Chhibber, *Bansāvalīnāmā*, pp. 118, 151, 165–7, 169, 226.

39. Chhibber, *Bansāvalīnāmā*, pp. 127, 132–3, 160, 197.

40. Chhibber, *Bansāvalīnāmā*, pp. 132, 224.

41. Chhibber, *Bansāvalīnāmā*, pp. 129, 132–4, 228, 230.

42. Bhai Sukha Singh, *Gurbilās Pātsāhī 10*, ed. Gursharan Kaur Jaggi (Patiala: Punjab Languages Department, 1989), p. 174.

43. Qazi Nur Muhammad, *Jangnāma*, in *Sikh History from Persian Sources: Translations of Major Texts*, ed. J.S. Grewal and Irfan Habib (New Delhi: Tulika/Indian History Congress, 2001), p. 209.

44. George Surman and Edward Stephenson, 'Massacre of the Sikhs at Delhi in 1716', in *Early European Accounts of the Sikhs*, ed. Ganda Singh (Calcutta: Indian Studies Past & Present, 1962), p. 50.

45. Major James Browne, *History of Origin and Progress of the Sikhs*, in Ganda Singh, *Early European Accounts of the Sikhs*, p. 18.
46. Colonel A.L.H. Polier, 'An Account of the Sikhs', in Ganda Singh, *Early European Accounts of the Sikhs*, p. 63, and William Francklin, 'The Sikhs and Their Country', in Ganda Singh, *Early European Accounts of the Sikhs*, p. 104. See also John Malcolm, *Sketch of the Sikhs* (New Delhi: Asian Educational Services, 1986 [1812]), pp. 138–9.
47. Polier, 'An Account of the Sikhs', in Ganda Singh, *Early European Accounts of the Sikhs*, p. 61.
48. Malcolm, *Sketch of the Sikhs*, pp. 190, 195–6.
49. James Skinner, *Tashrīḥu'l Aqwām*, in J.S. Grewal and Habib, *Sikh History from Persian Sources*, pp. 218–19.

# 6   The Sikh Social Order
## *Composition, Caste, and Gender*

The Sikh social order was evolving in the changing context of the eighteenth century. Contemporary writers consciously and unconsciously provide information about the composition of the Sikhs: their numbers and distribution, their different segments, and the relative position of the Khalsa among them. Any discussion on the Sikh social order would, however, be incomplete without taking note of the issues of caste and gender.

## COMPOSITION

Contemporary writers do not have much to say about the numbers and distribution of the Sikh population, but it may still be possible to form a general impression from the qualitative and quantitative statements in our sources. The author of the *Dabistān* observes around 1650 that Sikhs became very numerous in the time of Guru Arjan. 'Not many cities remained in the inhabited region, where the Sikhs had not settled in some number.'[1] Bhimsen observes in 1708 that 'no country, city, township and village' was without people having faith in Guru Nanak.[2] Another kind of statement is made by Muhammad Qasim: 'lakh upon lakh' of Sikhs came to Amritsar on the Baisākhī day.[3] On the appearance of Banda in the Punjab, the Sikhs rose reportedly 'in every village'.[4] Muhammad Hadi Kamwar Khan says that Sikhs were 'as numerous as ants and locusts' who converged on Sarhind in a twinkling of the eye after the defeat of Wazir Khan.[5] Writing about the same time Muhammad Shafi 'Warid' says that no village or city was without these people.[6] Nearly a hundred years later, Ghulam Ali Khan states that apart from the army or the Dal, the number of Sikhs in the Punjab reached 'thousands of thousands'.[7] These observations leave the impression that the Sikh population was quite widespread but with a clear concentration in the Punjab region.

Contemporaries also comment on the distribution of Sikhs. In the early eighteenth century, Warid thinks that those Sikhs who gathered around Banda came from all parts of Hindustan, notably from Kabul, Kashmir, and the Dakhin. Late eighteenth century European writers are aware of the Sikh presence in northern India from the Bay of Bengal to the River Indus. However, they regard the region between the Rivers Jamuna and the Indus, where Sikhs had occupied territories as rulers, as the country of the Sikhs. At the turn of the century, George Thomas makes a further distinction between what he calls Haryana and the Punjab. The latter covered the province of Lahore and the chaklah (circle) of Sarhind. Cutting across the provincial boundaries of the erstwhile Mughal Empire, this was the country of the Sikhs for Thomas.[8] For Malcolm, their country included the whole of the Punjab (province of Lahore), a small part of Multan, and most of the region between the Sutlej and the Jamuna. Malcolm is also aware of the subregions. The Sikhs who inhabited the tract between the Sutlej and the Jamuna were called the 'Malwa' Singhs. The Sikhs of the Jalandhar Doāb were known as the 'Doaba' Singhs. The Sikhs of the Bari Doāb were called the 'Majha' Singhs. The Sikhs of the Rachna Doāb, between the Rivers Ravi and the Chenab, were called the 'Dharpī' Singhs. The 'Nakkaī' Singhs resided in lower Bari Doāb in the province of Multan in the upland called Nakka.[9]

On the question of correspondence between territories and numbers, John Malcolm thinks that it is difficult, if not impracticable, to ascertain the number of Sikhs in the territories under their control. Even the number in their armies was difficult to compute. He is prepared to accept the estimate that the Sikhs could raise more than 1,00,000 horse.[10] In 1849, Joseph Davey Cunningham makes a general statement on the numbers and distribution of Sikhs in his *History of the Sikhs*. The particular country of the Sikhs, he observes, could be regarded as lying around Lahore, Amritsar, and Gujrat to the north of the Sutlej, and around Bhatinda (modern Bathinda) and Sunam to its south. In the latter region, called Malwa, the Sikh population was found to be unmixed: 'The priest, the soldier, the mechanic, the shopkeeper, and the ploughman are all equally Sikh.' Cunningham notices that the Sikh population of the Punjab and the adjoining districts had been estimated at 5,00,000 in all, which appears to him to be too small. In his view, even when there were no exact data, the gross Sikh population could probably amount to 'a million and a quarter or a million and a half of souls, men, women and children'.[11]

Nearly two decades after the annexation, the Sikh population of the British Punjab was enumerated at a little less than 11,45,000, constituting 6.5 per cent of the total population of the province. Much of this population was confined to the districts of Lahore, Amritsar, Jullundur (Jalandhar), Ludhiana, and Ferozepur. The Sikh population of these five districts was more than half of the total Sikh population.[12] In 1901, there were 9,43,121 Sikhs in these districts, forming over 60 per cent of the total population of the Sikhs in the British Punjab.[13] It is important to note that the early British administrators of the province counted only the Khalsa Singhs in the first census taken in 1855 and that too in the central districts. Cunningham had estimated the number of Singhs and not of all Sikhs. There is hardly any doubt that the British writers thought of 'Singh' as the predominant identity among Sikhs in the early nineteenth century.[14]

From the very beginning, the Sikh community was composed of persons coming from different background in terms of castes and occupations. Some dissenting groups emerged during the seventeenth century. Interestingly, at its inception, the Khalsa order was viewed by some Sikhs as a kind of divergence. During the course of the eighteenth century, the distinction between the Khalsa and other groups who subscribed to the tenets of Guru Nanak got sharpened. By the end of the century, significantly, the Khalsa emerged as the mainstream in the Sikh social order.

In the *Dabistān* the Sikhs of the Guru are referred to as Nanak-Panthīs. However, the author talks also of the category of Sikhs called *melī* and *sahlang*, who were initiated into the Sikh faith by the

Masands of Guru Arjan. It is also stated that Guru Arjan's brother Pirthia (Prithi Chand) sat in his place (after his martyrdom). Pirthia's followers called him 'Guru Mihrbān', and they called themselves '*bhagats*' or devotees of God. But the followers of Guru Hargobind called them 'Mīṇā', a name that was clearly regarded as derogatory.[15] Thus, in the middle of the seventeenth century, there were three categories of Nanak-Panthīs: the direct followers of Guru Nanak and his successors up to Guru Hargobind, the Sikhs initiated by the Masands, and the followers of Prithi Chand and his successors.

Writing in the 1690s, Sujan Rai Bhandari notices that the Udāsī followers of Baba Nanak were bracketed with sanyāsīs, jogīs, and bairāgīs as ascetics of north India. Bhandari appears to make a distinction between the householder Sikhs and the Udāsī renunciates.[16]

Mughal documents from the first decade of the eighteenth century point to both continuity and change. In an order of Aurangzeb the term used for Sikhs in general is the 'worshippers of Nanak' (*Nanak-Prastān*). In another order, Guru Gobind Singh is included among them. In yet another order, he is called the chief of the worshippers of Nanak (Nanak-Prastān).[17] One and the same words are used here for both the Sikhs and the Khalsa of Guru Gobind Singh. In a news report of August 1707 from the court of Bahadur Shah, Guru Gobind Singh is referred to as 'Nanaki'. In November 1708, he is referred to as 'Nanakpanthī'. According to a report of May 1710, to which a reference has been made earlier, Guru Gobind Singh had dismissed the Masands by one stroke of his pen and established the Khalsa who, in another report, are referred to as 'the Sikhs of the Khalsa'.[18] The Mughal news reports on which these documents are based seem to treat the 'Sikhs' of Guru Nanak and the Khalsa of Guru Gobind Singh as representing two components of the Nanak-Panthīs.

For the Persian chroniclers of the early eighteenth century too, the term 'Nanak-Panthī' generally covered both the Sikh and the Khalsa. Muhammad Qasim Lahauri distinguishes the Khalsa of Guru Gobind Singh from the Sikhs in general.[19] Mirza Muhammad refers to the Sikhs in general as the disciples of the Guru, and to the followers of Guru Gobind Singh as the Khalsa or the Sikhs of the Khalsa.[20] At the same time, he goes on to use the term 'Sikhs' for the supporters of Banda Bahadur.[21] Muhammad Shafi 'Warid' states that the followers of Guru Nanak and his successors were known as 'Sikhs' since the times of Guru Nanak.[22]

Writing in 1759–60, Rai Chaturman Saksena refers to the 'Nanak-Panthīs' as having a way of life and appearance different from that of others. Apparently, he is talking of the Khalsa of the eighteenth century, equating them with 'Nanak-Panthīs'. The ten Gurus from Guru Nanak to Guru Gobind Singh were regarded as eminently authoritative. However, Ajit Singh sat on the spiritual seat in 1711–12 to guide Guru Gobind Singh's disciples, taking permission from the imperial court on the plea that the tenth Guru had recognized him to be his son. The 'guruship' of Ajit Singh lasted for fourteen years and he was succeeded by his son Hathi Singh. In 1759–60, the latter was reportedly living in Mathura with a hundred or two hundred followers. Some 'Nanakshāhīs' are said to have turned away from him. In fact, continues the writer, Sikhs had begun deserting his father when Mata Sundari established a separate spiritual seat in Delhi in the reign of Farrukh Siyar. On her death, the Sikhs were drawn towards Mata Sahib Devi, known as Kuwārā Dolā (virgin bride), who died a year later.[23]

In the 1760s, the Khalsa were clearly emerging as the most prominent segment among Sikhs. We have made a reference to the news reports sent from Delhi to the Nizam of Hyderabad in 1759–65 which refer to the Khalsa Singhs as 'the Sikhs'.[24] Qazi Nur Muhammad refers to 'Sikhs' and 'Singhs' in his *Jangnāma* as the same set of people and looks upon them as different from the Hindus.[25] Tahmas Khan refers to the Khalsa as 'Sikhs', and mentions a sardār of some note who enjoyed the reputation of a spiritual guide among the Sikhs (*murshid-i Sikhān*).[26] Tahmas Khan was not aware that he was talking of a descendant of Dhir Mal at Kartarpur who represented a dissenting group like the descendants of Prithi Chand.

Ghulam Ali Khan, who wrote his account for the British Resident in 1808, talks of two categories of Sikhs: the Khalsa and the Khulāsā. The former were Singhs and the latter non-Singhs. However, he also refers to a disciple of Guru Gobind Singh, named Suthra, whose followers were known as Suthrā-Shāhīs. They insisted on getting a copper coin or a seer of flour or whatever they demanded from every shop and house. The term 'Sikhs' is used for all the categories mentioned by the author.[27] In 1825, James Skinner refers to the followers of Guru Gobind Singh as 'the Sikhs'. He talks of two categories among the Singhs: the Akālīs who followed the code of Guru Gobind Singh very strictly and the other Singhs now simply called Sikhs.[28]

Among the European writers, George Forster says that the Sikh nation was composed of 'two distinct sects' or orders of people: the Khulāsā and the Khalsa. The former was the most ancient and, with little deviation, adhered to the institutions of Guru Nanak and his eight successors. They were occupied in civil and domestic duties. They cut off the hair of their heads and beards, and resembled the ordinary classes of Hindus in their manners and appearance. The Khalsa or the Singhs constituted the 'modern order' founded by Guru Gobind Singh.[29] Significantly, Malcolm looked upon the Khulāsā as a sect of 'non-conformist Sikhs' who believed in the Ādi Granth but did not conform to the institutions of Guru Gobind Singh. The term was interpreted as free or exempt from the usages imposed on the Khalsa or Kesdhārī Singhs who were politically active as mainstream Sikhs.[30] The Khulāsā were generally employed as civil officers to manage the property and revenue concerns of the chief and to conduct negotiations on his behalf; they were not devoted to arms, but educated for peaceful occupations. Mir Mannu's dīvān, Kaurā Mal, was a Sikh of this category.[31] Malcolm seems to have little appreciation for the Khulāsā Sikhs who were full of intrigue, and had all the art of 'the lower classes of Hindus' from whom they were difficult to be distinguished.[32]

Malcolm also talks of three 'religious tribes' among the Singhs: the Akālīs, the Nirmalās, and the Shahids. The Akālīs were staunch Singhs of the days of Guru Gobind Singh. They had the sole direction of the religious ceremonies in Amritsar where they resided as its guardians. They had a bungā on the bank of the sacred tank. They imposed fines on Sikh chiefs and, if they did not pay, the Akālīs did not allow them to go through any of the religious ceremonies in Amritsar. The Akālīs used to convene the 'national council' and conduct its proceedings.[33] The Nirmalās were known for their quiet and peaceable habits. They had a bungā on the sacred tank. Their duty was to read and expound the Ādi Granth. Any Sikh could join their order. Malcolm brackets the Shahids with the Nirmalās.[34] He mentions yet 'another tribe' among the Sikhs, called the Nanak-Putrās (the descendants of Guru Nanak), who did not recognize the institutions of Guru Gobind Singh, but who were revered by his followers. They did not carry arms, and professed to be at peace with all. They enjoyed a general protection and could travel all over the country without molestation even during warfare.[35]

While tracing the history of the Sikhs, Malcolm refers to the 'schismatic sect' of the Bandaīs, or the followers of Banda who believed that he did not die in Delhi, but took refuge in Bhimbar. Banda's two sons propagated his doctrines. The Bandaīs revered the Ādi Granth but not the 'Dasamā Pādshāh kā Granth'. Malcolm thinks that the memory of Banda was not revered by the Khalsa because in their view he tried to change the religious institutions and laws of Guru Gobind Singh—Banda had abandoned the blue dress, refrained from drinking and eating flesh, and replaced the salutation 'Vāhegurūjī kā Khālsā, Vāhegurūjī kī fateh' by 'Fateh Darshan'. Therefore, he was opposed by the Akālīs. The Bandaīs were said to reside in Multan, Thatta, and the other cities on the banks of the Indus.[36]

The evidence of contemporary sources in Persian and English cited above leaves no doubt that the term 'Nanak-Panthī' (or Nanaki or NanakShāhī or Nanak-Prastān) was used for the Sikhs in general. There were sectarian groups among the Sikhs, like the Mīṇās, the Dhir Mallias, and the followers of Ajit Singh, besides other personal gurus claiming descent from the Sikh Gurus and Banda Singh. However, before the end of the eighteenth century, all these appear to have been overshadowed by the Khalsa, and lumped together as a residual category. European writers used the term 'Khulāsā' for this category. The quietist Nirmalās and the fanatical Akālīs among the Kesdhārī Singhs belonged to the Khalsa order.

For intricacies in the composition of the Sikh social order, we have to turn to Sikh sources. First of all, the term 'Khalsa' itself held different meanings over time. Beginning with the seventeenth century, we notice that in a hukamnāmā of Guru Hargobind the sangat of the east is referred to as the Guru's 'Khalsa'. Guru Tegh Bahadur refers to the sangat of Pattan Farid (Pakpattan) in the lower Bari Doāb as the 'Khalsa' of the Guru. A hukamnāmā of Guru Gobind Singh issued before the Baisākhī of 1698 contains the statement, 'the sangat is my Khalsa'. In another hukamnāmā issued on 25 April 1699, the sangat of the village Phaphre is referred to as 'sahlang'.[37] It seems that the term 'Khalsa', which makes its appearance in the hukamnāmā of Guru Hargobind, was meant to make a distinction between the 'sahlang' and the 'Khalsa', the former as the Sikhs initiated by a Masand, and the latter by the Gurus of the main line of successors. We have firm evidence in the hukamnāmās of Guru Gobind Singh that the removal of the Masands was meant to establish a direct link between the Guru and the 'sahlang'.[38]

Furthermore, in Guru Gobind Singh's hukamnāmā of 3 February 1708, the sangat of Benares is called 'the Khalsa of Vāhegurūjī'.[39] In the hukamnāmās issued by Banda Singh, Mata Sundari, and Mata Sahib Devi, the Sikhs are addressed as the 'Khalsa of Akāl Purkh', or 'the Khalsa of Vāhegurū'. In a hukamnāmā of Mata Sundari, dated 20 September 1722, all the Sikhs mentioned are 'Singhs', but in another hukamnāmā of the same date, there is no Singh amongst the fifty persons mentioned by name. Both these hukamnāmās are addressed to the 'Khalsa' of Patna. Evidently, there were two 'Khalsa' sangats in Patna: one consisted of Singhs and the other of non-Singhs. Thus, the Khalsa in the early eighteenth century denoted both Singhs and non-Singhs, linked with the Guru directly.[40]

In the *Tankhānāmā* associated with Bhai Nand Lal, the terms used for the Sikh are Khalsa and Singh. There is enough indication that the author is addressing himself solely to the Khalsa Singhs. A certain degree of preference for them is built into this usage. Even when he does not use the term 'Singh', the author of the *Sākhī Rahit* is rather emphatic in using the term 'Sikh' for the one who had taken khande kī pahul.[41]

The concern of the author of the *Prem Sumārag* similarly is solely with the Khalsa of Srī Akāl Purkh Jī. Another term used for the Khalsa is 'Sant Khalsa', though Gurmukh, Sikh, and Singh are also used interchangeably. The author leaves no doubt that he is talking of one and the same entity. The sangat of the *Prem Sumārag* is Khalsa sangat. The Sikh of the Khalsa of Srī Akāl Purkh is to be addressed as 'Singh jī'.[42] In the *Parchiān Sewādās*, the terms used for the followers of Guru Nanak and his successors are the 'Sikh' and the 'Khalsa'. The term 'Khalsa Panth' is also used. Its members must 'never remain without kes and arms'. There is a good deal of emphasis on the misdemeanour and misconduct of the Masands who had begun to think of themselves as rivals to the authority of the Guru and because of which they were removed.[43] According to the *Vār Bhagautī* of Gurdas (Singh), Guru Gobind Singh transformed the Sikh sangat into 'Khalsa' by administering pahul of the double-edged sword (*khandedhār*). The Singhs, who represented a third social entity (tīsar panth), are the only category of Sikhs recognized and upheld in the *Vār Bhagautī*.[44]

For Sainapat, the Sikhs who refuse to accept the new Khalsa rahit become Khulāsā. The most important category of Sikhs for him consists of the 'Khalsa Singhs'. The *Gur Sobhā* is emphatic that the primary connotation of the Khalsa is the direct link established with the Sikhs by the removal of the Masands. However, Sainapat tends to use the term 'Khalsa Singh' or simply Singh for the Khalsa of his definition. The equation of the Khalsa with the Singh carries the implication that Sainapat is talking of the Khalsa who have been initiated afresh through pahul of the double-edged sword. He also refers to five categories of people (*panj-mel*) with whom the Singhs should not have any connection.[45]

*The Chaupa Singh Rahit-Nama* refers to the Sikhs of the Guru (the Khalsa) as consisting of two distinct components: Kesdhārī and Sahajdhārī, the former initiated through pahul of the double-edged sword, and the latter through charan-pahul. However, belief in the ten Gurus, Guru Granth, and Guru Panth was common to the Kesdhārī Singhs and the Sahajdhārī Sikhs, and nearly the same rahit is prescribed for them. Significantly, the Sahajdhārī Sikhs did not include the followers of the Masands, nor did they include the Mīnās, the Dhir Mallias, and the Ram Raiyās. A degree of preference for a Kesdhārī Singh is indicated by the injunction that he should not distribute parsād in a gathering of the Sahajdhārīs.[46] The connotation of Sahajdhārī in this *rahitnāmā* is very different from the one in the census reports of the late nineteenth century which equate all non-Singhs with Sahajdhārīs.

Turning to the works produced in the second half of the eighteenth century, Koer Singh uses the terms Gurmukh, Sikh, and Gursikh Khalsa. The only other category is that of the excommunicated groups among the Sikhs. In other words, the Sikh Panth and the Khalsa Panth for Koer Singh are synonymous.[47] In his *Bansāvalīnāmā*, Kesar Singh Chhibber refers to four Sikhs accompanying Guru Gobind Singh from Chamkaur Sahib to Machhiwara; two of them were Kesdhārī and the other two Sahajdhārī.[48] Chhibber recognizes the Sahajdhārīs as Sikhs, but he tends to equate the Khalsa with the Singh. In other words, the Sahajdhārīs are Sikhs but the term 'Khalsa' is used for the Kesdhārī Singhs alone.

The growing tendency towards the consolidation of the Khalsa order is reflected in Sarup Das Bhalla's *Mahimā Prakāsh*. The followers of Guru Nanak and his successors were 'Sikhs' or the Sikhs of the Guru. The mediacy of the Masands was abolished to institute the Khalsa, and the entire sangat became the Guru's Khalsa. Guru Gobind Singh introduced khande kī pahul in place of the charan-pahul. The Khalsa kept their kes uncut, adopted the epithet Singh and put on blue clothes. Thus, the Khalsa are equated by Bhalla with Kesdhārī Singhs. Significantly, towards the end of his work, the term 'Sikh' is appropriated for the Khalsa and the rahit of the Khalsa becomes the Sikh rahit.[49]

Among the other important works of this phase, Sukha Singh refers to the followers of Guru Nanak and his successors as Sikhs or Sikhs of the Guru. The term 'sangat' or sādh-sangat is used for local congregations of Sikhs. The new order instituted by Guru Gobind Singh is called 'Panth Khalsa'. Like Sarup Das Bhalla, Sukha Singh thinks primarily of two categories of Sikhs: the pre-Khalsa Sikhs and the Khalsa Singhs. Towards the end of his work the Khalsa Singhs are regarded simply as the 'Sikhs'.[50]

In this context, it is not surprising that Bhai Desa Singh uses the term 'Singh' most frequently in his rahitnāmā. Rather, the terms 'Khalsa' and 'Sikh' are used as synonyms for the term 'Singh'.[51] Bhai Daya Singh also uses the terms Khalsa, Sikh, and Singh for one and the same entity, that is the Kesdhārī Singhs.[52]

We can see in retrospect that the institution of the Khalsa was meant to unify the Sikhs into a single whole. At its inception there were several groups among the Sikhs. First of all, there were the followers of the line of Gurus from Guru Nanak to Guru Gobind Singh, or 'Khalsa', who were distinct from the Sikhs initiated by the Masands, who were called 'sahlangs'. There were also a number of sectarian groups among the Sikhs. However, the only entity addressed, and thereby recognized in the early rahitnāmās, is that of the Khalsa Singhs. Among the other Sikhs, there were the followers of Prithi Chand and his successors, Dhir Mal and his successors, and Ram Rai and his successors. Guru Gobind Singh's decision to remove the mediacy of the Masands appears to have become effective in his lifetime and we do not hear of any Masandias, or the followers of a Masand, during the eighteenth century. But the other groups remained in existence. We get references to their presence in contemporary literature mostly as reprobate groups who were clearly overshadowed by the Khalsa. The Sodhi gurus at Guru Harsahai (the descendants of Prithi Chand) and at Kartarpur (the descendants of Dhir Mal) joined the Khalsa fold sometime in the late eighteenth century, like the Sodhis in Anandpur.[53] They do not appear to have renounced their position as gurus for a decreasing number of their followers. Some of the Bedis also became Singhs,[54] with a separate following of their own, like Sahib Singh Bedi.

Furthermore, the evidence of the hukamnāmās leaves no doubt that the term 'Khalsa' denoted Sikhs who were directly linked with the Gurus, all of whom did not take pahul of the double-edged sword. *The Chaupa Singh Rahit-Nama* talks of the Sahajdhārīs as the Khalsa who did not become Kesdhārī Singhs. The Sahajdhārī Sikhs appear to have shared common doctrines and beliefs with the Singhs, and many of their practices were the same.[55] In the course of the eighteenth century, the Kesdhārī Khalsa became far more important than the Sahajdhārī Khalsa, so much so that the 'Khalsa' and the 'Singh' became synonymous and they came to be equated with 'the Sikhs'. Some peripheral groups also emerged clearly during the eighteenth century, like the renunciate Udāsīs. Non-Sikh writers of the late eighteenth century generally looked upon the Sikhs as consisting of two components: the Khalsa, or the followers of Guru Gobind Singh, and the Khulāsā, or the Sikhs of Guru Nanak. The preponderance of the former by the turn of the century is evident from a telling statement about their relative proportions: 'Out of one thousand, or rather ten thousand persons, one can find only one or two persons who cut their hair.'[56] This is an exaggeration but there is hardly any doubt that the Singhs formed the dominant component by the end of our period, not only numerically but also socially and politically, and in terms of the centrality of their doctrines. With the emergence of the Kesdhārī Singhs as the mainstream, those who believed in personal gurus, or became renunciates, were bound to remain on the periphery of the Sikh social order.

## THE ISSUE OF CASTE

Simply put, caste system denoting occupation, commensality, and marriages based on birth, has been a hallmark of the Hindu social order. The relevance of caste for the Sikh social order, however, has been a problem for scholars. One extreme view is that the ideal of social equality was actually operative in the Sikh social order of the eighteenth century. The other extreme is the assertion that the caste system survived among eighteenth-century Sikhs, though somewhat differently from the Hindu social order. Considering the evidence from contemporaries, both Sikh and non-Sikh, may help to arrive at a more nuanced understanding of the caste issue during the eighteenth century.

Persian sources give some indication of the social background or occupations of the Sikhs. The importance of Jāt Masands is emphasized in the *Dabistān*.[57] Muhammad Hadi Kamwar Khan talks of the 'base and lowly castes', like sweepers, tanners, and *banjārās* who gathered around Banda.[58] Around 1731, Khafi Khan also notes that the followers of Banda came largely from 'the lower castes of Hindus', including the Jāts.[59]

In fact, any Sikh could hold a position of power. Putting it graphically, Muhammad Shafi 'Warid' says that a lowly sweeper or cobbler (Chamār), more impure than whom there was no social group (*qaum*) in Hindustan, could attend on Banda and be appointed to govern his own town. The moment he stepped into the territory, or town, or village, all the gentry and notables went out to receive him and stood before him with folded hands.[60] Continuing, the writer says that after the death of Wazir Khan in 1710, the Singhs were told to take their meals together 'so that the distinction in honour between the lowly and the well born was entirely removed and all achieved mutual unison, acting together'. Indeed, Warid emphasizes that a sweeper sat with a raja of great status, and 'they felt no hostility to each other'.[61]

In the first decade of the nineteenth century, Ghulam Ali Khan notes that the leaders of the Sikhs were mostly from the lower classes, such as yogurt-sellers, confectioners, fodder-vendors, grain-sellers, barbers, and washermen.[62] Writing nearly two decades later, James Skinner observes that any one from any social group (qaum), whether a Brahman or a sweeper could join the Sikh faith, and that the Sikhs allowed no distinction among them in eating and drinking. They did not recognize any difference between one another.[63] The works in Persian, on the whole, emphasize the plebeian background of the Sikhs, their egalitarian ethos, and social mobility.

Early European observers talk of both Hindus and Muslims becoming Sikhs. According to John Griffiths, the Sikhs received proselytes from all castes of Hindus and they admitted Muslims too.[64] Forster observes that Sikhs were not very strict about the injunctions for Muslim converts; they were concerned chiefly with preserving the hair of the head and cremating the dead. In all other articles of faith they were rather indulgent.[65] Evidently, in ethnic and occupational terms, European writers tended to equate the Khalsa with the Jāts. For Polier, the Sikhs, especially Jāts, were generally cultivators of land.[66] Griffiths sees similarities between the Sikhs and the Jāts of Sind and Haryana.[67] Thus, Singhs among the Sikhs, and Jāts among the Singhs appeared to be preponderant.

European writers have a few other observations to make on the relevance of caste for the egalitarian Sikh social order. George Forster thinks that there is no difference between Sikhs and Hindus so far as the patterns of matrimony and commensality are concerned. The only item of food that is shared by all Sikhs is parsād (sacred food).[68] In the *Military Memoirs* of George Thomas, it is noted that Sikhs allow 'foreigners of every description' to join their standard, to sit in their company, and to shave their beards, but they do not consent to intermarriages. The only exceptions in this matter are the Jāt Sikhs who presumably would intermarry with non-Sikh or non-Singh Jāts. Thomas thinks that the Sikhs did not eat or drink from the hands of an alien, except from Brahmans for whom they profess the highest veneration.[69] In all probability, he is not talking of relations of the Sikhs among themselves but with outsiders.

John Malcolm sees a close link between Guru Gobind Singh's political purpose and his attitude towards caste distinctions. Converts are admitted from all 'tribes' and the rules that had so long chained Hindus are broken. The old institutions of Brahmanical order have been subverted. Guru Gobind Singh adopted all the religious usages of Guru Nanak, and declared that all the four castes would be made one. He opened the dazzling prospect of earthly glory to men of the lowest 'tribe'. He rewarded the sweepers with high rank and employment for bringing away the corpse (actually the head) of Guru Tegh Bahadur from Delhi. Several men of this 'tribe' became Sikhs. Known as 'Ran-Rata' (Ranghretā) Singhs, they showed remarkable valour and attained great reputation. Thus, the Brahman who enters the Khalsa order has no higher claims to eminence than the lowest Shudra who swept his house. The honourable title of 'Singh' raised every Sikh to the rank of a Rajput. It was Guru Gobind Singh's object to make all Sikhs equal in civil rights. Malcolm observes, however, that due to the deep-rooted prejudices of the Hindus, some distinct features of the background of Sikhs are still kept up, 'particularly those relating to intermarriage'.[70]

The Sikh converts continue to observe the 'civil usages and customs' of the 'tribes' from which they came but only so long as they did not infringe the tenets of Guru Nanak and the institutions of Guru Gobind Singh. Coming from the higher caste of Hindus, the Brahman and Khatri Sikhs continue to intermarry 'with converts of their own tribes, but not with Hindus of the caste they had abandoned'. This was not true of the Jāt and Gujjar Sikhs who preserve an intimate intercourse with their original 'tribes' for both intermarriage and commensality. As an example, Malcolm refers to the marriage between the Jāt Sikh House of Patiala and the Hindu Jāt

House of Bharatpur. The Muslim converts to the Sikh faith intermarry among themselves. At the time of the meeting of the Sarbat
Khalsa, however, the Jāt Sikhs and others ate together.[71]

The most radical of the early Sikh writers on the issue of caste
is the author of *Prem Sumārag*. The Khalsa order for him is meant
to be casteless. As he puts it, the *baran* (varna) of the entire Khalsa
was pure (*pavittar*). If anyone asks a member of the Khalsa for his
jātī, he should reply, 'I am a Sodhi Khatrī', the caste background of
Guru Gobind Singh. As a single caste order the Khalsa could not
have hierarchy: 'There is no difference amongst the Khalsa of Srī
Akāl Purkh: they all belong to one *baran*.'[72]

In the *varnāshrama* ideal, jātīs were linked with occupations,
and occupations were regarded as hereditary. It is important,
therefore, to note that the author of *Prem Sumārag* imposes only
one restriction, and that too is ethical: the Khalsa of Akāl Purkh
should pursue an honest occupation (dharam dī kirt). There is no
reference to a hereditary calling.[73] The *Prem Sumārag* emphasizes
that as the progeny of Akāl Purkh and sharing the same faith, the
Khalsa should never hesitate to eat with one another. However, if
a Chūhrā, a Chamār, a Sānsī, a Dhānak, or a Kalāl, who actually
distils liquor, wishes to offer food to the Khalsa, he should provide
rations in kind or give cash to a Khalsa of another jātī for the food
to be cooked. But they all belong to Akāl Purkh and follow the
same path; all those who say, 'I am (the Khalsa) of Sri Guru Akāl
Purkh' should be seen as equal. They should all eat together, and
they should never bother about the caste norms of chaukā.[74]

In matters of matrimony, the author of the *Prem Sumārag* is
prepared to compromise a little more. For the marriage of a son,
a Khalsa should have no consideration (of caste or jātī), but in the
case of a daughter, the first preference should be for a Sikh boy of
the same caste. Within the caste, however, no further distinctions
should be made. Furthermore, if a boy from the same caste or jātī
is not found for any reason, a daughter may be married to a young
man of another jātī. No consideration should be given to the jātī
of the girl's mother. Rather, the one who entertains the idea of
the high and the low is punished in the divine court. Eventually,
with the passage of time, all shall belong to one baran. The author
clearly visualizes marriage between boys and girls of different

castes. Even a Sikh boy's marriage with a slave girl or a Muslim girl is envisaged.[75]

Paradoxically, but understandably, the author of the rahitnāmā associated with Chaupa Singh upholds the ideal of equality as well as the varna norms. The Sikhs of the Guru from all the four barans share the same faith and follow the same ethical principles, but each baran has its own social norms and practices. The Khatris, as servants (*sevaks*) of the Brahmans, were not equal to them. In serving others, a Khalsa should give greater consideration to Brahman Sikhs. A Sikh of the Guru should make a distinction between dhān (what is to be eaten) and kudhān (what is not to be eaten), and also between a suitable place (*thāv*) and an unsuitable place (*kuthāv*). He should not infringe the customary practices (*maryādā*). There is great emphasis on honest occupation (dharam dī kirt) for all members of the Khalsa order. There is no suggestion of a hereditary occupation. A Khalsa should disregard the differences of wealth. It is commendable to forge matrimonial ties with a poor Sikh: it pleases the Guru.[76] Differences of background are thus disregarded in matters religious and political, but not in all the traditional practices of commensality and connubium. In other words, for the author of this rahitnāmā, the Khalsa are more equal in religious and political matters than in social matters.

Sikh writers from other caste backgrounds tend to minimize the caste differences. In the *Tankhānāmā*, Guru Gobind Singh says: 'I shall make one baran of all the four barans, and they will all recite (the name of) Vāhegurū.'[77] As a poet at the Guru's court, Sainapat gives no thought to caste or jātī, but he does notice the reluctance of Khatris and Brahmans to accept the new norms of the Khalsa in matters affecting their traditional practices.[78] Among the names and jātīs of the five Sikhs that Koer Singh, a Kalāl, gives of those who offered their heads to Guru Gobind Singh in Anandpur on the Baisākhī day, at least three were Shudras in the traditional social order: a Chhīpa, a Nāī, and a Jhīvar. He goes on to say that people criticize Guru Gobind Singh for abolishing all distinctions between the four castes. The Shudra, the Vaish, the Khatri, and the Brahman eat together at one place. The Rajput Rajas of the hills refused to become members of the Khalsa because their *kula dharam* (family tradition) did not permit them to eat with the lower castes. Guru Gobind Singh then decided to give rulership to the Shudras.[79]

Kesar Singh, a Chhibber Brahman, takes a somewhat middling position. He looks upon the Khalsa as the abode (*ghar*) of Akāl Purkh in which all sins are washed away. Three of the five Sikhs who responded to Guru Gobind Singh's call for sacrifice were Shudras. Though all the four barans had taken refuge in the Panth of the Guru, rulership was given to the Shudras. However, Chhibber invokes the authority of Guru Gobind Singh in favour of the sacred mark and the sacred thread for the higher castes, and for marriage within the caste. But if a Sikh wishes that the conjugal knot should be tied between his son and the daughter of his Sikh sevak, he should not delay the matter; he could seek forgiveness afterwards. On the question of commensality, Chhibber keeps the 'untouchable' Sikhs strictly out. In fact he refers to an incident in which a Mazhabī Sikh, who had posed as a Jāt and shared food with Sandhu zamīndārs, was hanged by Kahan Singh Trehan, and his action is said to have been appreciated by all the Singhs.[80]

At any rate, the works produced in the last quarter of the eighteenth century appear to be less concerned about the caste background of the Khalsa. Sarup Das Bhalla states that the Sikhs coming to Anandpur for darshan of Guru Gobind Singh from different 'countries' belonged to all the four castes. There was a common langar for them all. Guru Gobind Singh adopted the outward appearance of the Khalsa to become one of them. The sacred thread was replaced by the sword belt.[81] In the *Gurū Kīān Sākhīān* there is no general statement about the kind of people who joined the Khalsa but individual cases are mentioned. Bhai Jaita, who brought the head of Guru Tegh Bahadur from Delhi to Anandpur, was an outcaste (Ranghretā); he was declared to be the Guru's son (*Guru kā betā*); he was initiated into the Khalsa order as Jiwan Singh. He became a commandant and died fighting in the battle of Chamkaur. Among the five Sikhs who offered their heads to the Guru, one was a Khatri, another a Chhīpa, the third a Nāī, the fourth a Jāt, and the fifth a Mehra (Jhīvar).[82]

Sukha Singh makes the explicit statement that Guru Gobind Singh transformed men into gods, and created the third Panth, the

Guru Khalsa. The sacred thread was replaced by the sword. Fools began to say that he had initiated men from all the four barans indiscriminately and asked them to eat together; the practice of the earlier Gurus was discarded, and there was no Veda, no pandit, and nothing else of the kind now. The hill rajas reported to the Mughal emperor that Guru Gobind Singh had created the Khalsa to destroy the mlechh and to establish Khalsa rule over all the lands where the sun rose and set.[83]

According to Bhai Daya Singh, pahul of the double-edged sword was meant for all the four barans. A Sikh should marry his daughter to the son of a Sikh. The Bedis, Bhallas, and Sodhis should observe the rahit of the Khalsa and worship in accordance with the Sikh dharam. Dress, or appearance (bhekh), and baran were not dear to the Guru; what was dear to the Guru was the actual conduct in life. A Sikh initiated by pahul of the double-edged sword should not associate with a Brahman, a Sarvariā (a follower of Sakhī Sarvar), or a fakir.[84] According to Bhai Desa Singh, men of all the four barans should be induced to take pahul of the doubled-edged sword. A Sikh should pursue any occupation that did not infringe dharam. Agriculture, trade, and craft were commendable. Any other honest occupation that one liked could be adopted. However, marriage within the caste is recommended.[85]

On the whole, the plebeian background of the Khalsa and the operation of the idea of equality seem to have reflected in the rise of Jāts, Tarkhāns, and Kalāls to political power in the eighteenth century. Significantly, there was no Rajput or Brahman ruler among the Sikhs. There was probably only one rather insignificant Khatri among the early Sikh rulers. There is no doubt that the lower castes were dominant in the order of the Khalsa. In the census of 1881, there were more than 11,25,000 Jāts and more than 1,45,000 Chamārs and Chūhrās, with about the same number of Tarkhāns, Nāis, and Kalāls among the Singhs. On the other hand, Aroras, Khatris, and Banias accounted for less than 80,000 Sikhs. The preponderance of Jāts, followed by the outcastes and the service-performing groups, is evident from these figures.

There is no indication in contemporary literature that any hierarchy of caste, or class was propounded or upheld. On the contrary, the ideal of equality is espoused and recognized by nearly all contemporary writers. In the sphere of religion and politics no distinction on the basis of caste is made by any Sikh writer. The older patterns of matrimony appear to have continued, but largely within the Sikh social order and not in relation to non-Sikhs. In matters of commensality, only the erstwhile untouchables were excluded from inter-dining. This in itself was a radical departure. We do not know the social background of all the Sikh writers, but the known Brahman writers are rather conservative and somewhat reactionary in their social stance, and the known Jāt and Kalāl writers are relatively egalitarian. There was probably an ongoing tension between the new ideology and the social background of the entrants into the Khalsa order.

## THE ISSUE OF GENDER

Several scholars have written on gender relations among eighteenth-century Sikhs, expressing widely divergent views on the relative position of women in the Khalsa order.[86] However, none of them has used the whole of contemporary evidence. We propose to take into account both the normative and the empirical evidence of the eighteenth century for a balanced view on this issue.

The normative evidence comes largely from the rahitnāmās and we may turn to these first of all, starting with the *Prem Sumārag*. The first chapter of this rahitnāmā states that a person who follows the prescribed rahit would attain liberation, whether a man or a woman. Mutual fidelity on the part of married men and women is underlined. The second chapter clarifies that the religious beliefs and practices, ethical life, and initiation of the khande kī pahul prescribed in the first two chapters are meant for both men and women entering the Khalsa order. It is important, therefore, to note that a woman could exercise the option of taking the path of sikhi as enjoined in the institution of the Khalsa. The procedure by which a married woman is to be initiated is laid down. Whereas five Singhs should initiate a Sikh, a woman could be initiated by one devout Sikh (Gurmukh). Like Sikh men, she should acquire Gurmukhi learning, and read shabad-bāṇī. Sikhṇīs should associate with one another to reflect on the shabad. For the gift of true Sikh faith, however, every Sikhṇī should serve her husband and obey him. A widow too could be initiated through the double-edged sword with a slight variation in the procedure.[87]

The most elaborate references to women are in the five chapters that relate to the ceremonies of birth, marriage, death, rulership, and justice. The prenatal ceremonies begin with conception. The woman who has conceived should be administered khande kī pahul and she should keep in sight the unsheathed khaṇḍā, the bow and arrow, and the sword. The procedure detailed for the ceremony on the birth of a son is to be followed on the birth of a girl, with appropriate variations. The baby girl should be given khande kī pahul and the epithet 'Devī' added to her name; karāh parsād should be distributed, and ardās performed in the same manner as for the boy.[88]

The prescriptions regarding marriage (*sanjog*) require that the girl should be married at a suitable age, preferably at the young age in the Kaliyuga. The ninth section of the chapter, however, recommends that the girl and the boy should be married at the age of seventeen when both of them are grown up. The parents of the girl should give their daughter in marriage to a Khalsa Sikh who may be poor but earnest in his occupation. Reference is also made to betrothal and other customary ceremonies and exchange of gifts, but the parents on both sides should not spend more than one-fourth of the cash in their possession. Two important features of the detail are the wearing of arms by the bridegroom when he rides the mare; and the marriage party singing or hearing shabad-bāṇī and the *Ānand*.[89]

In the detail about the actual rite of marriage, customs of both the families are to be followed with an ardās seeking peace and mutual love for the couple. The parents on both sides should regard themselves as equal and none should try to demonstrate superiority in any way. The bride should serve the groom as her lord and should always be faithful to him; the groom in turn should regard her as the other half of his body (*ardh-sarīrī*) and be kind to her; he should share with her whatever he earns; the wife should look towards only her husband and no one else for everything. Not to take anything from the bride's parents has a merit equal to millions of Gurpurabs. In the ardās meant to be performed on the first night of the union, the primary purpose of marriage is stated to be procreation (and not sensual pleasure). When the parents of the bride visit the place of her in-laws, they should eat and drink without any hesitation as it is done between two Khalsa families, implying that the relationship of faith is primary and the social tie (which customarily gives an inferior position to the bride's family) is secondary.[90]

Remarriage of widows (*par-sanjog*) is recommended on the assumption that a woman has far greater sexual urge than a man, and if a man could not live without a woman, how could a woman be expected to live without a man? This, however, is followed by a series of qualifications. But in certain situations, the widow can get married to a good person irrespective of his caste (*jātī* or baran).[91] The basic procedure for widow remarriage is very much similar to that followed in the case of the first marriage. The woman should be administered pahul of the double-edged sword in this case, as in the other.[92]

For the marriage of a slave girl too, the initiation of the double-edged sword is recommended. The procedure is largely similar to the procedure in the case of the widow. The daughter of a Muslim could also be married to a Khalsa Sikh in a similar manner. However, she is to be given pork to eat for fifty-one days before she is married. Initiation of the double-edged sword in her case too is obligatory. Even a Muslim widow could thus be remarried to a Khalsa Sikh. The *Prem Sumārag* is emphatic that the treatment of children born from a remarriage is to be exactly the same as that of the children born from an earlier marriage; an infringement of this injunction made a person liable to excommunication.[93]

The ceremony to be performed on the death of females is similar to that performed on the death of males. Similarly, the ceremony to be performed on the death of a girl is to be almost the same as for the boy. Only slight variations are mentioned for the ceremonies in case of married and unmarried women, and widows. The death of a childless widow too should be followed by kīrtan instead of lamentation.[94]

In the ideal Sikh state visualized in a separate chapter, it is the ruler's duty to ensure that education is imparted to Sikh girls and boys. It is obligatory for every young man and young woman to get married. The ruler should provide assistance to the parents who do not have sufficient means to marry off their daughters. The *pātars* (dancing girls) patronized by the state could tempt jogīs, sanyāsīs, baīrāgīs, Udāsīs, Jain monks, and pīrs, and whoever gets tempted should be obliged by the ruler to adopt the life of a householder.[95]

All men, women, boys, and girls should dress well to join the celebration on the night of the full moon (*pūran-māshī*). They should all sing the praises of Srī Akāl Purkh. If a man indulges in illicit sexual intercourse with a woman, both of them are to be seated on a donkey, with their faces blackened, and then ordered to get married. The quarters of the prostitutes should be clearly demarcated and separated from the rest of the people. Relationship with a prostitute is undesirable, but not so much as adultery. The 'Maharaja' has only one wife. However, if she does not bear any children, he can marry another woman. Intercourse with a slave girl is bad, but it is better than turning to another woman.[96]

The women's right in family earnings and property is spelt out in the chapter on justice. A man is asked to give a certain amount of his income to his wife. If a deceased person has only a daughter who has given birth to a son, the property of the deceased goes to his daughter's son. If the deceased has only a daughter who has no son, the property goes to her. It is clear that the daughter's son and daughter (*dohtrā* and *dohtrī*) are equally entitled to inherit the property of their grandfather in certain circumstances.

The wife's share in the property of her husband is stated to be one-fourth, and if he has two wives, this share is to be divided equally between them. It is explicitly stated that if a daughter is the only legal claimant to the property, it goes to her. If a person has no sons but only daughters and their mother is alive, then his property goes to the wife. When the property is to go to the daughters, the one who is unmarried gets the equivalent of expenditure on marriage, in addition to her equal share in the rest of the property. If one of the daughters is a widow, she gets the double share. No distinction is to be made between a real mother and a stepmother, a real brother and a stepbrother, or a real sister and a stepsister.[97] Evidently, the ideal of equality is important for the author, and he appears to recommend radical modification in the customary practices.

This position is somewhat qualified in the admonitory (tankhā) part of *The Chaupa Singh Rahit-Nama*, which categorically says that a Sikh who administers pahul of the double-edged sword to a Sikh woman is a defaulter (*tankhāiyā*) and liable to penance. A Sikh should not give his daughter in marriage to a person who cuts his hair (*monā*). However, the daughter of a monā could be married to a Sikh boy after she has been administered charan-pahul in which the foot of the *manjī* (lectern) of Guru Granth Sahib has been washed and over which Gurbāṇī has been recited.[98]

The prescriptive part of this rahitnāmā placed earlier extols married life as the ideal for a woman. The wife is expected to be loyal to her husband, and he too should not covet another woman. A Sikhṇī should have proper respect for food (parsād). The authority of Mata Gujri is recognized by the Masands and the Sikhs: they all request her that the succession ceremony (*rāj-tilak*) of the *sāhibzādā* (Guru Gobind Singh) should be performed. The rahitnāmā is emphatic that a Gursikh should never kill his infant daughter. It is commendable for a Sikh or a Sikhṇī to remain detached even in rulership (rāj), looking upon it as the rāj of Vāhegurū.[99] Significantly, the fundamental injunction in this rahitnāmā is common for both men and women: not to miss the opportunity for liberation.

Some injunctions are addressed directly to Sikh women. A Gursikhṇī should go to the dharamsāl twice a day; sitting in the sangat she should keep her head covered to pay homage (to Granth Sahib), and concentrate on shabad-bāṇī of the Guru. She should take something in kind as an offering, like a ball of cotton thread, a sheet, or a small piece of cloth according to her means. She should also save a part of her raw food in the name of the Guru and take it to the dharamsāl, or give it to a needy Sikh. She should offer better food to a needy Sikh than to a member of her own family. Men in the Kaliyuga listen more to women than to their fellow men; the instructions given by the wife are expected to be very effective.[100] Thus, correct religious, social, and domestic practices depended on the Gursikhṇī.

A Sikhṇī should read and understand Granth Sahib. She should not believe in anything except the Guru, her husband, and the satsangat. She should remain faithful to her husband and observe dharam, adopting all the good qualities of a person mentioned in Granth Sahib. She should never associate with a man other than her husband, and she should not sit alone with a woman of ill-repute.[101]

Instructions in the other rahitnāmās are not many nor new. The *Nasīhatnāmā* emphasizes that a Sikh should 'observe strict fidelity to his wife'; he should never go to a prostitute or have sexual relations with other women.[102] The *Sākhī Rahit* exhorts a Sikh to consider a woman older than his age as a mother and a woman of his age as a sister, and to never look with lust on another man's daughter and sister. But he should never trust a woman, nor should he share his thoughts with her.[103] There is a strong injunction in this and several other rahitnāmās to shun those who killed their daughters [104] Among other things, the rahitnāmā of Bhai Desa Singh has the injunction that a Sikh should give his daughter in marriage only to a *pahuliā* (Khalsa Singh). No distinction should be made between men and women when deg (sacred food) is distributed.[105] In the rahitnāmā of Bhai Daya Singh too, the marriage of a Sikh with the daughter of a Sikh is like mingling amrit (nectar) with amrit, but to give the daughter of a Singh in marriage to a non-Singh is like entrusting a goat to a butcher.[106]

Sikh literature in other forms, with its empirical evidence, supplements or complements the picture emerging from the rahitnāmās. Koer Singh's *Gurbilās* alludes to the undesirability of the practice of satī. When the tenth Guru announced that he was going to depart from this world, it was reported to him that Mata Sahib Devi would not be able to live without him (and would like to burn herself on his funeral pyre). Guru Gobind Singh made it absolutely clear that this was forbidden.[107] Women figure in several episodes of Kesar Singh Chhibber's *Bansāvalīnāmā*. He comments on a mismatch in which the wife is unhappy because the husband is much less intelligent than herself. She says, in fact that it is better to be a widow rather than the wife of such an idiot. The women in the Guru's household played an important role in the trying circumstances of the early eighteenth century. Mata Gujri and Mata Jito figure in the developments before the institution of the Khalsa; Mata Sundari and Mata Sahib Devi successively became leaders of Guru Gobind Singh's followers after his death.[108]

Chhibber devotes a separate chapter to Mata Sahib Devi who is said to have succeeded Mata Sundari on her death as the leader of the sangat. Sikhs used to come to her presence from all sides, especially at the time of Baisākhī and Diwali. Thinking of their insecurity in Delhi, Mata Sahib Devi thought of stopping the gatherings of Sikhs on these festivals. 'Bebe Gulabo' is mentioned among the eminent Sikhs who discussed the whole matter with Mata Sahib Devi. The term used for the decision to hold the gatherings on Baisākhī and Diwali in Amritsar is 'Gurmatā'. As pointed out in Chapter 3, Mata Sahib Devi was instrumental in getting appropriate arrangements made for the biannual gatherings and the revival of traditions associated with the Harmandar Sahib. After her death, 'Bebe Gulabo' looked after the establishment (derā) in Delhi for some time.[109]

Another episode given by Chhibber reveals an ordinary woman's steadfastness, grit, and determination. Her husband had been killed by a Sikh sardār under Banda Singh. With her deceased husband's head covered with a piece of cloth, she hurried to the presence of Banda Singh; she placed her husband's head before him and told him how her husband had been killed and that she was forced to remarry his killer. 'I have taken refuge with you for justice', she said, 'I shall hold you responsible in the divine court'. Banda Singh sent his men to bring the faujdār and to confront that woman. He was interrogated and it became clear that the Sikh was a liar. Banda Singh ordered that he should be blown with cannon. Some sardārs took him away for execution. But they allowed him to escape and a wooden effigy was blown by the cannon in her presence. That woman came to Banda Singh again, complaining that she had not received justice. The faujdār who had been kept alive in hiding was called and blown by the cannon.[110]

Sarup Das Bhalla states that Mata Gujri persuaded Guru Gobind Singh to evacuate Anandpur, giving him the assurance that the hill Rajas would honour their oath and would not attack the Sikhs. Another sākhī in the *Mahimā Prakāsh* relates that on his way from Damdama towards the south, Guru Gobind Singh had gone to the house of a devout Jāt Sikh woman who chided him for not taking revenge for the death of his sons (sāhibzādās), adding that 'if anyone kills one of our men we are never at peace until we have taken revenge'. Guru Gobind Singh replied: 'If I shake the sleeve of my garment (āstīn) many sāhibzādās would be produced.' Then he asked the old lady to draw a line on the ground. She did as she was told. The Guru asked her to undo what she had done. She did as she was told. The Guru asked her, 'Did you feel any pain?' She said, 'How could I feel any pain about the lines drawn on the ground?' 'In the same way', said the Guru, 'I feel no pain on account of the sāhibzādās. How can I accept your suggestion?' He added, however, that 'a *bandā* of mine would take revenge'.[111] In his *Gurbilās Pātshāhī 10*, Sukha Singh notices women becoming Sikhs of the Guru, and brackets men and women as the Guru's followers. Guru Tegh Bahadur's mother is referred to as 'Jagg Mata Nanakī'.[112]

In a poem recorded on the opening folio of the *Ānandpur Bīṛ* (recension), compiled in the 1690s at the court of Guru Gobind Singh, a poet named Mangal addresses a short poem to Mata Jito as the overseer of the community to ensure every family's welfare. The poem begins with a prayer that her glory may be like that of the sun and the moon, that her sons, Jujhar and Zorawar, may live long, and that her husband Guru Gobind Singh, 'the ruler of the three worlds', may have eternal life. Mata Jito is called the Jagat Mata who grants wishes of all who come to her. The poet requests for financial support to enable him to perform the marriage of his daughter in Pasrur (near Sialkot). He hopes to return to Anandpur in order to serve Mata Jito without any anxiety on his mind. Apparently, his prayer was granted. The place of Mata Jito's cremation in Anandpur was later marked with a gurdwārā.[113]

Two works composed in Nandeṛ in 1708 yield interesting insights. The *Amarnāma* contains an episode in which the wife receives great consideration from her husband in all decisions on matters important to the family.[114] An episode in the *Parchiān Sewādās* underlines that service of the poor and the needy was undertaken by the Guru's mother who was persuaded that the ideal of service (*sevā*) was meant as much for women as for men.[115]

In this context, and as alluded earlier, it is not surprising that after the death of Guru Gobind Singh, Mata Sundari and Mata Sahib Devi assumed leadership of the Sikh community on their own. The published hukamnāmās of Mata Sundari, nine in all, are addressed to the sangats of Patna and Ghazipur, and to the family (*kabīlā*) of Bhai Rama (son of Phul), from 1717 to 1730. The available nine hukamnāmās of Mata Sahib Devi, from 1726 to

1734, are addressed to the sangats of Patna, Benares, Pattan Shaikh Farid, and Naushehra Pannuan; to Alam Singh Jama'tdar, and to the family of Bhai Rama of Phul. The Sikhs are called 'sons' in both sets of hukamnāmās, and are asked to send the stipulated amount of money through a bill of exchange (hundī) handed over to the authorized messenger. This amount is meant for the open kitchens (langar) in Delhi which were maintained in two separate establishments by Mata Sundari and Mata Sahib Devi.[116]

The authority of Mata Sundari and Mata Sahib Devi was acceptable to the Sikhs equally because of their personalities. A few of their hukamnāmās are interesting in this connection. The hukamnāmā of Mata Sundari, dated 13 September 1726, addressed to some leading Sikhs simply acknowledges the receipt of rupees 21 sent by them. However, the hukamnāmā of Mata Sahib Devi of probably the same year and addressed largely to the same set of people states that they had never sent anything for her, and that they should make no distinction between her and Mata Sundari, both of whom belonged to the same house. All the persons addressed in these hukamnāmās were important individuals, especially Ala Singh, the founder of Patiala state, who had by then established his control over Barnala and a number of villages.[117] They are addressed like other Sikhs as 'the sons' of Mata Sundari or Mata Sahib Devi who appear to exercise their authority essentially on moral grounds.

However, they took interest in the mundane affairs of Sikhs as well. The hukamnāmā of Mata Sundari, dated 18 October 1723 and addressed to five respectable Sikhs by name, asks them to do impartial justice to two contending parties (on behalf of the entire Khalsa of Vāhegurū), and to ensure that their decision was based on moral justice (dharam-niān). It is significant that instead of going to a panchayat or a court, the disputants went to Mata Sundari to seek justice, and she appointed arbitrators on behalf of the Khalsa.[118] In the hukamnāmā of Mata Sahib Devi dated 30 December 1734, there is the order to construct a well in Pattan Shaikh Farid for use of Sikhs. Expenditure on the construction of the well through Bhai Binta is to be debited to Mata Sahib Devi.[119]

There is hardly any doubt, thus, that both Mata Sundari and Mata Sahib Devi maintained regular establishments in Delhi with

the help of Sikhs employed for various purposes, including sec-
retarial work. The institution of langar was maintained as a part
of each establishment. The hukamnāmās indicate that in secular
matters as well the wives of the Guru took initiatives on their own,
and that their authority was recognized by the Sikh sangats within
and outside the Punjab. Incidentally, this evidence also shows that
Mata Sahib Devi had begun to issue hukamnāmās and exercise
authority during the lifetime of Mata Sundari.

This section may be aptly concluded with reference to J.S.
Grewal's recent analysis of the so-called *Mahimā Prakāsh Vārtak*.[120]
He notices three categories of women in this work: non-Sikh
women, Sikh women, and the women of the families of the Gurus.
Analysing each sākhī related to the women of these categories,
Grewal notes that a large space appears to have been created for
women in the Sikh social order. Sikh women figure as respectable
autonomous individuals who could attain to liberation. However,
more space is created for them within the framework of the patriarchal family, which remains the key institution of the Sikh social
order. Significantly, no conflict is postulated between the demands
of the faith and the demands of the family. In short, equilibrium
is sought to be created between the principle of equality and the
inegalitarian social reality.[121]

Persian and early European sources of the eighteenth century
show little interest in the position of women among Sikhs. Non-
Sikh writers were interested, almost exclusively, in the political
activity of the Khalsa. Consequently, they take notice mostly of
men and women directly involved in politics. A few stray references, nevertheless, support the impressions gathered from Sikh
sources. As noticed before, Rai Chaturman refers to Mata Sundari
establishing a separate spiritual seat in Delhi, the Sikhs turning
to her, and after her death, Mata Sahib Devi taking her place.[122]
Resourcefulness of an ordinary Sikh woman is reflected in an
incident recounted by Khafi Khan. This woman's son had been
made captive along with Banda Singh and his companions who
were being executed in Delhi in 1716. She managed to find the
means and a patron to enable her to make a representation to the
emperor and the wazir, contending that her son had actually been
captured by the Sikhs, and since he did not join them voluntarily

he was innocent of any crime against the state. The emperor sent a mace-bearer with the order to secure the release of her son who, however, refused to be freed.[123]

Among the Europeans, the first to take notice of Sikh women or the attitude of Sikh men towards Sikh women is the Irish adventurer George Thomas, who was active in southeastern Punjab around Hansi (in Haryana). He observes that the women attended to their domestic concerns with diligence. However, they were held in little esteem among the Sikhs: they were prohibited from accompanying them in their wars. At the same time, he notes that there were frequent occasions on which Sikh women had taken up arms to defend their habitations from desultory attacks, and conducted themselves throughout the contest with a highly praiseworthy spirit of intrepidity.[124]

At the turn of the century, two British officers leave some impressions about the relative position of ordinary as well as upper-class Sikh women. Travelling through the Sikh territories in 1808, Captain Matthews, an officer of the Bengal Army, observes that both Sikhs and Singhs marry one wife. In the event of her death, they could marry again. But if the husband died, the widow does not remarry, except in the case of Jāts who allow widows to marry a second, or a third husband. Sikh widows rarely become satis in the Punjab, though the practice is common in Jammu.[125] Writing his *Sketch of the Sikhs* about the same time, John Malcolm comments on the conduct of the contemporary Sikhs towards their women, making a few general statements which are likely to be misleading.[126] Malcolm probably has in mind the examples of a few members of the Sikh ruling class in relation to their conduct with prostitutes and professional dancing girls who were mostly Muslim. It may be added that early European writers, including Malcolm, base their observations on limited evidence, quite often relying on hearsay. Moreover, gender relations formed an unimportant aspect of any social order in their time. At best, they remain distant and cursory observers of issues of gender among the Sikhs.[127]

The British, however, became interested in the ground realities immediately before and after annexation. In Chapter 2 we have noted that their summary settlements and land surveys unearthed several landed estates held by the Sikh women, and numerous charitable grants (dharmarth) made by them during the last quarter of the eighteenth century when a large number of autonomous principalities and pockets created by Sikhs had come into existence. The women exercised authority or held estates and landed property generally as the wives, widows, and regents of the emergent rulers and pattidars (cosharers in a joint conquest).[128]

## IN RETROSPECT

The principle of equality was upheld by most Sikh writers of the eighteenth century. For entry into the Khalsa Panth, no distinction was made between Hindus and Muslims, or between a Brahman and a Chandāl, and no distinction was made between one Sikh and another in terms of religious beliefs and practices. The dharamsāl was the place where the Khalsa met as equals and ate together. The background of creed and caste was seen as irrelevant for the religious life of the Khalsa. Even the granthīs, ragīs, and other persons associated with gurdwaras, including the Harmandar Sahib, came from different social backgrounds.

In the public sphere, equal right and equal opportunity was given to Sikh men. The individual Khalsa was duty-bound to carry arms and to fight; he had the right to conquer and rule. However, no democratic institutions were formalized or even visualized for the exercise of political power. The differences of caste were irrelevant but so were the differences of wealth. It is significant, therefore, that 'class' differences within the Khalsa tended to become increasingly important with the establishment of Sikh rule.

In matters of commensality outside the dharamsāl, a distinction appears to have been made only between the erstwhile untouchable jātīs and the rest of the Khalsa. The ideal of chaukā with the notion of impurity was discarded. In matters of matrimony, inter-caste marriages among Sikhs were not unknown in the early eighteenth century, but in the course of the century, and even when the most important criterion was still the Sikh faith, adjustments began to be made with the traditional patterns of marriage within the caste. This trend could be reinforced under Sikh rule. Significantly, the rahitnāmās of this phase hold on to the ideal of equality but do not see its bearing on the patterns of matrimony. Tension between the norm and the praxis appears to be built into this process. There was no caste system but the caste background retained relevance for certain practices.

The most comprehensive statement about the relative position of Sikh women is found in the *Prem Sumārag*, which is closer in time and spirit to the institution of the Khalsa. The religious life was as much open to women as to men, though for initiation a few differences of detail are mentioned. Monogamy and mutual fidelity were the cornerstones of the domestic life of Sikhs. For the ceremonies at birth, marriage, and death also the differences between men and women were of degree and not of kind. Satī was clearly disapproved of, and widow remarriage was allowed in certain situations. Within the general social and patriarchal framework, thus, a large degree of equality was sought to be made operative. The most radical feature figuring in the *Prem Sumārag* is the right of women to hold property in certain situations. *The Chaupa Singh Rahit-Nama* too visualizes a large space for women. When seen in totality, its relatively conservative stance gets considerably mitigated. The remaining rahitnāmās say very little about women and little that is new.

In other Sikh literature men and women are bracketed for religious life, and women of the Guru's household play a considerable role in Sikh affairs. Their role in public affairs is emphasized by the empirical evidence in the Gurbilās literature and the hukamnāmās. Significantly, all women noticed in public life did not belong to the Guru's house. In the second half of the eighteenth century, more women are mentioned as taking part in politics and administration, holding property, and giving charitable grants. Despite their relative indifference to gender relations, non-Sikh sources of the later period point to their initiative and active role both within and outside the family. On the whole, there was an attempt at reduction of inequalities in the life of a Sikh woman in all conceivable situations. Tension between the norm and practice appears to be inherent in the situation in which the inegalitarian patriarchal family was taken for granted.

The institution of the Khalsa proclaimed new political and socio-religious agenda based on the principle of equality. The literature of the early decades of the eighteenth century projected the salient features of a new ideology of change in the Sikh social order. However, it was not easy to bring about revolutionary change, partly because of the way in which equality was conceptualized, but largely because of the intractability of institutionalized inequalities in contemporary society from which the members of the Khalsa got inducted. Nevertheless, the Kesdhārī Singhs emerged as the predominant component of the Sikh social order before the end of the eighteenth century to overshadow all the other components. Included among them were the rulers and members of the ruling class. Thus, a political revolution was accompanied by a radical social change. A lot of space was created for the erstwhile low castes, with a considerable space for women. There is hardly any doubt that the eighteenth-century Sikh social order was more egalitarian than the Indian society of the period, even though the process of state-formation tended to create social stratification among the Kesdhārī Singhs who represented the most egalitarian section. The eighteenth century in Sikh history became important not only for its political revolution but also for its social legacy.

## NOTES AND REFERENCES

1.  'Mobad', *Dabistān-i Mazahib*, in *Sikh History from Persian Sources: Translations of Major Texts*, ed. J.S. Grewal and Irfan Habib (New Delhi: Tulika/Indian History Congress, 2001), pp. 64, 66.
2.  Bhimsen, *Nuskha-i Dilkushā*, in J.S. Grewal and Habib, *Sikh History from Persian Sources*, p. 105.
3.  Muhammad Qasim, '*Ibratnāma*, in J.S. Grewal and Habib, *Sikh History from Persian Sources*, p. 118.
4.  Mirza Muhammad, '*Ibratnāma*, in J.S. Grewal and Habib, *Sikh History from Persian Sources*, p. 133.
5.  Muhammad Hadi Kamwar Khan, *Tazkiratu's Salātīn Chaghatā*, in J.S. Grewal and Habib, *Sikh History from Persian Sources*, p. 143.
6.  Muhammad Shafi, 'Warid', *Mir'at-i Wāridāt*, in J.S. Grewal and Habib, *Sikh History from Persian Sources*, p. 161.
7.  Ghulam 'Ali Khan', '*Imādu's Sa'ādat*', in J.S. Grewal and Habib, *Sikh History from Persian Sources*, p. 215.
8.  'Memoirs of an Irish Maharaja, 1803', in *"Sicques, Tigers or Thieves": Eyewitness Accounts of the Sikhs (1609–1809)*, ed. Amandeep Singh Madra and Parmjit Singh (New York: Palgrave Macmillan, 2004), p. 204.

9. John Malcolm, *Sketch of the Sikhs* (New Delhi: Asian Educational Services, 1986 [1812]), pp. 108–14.

10. Malcolm, *Sketch of the Sikhs*, pp. 142–3.

11. Joseph Davey Cunningham, *History of the Sikhs: From the Origin of the Nation to the Battles of the Sutlej* (New Delhi: Rupa & Co, 2003 [1849]), pp. 10, 343–4.

12. *Report on the Census of the Punjab Taken on 10 January 1868* (Lahore: Indian Public Opinion Press, 1870); General Statement No. III A: 'Return of Population According to Religion', pp. 7, 22–3.

13. *Report on the Census of the Punjab, 1901* (Simla: Government Central Printing Office, 1902), Subsidiary Table 1B., p. 169.

14. Anurupita Kaur, 'Sikhs in the Early Census Reports', in *Five Centuries of Sikh Tradition: Ideology, Society, Politics and Culture*, ed. Reeta Grewal and Sheena Pall (New Delhi: Manohar, 2005), pp. 121–50.

15. 'Mobad', *Dabistān*, pp. 61, 66–8.

16. Sujan Rai Bhandari, *Khulāṣatu't Tawārīkh*, in J.S. Grewal and Habib, *Sikh History from Persian Sources*, pp. 92–3.

    The Udāsīs are generally seen as representing a sect of Sikhism, because they traced their origin to Guru Nanak through his son Sri Chand who is regarded as the real founder of the path of renunciation (*udās*). However, the Udāsī version of Sikhism was in some essential ways different from what the Singhs believed in. The Udāsīs showed no great respect for Granth Sahib, and interpreted its essential message in Vedantic terms, shifting the emphasis from a personal God to an impersonal reality. They did not subscribe to the twin doctrine of Guru Panth and Guru Granth. For some detail, see J.S. Grewal, *The Sikhs of the Punjab* (The New Cambridge History of India, II.3) (Cambridge: Cambridge University Press, 2014 [1990]), p. 117.

17. *Ahkām-i 'Ālamgīrī* (1703–7), in J.S. Grewal and Habib, *Sikh History from Persian Sources*, pp. 97–8.

18. 'News Reports from Bahadur Shah's Court, 1707–10', in J.S. Grewal and Habib, *Sikh History from Persian Sources*, pp. 106–8.

19. Muhammad Qasim, '*Ibratnāma*, p. 114.

20. Mirza Muhammad, '*Ibratnāma*, pp. 132–3.

21. Mirza Muhammad, '*Ibratnāma*, pp. 134–5.

22. Muhammad Shafi, 'Warid', *Mir'āt-i Wāridāt*, p. 161.

23. Rai Chaturman Saksena, *Chahār Gulshan*, in J.S. Grewal and Habib, *Sikh History from Persian Sources*, pp. 164–7.

24. 'News Reports from Delhi, 1759–65', in J.S. Grewal and Habib, *Sikh History from Persian Sources*, pp. 187–203.

25. Qazi Nur Muhammad, *Jangnāma*, in J.S. Grewal and Habib, *Sikh History from Persian Sources*, p. 209.

26. Tahmas Khan, *Qissa-i Ṭahmās-i Miskīn* or *Tahmās Nāma*, in J.S. Grewal and Habib, *Sikh History from Persian Sources*, p. 176.

27. Ghulam Ali Khan, '*Imādu's Sa'ādat*, pp. 213–14.

28. James Skinner, *Tashrīḥu'l Aqwām*, in J.S. Grewal and Habib, *Sikh History from Persian Sources*, pp. 217–19.

29. George Forster, *A Journey from Bengal to England through the Northern Part of India, Kashmire, Afghanistan, and Persia, and into Russia by the Caspian-Sea*, 2 vols (Patiala: Punjab Languages Department, 1970 [1798]), vol. 1, pp. 309–10.

30. Malcolm, *Sketch of the Sikhs*, pp. 91–2 and note.

31. Malcolm, *Sketch of the Sikhs*, pp. 91, 125.

32. Malcolm, *Sketch of the Sikhs*, pp. 132–3.

33. Malcolm, *Sketch of the Sikhs*, pp. 116–20 and 118n.

34. Malcolm, *Sketch of the Sikhs*, pp. 118n, 133–4.

35. Malcolm, *Sketch of the Sikhs*, pp. 91, 134–5 and note.

36. Malcolm, *Sketch of the Sikhs*, pp. 82–4 and note.

37. Ganda Singh, ed., *Hukamnāme: Gurū Sāhibān, Mata Sāhibān, Banda Singh Ate Khalsa Jī De* (Patiala: Punjabi University, 1967), pp. 66–7, 76–7, 152–3, 155. Also, Ajit Singh Baagha, *Banur Had Orders: A Critical Study of an Hitherto Unknown 'Hukamnāmāh' of Guru Gobind Singh* (Delhi: Ranjit Printers and Publishers, 1980), pp. 54–5.

38. Ganda Singh, *Hukamnāme*, pp. 66–7, 152–3, 155.

39. Ganda Singh, *Hukamnāme*, pp. 190–1.

40. Ganda Singh, *Hukamnāme*, pp. 192–7, 200–3, 205, 206–7, 209–11, 214–17.

41. Respectively *Tankhānāmā*, in *Bhai Nand Lal Granthāvalī*, ed. Ganda Singh (Malacca [Malaysia]: Sant Sohan Singh, 1968), pp. 195–9; *Sākhī Rahit Pātisāhī* 10, in *The Chaupa Singh Rahit-Nama*, trans. and ed. W.H. McLeod (Dunedin, New Zealand: University of Otago Press, 1987) [hereafter *Sākhī Rahit Pātisāhī* 10], pp. 133–8.

42. Randhir Singh, ed., *Prem Sumārag Granth arthāt Khalsai Jīvan Jāch (Pātshāhī Dasvīn)* (Jalandhar: New Book Company, 1965 [1953]), pp. 2–5, 8, 10–18, 20–2, 24–6, 32–5, 42–5, 60, 62, 68, 70, 80, 83–4, 86, 92, 104, 149, 150.

43. *Parchiān Sewādās* contains fifty episodes of which thirty-eight relate to Guru Gobind Singh.

44. Gurdas (Singh), *Rāmkalī Vār*, in *Vārān Bhai Gurdas*, ed. Giani Hazara Singh (Amritsar: Khalsa Samachar, 1962 [1911]), pp. 662–7.

45. Sainapat, *Shri Gur Sobhā*, ed. Shamsher Singh Ashok (Amritsar: Shiromani Gurdwara Prabandhak Committee, 1967), pp. 29–41, 43, 47, 51–5, 73–8, 83, 100, 111.

46. McLeod, *The Chaupa Singh Rahit-Nama*, pp. 57, 60, 62, 65, 68, 72, 74–6, 78, 111.

47. Koer Singh *Gurbilās Pātshāhī 10*, ed. Shamsher Singh Ashok (Patiala: Punjabi University, 1968), pp. 17, 114, 127, 129–30, 132.

48. Kesar Singh Chhibber, *Bansāvalīnāmā Dasān Pātshāhiān Kā*, in *Parkh*, vol. 2, ed. Ratan Singh Jaggi (Chandigarh: Panjab University, 1972), p. 152.

49. Sarup Das Bhalla, *Mahimā Prakāsh*, ed. Gobind Singh Lamba and Khazan Singh (Patiala: Punjab Languages Department, 1971), part II, pp. 777–8, 805–6, 810, 825–8, 892–3.

50. Bhai Sukha Singh, *Gurbilās Pātsāhī 10*, ed. Gursharan Kaur Jaggi (Patiala: Punjab Languages Department, 1989), pp. 29, 35–7, 41, 43, 45–7, 49, 57, 67, 71, 94, 118, 126, 130, 145, 153, 171, 177–80, 307, 319, 358, 439, 446.

51. *Rahitnāmā Bhai Desa Singh*, in *Rahitnāme*, ed. Piara Singh Padam (Amritsar: Singh Brothers, 1995), pp. 128–37.

52. *Rahitnāmā Bhai Daya Singh*, in Piara Singh Padam, *Rahitnāme*, pp. 68–75.

53. J.S. Grewal, 'Cleavage in the Panth', in J.S. Grewal, *Sikh Ideology, Polity and Social Order: From Guru Nanak to Maharaja Ranjit Singh* (New Delhi: Manohar, 2007 [1996]), pp. 78–85. In the sources of the late eighteenth and early nineteenth centuries, the Sodhis of Guru Harsahai, Kartarpur, and Anandpur begin to figure as 'Singhs'. See also NAI, Foreign/Political Proceedings, 31 December 1847, No. 2204; 21 February 1851, No. 142 A; 21–8 February 1851, No. 218 A; 16 April 1852, No. 49; 20 November 1857, No. 183.

54. NAI, Foreign/Political Proceedings, 6–13 August 1852, No. 49; 14 January 1853, Nos 213, 216, 219, 220, 223; 15 October 1858, No. 372.

55. McLeod, *The Chaupa Singh Rahit-Nama*, pp. 57–78, 100.

56. Ghulam Ali Khan, '*Imādu's Sa'ādat*, p. 213.

57. 'Mobad', *Dabistān*, p. 66.

58. Kamwar Khan, *Tazkiratu's Salātīn Chaghatā*, p. 143.

59. Khafi Khan, *Muntakhabu'l Lubāb*, in J.S. Grewal and Habib, *Sikh History from Persian Sources*, p. 157.

60. Muhammad Shafi 'Warid', *Mir'āt-i Wāridāt*, p. 162.

61. Muhammad Shafi 'Warid', *Mir'āt-i Wāridāt*, p. 161.

62. Ghulam Ali Khan, '*Imādu's Sa'ādat*, p. 215.

63. Skinner, *Tashrīhū'l Aqwām*, p. 218.

64. John Griffiths, 'A Memorandum on the Panjab and Kandahar', in Ganda Singh, *Early European Accounts of the Sikhs* (Calcutta: Indian Studies, Past & Present, 1962), p. 92.

65. Forster, *A Journey from Bengal to England*, vol. 1, pp. 338–9.

66. Colonel A.L.H. Polier 'An Account of the Sikhs', in Ganda Singh, *Early European Accounts of the Sikhs*, p. 56.

67. Griffiths, 'A Memorandum on the Panjab and Kandahar', in Ganda Singh, *Early European Accounts of the Sikhs*, p. 88.

68. Forster, *A Journey from Bengal to England*, vol. 1, pp. 294–5.

69. 'Memoirs of an Irish Maharaja 1803', in "*Sicques, Tigers, or Thieves*", p. 202.

70. Malcolm, *Sketch of the Sikhs*, pp. 45–6n, 47–8 and note.

71. Malcolm, *Sketch of the Sikhs*, pp. 135–7 and note.

72. For the text see Randhir Singh, *Prem Sumārag Granth*, pp. 44–6.

73. Randhir Singh, *Prem Sumārag Granth*, pp. 73–4. For a reference to the prescribed occupations in this work, see Chapter 5, pp. 173–4.

74. Randhir Singh, *Prem Sumārag Granth*, pp. 45, 61–6.

75. Randhir Singh, *Prem Sumārag Granth*, pp. 43–6, 55–7.

76. McLeod, *The Chaupa Singh Rahit-Nama*, pp. 57, 59–60, 61, 67, 68, 72–4.

77. *Tankhānāmā*, in Ganda Singh, *Bhai Nand Lal Granthāvalī*, pp. 195–9.

78. Sainapat, *Shri Gur Sobhā*, ed. Shamsher Singh Ashok, p. 43.

79. Koer Singh, *Gurbilās Pātshāhī* 10, pp. 129, 131, 133–4, 136–9.

80. Chhibber, *Bansāvalīnāmā*, pp. 111–12, 132, 137–8, 142–3, 144, 147, 187–8, 192, 204, 216, 222, 224, 226.

81. Bhalla, *Mahimā Prakāsh*, part II, pp. 784–6, 825–31.

82. Bhai Svarup Singh Kaushish, *Gurū Kiān Sākhiān*, ed. Piara Singh Padam (Amritsar: Singh Brothers, 1999 [1986]), pp. 84–5, 120–2.

83. Sukha Singh, *Gurbilās Pātsāhī*, pp. 171–85.

84. For the text see *Rahitnāmā Bhai Daya Singh*, pp. 68–74.

85. *Rahitnāmā Bhai Desa Singh*, pp. 128–31.

86. For a brief discussion on the conflicting interpretations, see Karamjit K. Malhotra, 'Issues of Gender among the Sikhs: Eighteenth-Century Literature', *Journal of Punjab Studies* 20, nos 1 and 2 (Spring–Fall 2013): 54–7. The Sikh scholars covered are Teja Singh and Kapur Singh, and the professional historians discussed are J.S. Grewal, W.H. McLeod, Nikky Guninder Kaur Singh, Doris R. Jakobsh, and Purnima Dhavan.

87. Randhir Singh, *Prem Sumārag Granth*, pp. 15–21.

88. Randhir Singh, *Prem Sumārag Granth*, pp. 22–6.

89. Randhir Singh, *Prem Sumārag Granth*, pp. 27–38.

90. Randhir Singh, *Prem Sumārag Granth*, pp. 38–42.

91. Randhir Singh, *Prem Sumārag Granth*, pp. 46–8.

92. Randhir Singh, *Prem Sumārag Granth*, pp. 49–56.

93. Randhir Singh, *Prem Sumārag Granth*, pp. 56–8.

94. Randhir Singh, *Prem Sumārag Granth*, pp. 80–91.

95. Randhir Singh, *Prem Sumārag Granth*, pp. 103, 105–6, 108, 110.

96. Randhir Singh, *Prem Sumārag Granth*, pp. 103, 108–9, 121–2, 123, 142.

97. Randhir Singh, *Prem Sumārag Granth*, pp. 125–31, 133–4.

98. McLeod, *The Chaupa Singh Rahit-Nama*, pp. 59–60, 111. For Sikh rites and ceremonies, refer to Chapter 4.

99. McLeod, *The Chaupa Singh Rahit-Nama*, pp. 59, 60, 66, 69, 81, 102, 103, 104, 114, 115, 123, 127.

100. McLeod, *The Chaupa Singh Rahit-Nama*, pp. 114, 115.

101. McLeod, *The Chaupa Singh Rahit-Nama*, pp. 114–16.

102. For English translation of the text and discussion of the *Nasīhatnāmā*, see Karamjit K. Malhotra, 'Earliest Manual on the Sikh Way of Life', in Grewal and Pall, *Five Centuries of Sikh Tradition*, pp. 69, 74–5.

103. *Sākhī Rahit Pātisāhī 10*, p. 137. See also *Sākhī Rahit Kī*, in Piara Singh Padam, *Rahitnāme*, p. 63.

104. *Rahitnāmā Bhai Prahilad Singh*, pp. 65–6, and notes 105, 106.

105. *Rahitnāmā Bhai Desa Singh*, pp. 128–34.

106. *Rahitnāmā Bhai Daya Singh*, pp. 69, 70, 72–4.

107. Koer Singh, *Gurbilās Pātshāhī 10*, pp. 17–18, 103–26, 133, 153, 272, 286–7.

108. Chhibber, *Bansāvalīnāmā*, pp. 99, 100, 106–7, 113, 124–7, 134, 153, 157–8, 174, 178–86, 191, 235.

109. Chhibber, *Bansāvalīnāmā*, pp. 182–6.

110. Karamjit K. Malhotra, 'Banda Singh in Chhibber's *Bansavalinama*: Image, Idea and Reality', *Panjab Journal of Sikh Studies* 2 (2012): 119–20.

111. Bhalla, *Mahimā Prakāsh*, part II, pp. 801, 818–28, 876–8, 881–2.

112. Sukha Singh, *Gurbilās Pātsāhī 10*, pp. 8–9, 126–57, 208–10.

113. Gurinder Singh Mann, 'Sources for the Study of Guru Gobind Singh's Life and Times', *Journal of Punjab Studies* (Special Issue on Guru Gobind Singh) 15, nos 1 and 2 (Spring–Fall 2008): 246, 257–8.

114. Nath Mal, *Amarnāma*, trans. and ed. Ganda Singh (Amritsar: Sikh History Society, 1953), p. 31.

115. Sewadas, *Episodes from Lives of the Gurus: Parchiān Sewādās*, trans. and ed. Kharak Singh and Gurtej Singh (Chandigarh: Institute of Sikh Studies, 1995), sākhī 33, p. 148.

116. For Mata Sundari, see document nos 68–73, 79, 80; and for Mata Sahib Devi, document nos 74–5, 77–8, 81–5, in Ganda Singh, *Hukamnāme*, pp. 196–231.

117. Ganda Singh, *Hukamnāme*, pp. 209, 292–3. See also Indu Banga 'Alha Singh: The Founder of Patiala State', in *The Panjab Past and*

*Present: Essays in Honour of Dr Ganda Singh*, ed. Harbans Singh and N. Gerald Barrier (Patiala: Punjabi University, 1976), pp. 150–60.

118. Ganda Singh, *Hukamnāme*, pp. 206–7.

119. Ganda Singh, *Hukamnāme*, pp. 230–1.

120. As discussed in 'Introduction', the prose work called the *Mahimā Prakāsh Vārtak* was probably written in 1824, but it was based entirely on the two eighteenth-century texts—*Parchiān* by Sewa Das Udāsī and *Mahimā Prakāsh* by Sarup Das Bhalla.

121. J.S. Grewal, 'Gender Relations in the *Mahimā Prakāsh (Vārtak)*', Forty-Fourth session, *Proceedings Punjab History Conference* (Patiala: Punjabi University, 2013), pp. 124–34.

122. Rai Chaturman Saksena, *Chahār Gulshan*, pp. 166–7.

123. The executioner was ready to strike when the order was handed over to him, but the son emphatically refused to be released. Khafi Khan, *Muntakhabu'l Lubāb*, pp. 158–9.

124. 'Memoirs of an Irish Maharaja, 1803', in *"Sicques, Tigers, or Thieves"*, p. 202.

125. [Captain Matthews], An Officer of the Bengal Army, 'A Tour to Lahore in 1808', in *The Panjab Past and Present* (Patiala: Punjabi University, 1967), vol. 1, part I–II, pp. 112–13.

126. Malcolm, *Sketch of the Sikhs*, pp. 139–40.

127. For a critical analysis of John Malcolm's work, see J.S. Grewal, *Historical Writings on the Sikhs (1784–2011): Western Enterprise and Indian Response* (New Delhi: Manohar, 2012), pp. 40–59.

128. NAI, Foreign/Political Proceedings, 21–8 February 1851, No. 218A; 14 January 1853, Nos 213, 216, 223. See also Indu Banga, *Agrarian System of the Sikhs: Late Eighteenth and Early Nineteenth Century* (New Delhi: Manohar, 1978), pp. 131n58, 135n68.

# Part III
# Cultural Articulation

# 7   The Old and New Literary Forms

We have made ample use of Sikh literature of the eighteenth century as a source of empirical evidence and ideas, values, and attitudes. It needs to be emphasized, however, that literary articulation in itself is a form of cultural expression. The production of a large volume of literature by Sikh writers in their responses to the changing situations is an integral part of the historical process, linking literature with religious, social, and political developments. With its representation of the Sikh past and vision of the future, this literature entered history in terms of its influence on its readers and listeners.

Three main approaches have been adopted by historians in dealing with Sikh literature of the eighteenth century. W.H. McLeod has examined different works for piecemeal evidence on themes of Sikh history. Surjit Hans has analysed each literary work for 'reconstructing' Sikh history. Generally, he makes a few major points on a work, supporting each with a string of quotations. Quite often, the points made reinforce his prior understanding of Sikh history. J.S. Grewal, who was the first historian to introduce the method of analysing each work as a whole, is concerned primarily with what appeared to be important to its author.[1] There is a growing historical sense in this literature, which is just beginning to be studied. It may be added that the historians of Punjabi literature have, by and large, not shown much interest in Sikh literature of the eighteenth century because all the works were not written in Punjabi.

Furthermore, a literary work not only reflects the purposes and interests of the author, but also the major interests of some of his contemporaries. There may even be overlapping of purposes and features in different literary forms. The use of earlier works by later writers indicates their importance. The worldviews of the authors and their attitudes can be seen in relation to the Sikh faith, including sectarian affiliations in some cases, and the pull of their cultural heritage.

It may be recalled that the major forms of Sikh literature of the period identified in the course of this study are the rahitnāmā (a written code of injunctions on the Sikh way of life), the vār (generally regarded as heroic poetry), the *gurbilās* (poetical work in praise of the Guru/s), the *sākhī* (an episode in the life of a Guru), the *ustat* (a eulogistic composition), and the *shahīd bilās* (an appreciative account of a Sikh martyr). While the vār and the sākhī came down from the earlier period, the other forms originated broadly in the eighteenth century. The emergence of new forms of literature is a reflection of historical change, and new needs of the community. Furthermore, some composite *janamsākhī*s depicting the life and message of Guru Nanak also emerged in the period, drawing upon various Janamsākhī traditions, notably the Purātan, Miharbān, and Bālā.

## THE VĀR

The vār as a poetic form was popular in the Punjab before it was adapted by Guru Nanak for his compositions. His example was followed by some of his early successors. There are over a score of vārs in Granth Sahib. Bhai Gurdas popularized this form in the early seventeenth century, and it figures prominently in Punjabi literature of the eighteenth century.[2] It is not surprising, therefore, that we find some Sikh writers of the period making use of the vār for giving expression to their ideas on themes related directly or indirectly to the Sikh tradition. Sung by the dhādīs, the vār could serve as a source of inspiration.

One of the best known vārs in Sikh literature is the *Chandī dī Vār* composed in Punjabi, and attributed generally to Guru Gobind Singh.[3] It consists of fifty-five stanzas (pauṛīs) and one couplet (dohrā). The opening pauṛī starts with '*Pritham bhagautī simarke*', which now forms the opening part of the Sikh ardās. Contrary to the popular impression, the term 'bhagautī' does not refer to Goddess Durga but to God as the Supreme Deity who created the khandā first and then Brahma, Vishnu, and Mahesh for the manifestation of his power; he created the earth and the sky, the mountains, and the seas; he created demons and gods and a constant clash between them; and he created Durga to destroy the demons. She is like Rama who killed the ten-headed (Ravana), and like Krishna who held Kans by the hair and dashed him to the ground. Like Rama and Krishna, Durga derives her power from God, takes the side of God's devotees, and uses physical force with great effect. These are the traits which Guru Gobind Singh appreciates. The *Chandī dī Vār* is a heroic composition in which the power of Durga, and not her beauty, comes to the fore. It could inspire warriors to fight for the right cause, that is, the welfare of the pious.[4]

Another well-known composition, to which we have made a reference in the Introduction, is the *Vār Bhagautī* of Gurdas (Singh). Written in praise of Guru Gobind Singh and the Khalsa, it embodies a triumphant spirit, which makes it a celebration of both spiritual liberation and political freedom. The date of composition of its first fourteen pauṛīs is placed around 1700, and these have a remarkable consonance with the literature of Guru Gobind Singh's period. As noticed before, its last six pauṛīs appear to have been added by another poet towards the end of the eighteenth century. Together, the two parts talk of the Singhs and their great prowess as warriors. Their religious life is as important as their political activity. In fact, these spiritual and temporal activities present two sides of the same coin.[5]

As argued by Ganda Singh, the work known as the *Amarnāma* was completed by Dhadi Nath Mal in Nander within a few days of Guru Gobind Singh's death in October 1708. The *Amarnāma* is a kind of vār composed in Persian, though rather inelegantly, to be sung in the presence of Guru Gobind Singh. This work celebrates a few incidents of the life of the tenth Guru in Nander, and propagates the Sikh beliefs and the Khalsa rahit to the exclusion of Brahmanical practices. It is emphasized that Sikhs should attend

the assemblage of *dhādhī*s (dhādī darbar) where vārs are sung. Just
as Guru Nanak always kept Mardana with him, the Singhs should
keep dhādīs with them at all times.[6]

The *Vār Amritsar Kī*, composed by Darshan Bhagat in 1709, is
a heroic composition about a battle fought in Ramdaspur by the
Singhs against the representatives of the Mughal government soon
after the Baisākhī of 1699. It depicts the bravery of the Singhs in
the face of the strength of their opponents. The House of Nanak,
the Chak of the Guru, and the sacred tank known as *amritsar* are
praised by the poet. This vār aims at inspiring the Khalsa to fight
for the protection of their sacred space.[7] It may be added that this
event appears later in the *Bansāvalīnāmā* of Kesar Singh Chhibber
and the *Shahīd Bilās* of Sewa Singh. However, the spirit in which
Darshan Bhagat presents the event with the Khalsa as the hero is
absent in the later works.

## THE SĀKHĪ

The episodic narrative form used for the janamsākhīs remained
important in Sikh literature of the eighteenth century also. Apart
from the *B40 Janamsākhī* and the *Giān Ratnāvalī*, which are better
known, we have referred to the *Parchīan Pātshāhī Dasvīn Kīan* and
the *Gurū Kīan Sākhīan*, all of which are in prose. The *Mahimā
Prakāsh* of Sarup Das Bhalla, which is in verse, also uses the sākhī
form for the lives of the ten Gurus and Banda Singh.

As noted earlier, the *Parchīan Pātshāhī Dasvin Kian* was completed in October 1708 by Sewa Das Udāsī who prepared this
'parchī' (lit. document) in praise of the Guru (*Gur-ustat*). At the
end, it is again referred to as 'parchī' of Guru Gobind Singh.
Out of its fifty sākhīs, thirty-eight relate to Guru Gobind Singh.
Only four sākhīs relate to Guru Tegh Bahadur, and one sākhī
each to the first eight Gurus. The names of the ten Gurus are
given at the outset, followed by thirteen *sloka*s in their praise.
While underlining the importance of this work for its evidence
on Sikh doctrines and values, its editors point out that Sewa
Das could not altogether discard his Brahmanical values and
notions, and at places, he even appears to project his own Udāsī
cult rather than Gurmat.[8] A close reading of the text suggests,

however, that the Udāsī concerns are far stronger in this work than what is suggested by the learned editors. It is doubtful, therefore, that the primary purpose of Sewa Das was to write in praise of the Gurus. Sewa Das had a sort of hidden agenda. The import of his sākhīs generally is to project the Udāsī position with approval.

The *B40* (due to the number given to its manuscript in the British Library) is one of the dated Janamsākhīs completed in 1733. Its sākhīs are selected from different Janamsākhī traditions, besides the oral tradition current in the early eighteenth century. Despite a broad chronological order, each sākhī constitutes a separate unit. The compilation fails to present a unified and coherent image of Guru Nanak in terms of his doctrines and ethics, and his attitude towards the contemporary systems of religious beliefs and practices. As a corollary probably of its composite character, this Janamsākhī does not appear to project any conscious concern very strongly. Guru Nanak, on the whole, remains somewhat close to the image that emerges from his own compositions, but two features go against the spirit of his bāṇī: practise of austerities and performance of miracles. At the same time, remarkable importance is given to the sangat and the shabad, which suggests that the patron of this Janamsākhī did not belong to any sectarian group.[9]

Another composite janamsākhī, the *Giān Ratnāvalī*, has been a subject of considerable debate about its character, authorship, and date, as noted in the Introduction. Its editor, Jasbir Singh Sabar, argues that Bhai Mani Singh gave an exposition of the first vār of Bhai Gurdas, adding information received at the court of Guru Gobind Singh. A disciple of Bhai Mani Singh, Giani Surat Singh gave it a literary form with additions from the earlier Janamsākhīs, including the *B40*, presented in his own way. This makes the *Giān Ratnāvalī* a new and a non-sectarian work. In other words, Sabar does not agree with McLeod about the influence of the Bālā tradition or with Hans about the Udāsī influence over the *Giān Ratnāvalī*. The primary concern of the author is to use his understanding of traditional learning, the Gurbāṇī, and philosophic knowledge for projecting the new ideals and ethical principles of Guru Nanak. The work was meant to inspire the reader to strive to know the truth for himself and attain liberation. This, the author tries to recapture and convey the essential message of the Guru.[10] One may not agree with Sabar that the *Giān Ratnāvalī* depicts the religious and social environment of Guru Nanak, but there is hardly any doubt about the distinctive position of Guru Nanak in the larger context of the Indian and Islamic traditions.

The *Gurū Kiān Sākhiān* by Kaushish has no introductory statement,[11] and its editor, Piara Singh Padam, suggests that the extant work may be incomplete; possibly, the original was meant to cover all the ten Gurus. At any rate, out of its 112 sākhīs on the period of the last five Gurus, four relate to Guru Hargobind. Of the eight sākhīs for Guru Har Rai, six relate actually to Ram Rai. Three sākhīs relate to Guru Har Krishan, and four sākhīs relate to Dhirmal and his successors. The number of sākhīs on Guru Tegh Bahadur is fifteen, and there are seventy-six sākhīs on Guru Gobind Singh alone. The relations of the Gurus with Dhirmal and Ram Rai as well as with the descendants of Prithi Chand, called Mīṇās, are presented as cordial. The dissident groups nevertheless stand excommunicated in this account and the author does not see the contradiction. Furthermore, the *Gurū Kiān Sākhiān* is generally thought to be based on Bhatt Vahīs. As pointed out by Padam, all the dates given in Bhatt Vahīs are not necessarily correct because all entries were not based on personal observation or made contemporaneously. A close study of this work shows that its author used other sources too, both literary and oral. He seems to have seen a number of the places he mentions in the text. In any case, the *Gurū Kiān Sākhiān* is remarkable for its empirical content in terms of dates, persons, and places. Even though each sākhī is an independent unit, there is a considerable degree of coherence in the sākhīs selected for inclusion. Miracles are not ruled out, but the frequency with which reading of Granth Sahib, kīrtan, ardās, and distribution of kaṛāh parsād are mentioned is remarkable. We have already noted that five kakārs are mentioned, though keskī takes the place of kes. Quite explicitly and emphatically, '*Gurtā*' (Guruship) is passed on to 'Sri Granth Sahib' before the death of Guru Gobind Singh.

## THE GURBILĀS

Unlike the sākhī, which by definition is episodic, the gurbilās narrates events in the life of Guru Gobind Singh in a broad chronological sequence. Though composed in praise of the tenth Guru, the accounts of his life before and after the institution of the Khalsa are essentially historical in character. As the first work of this genre, Sainapat's *Gur Sobhā* was inspired by the *Bachittar Nātak*. Covering the same ground briefly in the third person, Sainapat's work became a model for the narratives produced in the second half of the eighteenth century. Koer Singh and the later writers, however, bring in the Goddess in their descriptions of the institution of the Khalsa, which require a separate notice (see Appendix).

It may be in order to begin with the narrative in verse in autobiographical form, entitled *Sarab Kāl Kī Benatī*, which was completed around 1698, to head the compositions included in the *Bachittar Nātak Granth*. Generally known as the *Bachittar Nātak*, it is now included in the *Dasam Granth*. The *Bachittar Nātak* projects the dispensation of Guru Nanak as the only dispensation meant for the Kaliyuga, and Guru Gobind Singh as his true successor and God's instrument for destroying the enemies of this dispensation. The events of Guru Gobind Singh's life from his birth to the mid-1690s underline that he was under the protection of the Supreme Being who ensured his success in battles against his opponents. The supporters of Guru Gobind Singh, therefore, remained safe and those who left his side came to grief. The *Bachittar Nātak* becomes in a sense an open declaration of, and justification for, Guru Gobind Singh's mission on the eve of instituting the Khalsa.[12]

Begun in 1701 and completed soon after the death of Guru Gobind Singh in October 1708, the *Gur Sobhā* may be regarded as an extension of the *Bachittar Nātak*. As a narrative (*kathā*) of the events (sākhīs) of Guru Gobind Singh's life, the *Gur Sobhā* was written explicitly in his praise (*sobhā, upmā*) to highlight his wondrous deeds (*chalittar, kautak*). The Guru's mission was to protect the sants and to destroy their enemies, for which he created the pure (*nirmal*) Panth of the Khalsa to be ever ascendant in the world. The chronological order in which the events are presented is indicated by mentioning the number of days, months, or years between two events. The major events, both before and after the institution of the Khalsa, are the battles which depict the valour and martial prowess of Guru Gobind Singh and his warriors. However, the core event of his life is the creation of the Khalsa, which transforms the Sikh sangat into the Khalsa Panth as the source of liberation. The Khalsa are as much the subject of the *Gur Sobhā* as Guru Gobind Singh himself. As mentioned earlier, the Khalsa become his heirs as the Guru, like Granth Sahib. Their ultimate triumph as a sovereign entity is said to be built into their creation with divine sanction. The *Gur Sobhā* was meant to inspire the reader and the listener with firm faith in the Khalsa as the instrument of universal redemption.[13]

Koer Singh's *Gurbilās Pātshāhī* 10 covers the same ground as the *Gur Sobhā*. Indeed, 'gurbilās' bears the same connotation as 'gursobhā'. Apart from literary sources like the *Bachittar Nātak* and the *Gur Sobhā*, Koer Singh used the oral evidence provided by Bhai Mani Singh who was an eyewitness to many events in the life of Guru Gobind Singh. However, a few of the dates given for events are incorrect. The episode of the Goddess is given in a separate chapter. Guru Gobind Singh is projected not so much as a religious leader but as a hero fighting against the 'Turks' in a struggle for freedom. The martyrdom of Guru Tegh Bahadur is seen as the means of taking over rulership from the 'Turks' who are explicitly stated in the *Gurbilās* to be the 'enemy'. Their destruction is necessary for establishing 'Khalsa Rāj' in Delhi. The Guru remains present among the Khalsa to ensure their ultimate triumph. By hearing the kathā of the *Gurbilās* all one's desires could be fulfilled, including the attainment of Rāj. Written probably in 1751, Koer Singh's *Gurbilās* could inspire people to support the Khalsa in their ongoing struggle for sovereign power.[14]

Sukha Singh's *Gurbilās Pātshāhī* 10 follows the pattern of Koer Singh and remains rather close to it in many ways. Three chapters are devoted to the episode of the Goddess. Like Koer Singh, he places the episode after the battle of Nadaun and before the institution of the Khalsa. Writing at a time when Sikh rule was firmly established, Sukha Singh does not talk of the struggle for political power, a theme that was all important for Koer Singh. Sukha Singh's *Gurbilās* is composed in love (*prem*) and loving devotion (*bhagtī-bhāo*). He who reads it and listens to it has all his hopes fulfilled. It is a work of piety meant to generate piety. Three places are specifically sanctified by Guru Gobind Singh: Patna, where he was born; Anandpur, where he administered pahul of the double-edged sword to the five Sikhs; and Nander, where he assumed his eternal form.[15]

The *Bansāvalīnāmā* of Kesar Singh Chhibber and the *Mahimā Prakāsh* of Sarup Das Bhalla, which cover all the ten Gurus, reflect the increasing concern of Sikhs in the eighteenth century with the ten personal Gurus as a single entity before their office passes on to the Ādi Granth and the entire Khalsa. Their interest is not confined to the ten Gurus. Chhibber's work has fourteen chapters, one each on the ten Gurus, and one each on 'Banda Sahib', Ajit Singh, Mata Sahib Devi, and contemporary Sikhs. In his own way, Chhibber covers the whole of Sikh history from the time of Guru Nanak to his own. Though he underlines that Guruship was vested in the Ādi Granth, he advocates that the Granth of Guru Gobind Singh may also be regarded as the Guru, and he even talks of the guruship of Banda Sahib, Ajit Singh, and Mata Sahib Devi.[16]

Sarup Das Bhalla's work consists of sākhīs of all the ten Gurus, with the maximum number for Guru Nanak, followed by Guru Gobind Singh. A few sākhīs related to Guru Gobind Singh are in prose. There is one sākhī on Banda Singh. Unlike Chhibber who admires Banda Singh for taking revenge on the Muslim oppressors of the Guru and his Sikhs, Bhalla has little appreciation for Banda because he is believed to have turned away from the Guru.[17] However, both Chhibber and Bhalla introduce the Goddess. Whereas Kesar Singh tends to Brahmanize the Sikh tradition in his presentation of the Gurus, Sarup Das tends to maximize the role of the Bhallas in the affairs of the Sikh Panth and to minimize the tensions amongst the descendants of the Gurus. Both the writers are aware of the establishment of Sikh rule and both try to highlight the close association of their ancestors with the Gurus. Kesar Singh's ancestors had served the Gurus as dīvāns, and Sarup Das was actually a descendant of Guru Amar Das. Both appear to write for seeking patronage through their works which, consequently, appear to lack any kind of unity or cohesion.

## THE RAHITNĀMĀ

The word rahit occurs in the compositions of Guru Nanak for a way of life that accords well with one's professed beliefs and values. His successors too were seriously concerned with the actual conduct of life in accordance with their ethical values. Certain statements about rahit are also attributed to them. As noticed earlier, the formal works on rahit, now known as rahitnāmās, made their appearance in the time of Guru Gobind Singh. After a phase of scholarly scepticism, the serious scholars of the Sikh tradition are now inclined to place a number of rahitnāmās in the time of Guru Gobind Singh, highlighting the close link between the institution of the Khalsa and the production of rahitnāmās.

It may be recalled that the *Prashan-uttar* of Bhai Nand Lal is now placed in 1695, while the rahitnāmā of Prahilad Singh is placed before the institution of the Khalsa. The preface and rahit parts of the rahitnāmā associated with Chaupa Singh is accepted as composed in 1700, though the two narratives and the 'tankhā' part were appended to this rahitnāmā in the 1740s, with the entire work attributed to Chaupa Singh Chhibber. The *Prem Sumārag*, the most comprehensive rahitnāmā, was composed at the time of Guru Gobind Singh, like the short rahitnāmās known as the *Tankhānāmā* and the *Sākhī Rahit*, both associated with Bhai Nand Lal. Thus, the largest rahitnāmā, the four short rahitnāmās, and a substantial part of the second-largest one can be placed in the years from 1695 to 1708. Only two works in the genre are placed in the period of Sikh rule—the rahitnāmās of Bhai Desa Singh and Bhai Daya Singh.[18] These works are important not simply because of their contents, but also because they enable us to compare the concerns of the writers of these two phases, separated by time and a major change in the historical situation. The large, common ground between them, therefore, becomes very important.

The earliest rahitnāmā, *Prashan-uttar*, is also the shortest. It opens with a statement of Guru Gobind Singh on how a Sikh of the Guru should observe his daily worship, individually and in congregation. On a request from Bhai Nand Lal, Guru Gobind Singh explains that there are three forms of the Guru: one is beyond attributes and, therefore, can never be known; another is the Granth Jī, the visible body of the Guru; and the third is the Sikh who is nurtured on Gurbāṇī and lives in accordance with its principles to attain liberation. Thus, the Guru is nirguṇ, Guru-Shabad, and sarguṇ (sagun). The foremost obligation of the Sikh is service (sevā). We can see that the *Prashan-uttar* is concerned with the basic beliefs, the daily worship, and the ideal of service.[19]

The rahitnāmā of Bhai Prahilad Singh has only seventy-six lines but it is rich in content. It lays emphasis on the exclusive worship of Akāl Purkh, and on the Guru and Gurbāṇī, especially the *Japu*, the *Jāp*, and the *Rahirās*. Only he who follows the Guru's injunctions about the Sikh way of life is a true Sikh. A Sikh should never hesitate to send offerings on account of kār, bhet, sukh, and mannat. Sanctity of the kes is embodied in the injunction that a Sikh shall never eat his food without a turban on his head. He should regard the Khalsa as the Guru, the body manifest of the Guru, and the Granth as the Guru. The Khalsa Panth was created in accordance with the order of Akāl Purkh. A Sikh should serve the other Sikhs. There is nothing like the service of Sikhs, who are the image of God. All the dealings of the Sikh should be with the Khalsa. A Sikh should not worship idols, or visit sepulchres and tombs. He should not follow any of the six systems of philosophy. He should not trust a jogī or a 'Turk'. He should not bow to a person wearing a cap, nor should he himself wear a cap. He should not wear a sacred thread. A Sikh should have no dealings with the Mīṇās, the Masandias, the *monās*, and the killers of infant daughters; he should not even eat with these reprobate groups.[20] In relation to the debate about the date of this rahitnāmā, it may be added that there is nothing in its content that goes against the assumption that it was composed in the early phase.

In the *Sākhī Rahit*, the terms Khalsa and Sikh are used for the same entity but there is clear indication that the author is thinking of the Kesdhārī Singhs. To use the razor and to cut the beard is as heinous as incest. A Khalsa stands distinguished in a crowd of Hindus and Musalmans due to his kes and flowing beard. This rahitnāmā is remarkable for its emphatic rejection of all Brahmanical rites and rituals. The recitation of the *Ānand* and the performance of ardās are the common substitutes for all rites and ceremonies. There is great emphasis on strictly Sikh beliefs and there is strong injunction against having anything to do with the representatives and institutions of the contemporary systems of religious beliefs and practices. The service of the hungry and the naked is highly commendable. Fellow Sikhs are raised to the status of the Guru in terms of the importance given to them.[21]

The *Tankhānāmā*, also called *Nasīhatnāmā* in its earliest known copy, opens with a question by Bhai Nand Lal: what was and what was not commendable for a Sikh? The response of Guru Gobind Singh is much longer now, with much detail. The daily individual and congregational worship in the sangat brings in the distribution of kaṟāh parsād, and how it is to be prepared to ensure grace. It also dwells on how a Sikh should conduct himself in relation to the men and women in the sangat. Other injunctions relate to dress, food and intoxicants, dasvandh, golak, and bhet, and the attitude towards women in general and towards prostitutes in particular. The rahitnāmā is addressed to the Sikh and the Khalsa as one entity. Not to injure human beings (*khalk*) is the basic principle for all. However, the Khalsa has to fight every day, to ride the horse, and to attack the mlechh. Guru Gobind Singh says that he would establish his own rule (rāj) and conquer all quarters of the world. Significantly, the rahitnāmā ends with the well-known couplet of the Sikh anthem on 'rāj karegā khālsā'. It is obligatory for the Khalsa to bear arms, to fight, to conquer, and to establish their rāj.[22]

The *Prem Sumārag* stands distinguished from the other rahitnāmās by its large size and the wide scope of its contents. It has been remarked by J.S. Grewal that this work is so comprehensive in scope that it is little short of an exposition of a whole social order. It sets out in detail what a Sant Khalsa is expected to do in the religious, social, and political spheres of his life. A number of important questions are answered by the author about the personal religious beliefs and practices of a member of the ideal community, his moral duties as an individual, his obligations towards the other members of the Sikh community, his attitude towards the non-Khalsa and the non-Sikh groups as well as the issues of caste and gender in the Sikh social order. The author of the *Prem Sumārag* is remarkably egalitarian in his outlook, particularly in matters religious, and partly also in social and political matters. But there are some basic limitations with regard to equality in its very conception. In the ideal Sikh state, for example, political power is held by an individual, the maharaja, like the bādshāh. Nevertheless, even the maharaja has to appear before the court of justice on receiving summons, and he is to be judged impartially, on the merit of the case. Similarly, the Khalsa Panth, though ideally a casteless society, has its own social stratification. There is also a deliberate, though temporary, compromise between the ideal Sikh norms and the actual practice in matters of matrimony and commensality.[23] On the whole, the *Prem Sumārag* remains a precious document on Sikh religious, social, and political thought in the early decades of the eighteenth century.

In the Preface of the rahitnāmā associated with Chaupa Singh, the mukte (redeemed) Gurmukhs, who give instruction to the Sikhs visiting Anandpur, insist on rejection of the traditional patterns of matrimony and the ceremony of marriage. This is brought to the notice of Guru Gobind Singh who orders that a manual of rahit should be prepared in accordance with the teaching of Granth Sahib. A manual is prepared in six days. The Guru listens to a part of it and approves of it. The rahit part in the present text ends with the statement that this rahit has been prepared for the Sikhs by the Guru's order and with the consent of the Sikhs. In addition to this rahit, the Sikhs could adopt 'Gurmat-rahit', that is, the rahit in accordance with Granth Sahib, in consultation with one another. There are 154 injunctions in the rahit, which make it rather comprehensive in scope. Regarded as the Guru, Granth Sahib is quoted at many places. A lot of importance is given to the dharamsāl and its maintenance. The Khalsa consist of both Kesdhārī Singhs and the Sahajdhārī Sikhs. The sanctity of kes and respect for the sword are emphasized. The attitudes of a Sikh towards other Sikhs and that of the latter towards non-Sikhs figure prominently in the rahit. The five excommunicated groups are mentioned. The injunctions never to be infringed by any Sikh are against female infanticide, tonsure, and the use of tobacco. However, the Brahman Sikh is to be given preferential treatment. The ideal of varnāshrama is upheld for inter-dining and intermarriage. On this point, and as pointed out earlier, this rahitnāmā embodies a far more conservative view than what we find in the other rahitnāmās.[24]

In the 'tankhā' part placed at the later date, it is recorded that Guru Gobind Singh declared in his lifetime that 'the sarbat sangat is my Khalsa, and the Khalsa is the Guru'. It is emphasized that to bear arms, to fight, and to establish their rule (rāj) are the duties of the Khalsa. The last injunction in this part reiterates Guru Gobind Singh's declaration: 'I am present in the Sarbat; regard the Sarbat Sikh sangat as the Guru.' There are over 280 injunctions on acts of infringement (kurahit) which make Sikh men and Sikh women liable to penance. Many of these injunctions are common with those of the rahit part but others mention new situations introducing greater detail. Some preference is shown for the Kesdhārī Singh over the Sahajdhārī Sikh. Langar along with karāh parsād figures prominently in the 'tankhā' part. Respect for shahīdganj is enjoined. Specific injunctions for Sikh women are followed by the statement that the Guru's instruction is meant for both men and women.[25]

The narrative part of this rahitnāmā makes Chaupa Singh the narrator and, therefore, the author of the rahitnāmā. It narrates, at some length, the opposition to the Gurus from the very beginning, both internal and external. The episode of the Goddess is introduced for instituting the Khalsa. The concept of four categories of Sikhs (dīdārī, mukte, murīd, and mayikī) is brought in to create room for sin in the time of Sikh rule. Guru Gobind Singh's Savvayyās in praise of the Sikhs are presented as verses in praise of Brahmans who are regarded as superior to the Khatris. The role of Dharam Chand as the dīvān of Guru Gobind Singh is highlighted. Towards the end, Chaupa Singh is made the writer of the original document on the basis of which Gurbakhsh Singh Chhibber, son of Dharam Chand, prepares the present 'chiththā of rahitnāmā'.[26] Thus, the narrative serves two additional purposes: appropriation of the rahitnāmā by the Chhibber Brahmans, and reconciliation of Brahmanical elements to the Khalsa tradition.

At the outset, Bhai Desa Singh states how he was told by Guru Gobind Singh in a dream to write the rahitnāmā in a situation that could only be in the time of Sikh rule.[27] His rahitnāmā contains Guru Gobind Singh's response to Bhai Nand Lal's question about rahit. Much of the rahitnāmā reiterates the injunctions we find in the earlier rahitnāmās. The importance of the Khalsa rahit, dharamsāl, langar, and karāh parsād is underlined. Brahmanical rites and ceremonies are rejected. In the detailed rahit that follows, we may notice a few significant statements which reflect the changed circumstances of the last three decades of the eighteenth century. The phrase 'earnest livelihood' refers to actual manual work. A Singh should protect the cow and the Brahman. He should visit holy places like Anandpur, Amritsar, Patna, and Abchalnagar. He should serve the Khalsa who represent the Guru's form, but never a 'Turk'. A Sikh ruler should patronize Sikhs and help them; he should employ Singhs in his service. A Singh should look upon the Khalsa as the Guru and have proper respect. He should encourage men of all the four vārāns to become Singhs, and even hold out temptation, if necessary. Wealth and power are gifts from the Guru; a Singh, therefore, should never feel proud. He should never take bribe to do justice and he should never give false witness. He should confine matrimonial ties to the Sikhs of his own vārān. He should commit selected portions of 'the bānī of both the Granths' to memory. Finally, he should not love his family more than the Guru.[28]

The rahitnāmā associated with Bhai Daya Singh refers to Daya Singh's request to Guru Gobind Singh for stating a 'rahitnāmā' (not rahit) so that by listening to it one may attain liberation. The response given by the Guru is the rahitnāmā itself. When the Goddess appeared, all the gods came to contribute one thing or the other for the institution of the Khalsa.[29] All this may suggest infiltration of Brahmanical elements in the period of Sikh rule but the goddesses and the gods are subservient to Akāl Purkh. In fact, there is hardly anything else in the rahitnāmā to indicate Brahmanical influence. Most of the injunctions come from the earlier rahitnāmās. There is greater emphasis on some of the familiar injunctions. For example, Guru Gobind Singh says that, 'whosoever from amongst the four vārāns takes amrit represents my form (*sarūp*)'. In his eyes, his own faith is like the (mythical) Sumer Mountain and that of another, like a grain of mustard.

'Where there is the Granth, there is the door to liberation.' 'The body of the Guru-Khalsa is the manifest form of God.' 'Regard the Granth and the Panth as the Guru.' One cannot become pure without bathing in Amritsar; one cannot attain sikhi without having darshan of Kesgaṛh (in Anandpur). By bathing in Muktsar one attains liberation. A Sikh should celebrate Baisākhī and Diwali in Amritsar, Hola in Anandpur, and go to Abchalnagar (Nandeṛ) for the liberation of his whole family.[30]

## NEW LITERARY FORMS OF THE LATE EIGHTEENTH CENTURY

The eminent Sikhs of the Gurus came to be seen as the embodiment of Sikh principles and values. The work known as *Sikhān dī Bhagatmālā* is an elaborate version of the eleventh vār of Bhai Gurdas in which he gives the names of the eminent Sikhs of Guru Nanak and his five successors. The *Bhagatmālā* mentions 21 Sikhs of Guru Nanak, 15 Sikhs of Guru Angad, 11 Sikhs of Guru Amar Das, 20 Sikhs of Guru Ram Das, 209 Sikhs of Guru Arjan, and 37 Sikhs of Guru Hargobind. They are located in the former Mughal province of Lahore and at many other places outside that province, like Sarhind, Thanesar, Delhi, Agra, Lucknow, Benares, Patna, and Burhanpur, and in the provinces of Gujarat and Kashmir. The sangats of Dalla, Sabharwal, and Sultanpur are collectively mentioned.[31] Towards the end of this work there are several sākhīs on Guru Gobind Singh. All the sākhīs are used to project mostly the Sikh values through the lives of the eminent Sikhs of the ten Gurus.

Sikh martyrs were reverentially remembered for laying down their lives selflessly for their faith and the Sikh Panth. Bhai Mani Singh is the subject of the *Shahīd Bilās* of Sewa Singh, the younger brother of Bhai Svarup Singh Kaushish, the author of the *Gurū Kiān Sākhīan*. They were descendants of Bhatt Bhikha whose Savvayyas are included in Granth Sahib. Based on a number of sources, including Bhatt Vahīs, the *Shahīd Bilās* was written in Bhattakharī in the early years of the nineteenth century and transliterated into Gurmukhi later by Bhatt Chhajju Singh of Bhadson. According to the author, before acquiring importance as a Sikh of

Guru Gobind Singh, Bhai Mani Singh, who was born in 1644, was associated with Guru Tegh Bahadur. For a long time Bhai Mani Singh looked after the affairs of the Khalsa as a custodian of the Harmandar and the Akāl Bungā. He used to preach the Sikh doctrine and propagate the Khalsa rahit. The political struggle of the Singhs against the Mughals revolved around Ramdaspur where Bhai Mani Singh was the kingpin. He died as a martyr in Lahore in 1734 when Zakariya Khan, the Mughal governor, tried to suppress the Singhs as a threat to his power. Bhai Mani Singh is projected as a staunch Sikh who died as an embodiment of the Sikh faith. A number of other eminent Singhs also became martyrs with him.[32]

The emergence of ustat of the sacred place as a genre synchronizes with the beginning of the reconstruction and embellishment of amritsar under Sikh rule. Independent works on the subject of the sacred tank began to appear in the last quarter of the eighteenth century. Kavi Kankan in his *Das Gur Kathā*, which was written in praise of the ten Gurus, refers to Ramdaspur as superior to 'Indarpurī', 'Shivpurī' and (the golden) 'Lankā'; he praises the *amrit sarovar* as a unique tīrath in the world.[33] Kavi Sant Das in his *Amritsar Sarovar Ustat* brings in mythology to exalt amritsar above all other sacred places during the Kaliyuga. Known by different names, it was believed to be a supreme tīrath in the earlier cosmic ages too. The desecration of amritsar by Ahmad Shah Abdali induces the poet to remark that whoever shows disrespect to this place incurs the curse of all the gods. Granth (installed in the Harmandar) is the essence of all the four Vedas, eight Shāstras, and eighteen Puranas.[34]

Towards the end of the eighteenth century, Kavi Saundha wrote *Ustat Sri Amritsar Jī Kī* to pay his homage to this sacred place. There is no pool like amritsar in the three worlds; the Harmandar in its midst is like the house of Ram; it is studded with priceless pearls, gems, and diamonds. The Khalsa obtained ruler-ship by bathing in amritsar. Whosoever bathes here finds all his wishes fulfilled. The people of Rūm, Shām, Arabia, and Ājam would bow before it and none would remain obdurate in the east or the west, in the north, or the south.[35] With the centrality of Amritsar under Sikh rule, thus emerges a new literary form in praise of this supreme centre of Sikh pilgrimage.

## THE CHARACTER OF EIGHTEENTH-CENTURY
## SIKH LITERATURE

Despite the differences of detail, and some contradictory statements, the works in all the literary forms collectively reveal serious concern with the ten Gurus, especially Guru Nanak and Guru
Gobind Singh. The Khalsa and the rahit of the Khalsa are almost
equally important. The Sikh sacred space known as amritsar
emerges as the most sanctified centre. Next in importance are the
Sikh martyrs and eminent Sikhs of the earlier Gurus. Much of
this literature was produced to influence and inform Sikh beliefs
and attitudes and to inspire the Sikhs with the underlying ideology. Even when the bulk of this literature was quasi-religious in
character and purpose, it is possible to discern a growing historical
consciousness in different literary forms.

The expanding scope of literature becomes also an expanding
scope of interest in Sikh history. For evidence of a historical sense,
we may turn first to the Janamsākhīs, which are not biographies of
Guru Nanak but they do tend to place the happenings of his life in
a broad sequence suggestive of the passage of time though not of
strict chronology. The gurbilās form shares a greater sense of the
events in a chronological order. In fact, Anne Murphy has recently
argued that the author of *Gur Sobhā* shows a keen sense of history
not only in relation to the life of Guru Gobind Singh but also to the
evolution of the Khalsa.[36] When we come to the *Bansāvalīnāmā* we
find that the ten Gurus are presented in the order of their succession, covering a span of about 200 years. The accounts of Banda,
Mata Sundari, and Mata Sahib Devi are added to extend the period
to the 1730s, and then the author goes on to talk of the contemporary Sikhs. In its own way the *Bansāvalīnāmā* tends to become
a work of history. A sense of an evolving situation is evident in
other literary forms too. In the vār form the scope is extended from
God, to a goddess, to the Guru, and then to the Khalsa. In the
sākhī form too there is extension of scope from Guru Nanak to all
the ten Gurus, Sikh martyrs, and eminent Sikhs. A new subject
for praise is Sri Amritsar, the town as well as the Darbār Sāhib
and the Akāl Bungā. The writers of the eighteenth century take
notice of the expanding activities of the Guru and their followers.

The dominant concern is with the present and writers delve in the past and entertain a vision of the future. This comes into sharp focus in Ratan Singh Bhangu's *Sri Gur Panth Prakāsh*, which evinces a keen sense of history. Written in the early years of the nineteenth century, the entire work is professedly meant to answer one question: 'How did the Sikhs become sovereign?' In Bhangu's treatment, thus, the whole Sikh movement is moving towards the present and pointing to the future.

## NOTES AND REFERENCES

1.  For a detailed analysis of the works of W.H. McLeod, Surjit Hans, and J.S. Grewal, see Karamjit K. Malhotra, 'Expanding Scope of Sikh Studies on the Eighteenth Century', *Panjab Journal of Sikh Studies* 3 (2013): 52–61. Sekhon and Duggal take notice of only four eighteenth-century works of Sikh literature: the *Giān Ratnāvalī*, *Bhagat Ratnāvalī* or *Bhagatmālā*, the *Prem Sumārag* and the *Parchiān*, which showed a strong influence of Braj Bhāshā. According to them, this 'trend in the writings of the Sikhs that had set in probably from the time of Guru Gobind Singh himself' militated against the writing of Punjabi is visible in the poetry of the period. See Sant Singh Sekhon and Kartar Singh Duggal, *A History of Punjabi Literature* (New Delhi: Sahitya Akademi, 1992), pp. 98–100.

2.  Sekhon and Duggal point out that ballads or vārs were next to the stories of love as significant works of medieval Punjabi poetry. They refer to the popularity of the vārs of Dulla Bhatti and Jaimal Fatta. The vār of Nadir Shah relates to his invasion of India in the first half of the eighteenth century. The vār of Hakikat Rai pertains to the time of Zakariya Khan. The *Chaththiyān-dī-Vār* describes the battles between the Chaththā Sardārs and Mahan Singh Sukarchakia. The tradition continued into the early nineteenth century. Sekhon and Duggal, *A History of Punjabi Literature*, pp. 91–7.

3.  It is generally held that the *Chandī dī Vār* is one of the three versions of the myth of Durga included in the *Dasam Granth*. The other two versions are in Braj. For a discussion, see Appendix.

4.  Kala Singh Bedi, ed., *Vār Sri Bhagautī Jī Kī (Chandī dī Vār)* (New Delhi: Punjab Book Store, 1965), pp. 662–76.

5.  Gurdas (Singh), *Rāmkalī Vār*, in *Vārān Bhai Gurdas*, ed. Giani Hazara Singh (Amritsar: Khalsa Samachar, 1962 [1911]), pp. 662–76.

6.  Nath Mal, *Amarnāma*, trans. and ed. Ganda Singh (Amritsar: Sikh History Society, 1953). The internal evidence of this work suggests

that Nath Mal always accompanied Guru Gobind Singh who gave the 'amarnāmā' as a reward. The term carries the same significance as 'hukamnāmā'. Sikhs are told to patronize the dhādī after the Guru's death. It is not surprising that this composition was carefully preserved by the descendants of Nath Mal for eight generations covering more than two centuries. His last known descendant, Bhai Fatta, handed it over to a patron before leaving for Pakistan in 1947.

For the early dhādī tradition in the Punjab and among Sikhs, see Michael Nijhawan, *Dhadi Darbar: Religion, Violence and the Performance of Sikh History* (New Delhi: Oxford University Press, 2006), pp. 27–36, 39–40, 47–64.

7. Darshan Bhagat, *Vār Amritsar Kī*, in *Punjābī Vārān*, ed. Piara Singh Padam (Amritsar: Singh Brothers, 2008), pp. 226–33.

8. Sewadas, *Episodes from Lives of the Gurus: Parchiān Sewādās*, trans. and ed. Kharak Singh and Gurtej Singh (Chandigarh: Institute of Sikh Studies, 1995), pp. 1–8, 162. At the beginning of the text published by Kharak Singh and Gurtej Singh, the word used is *Parchī* and not *Parchiān*. At the end of the text, the name of the author is given as Sewa Das 'Udās'. For the essential difference between the Udāsī and orthodox Sikh positions, see Chapter 6, note 16.

9. For the text, see Piar Singh, ed., *Janam Sākhī Srī Guru Nanak Dev Jī* (Amritsar: Guru Nanak Dev University, 1974). It has been translated by W.H. McLeod as *The B40 Janam-Sākhī*. For a detailed analysis of this *Janamsākhī*, see J.S. Grewal, 'The B40 *Janamsākhī*', *Lectures on History, Society and Culture of the Punjab* (Patiala: Punjabi University, 2007), pp. 167–217. It may be added that this *Janamsākhī* was commissioned by Bhai Sangu Mal on behalf of the local sangat, inscribed by Daya Ram Abrol, and illustrated by Alam Chand Rāj (rāj or mason by profession).

10. Jasbir Singh Sabar, ed., *Giān Ratnāvalī: Janamsākhī Srī Guru Nanak Dev Jī* (Amritsar: Guru Nanak Dev University, 1993), pp. 36–89.

After evaluating the views of earlier scholars, Sabar comes to the conclusion that, by and large, their study of the *Giān Ratnāvalī* has been rather superficial. In his assessment, W.H. McLeod is somewhat close to Sabar's own understanding of the date, authorship, and character of the work, but Surjit Hans is wide off the mark. It may be pointed out that a large number of quotations from the compositions of Guru Nanak and their exposition, notably the larger compositions like the *Japujī*, the *Āsā dī Vār*, and the *Siddh-Gosht*, represent the position of Guru Nanak in its true light.

11. Bhai Svarup Singh Kaushish, *Gurū Kiān Sākhiān*, ed. Piara Singh Padam (Amritsar: Singh Brothers, 1999 [1986]). As mentioned

earlier, the available text of the *Gurū Kiān Sākhiān* was prepared by Padam on the basis of only one manuscript, partly edited by Giani Garja Singh. Written originally in Bhadson in Bhattakharī in 1790 by Bhai Svarup Singh Kaushish, this work was transliterated into Gurmukhi in 1868 by a descendant, Bhatt Chhajju Singh of Bhadson near Thanesar.

12. *Bachittar Nātak*, in *Sri Dasam Granth Sāhib*, ed. Ratan Singh Jaggi and Gursharan Kaur Jaggi (New Delhi: Gobind Sadan, 1999), vol. 1, pp. 104–91. For an analysis of this work, see J.S. Grewal, '*Bachittar Nātak*', in *Sikh Ideology, Polity and Social Order: From Guru Nanak to Maharaja Ranjit Singh* (New Delhi: Manohar, 2007 [1996]), pp. 92–5. See also Surjit Hans, *A Reconstruction of Sikh History from Sikh Literature* (Patiala: Madaan Publications, 2005 [1987]), pp. 212–17. It may be added that its autobiographical form has given rise to the idea that the *Bachittar Nātak* was written by Guru Gobind Singh himself. The alternative view is that it was the work of a poet at the Guru's court, but its contents had his approval.

13. As mentioned earlier, the two editions of Sainapat's, *Sri Gur Sobhā*, have been brought out by Ganda Singh and Shamsher Singh Ashok. For an analysis of this work, see J.S. Grewal, '*Gursobhā*: In Praise of the Khalsa', *Sikh Ideology, Polity and Social Order*, pp. 107–10. See also Hans, *Reconstruction of Sikh History from Sikh Literature*, pp. 227–32.

14. Koer Singh, *Gurbilās Pātshāhī 10*, ed. Shamsher Singh Ashok (Patiala: Punjabi University, 1968). For analyses of this work, see Hans, *Reconstruction of Sikh History from Sikh Literature*, pp. 247–50. Madanjit Kaur, 'Koer Singh's *Gurbilās Pātshāhī 10*: An Eighteenth Century Sikh Literature', in *Sikhism*, ed. Jasbir Singh Mann and Kharak Singh (Patiala: Punjabi University, 1992), pp. 161–72. Gurtej Singh, 'Compromising the Khalsa Tradition: Koer Singh's *Gurbilas*', in *The Khalsa: Sikh and Non-Sikh Perspectives*, ed. J.S. Grewal (New Delhi: Manohar, 2004), pp. 47–58.

15. Bhai Sukha Singh, *Gurbilās Pātsāhī 10*, ed. Gursharan Kaur Jaggi (Patiala: Punjab Languages Department, 1989). See also Hans, *Reconstruction of Sikh History from Sikh Literature*, pp. 232–4.

16. See Kesar Singh Chhibber, *Bansāvalīnāmā Dasān Pātshāhiān Kā*, in *Parkh*, vol. 2, ed. Ratan Singh Jaggi (Chandigarh: Panjab University, 1972).

17. See Sarup Das Bhalla, *Guru Nanak Mahimā arthāt Mahimā Prakāsh*, ed. Shamsher Singh Ashok and Gobind Singh Lamba (Patiala: Punjab Languages Department, 1970), part I, and Sarup Das Bhalla,

*Mahimā Prakāsh*, ed. Gobind Singh Lamba and Khazan Singh (Patiala: Punjab Languages Department, 1971), part II.

18. For the recent understanding about the dates of the rahitnāmās, refer to 'Introduction', pp. 5–12.

19. *Rahitnāmā*, in *Bhai Nand Lal Granthāvalī*, ed. Ganda Singh (Malacca [Malaysia]: Sant Sohan Singh, 1968), pp. 191–4.

20. *Rahitnāmā Bhai Prahilad Singh*, in *Rahitnāme*, ed. Piara Singh Padam (Amritsar: Singh Brothers, 1995), pp. 65–7.

21. *Sākhī Rahit Pātisāhī 10*, in *The Chaupa Singh Rahit-Nama*, trans. and ed. W.H. McLeod (Dunedin, New Zealand: University of Otago Press, 1987), pp. 133–8.

22. For a detailed analysis see Karamjit K. Malhotra, 'Earliest Manual on the Sikh Way of Life', in *Five Centuries of Sikh Tradition: Ideology, Society, Politics and Culture*, ed. Reeta Grewal and Sheena Pall (New Delhi: Manohar, 2005), pp. 55–81.

23. J.S. Grewal, 'The Prem Sumārag: A Theory of Sikh Social Order', in *Panjab Past and Present (Essays in Honour of Dr Ganda Singh)*, ed. Harbans Singh and N. Gerald Barrier (Patiala: Punjabi University, 1976 [1965]), pp. 165–75.

24. For the Preface see *Rahitnāmā Hūzūrī, Bhai Chaupa Singh Chhibber*, in Piara Singh Padam, *Rahitnāme*, pp. 77–8. For the text of the rahit portion, see McLeod, *The Chaupa Singh Rahit-Nama*, pp. 57–78.

25. For the tankhā part, see McLeod, *The Chaupa Singh Rahit-Nama*, pp. 97–116.

26. McLeod, *The Chaupa Singh Rahit-Nama*, pp. 79–97, 116–38. This version containing the narrative part was composed later on.

27. *Rahitnāmā Bhai Desa Singh*, in Piara Singh Padam, *Rahitnāme*, pp. 136–7. Bhai Desa Singh narrates that he wrote his Rahitnāmā after having lived in the Muraliwala Bungā in Amritsar in the time of Jassa Singh. He left the place in old age, went to Patna, and had the darshan of Harmandar there. He stayed there for twenty days and moved on. On the way, one day he felt tired and went to sleep. Guru Gobind Singh appeared in a dream in all his regal majesty and told him that he had composed the *Jāp*, the *Akāl Ustat*, the *Bachittar Nātak*, the *Chaubīs Avtār*, the *Charitra Pakhyān*, and the *Shabad Hazāre*. The Guru then spoke about the rahit of the Khalsa, which was not inscribed. He told Desa Singh to write the rahit. When Desa Singh expressed his inability to perform such a difficult task, the Guru assured him that he would guide him.

28. *Rahitnāmā Bhai Desa Singh*, pp. 128–36.

29. *Rahitnāmā Bhai Daya Singh*, in Piara Singh Padam, *Rahitnāme*, pp. 68–9. The contribution from mythical entities was combined with Guru Nanak's mantar of '1 onkār satnām' and his *Japūjī* for liberation, the *Ānand* of Guru Amar Das for peaceful disposition, and the *Chaupaī* and *Savvāyyās* of Guru Gobind Singh for the firm intention to fight. Daya Singh further says that the qualities of sages like Sukdev (Shukdev), Durbasa (Durvasa), Krishan, Vashisht, Bisvamittar (Vishvamitra), Bias, Kapil, Jagnavalik (Yajnavalkya), Jaimini, and Patanjali are brought together in Guru Gobind Singh.

30. *Rahitnāmā Bhai Daya Singh*, pp. 69–76.

31. Giani Hazara Singh, ed., *Vārān Bhai Gurdas*, vār XI, pp. 183–206. See also S.S. Padam, ed., *Sikhān dī Bhagatmālā* (Amritsar: Singh Brothers, 2013), pp. 352–65.

32. Sewa Singh, *Shahīd Bilās* (Bhai Mani Singh), ed. Giani Garja Singh (Ludhiana: Punjabi Sahit Akademi, 1961).

33. Kankan Kavi, *Das Gur Kathā*, in Sarwan Singh, 'Amritsar in Medieval Punjabi Literature: An Historical Analysis' (PhD diss., Guru Nanak Dev University, Amritsar, 1994), p. 208.

34. For the text of this work, see Sarwan Singh, 'Sant Das Chhibber, *Ustat Sri Amritsar Jī Kī*' (M. Phil diss., Guru Nanak Dev University, Amritsar, 1988), pp. 46–97.

35. Kavi Saundha, *Ustat Sri Amritsar Jī Kī*, in 'Amritsar in Medieval Punjabi Literature', pp. 212–29.

36. Anne Murphy, 'History in the Sikh Past', *History and Theory* 46, no. 3 (October 2007): 345–65.

# 8 Painting and Architecture

Political, religious, and social developments of the eighteenth century were reflected in the painting and architecture of the period as well. Scholarly interest in Sikh painting and architecture is relatively recent, with more work produced on the nineteenth and twentieth centuries. However, we know enough now about the artistic activity of the Sikhs during the eighteenth century to attempt an overview. Like the content and forms of Sikh literature, themes, styles, structures, and features associated with Sikh painting and architecture were evolving in relation to the changing context of the period and its background. B.N. Goswamy talks of 'piety and splendour' becoming the Sikh heritage in art. This felicitous expression is no less appropriate for Sikh heritage in architecture.

## THE SEVENTEENTH-CENTURY BACKGROUND

Sikh interest in the art of painting first appeared in the scriptural texts.[1] Most notable of the early examples is the Pothī compiled by Guru Arjan in 1604 with its opening folio extensively illuminated in blue and gold. The section on *Rāg Sūhī* is also extensively illuminated in a style designated as Islamicate.[2] Some of the early manuscripts have *nishān*s on their opening folios, that is, the words '1 Onkār sat nām kartā purakh nirbhau nirvair akāl mūrit ajūnī saibhan' inscribed in the hand of a Guru. In a number of seventeenth-century manuscripts, nishāns are found with simple ornamentation as a frame. The opening folio of a manuscript from Patna, which bears the nishān of the tenth Guru, differs from most of the seventeenth-century examples: it has a floral decoration in yellow, gold, and blue instead of the usual Islamicate blue and gold geometric patterns of illumination. A typical example of the latter is a blank folio in a Banno manuscript of 1679, presumably prepared in the hope of getting a nishān. The nishāns of Guru Arjan, Guru Hargobind, Guru Har Rai, Guru Tegh Bahadur, and Guru Gobind Singh have been identified. These nishāns were evidently inscribed between 1600 and 1708. Among the other examples of nishāns with decorations are a manuscript of 1666 in the north Indian Islamicate style in gold and blue, and a nishān of 1691 which carries a simpler ornamentation.[3]

Like the nishāns, the hukamnāmās of the Gurus began to appear in the early seventeenth century in the time of Guru Hargobind. A considerable number of the hukamnāmās of Guru Tegh Bahadur and Guru Gobind Singh are available. Among these are a few decorated ones. The earliest known example is a hukamnāmā of Guru Hargobind.[4] A decorated hukamnāmā of Guru Tegh Bahadur is addressed to Ramdas Ugar Sain who was a Masand.[5] A hukamnāmā of Guru Gobind Singh, issued in 1696 to Bhai Tiloka and Bhai Rama, respectively the ancestors of the founders of the Nabha and Patiala states, has an ornamental border on all its four sides.[6] Another hukamnāmā of Guru Gobind Singh, addressed to the Khalsa sangat of Benares in February 1708, has a simple border.[7] However, two hukamnāmās of Guru Gobind Singh, dated 1698 and 1699, are elaborately decorated with floral patterns. They represent the best examples of illuminated hukamnāmās.[8]

There is a reference to a painter arriving in Ramdaspur for making a portrait of Guru Hargobind. At Sur Singh near Amritsar, where there is the seat of Bidhi Chand—a well-known Masand of Guru Hargobind—there are two portraits of the Guru. These portraits resemble his portraits available at two other places: Bhai Rupa, and Dehra Ram Rai.[9] A portrait of Guru Tegh Bahadur is ascribed to the 'Mughal school' and placed in 1670.[10] A portrait of a young Guru Gobind Singh is in the possession of Anurag Singh in Ludhiana.[11] In the National Museum, New Delhi, there is a portrait of Guru Gobind Singh, which is stated to have been prepared during his lifetime.[12] Two portraits of Guru Gobind Singh are pasted on the opening folios in the *Ānandpur Bīr*, a composite manuscript completed in the 1690s. One shows him sitting on the throne with an attendant waving the ceremonial whisk, and the other shows him riding a horse and shooting arrows at a lion. These portraits leave little doubt that some of the accomplished artists of the time had moved to Anandpur to work under Sikh patronage. The portraits compare easily with the finest paintings of the period.[13]

We can, thus, see that Sikh interest in painting was surely in evidence at the beginning of the seventeenth century, with the folios of scriptural manuscripts illuminated in geometric designs of the Islamicate tradition. Towards the end of the seventeenth century, the geometric designs were being replaced by floral designs, a trend that continued in the eighteenth century. Some of the nishāns of the Gurus and their hukamnāmās were also illuminated. The painting of portraits appears to have begun with Guru Hargobind. A few known portraits of Guru Tegh Bahadur and Guru Gobind Singh suggest that painters were regularly patronized by them. The increasing importance of the Guru's court added a new dimension to Sikh interest in the art of painting. Contemporary portraits, nishāns, and hukamnāmās of the Gurus, however, could not continue after Guru Gobind Singh, the last personal Guru for most of the Sikhs.

## ILLUSTRATED MANUSCRIPTS OF THE EIGHTEENTH CENTURY

Sikh painting has received scholarly attention from historians, including art historians, and scholars of Sikh religion and literature. We proceed with reference to the spade work done by them, but examine their assumptions and findings in the light of our understanding of the eighteenth century sources.

Jeevan Singh Deol observes that illuminations in scriptural manuscripts move away from purely Islamicate models during the eighteenth century. 'Most illuminated manuscripts produced in the mid to late 18th century already exhibit the vine and floral decorations characteristic of Kashmiri illumination work.' He gives the impression that the bulk of the relevant manuscripts of the eighteenth century were illuminated. However, he cites only one example of an illustrated manuscript: a painting of Guru Nanak, Mardana, and Bala facing the final index folio of a Banno recension of 1776.[14]

Piar Singh, the editor of the *B40 Janamsākhī*, refers to a number of illustrated Janamsākhīs of the eighteenth century. One such manuscript of 1724 is in the library of Bhai Ardaman Singh of Bagaṛian. Another illustrated Janamsākhī of 1740 was in the possession of 'Harbhajan Singh Harcharan Singh Chawla' of Bazar Mai Sewan, Amritsar. Yet another such manuscript of 1743 is in the library of the Maharaja of Patiala. On the basis of his familiarity with Janamsākhī illustrations of the eighteenth century, Piar Singh disagrees with scholars like Kirpal Singh and Fauja Singh, who are inclined to attribute these paintings to Pahāṛī artists. In Piar Singh's view, a Sikh tradition of painting was developing in the Punjab plains during the eighteenth century.[15] A manuscript of 1793 illustrated in Pahāṛī style, made for Sardār Baghel Singh Karoṛasinghia, and scripted by Jawahar Singh, has also been noticed.[16]

Of all the illustrated Janamsākhīs of the early eighteenth century, the *B40* has received the greatest attention. One of its illustrations was published in 1952 and another in 1965, both in black and white.[17] Piar Singh has reproduced six illustrations in black and white. He notices that the name of the artist given in the text is Alam Chand 'Rāj', and points out that the word 'Rāj' indicated his profession of a mason; it should not be seen as an indication of his connection with any state or royal court (as Kirpal Singh had done). Alam Chand was one of the numerous masons who used to paint pictures on walls and, when an opportunity arose, on paper as well. He does not appear to be familiar with the Gurmukhi script because the titles on the illustrations are given in Persian script. A separate sheet of paper is used for each painting, and it is pasted on the relevant folio of the Janamsākhī or in the space left blank for the purpose.[18]

W.H. McLeod, in his translation of the *B40 Janamsākhī*, published in 1980, notes that thirty of the illustrations are full-page; sixteen occupy two-thirds to three quarters of a page; and the remaining eleven only half a page each. Nearly all the illustrations appear at the beginning of individual *sākhīs* and depict a scene from the narrative that follows. Sākhī twenty-four has an extra illustration, and sākhī thirty-four has three extra illustrations. But, four sākhīs have no illustration. The captions in most cases appear in Persian script in the margin. Gurmukhi captions are added to eleven illustrations later in a different hand. Six illustrations reproduced by McLeod in black and white in his translation are the same as in Piar Singh's text. The painter Alam Chand 'Rāj' is referred to as a distinguished forbear in terms of professional skill of the masons included later in the Ramgaṛhia 'caste' who made distinctive contribution as artists and interior decorators of gurdwaras. Like the other Punjab art of the period, the *B40* illustrations display only a rudimentary notion of perspective, according to McLeod. However, they are expertly executed in attractive colours.[19] He comments later on that the iconography that surrounds Guru Nanak in the *B40 Janamsākhī* is patently Sikh. In a sense, the tradition of a distinctively Sikh art was well established before the middle of the eighteenth century. At the same time, it could not be affirmed that 'the style' was 'uniquely Sikh' because the debt of Sūfī patterns is too marked to allow any such claims. McLeod suggests, therefore, that the style could be seen as borrowed, but the purpose was distinctively Sikh.[20]

The complete set of fifty-seven illustrations of the *B40 Janamsākhī* was published in 1987, with a brief introduction by Surjit Hans. He looks upon the *B40* manuscript as 'the oldest extant manuscript of the Punjabi language'. Its illustrations constitute for him 'a unique achievement of Sikh art'. They were not only painted by a Sikh and for the Sikhs, but also embodied the basic doctrines of Sikhism. 'No other group of paintings has been found to fulfil an ideological function so far.'[21]

Hans goes on to underscore the extraordinary merit of these paintings. Alam Chand is stated to have had a profound understanding of Sikhism, and he had the technical inventiveness to convey its ideas through his paintings. Some of the paintings are divided into two planes. Baba Nanak belongs to a higher world, corresponding to *parlok* (transcendental reality) as distinct from *lok* (the world). Baba Nanak grows spiritually: his beard starts greying after his meeting with God. Like a sākhī, an illustration successfully depicts the Sikh doctrine.[22] In fact, Alam Chand uses a number of devices to portray the spiritual sovereignty of Guru Nanak. His face is painted three-fourth while all other major characters are painted in profile. The minor figures whose faces are shown three-fourth are in the lower panel. Only Kabir is painted like Guru Nanak; his face is only slightly smaller in size; he is just a little lower. The same colour of the head gear of Baba Nanak and Kabir suggests their spiritual affinity.[23]

Several other devices are used by Alam Chand to enhance the centrality of Guru Nanak. Apart from occupying a higher elevation, he is more richly dressed. The area covered by him in a painting is more than by any other person. A tree over his head denotes his spiritual royalty. The characters in paintings focus their eyes on the centre of action, or on Guru Nanak who looks beyond them. The perspective in the picture has the quality of 'being on the end of the world'; it is a means of fostering a spiritual frame of mind. There is hardly any sky; it is filled by the flight of birds. The gesture made by hands portrays spiritual combat with exquisite facility. Moreover, the repertory of technical devices to establish the spiritual sovereignty of Guru Nanak is always used selectively according to the requirements of the doctrine and the context.[24]

After Guru Nanak, the most painted person is Guru Angad. The representations of Guru Angad pictorially proclaim the orthodox line of succession: he is always painted in the image of Guru Gobind Singh. Here, the image is the argument. The picture of Kaliyuga makes an important point of Sikh theology. His submission to Guru Nanak in the picture corroborates his promise in the text that his Sikhs would not be harmed in Kaliyuga. Baba Nanak's ecstasy in the court of God is a beautiful picture of 'inspiration'. The 'wilderness' in the paintings depicts a contemporary appreciation of nature. There is social history, and there is theology. Surjit Hans looks upon this group of fifty-seven paintings as a 'supreme example of Sikh aesthetics in paintings'. The *B40* paintings pictorially match the art of the *B40 Janamsākhī* narrative. Indeed, 'a higher praise is difficult to imagine'.[25]

Surjit Hans is not an art historian. His perception of the aesthetic merit of the *B40* paintings is based on his sensibility and his understanding of Sikh aesthetics and Sikh theology. He points out that these paintings were supposed to be poor specimens of one school of art or another. 'Nothing could be far from the truth.' There is a good case for the existence of 'Sikh school' of painting in the early eighteenth century.[26] This gives further support to Piar Singh's view based on three illustrated manuscripts of the first half of the eighteenth century. However, the art historian Robert J. Del Bonta comments that the style of these paintings is not discussed by Surjit Hans. He himself thinks of the *B40* illustrations as derived from the Rajasthani School. Indeed, he talks only of Kashmiri, Kangra, and Rajasthani styles in Sikh painting.[27]

We find that five illustrations of the *B40 Janamsākhī* have two panels. The boy Nanak's father takes him to the schoolteacher and all the three are shown in the upper panel, and the boys who have come to the school are shown in the lower one. The nature of the subject appears to suggest two distinct panels. The two parts of the illustrations depict one and the same situation (plate 1). When Guru Nanak goes to Mecca he sleeps in the mosque with his feet towards the Kāba. This is shown in the upper panel. His companion Mardana and a mullāh are in the lower panel. The two parts relate to the same situation (plate 12). In Saidpur, Guru Nanak observes the Pathans singing and dancing, oblivious of the need of the hungry fakirs shown in the lower panel, while in the upper panel Guru Nanak is singing a verse of his own to the accompaniment of Mardana's rabāb (plate 16). On his way to Mecca in company of Muslim pilgrims, Guru Nanak and Mardana occupy the upper panel, and in the lower panel there are three pilgrims who are turning away from the Guru after they discover that he was not a Muslim (plate 30). Three eminent jogīs (*jogīsars*) come to see Guru Nanak with the symbolic message of his death. Guru Nanak sends his disciple Kamla to receive the message. Guru Nanak and Mardana are shown in the upper panel, and the lower panel is given to Kamla and the three jogīsars (plate 57). It is clear that two panels are seen as a more suitable device for depicting a situation that requires two connected scenes. All the single panels depict a single scene. However, the symbolism in terms of the upper panel representing parlok and the lower panel representing lok, suggested by Surjit Hans, is rather fanciful. The use of a double panel appears to enable the artist to handle the subject matter better.

Most of the illustrations reveal a close correspondence between the content or idea of the sākhī and the painting meant to illustrate it, though at times it is difficult to convey a verbally expressed idea through a pictorial representation. The artist is reasonably successful in representing Kaliyuga's submission to Guru Nanak through the posture adopted before the Guru (plate 10). Far more difficult is to portray Guru Nanak's meeting with God. It is shown through his posture of ecstasy, as if he were in God's presence (plate 28). Occasionally, however, the illustration represents the artist's own idea rather than the import of the sākhī. The most glaring example of this discord is the meeting of Kabir with Guru Nanak. Kabir is shown as almost an equal of Guru Nanak (plate 31). But in the sākhī, he feels honoured to be a disciple of Guru Nanak. In another case, the essential content of the sākhī is set aside in the illustration (plate 56). These instances leave the impression that Alam Chand 'Rāj' was not familiar with the Janamsākhī, much less with Sikh theology.

Guru Nanak stands distinguished from all other people who figure in the illustrations. A hasty impression would suggest that the umbrella-like tree over his head is the chief marker of distinction. Indeed, in twenty illustrations he has the tree over his head: in the presence of his parents, Abdul Rahman, the robber Bhola, Kaliyuga, a Sikh, (Shaikh) Rukn ud-Din, Shaikh Ibrahim, the Pathans, a Karori, Lehna and his companions, Ajita Randhawa, Muslim pilgrims, a shepherd, a magnate, a philosopher, Gorakh Nāth, and Guru Angad. In one illustration both Guru Nanak and Guru Angad have trees over their heads; the tree over Guru Angad's head is fully laden with bright flowers as if it is lighted. This is the situation in which Lehna is chosen as a successor, and the 'lighted' tree may have a symbolic significance (plate 54). Similarly, in the case of Guru Nanak's meeting with Kabir, there are two trees over their heads. This again suggests a symbolic near equality (plate 31). But in his meeting with the Thugs, the same tree covers their heads (plate 48). Even more important is the reversal in the case of the Siddhs. In two illustrations, the Siddhs have a tree over their heads but not Guru Nanak (plates 27, 44). In the text of the sākhīs the Siddhs are not superior to Guru Nanak. As we noticed earlier, Gorakh Nāth has nothing over his head while Guru Nanak has the tree (plate 53). In the sākhī, Gorakh Nāth is presented as far more important than the Siddhs. It seems, therefore, that the umbrella-like tree over Guru Nanak's head cannot always be seen as the symbol of his superiority.

In three illustrations the dress of Guru Nanak is white (plates 6, 10, 29). In these illustrations, Guru Nanak is sitting with his parents, with Kaliyuga standing before him in a submissive posture, and with a king. In Guru Nanak's meeting with Kabir, it is actually Kabir who is wearing a white dress (plate 31). In Guru Nanak's encounter with the robber Bhola, the robber is in white dress. It is evident that white dress is not symbolic of any spiritual status. In the case of the robber, the sākhī says that he used to wear white dress. It could surely be a symbol of respectability, as young Nanak's father also wears white dress in two illustrations (plates 4, 6). In five paintings, the dress of Guru Nanak is a shade of blue (plates 8, 12, 23, 30, and 50). These illustrations relate to Guru Nanak's encounter with a demon, the mosque in Mecca, the Muslim pilgrims, and Shaikh Sharaf. Here, again, the dress does not symbolize distinction. In most of the illustrations the dress of Guru Nanak is in shades of yellow. His dress, therefore, does not appear to be the distinctive marker of his persona.

For the headgear, the boy Nanak is shown with a turban. In the sākhī marking the beginning of his travels, he wears a cap-like headgear. There are other individuals in this set of illustrations who wear a cap, like Abdul Rahman and Mian Mitha (plate 7), Shaikh Kamāl (plate 15), the three Muslim pilgrims (plate 30), and the philosopher (plate 52). But the headgear of Guru Nanak is markedly different. He wears the same headgear in all the illustrations except in two: one in which he is bathing (plate 56), and the other in which the style is different and even he himself has on a black dress (plate 45). A number of individuals in the illustrations are without any headgear, but the majority wear turbans. It seems, therefore, that the hallmark of Guru Nanak's persona is his cap-like headgear. But it is not a cap. On the orange headgear there is a golden emblem, which gives it the appearance of a crown, as if Guru Nanak is the spiritual king of the world.

Next to Guru Nanak, Lehna is the most important figure in the Janamsākhī. He appears first with a group of pilgrims to the temple of the Goddess (plate 21). They decide to see Guru Nanak and they pay homage to him (plate 220). Much later, Lehna comes to Guru Nanak and converses with him; he is blessed by Guru Nanak. This is the illustration in which there is a tree in blossom over Lehna's head (plate 54). Not much later, Lehna expresses his exclusive dedication to Guru Nanak (plate 55). By now Lehna has become Angad, a part of Guru Nanak's body, and performs personal services for him (plate 56). These three sākhīs carry the implication that Lehna has been selected by Guru Nanak as his successor, and made into Guru Angad. In all these illustrations, Lehna (Angad) wears a turban, like the majority of persons in the illustrations. It is difficult to agree with Surjit Hans that he is portrayed in the image of Guru Gobind Singh.

We may take note of one more aspect of these illustrations that has remained unnoticed. The flora and fauna in the paintings and the dress of the people has been commented upon in passing. Architecture, however, is never mentioned, though architecture appears to be quite prominent in this set of illustrations. The school of the Pādhā appears actually to be his house, which is quite impressive as a residential structure (plate 1). Similarly, the house of the boy Nanak's father takes a larger space in the illustration that shows the physician examining the pulse of Nanak (plate 4). When the parents of Guru Nanak meet him in a forest, a part of the townscape is shown in the background (plate 6). The mosque of Mecca is beautifully depicted with its arches, domes, and decorations (plate 12). The mansion of the women ruling over a country occupies much space (plate 19). Mula Khatri's house is very impressive and occupies the whole space except where Guru Nanak is standing with Mardana and two fakirs (plate 23). Architectural features figure in a number of other illustrations depicting Guru Nanak's visit to different countries (plates 35–42, 45, 47, and 48). A very interesting illustration is the one which shows Shaikh Sharaf's city (plate 50). This interest in architecture may be due partly to the fact that the artist belonged to a family of masons. In any case, historians interested in secular history of the Punjab during the late seventeenth and early eighteenth century may find these illustrations and objects depicted in them as relevant for their interests. Though some of the detail may be conventional, the whole set of these illustrations is crowded not only with people from all walks of life, but also with beautiful birds, green trees, bushes, and shrubs of various kinds, plants bearing beautiful flowers, and, above all, with a wide range of religious and secular architectural features. A whole world appears to have been created with a new hope for human beings.

B.N. Goswamy comments on the quality of the paintings of Janamsākhīs in general. For him, many of them are

> routine productions, often in the hand of inadequately skilled provincial painters, or of itinerant Kashmiri scribes and painters: graphic and descriptive but rarely informed by feeling. Even the much written about illustrated manuscript, popularly designated as the 'B40 Janamsākhī', is painted in a prosaic, somewhat sterile, style.[28]

B.N. Goswamy has great appreciation for the set of drawings and a set of paintings in the collection of the Chandigarh Museum, which he places in the last quarter of the eighteenth century and ascribes to the family workshop of Nainsukh of Guler, a Pahāṛī 'master'. He takes up seven coloured paintings of this family as Guru Nanak's 'encounters', giving apt descriptions. In the first of these, Guru Nanak is shown in earnest conversation with a number of clean-shaven holy men. The inscription at the back seems to indicate Rameshwaram as the place of meeting but there is no cityscape. Two monkeys hold their playfulness in check, as if aware of the importance of the moment. Accompanied by Mardana and another person (Bhai Bala?), Guru Nanak is wearing a cap with a water pot by his side, an armrest under the left armpit and a rosary in his right hand.[29]

In the second illustration Guru Nanak subdues Kaliyuga. The divine sage Narad is standing on the left of Kaliyuga. Guru Nanak is lifting his staff as if to strike Kaliyuga and the latter throws up his hands in submission.[30] In the third illustration, a king pays homage to Guru Nanak who is sitting cross-legged in the open on a piece of cloth under a tree, with an open book in front, accompanied by Mardana and a devotee. A princely figure on a horseback approaches the group with his gaze on Guru Nanak (see Figure 8.1).[31]

In the fourth illustration Guru Nanak is looking at an ascetic, lying on a sheet of ochre-coloured cloth spread on a tiger skin on a patch of grass by the side of a stream. The inscription in Gurmukhi clarifies that the ascetic is the sage Dattatreya. However, a sense of mystery pervades the scene. There is no conversation.[32] In the fifth illustration, a couple of jogīs approach Guru Nanak; they are disciples of Bal Nāth (see Figure 8.2). They stand before Guru Nanak with folded hands as if asking to be accepted as disciples.[33]

The sixth illustration shows Guru Nanak in conversation with two Muslim holy men. The inscription in Gurmukhi clearly states, 'Bābā jī Uch gaye' (the Guru went to Uch, which was associated with Sūfī pīrs). The holy men are listening to Guru Nanak intently and appreciatively but 'there is no true air of engagement in the exchange'. The architecture is suggestive of a dargāh.[34] The last illustration depicts Guru Nanak and a young man besides a cistern as if ready to bathe. The inscription in Gurmukhi reads 'Dina Nāth Khatrete nū mile' (met Dina Nāth, the Khatri). The picture by itself does not carry any obvious import.[35]

In four of these seven paintings, Guru Nanak meets Hindu and Muslim holy men, two jogīs, and a sanyāsī. Whereas in the sākhīs Guru Nanak's triumph over all categories of individuals is quite emphatic, in these paintings it is merely suggestive. In two of these paintings, Guru Nanak meets a royal personage and an ordinary individual without a clear import. However, Kaliyuga is clearly subdued but not so emphatically or meaningfully as in the sākhī in the *B40*. Compared with the *B40* illustrations, these paintings are technically superior but their import becomes weak or it is lost altogether.

Goswamy has taken notice of two other paintings and a drawing of the eighteenth century, mentioning Guru Nanak as the subject. All the three are associated with the Pahāṛī style of Bilaspur, Mankot, and Guler respectively. The inscription in the first is 'Sri Guru awwal Nanak jī' in Persian script; in the second it is 'Shri Nanak jī' in Devanagri; and the third shows Guru Nanak with his followers. The general appearance in the first is that of a Muslim fakir, in the second that of an Udāsī ascetic, and in the third as the Guru. A certain degree of uncertainty persists about the first two figures.[36] The patrons of these portraits were possibly not Sikh.

B.N. Goswamy and Caron Smith have given five coloured illustrations which they place in the third quarter of the eighteenth century, all associated with Murshidabad in West Bengal. Four of these depict scenes in which young Nanak is taken to school, he is at Lalo's home as Guru Nanak, faces the priests of Kurukshetra, and meets the Mughal Emperor Babur. In the fifth illustration, Guru Angad is receiving homage.[37] There are strong similarities between the Murshidabad and Pahāṛī paintings. Goswamy and Smith refer to a 'template' of the eighteenth century in which sixty-four episodes from a Janamsākhī, with a brief inscription in Persian and Gurmukhi characters, are drawn clearly on a single sheet as 'thumbnail sketches'. Such sheets, they suggest, were used by painters in different parts of the country. It throws valuable light on 'the methods used by the artists in the eighteenth century and the means through which ideas and images seem to have disseminated'.[38]

## PORTRAITS OF THE SIKH GURUS AND SIKH CHIEFS

The successors of Guru Nanak were also the subjects of portraits in the eighteenth century. Portraits of Guru Ram Das, Guru Hargobind, and Guru Tegh Bahadur were produced in the Punjab plains during the first half of the eighteenth century. Guru Ram Das is seen seated, with an attendant standing behind, holding a fly-whisk (*chaurī*) over his shoulder. He is depicted in his quiet dignity, with an air of formality about his stance, as in Mughal portraits of princes and noblemen.[39] In the portrait of Guru Hargobind the setting is essentially the same as in the portraits of Guru Ram Das and his appearance is much like that of Guru Ram Das, but a falcon perches on the gloved hand of Guru Hargobind and an aigrette (*kalghī*) tops his turban. The falcon and the kalghī are appropriate to the image of Guru Hargobind as the master of temporal as well as spiritual power. Nothing in these portraits is based on observation. The painter attempts to introduce little variation upon the theme through these changes.[40] Guru Tegh Bahadur is shown standing, carrying a staff, and dressed in a long yellow cloak. The attendant carrying a fly-whisk stands just a little behind. The painter has tried to depict the qualities of forbearance, poetic disposition, indomitable spirit, and unwillingness to bend before injustice.[41] A portrait of Guru Hargobind, thought to have been produced in the Punjab plains in 1750, is perhaps not authentic. 'A measure of uncertainty about the identity of the person continues to cling to this work of luxuriant color and pattern.'[42] It is interesting to note, however, that this portrait appears on the dust jacket of the book.

In the second half of the eighteenth century, when the tradition of painting was well established in a number of hill principalities of the Punjab region, the emergent Sikh rulers came into increasing contact with the hill chiefs. It is not surprising, therefore, that the artists of the hills began to take interest in Sikh themes, including the Sikh Gurus.

To cite a few examples, a portrait of Guru Hargobind was made by an artist of the family of Purkhu of Kangra around 1790, and a portrait of Guru Gobind Singh was made by an artist of the family of Nainsukh of Guler around 1800. The portrait of Guru Ram Das produced around 1800 in the family workshop of Nainsukh is one of the most accomplished paintings of the Gurus.[43] The portrait of Guru Arjan produced around 1800 in the family workshop of Purkhu has no similarities with the other portraits of the Guru done in different styles by different artists in different regions or times. There is nothing to be sure that this is a portrait of Guru Arjan, but the inscription on the dust cover is very clear.[44]

Portraits of the Sikh chiefs were produced by the artists of Guler and Kangra. In a painting produced around 1775 in the family workshop of Nainsukh, Jai Singh Kanhiya is shown with hill chiefs. He alone is the person over whose head a fly-whisk is being waved. On his left are seated two Akālīs in blue dress, called 'Akal Bungiās'. Among the hill chiefs identified are Raja Raj Singh of Chamba, Raja Pragas Chand of Guler, Raja Jagrup Singh of Jaswan, and Raja Narain Singh of Siba. In the middle is seated the young prince, Sansar Chand of Kangra. 'Khalsa Jai Singh' is clearly in command. We know from other sources that some of the hill chiefs paid tribute to Jai Singh in recognition of his suzerain status. This painting is used on the front cover of this book.

The family of Purkhu produced portraits of Gurbakhsh Singh Kanhiya, Jassa Singh Ramgaṛhia, Bhag Singh Ahluwalia, Tara Singh Gheba, and Jai Singh Kanhiya. All these Sikh chiefs were situated rather close to the Kangra Hills. Whereas the Gurus were imaginatively 'recalled' in the late eighteenth century, the chiefs were realistically portrayed. Jai Singh Kanhiya is shown sitting alone with an attendant standing behind him, holding a fly-whisk over his head. He is dressed as a warrior, holding bow and an arrow in his hand, with a sword strapped to the waist with a cross-belt. In the portrait of Jassa Singh Ramgarhia, produced around 1760, the chief is shown sitting with his sons, Bir Singh and Jodh Singh. Their martial character is indicated by their weapons. Significantly, blue is the dominant colour in the painting. The portrait of Tara Singh Gheba produced in 1775 depicts him seated on a terrace in an informal posture and a simple dress (see Figure 8.3). He is wearing a sword, and the attendant standing behind him is wearing a blue turban and waving a fly-whisk over his head.

The portrait of Bhag Singh, the successor of Jassa Singh Ahluwalia, produced around 1785 shows him wearing a sword and holding a bow in his right hand and an arrow in his left. He is sitting in quiet dignity, with an air of self-assurance. The portrait of Jai Singh's son Gurbakhsh Singh Kanhiya shows him simply dressed, sitting on a decorated floral carpet spread out on a terrace. A long sword is attached to a cross-belt and he is holding an arrow in his left hand. Despite the weaponry, his figure appears to be rather benign.[45]

Before the eighteenth century, artists were patronized largely, if not exclusively, by the Gurus who had both the interest and the means. In the early eighteenth century, we find Bhai Sangu Shah commissioning a Janamsākhī and its illustration. His position in the sangat and the society is not known but he appears to have been a private person of some influence and means. In the case of the *B40 Janamsākhī* the artist named is a mason. It was quite common in the hills for *tarkhān*s (carpenters) to become *chitrerā*s (painters). Later on, in the Punjab plains too tarkhāns took to painting. Therefore, Alam Chand of the *B40* illustrations could be a tarkhān of the plains. Kashmiri scribes and painters are known to have worked in the Punjab during the eighteenth century, and so are the artists of the Punjab hills in the latter part of the century. The patrons of Sikh painting during this phase were largely the new Sikh rulers and, possibly, a few of their jāgīrdārs.

## SIKH ARCHITECTURE

The history of Sikh architecture from the sixteenth to the eighteenth centuries is most intimately linked with the religious and political history of the Sikhs. Gurmeet Rai and Kavita Singh have observed that architectural structures did not survive for a very long time in the Punjab. Architecture tended to be of brick rather than stone. Made from local earth and low-fired in wood-burning kilns, the bricks had to be small and thin to be fully baked. Most often, mud was used to bind them. Lime mortar was a luxury item, as it had to be imported from Rajasthan. It was used sometimes in mud mortar joints, but rarely for entire structures. In a small number of cases mud-mortar structures were plastered with lime and decorated with paintings.[46] It may, nevertheless, be possible to form some idea of the architectural interests of the Sikhs during the eighteenth century from the surviving monuments.

During the late sixteenth and the early seventeenth century, when Ramdaspur flourished as an autonomous town, Guru Arjan constructed the Harmandar and Guru Hargobind built the 'Akāl Takht'. The ground plan of the former has survived and the latter is now covered by the present building of the Akāl Bungā. The Guru's place of residence or the Guru-ke-Mahal has survived but there is no remnant of the fortress built by Guru Hargobind. Guru Arjan is associated with the building of water tanks not only in Ramdaspur but also in Tarn Taran, Guru ki Wadali, and Thatte Kheṛa. The tank of Thatte Kheṛa in Amritsar district is said to have come down from the days of Guru Arjan, like the painted pavilion in the complex. A small kiosk-like structure in Sri Hargobindpur is believed to have been built by Guru Hargobind. It has an octagonal plan and four doors. The blind faces have niches with foliated arches, and the roof has a squat dome. The Guru-kī-Masīt in Sri Hargobindpur of the days of Guru Hargobind is a modest three-bayed structure, with three square domes. The central arch is larger than the ones on the two sides, and the central dome is larger than the other two.[47]

Guru Tegh Bahadur chose Makhowal as the site of his headquarters and named it 'Chak Nanaki'. The Guru-ke-Mahal formed the nucleus of Chak Nanaki. There was a dharamsāl and a langar. The

Guru would hold his court, and there would be other buildings for running the whole establishment. Guru Gobind Singh extended the township. In 1688 he founded Anandpur adjoining Chak Nanaki. His residential quarters were surrounded by the houses of his battle-tested warriors of the days of Paonta (where a fortress had been built by Guru Gobind Singh). He held his court at a higher elevation called *uchā asthān*, which later came to be known as Kesgaṛh (fort of the blessed hair). Four other fortresses were built: Lohgaṛh and Holgaṛh across the Charan Ganga stream; Fatehgaṛh between the town and the Charan Ganga, and Anandgaṛh on the top of a hillock close to Kesgaṛh on the opposite side of Lohgaṛh. Anandgaṛh was the largest of the five fortresses, and had a well with stairs within its thick walls, which had provision for guns to be fitted in.[48] Thus, besides domestic architecture, Sikh architecture in the sixteenth and seventeenth centuries took two major forms: the gurdwārā and the fort.

In half a century from 1715 to 1765, when the Khalsa waged a protracted war to establish their rule, Ramdaspur emerged as the most important centre of their activity. Kesar Singh Chhibber refers to the Darbār Sāhib as 'Gurū kī jāgāh' (the Guru's place), and the 'Akāl Bungā' was a structure built over the platform later known as the Akāl Takht. Another structure was the 'Jhandā Bungā', used for keeping banners and standards, and probably also arms. As we have noted with reference to Chhibber, four masons were permanently employed for repair and new construction, as a part of the regular administrative set up in Ramdaspur in the late 1720s.[49]

Among the Sikh structures figuring in the contemporary Persian sources is Lohgaṛh in the north of Sadhaura as a place fortified by Banda Singh for defence against the Mughal forces.[50] Tahmas Khan refers to 900 Sikhs going into the fort of Ram Rauṇī, which was adjacent to Chak Guru.[51] It was destroyed probably during the invasions of Ahmad Shah Abdali, when the Harmandar and the Akāl Bungā were also destroyed. At the site of Ram Rauṇī, a new fortress called Ramgaṛh was built. We have noted Qazi Nur Muhammad's statement towards the end of 1764, referring to Ahmad Shah Abdali's destruction of Chak Guru, with the Harmadar as its central structure.[52] We have also noted the construction of a shahīdganj, the memorial at the spot where the thirty Sikh defenders of the shrine had been cremated together.[53]

Already by 1765 the phase of reconstruction on an extensive scale had started in Ramdaspur. The construction work on the sarovar, the Harmandar, the bridge, and the Darshanī Deoṛhī was completed by 1776. The work on subsidiary shrines was completed in 1784, and a number of bungās were constructed around the sarovar to serve various purposes. Out of over seventy bungās, probably twenty-five were constructed before 1800.[54] Every Sikh chief built a separate dwelling place, and in some cases, a fort with a bazaar which supplied his retainers with food and other necessities of life. Before the end of the century, there existed enclosed localities (katṛās) of the Kanhiyas, Baggas, Ramgaṛhias, and the Ahluwalias, with forts built by the Bhangis and the Ramgaṛhias.[55]

In his *The Golden Temple: History, Art and Architecture*, P.S. Arshi has given architectural drawings and illustrations, sources of the design of the Golden Temple, architectural details of the extant buildings in the complex, and the historical background.[56] His book is regarded as a pioneering work on the subject of art and architecture of the Golden Temple. It may be pointed out that the structures of the Harmandar, the Akāl Bungā, and several other bungās were raised in the late eighteenth century. S.S. Bhatti observes that the Golden Temple is 'the most celebrated example of Sikh architecture'. He refers to the characteristics of the Sikh style of architecture and structural ornamentation. A dome was the crowning feature of a gurdwārā.[57] Some of these features were evolved in the late eighteenth century.

In his account of the five Doabs, Ganesh Das mentions some Sikh places of the eighteenth century. Their number is not large but they include forts and samādhs as well as dharamsāls and gurdwaras. Besides the new forts built by Sikhs, a number of forts of the earlier times mentioned by Ganesh Das remained important, like Lahore, Rohtas, Attock, Gujrat, Sialkot, and Kangra. Such forts remained in use after their conquest by Sikh chiefs. The city and the fort of Sialkot, for example, were occupied by four sardārs: Jiwan Singh, Sahib Singh, Natha Singh Shahīd, and Mohar Singh Atariwala (before these were taken over in 1808 by Maharaja Ranjit Singh).[58] It is probable that some new structures came up within the forts according to the need of their Sikh masters. New forts were built by the rulers of Nabha, Jind, and Patiala during the eighteenth century.

As mentioned earlier, with the establishment of Sikh rule, new structures were raised on places associated with the Gurus and Sikh martyrs. Sialkot came to have two places associated with Guru Nanak: one was a ber (the jujube) tree and the other was a *baolī* (step-well). Both of these were well-known. Two places associated with Guru Hargobind figure as old places of worship: the dharamsāl of Bhai Qandhara Singh in Gujrat, and the dharamsāl called Kotha Guru in Wazirabad. A structure associated with Guru Har Rai in the Ghalotian village was a place of worship for Sikhs. Ganesh Das mentions two samādhs of the late eighteenth century: one of Sahib Singh Bedi, a descendant of Guru Nanak in Una, which became a place of pilgrimage (because of the sanctity acquired by Sahib Singh), and the other of Sahib Singh, the ruler of Gujrat, near Bajwat.[59]

Many of the gurdwaras figure in Iqbal Qaiser's study of Sikh shrines in Pakistan. He gives 181 coloured photographs relating to 165 places. Some of these belong to the categories of dargāh, darbār, *mazār*, or *makbara*. A number of samādhs are represented. A few of them are structures at the places of birth of the Gurus, and a few others are at the places of martyrdom of the Sikhs, called shahīdganj. The use of the terms 'dharamsālā', 'tibbā', and 'kothā' may actually represent a gurdwārā, which is the term used for the largest number of structures in this work. In a few cases, the land attached to gurdwaras is clearly said to be coming down from the time of Sikh rule. In other cases, it was given either by individuals or by village communities. A large number of structures are explicitly stated to be of the time of Maharaja Ranjit Singh; a still larger number are clearly later. Some structures appear to be old, but only a few can be placed in the eighteenth century with any degree of certainty.[60] The author is not seriously concerned with the dates of the structures, but his work is extremely useful for giving an overview of Sikh structures.

A solid, havelī-like two-storeyed structure in Gujranwala could have been built in the time of either Charhat Singh or Mahan Singh. The architectural features of this structure are similar to those generally associated with Sikh architecture, especially the arches for doors and windows.[61] The samādhs of Charhat Singh and Mahan Singh in Gujranwala were built in the time of Maharaja Ranjit Singh. The arches and domes of the structure are quite remarkable.[62] Two structures representing shahīdganj are those of Bhai Mani Singh and Bhai Taru Singh.[63] The gurdwaras known as 'Babe dī Ber' and 'Bāolī Sahib' in Sialkot were built by Natha Singh Shahīd, one of the earliest Sikh rulers of Sialkot.[64]

Some of the gurdwaras can be noted for stylistic interest, irrespective of their dates: Gurdwārā Sach Khand near Chuhar Kana for its large dome; Janam Asthān Bebe Nanaki at Dera Chahal in Lahore district for its dome and arches; Gurdwārā Tībba Nanaksar near Pakpattan for its dome and arch; Gurdwārā Fateh Bhinder in district Sialkot for its entrance; Gurdwārā Bucheki near Sheikhupura for its dome and arches; Kothā Guru in Wazirabad for its general structure and dome; and Gurdwārā Chhevīn Pātshāhī at Minhala in Lahore district for its tower.[65] It is important to note that these gurdwaras reveal subregional variations in style, highlighting the richness and variety of the evolving tradition of Sikh architecture.

In his arduous fieldwork, which enabled him to photograph architectural features of more than a hundred gurdwaras in the Punjab (Pakistan), Iqbal Qaiser refers at a few places to the sources of patronage: ruling chiefs, village communities, and private individuals.

## IN RETROSPECT

We can see that interest in painting among the Sikhs began in the late sixteenth and early seventeenth centuries, with illumination of the opening folios of scriptural manuscripts in geometric designs of the Islamicate tradition. Towards the end of the seventeenth century, geometric designs were replaced by floral ones, a trend that continued into the eighteenth century. The nishāns of the Gurus and their hukamnāmās were also decorated or illuminated. Portrait painting appears to have begun with Guru Hargobind, and a number of known portraits of Guru Tegh Bahadur and Guru

Gobind Singh suggest that the art of painting was patronized by them. Janamsākhī manuscripts began to be illustrated in the late seventeenth century and this art flourished in the eighteenth century in a number of styles, including 'Sikh'. Portraits of the Gurus were produced during the early part of the century in the Punjab plains in the provincial Mughal style, and in the later part in the Murshidabad style. To these were added the portraits in Pahāṛī style. The portraits of the Sikh rulers of the period in Pahāṛī style reflect the political change that had come about in the Punjab region by then.

The evidence on Sikh painting that has come to light in the recent decades raises the hope that more materials will be discovered. The names of artists or the families of artists who produced the paintings are known only in a few cases. It is quite clear that the art was not patronized by the hill chiefs alone. Patronage started with the Gurus and it was taken up by the Mughal nobility and the local communities and then by the Sikh rulers and, possibly, the members of the Sikh ruling class. The illuminations, illustrations, and portraits are directly linked with the Sikh faith: the Gurus and the scriptural manuscripts. The only exception to this is the portraits of the Sikh rulers of the late eighteenth century. In this, as in some other respects, they followed the practice of the earlier rulers of the land.

Architectural activity was an essential part of the towns founded by the Gurus in the sixteenth and seventeenth centuries. The dharamsāl, the Guru-ke-Mahal, and the Guru's court were some of the important features of these towns, apart from residential buildings. Guru Hargobind built a fort in Ramdaspur, and Guru Gobind Singh built a number of forts in Anandpur. In the eighteenth century, a large number of gurdwaras, a number of forts and havelīs, and some samādhs were built. The structures called dehurā and shahīdganj were, in a sense, the sacred samādhs. The resources for raising these structures came occasionally from local zamīndārs, affluent individuals, and members of the ruling class, but mostly from Sikh rulers in the late eighteenth century. The gurdwārā architecture exhibited important regional and subregional variations. In Amritsar, however, a distinct Sikh style of architecture was being evolved in the later part of the century.

It was represented at its best by the Darbār Sāhib, embellished subsequently by Ranjit Singh and popularly known now as the Golden Temple.

## NOTES AND REFERENCES

1. For some early studies of Sikh art, see M.S. Randhawa, 'Paintings of the Sikh Gurus in the collection of Mahant of Gurdwara Ram Rai, Dehradun', *Roopa Lekha* 39, no. 1 (nd): 13–20; Fauja Singh, 'A Study of the Paintings of Guru Nanak', *Proceedings Punjab History Conference* (Patiala: Punjabi University, 1970), pp. 122–59; and W.H. McLeod, *Popular Sikh Art* (Delhi: Oxford University Press, 1991).

2. Gurinder Singh Mann, *The Making of Sikh Scripture* (New York: Oxford University Press, 2001), pp. 45, 52, 65. Mann refers to earlier illuminations in the *Goindval Pothīs* and MS 1245 in Bhai Gurdas Library, Guru Nanak Dev University Amritsar. See also Gurinder Singh Mann, *The Goindval Pothīs: The Earliest Extant Source of the Sikh Canon* (Cambridge, Massachusetts: Harvard University Press, 1996), pp. 194, 195.

3. Ganda Singh, ed., *Hukamnāme: Gurū Sāhibān, Mata Sāhibān, Banda Singh Ate Khalsa Jī De* (Patiala: Punjabi University, 1967), p. 125. See also Shamsher Singh Ashok, ed., *Nishān Te Hukamnāme* (Amritsar: Shiromani Gurdwara Prabandhak Committee, 1967), documents 13, 17, 20, 57, 59, 61; MS M/341 (a copy of *Sri Guru Granth Sahib*), Punjab State Archives, Patiala; Jeevan Singh Deol, 'Illustration and Illumination in Sikh Scriptural Manuscripts', in *New Insights into Sikh Art*, ed. Kavita Singh (Mumbai: Marg Publications, 2003), pp. 50–2; Prithipal Singh Kapur and Mohinder Singh, eds, *Guru Arjan Dev: Life, Martyrdom and Legacy (1563–1606)* (New Delhi: Delhi Sikh Gurdwara Management Committee, 2006), pp. 116–17.

4. Ashok, *Nishān Te Hukamnāme*, document 9.

5. Sabinderjit Singh Sagar, ed., *Hukamnāmās of Guru Tegh Bahadur: A Historical Study* (Amritsar: Guru Nanak Dev University, 2002), p. 48.

6. Ganda Singh, *Hukamnāme*, p. 146. For its coloured reproduction, see Bhayee Sikander Singh and Roopinder Singh, *Sikh Heritage Ethos and Relics* (New Delhi: Rupa Publications, 2012), p. 158.

7. Ganda Singh, *Hukamnāme*, p. 190.

8. For the illuminated hukamnāmās dated 1698 and 1699, see Gurinder Singh Mann, 'Sources for the Study of Guru Gobind Singh's Life and Times', *Journal of Punjab Studies* (Special Issue

on Guru Gobind Singh) 15, nos 1 and 2 (Spring–Fall 2008): 237–8. For an illuminated hukamnāmā of 1704, see Ashok, *Nishān te Hukamnāme*, document 88.

9.  Mann, 'Sources for the Study of Guru Gobind Singh's Life and Times': 235, 268n45.

10.  The Guru is wearing a long cloak and a red turban, and a falcon is perched on his right hand. Kerry Brown, ed., *Sikh Art and Literature* (London and New York: Routledge, 1999), plate 5, 'Guru Tegh Bahadur', 1670, Mughal School.

11.  Trilochan Singh and Anurag Singh, *A Brief Account of Life and Works of Guru Gobind Singh* (Amritsar: Bhai Chattar Singh, Jiwan Singh, 2002), second illustration (unnumbered) after the foreword. See also Mann, 'Sources for the Study of Guru Gobind Singh's Life and Times': 244.

12.  Daljeet, 'A portrait of Guru Gobind Singh', *The Sikh Heritage: A Search for Totality* (New Delhi: Prakash Book Depot, 2004), pp. 126 and 127n. The author states that this portrait, with an inscription in Tākrī script, seems to have been made in the 1690s when Guru Gobind Singh visited Mandi.

13.  Piara Singh Padam, *Sri Guru Gobind Singh Jī de Darbārī Ratan* (Jalandhar: Hamdard Printing Press, 1994 [1974]), p. 13. For colour reproductions of these portraits see Mann, 'Sources for the Study of Guru Gobind Singh's Life and Times': 243–4.

14.  Deol, 'Illustration and Illumination in Sikh Scriptural Manuscripts', pp. 53, 55.

15.  Piar Singh, ed., *Janam Sākhī Sri Guru Nanak Dev Jī* (Amritsar: Guru Nanak Dev University, 1974), pp. 19–20. Photographs of Janamsākhī manuscripts of 1658 and 1724 are available in the Archives of the Department of Punjab Historical Studies, Punjabi University, Patiala.

16.  S.S. Dosanj and Rao Uttam Singh, 'A Dated Janam Sākhī of Guru Nanak', *Roop Lekha* 39, no. 1 (nd): 7–12.

17.  W.H. McLeod, trans. and ed., *The B40 Janam-Sākhī*, p. 8.

18.  Piar Singh, *Janam Sākhī Sri Guru Nanak Dev Jī*, p. 19, plates I–VI.

19.  McLeod, *The B40 Janam-Sākhī*, pp. 7–8, plates I–VI.

20.  McLeod, *Popular Sikh Art*, pp. 6–7.

21.  Surjit Hans, ed., *B40 Janamsākhī: Guru Baba Nanak Paintings* (Amritsar: Guru Nanak Dev University, 1987), p. 5.

22.  Hans, *B40 Janamsākhī*, pp. 5–6.

23.  Hans, *B40 Janamsākhī*, pp. 7–8.

24.  Hans, *B40 Janamsākhī*, pp. 9–10.

25.  Hans, *B40 Janamsākhī*, pp. 10–11.

26. Hans, *B40 Janamsākhī*, pp. 5–11.
27. Robert J. Del Bonta, 'An Illustrated Life: Guru Nanak in Narrative Art', in Brown, *Sikh Art and Literature*, pp. 53–71.
28. B.N. Goswamy, *Piety and Splendour: Sikh Heritage in Art* (New Delhi: National Museum, 2000), p. 15.
29. Goswamy, *Piety and Splendour*, pp. 16–17.
30. Goswamy, *Piety and Splendour*, p. 18
31. Goswamy, *Piety and Splendour*, pp. 19, 21.
32. Goswamy, *Piety and Splendour*, pp. 20–2.
33. Goswamy, *Piety and Splendour*, pp. 22–3.
34. Goswamy, *Piety and Splendour*, pp. 24–5.
35. Goswamy, *Piety and Splendour*, pp. 26–7.
36. Goswamy, *Piety and Splendour*, pp. 122–5, 130–1.
37. B.N. Goswamy and Caron Smith, *I See No Stranger: Early Sikh Art and Devotion* (New York and India: Rubin Museum of Art, in association with Mapin Publishing, 2006), pp. 46–7, 54–6, 92–5, 98–9.
38. Goswamy and Smith, *I See No Stranger*, pp. 100–1.
39. Goswamy, *Piety and Splendour*, p. 44.
40. Goswamy, *Piety and Splendour*, p. 45.
41. Goswamy, *Piety and Splendour*, p. 48.
42. Goswamy and Smith, *I see No Stranger*, pp. 138–9.
43. Goswamy and Smith, *I see No Stranger*, pp. 134–5, 142–3, 146–7.
44. Goswamy and Smith, *I see No Stranger*, pp. 136–7.
45. Goswamy and Smith, *I see No Stranger*, pp. 168–77.
46. Gurmeet Rai and Kavita Singh, 'Brick by Sacred Brick: Architectural Projects of Guru Arjan and Guru Hargobind', in *New Insights into Sikh Art*, ed. Kavita Singh (Mumbai: Marg Publications, 2003), p. 33.
47. Rai and Singh, 'Brick by Sacred Brick', pp. 33–49.
48. Reeta Grewal, 'Anandpur: The City of Guru Gobind Singh', *Journal of Punjab Studies* 15, nos 1 and 2 (Spring–Fall 2008): 67–8. Mann, 'Sources for the Study of Guru Gobind Singh's Life and Times': 232–3.
49. Kesar Singh Chhibber, *Bansāvalīnāmā Dasān Pātshāhiān Kā*, in *Parkh*, vol. 2, ed. Ratan Singh Jaggi (Chandigarh: Panjab University, 1972), pp. 184–5, 189–90, 192.
50. Muhammad Hadi Kamwar Khan, *Tazkiratu's Salātīn Chaghatā* in *Sikh History from Persian Sources : Translations of Major Texts*, ed. J.S. Grewal and Irfan Habib (New Delhi: Tulika/Indian History Congress, 2001), p. 150.
51. Tahmas Khan, *Tahmās Nāma*, in J.S. Grewal and Habib, *Sikh History from Persian Sources*, p. 172.

52. Qazi Nur Muhammad, *Janganāma*, in J.S. Grewal and Habib, *Sikh History from Persian Sources*, pp. 206–7.

53. Bhangu, *Sri Gur Panth Prakāsh*, ed. Balwant Singh Dhillon (Amritsar: Singh Brothers, 2004), pp. 386–94.

54. Madanjit Kaur, *The Golden Temple: Past and Present* (Amritsar: Guru Nanak Dev University, 1983), pp. 182–4.

55. V.N. Datta, *Amritsar: Past & Present* (Amritsar: The Municipal Committee, 1967), pp. 21–3.

56. P.S. Arshi, *The Golden Temple: History, Art and Architecture* (New Delhi: Harnam Publishing House, 1989).

57. S.S. Bhatti, 'The Golden Temple: A Spiritual Marvel in Architecture', in *Golden Temple*, ed. Parm Bakhshish Singh et al. (Patiala: Punjabi University, 1999), pp. 235, 237, 238.

58. J.S. Grewal and Indu Banga, trans and eds, *Early Nineteenth Century Punjab: From Ganesh Das's Chār Bāgh-i Panjāb* (Amritsar: Guru Nanak Dev University, 1975), pp. 28, 36, 38, 39, 45, 56, 57, 62, 69, 77, 84, 115–6, 133, 134.

59. Grewal and Banga, *From Ganesh Das's Chār Bāgh-i Panjāb*, pp. 51, 86, 95, 100, 136.

60. Iqbal Qaiser, *Historical Sikh Shrines in Pakistan* (Lahore: Punjabi History Board, 1998).

61. Qaiser, *Historical Sikh Shrines in Pakistan*, pp. 386–7.

62. Qaiser, *Historical Sikh Shrines in Pakistan*, pp. 382–5.

63. Qaiser, *Historical Sikh Shrines in Pakistan*, pp. 342–5.

64. Qaiser, *Historical Sikh Shrines in Pakistan*, pp. 152–7.

65. Qaiser, *Historical Sikh Shrines in Pakistan*, pp. 50–1, 68–9, 102–3, 188–9, 202–3, 238–9, 272–3.

# Conclusion
## Convergence on Sikh Identity

The eighteenth-century history of the Sikhs was marked by a political revolution that transformed rebels into rulers. In the lifetime of Guru Gobind Singh the 'Sikh' came to be identified with the 'Khalsa', and after his death the 'Khalsa' became identified with the 'Singh'. The Khalsa Panth at the end of the eighteenth century was radically different from the Sikh Panth at the time of Guru Tegh Bahadur's execution in Delhi in 1675. His successor's response to the situation was systematic and sustained. Essentially, Guru Gobind Singh instituted the Khalsa as a political community with the duty to fight, to conquer, and to rule. The aspiration for political ascendancy, articulated as 'rāj karegā Khālsā' (the Khalsa shall rule) was built into this situation.

Within two years of Guru Gobind Singh's death, this aspiration found a tangible form in the creation of a sovereign state. Though short-lived, it served as an example to reinforce the ideal. Ramdaspur (later called Amritsar) became the rallying centre of the political activity of the Khalsa. The doctrine of Guru Panth, as the source of total equality of each of its members with the others, imparted a peculiar authority to the resolutions of the Sarbat Khalsa as the Guru. These Gurmatās were morally binding even for those Sikhs who were not personally present at that time. Their resolutions were implemented by the combined forces of the Khalsa leaders. Thus, Sikh ideology, and the institutions and organizations based on Sikh ideology, largely, but not wholly, accounted for cohesion among the Khalsa in their protracted struggle for sovereign status against the Mughals and the Afghans. It is not an accident that 'deg, teg, fateh' appear on the seals of Guru Gobind Singh and Banda Singh, and the Sikh coin of 1765.

A hukamnāmā of 1759 explicitly equates the Khalsa Panth with the Guru, exercising authority at the Akāl Bungā in Amritsar. The frequent visits of the leaders of the Khalsa to Amritsar and their resolutions at the Akāl Bungā are highlighted in the Persian news reports of the early 1760s. The orders issued by the leaders from about 1750 to 1765 declared the authority of the individual Khalsa, exercised with God as the helper (Akāl Sahāi). The coin struck in Lahore in 1765 declared the sovereignty of the Khalsa through the grace of the Gurus.

The government and administration of the Sikhs in the late eighteenth century came to be designated by the later writers as the 'misaldārī system' in the territories ruled by twelve misals. This conceptualization does not take into account a very large number of Sikh chiefs, who were independent of others in the internal administration of their territories. Nor was it applicable to the Sikh zamīndārs of the Mughal state who established their power as rulers. Furthermore, the misal as a fighting unit had great relevance for conquest but not for governance. The territories conquered by a misal were divided among the leaders and their associates who ruled as autonomous chiefs. An early nineteenth-century British writer talks of 70,000 'sovereigns' in the territories of the Sikhs to underscore the autonomy of the Sikh chief. Every chief was succeeded by his heirs. The more powerful chiefs exercised suzerainty over others. The complete autonomy of the individual chief coexisted with the sovereign status of the Khalsa as a collective entity. Some of the autonomous chiefs, especially those in the former Mughal province of Lahore, had their mints to issue Sikh coins. The Sikh chief was sovereign not in spite of the coin but because of it.

On the whole, the picture that comes out of our evidence is that of a dynamic process. The Rākhī, the Gurmatā, and the Dal Khalsa were relevant much more for the process of conquest than for governance. More important for the institutionalization of the Khalsa Rāj was the conscious exercise of political power in a given territory by individual Sikhs as rulers. Land revenue, jāgīrdārī, state patronage, and suzerain–vassal relationship more or less assimilated the Sikh to the Mughal system. In institutional or constitutional terms, the political revolution of the eighteenth century did not lead to a new form of government or administration. However, the new rulers and their jāgīrdārs and retainers came largely from peasant and artisan backgrounds, and a substantial proportion of religious grantees and institutions received state patronage for the first time.

These political developments in the eighteenth century were intermeshed with significant changes in the religious and social life of Sikhs, and their cultural articulation. Most central to the religious beliefs and practices of the Khalsa were their conception of God and the Guru, and the institution of the gurdwārā. Contemporary sources, whether in Persian, Gurmukhi, or English, regard the Sikhs primarily as monotheists, with a firm belief in the unity and supremacy of Akāl Purkh or Vāhegurū. His name alone was the means of liberation. The Goddess appears in some major works of the period, but not as the supreme deity, and has only a restricted role to play in the situation in which the Khalsa is instituted. She does not figure in the rahit prescribed for the Khalsa. At any rate, the Khalsa had nothing in common with her worshippers for whom she was the Supreme Deity. Other gods, or their incarnations, which appear in some works, are meant to perform an assigned role, exercising power derived from God. In fact, there is a general emphasis on shunning gods and goddesses, worship of idols, sepulchres, monasteries, places of pilgrimage, fasting, shrādh, *gāyatrī*, *sandhyā*, and the mediacy of Brahmans. In the literature of the period, the pandit is shunned like the jogī, pīr, and the mullāh, and the religious systems represented by them.

As the hallmark of Sikh faith, Guruship is seen as continuous and eternal, vested first in the person of the ten Gurus and then in the Granth and the Khalsa Panth as decreed by the tenth Guru. The Granth in this connection was clearly identified with the Adi Granth, which now came to be referred to as Guru Granth Sahib. At the same time, some of the compositions of Guru Gobind Singh first and then the *Dasam Granth* acquired increasing importance, and they came to be placed next to the Ādi Granth in some gurdwaras. There is no contemporary evidence, however, in support of the view that the *Dasam Granth* too was regarded as the Guru. The presence of Guru Granth Sahib and the Khalsa sangat in the dharamsāl made it all the more important as the gurdwārā, the Guru's door. The gurdwaras associated with the Gurus became more important as much for congregational worship as for pilgrimage. They also received generous patronage from the new rulers and their jāgīrdārs. Amritsar emerged as by far the most important place of Sikh pilgrimage, followed by Anandpur, Patna, Nandeṛ, and several other places associated with the Gurus. The contemporaries notice the differences of beliefs and practices between the Khalsa Singhs and other Sikhs, and among each of the two. Rather than being deliberately cultivated or maintained, most of the differences were a legacy of the social background of those who entered the Khalsa order. What is far more important, there was a common core shared by the Khalsa.

The rite of initiation through khande kī pahul was essential for entering the order of the Khalsa and it was without any parallel in history. The foremost injunction to keep the hair uncut is followed by the injunction to bear arms, and prohibition against the use of tobacco. These three formed the core about which there was no difference of opinion ever since the time of Guru Gobind Singh. The Brahman, in theory, had no role to play in the performance of the rites and ceremonies for the Khalsa. The sectarian groups, evidently, did not adopt the new initiatory rite. Also, many Sikhs continued to use the services of the Brahmans for the rites related to birth, marriage, and death. The empirical evidence from the eighteenth-century sources, nevertheless, confirms the basic form of initiation into the order of the Khalsa in which the sacred thread had no meaning. It is pertinent to add that some compositions of Granth Sahib, including the *Ānand*, were meant to be recited or sung at the times of birth, marriage, and death, which was followed by the collective ardās and distribution of karāh parsād as integral to the religious and social life of the Khalsa.

The personal and social ethics of the Khalsa sprang from three principles: truthful conduct, social commitment, and welfare of others. All these three principles are drawn from Gurbāṇī. The importance of ethics is underlined by the enunciation that liberation is not possible without good conduct. Ethical living would vary from person to person but the non-Sikh contemporaries of the Khalsa have much to say in appreciation of their conduct in both war and peace.

The Sikh social order of the eighteenth century was marked by the difference between the Khalsa and the non-Khalsa. In the early part of the century, the Khalsa were divided into Kesdhārī Singhs and Sahajdhārī Sikhs. At the end of the century, the Kesdhārī Singhs were so visibly predominant that the Singh came to be identified with the Sikh. Nevertheless, the Sikhs consisted of two main categories: the Khalsa (now equated with the Kesdhārī Singhs) and the non-Khalsa Sikhs. Within the general category of the Khalsa there were two distinct groups: the Akālīs or Nihangs and the Nirmalās. Within the non-Khalsa (called Khulāsā by some Persian and European writers of the period) were the Udāsīs of various denominations, and the excommunicated Mīṇās, Dhir Mallias, and Ram Raiyās. Like some of the Bedi descendants of Guru Nanak, the Sodhi descendants of Prithi Chand, Dhir Mal, and Ram Rai did not discard their claim to personal guruship even when they became Kesdhārī Singhs. They continued to be regarded as gurus by the dwindling number of their sectarian followers. Towards the end of the eighteenth century, the total number of all the non-Khalsa was much smaller than that of the Kesdhārī Singhs who were spread largely over the upper portions of the Rachna and Bari Doabs, and between the Rivers Beas and the Ghaggar.

The Sikh social order in general and the Khalsa order in particular appear to be more egalitarian than the other socio-religious orders of the eighteenth century. The principle of equality was followed first by making the Khalsa order open to all, irrespective of creed, caste, class, or gender. All its members met as equals in the gurdwārā for common worship and commensality. Religious beliefs and practices and ethical norms were the same for all. The doctrine of Guru Panth enhanced the importance of the sangat in the gurdwārā and gave a sure degree of sanctity to the five Singhs nominated by the sangat for any specific purpose. Outside the sacred space, commensality was extended to all the erstwhile four castes, and perhaps also to the erstwhile untouchables in the early decades of the century. However, this uncompromisingly egalitarian situation could not be institutionalized, and there was an undercurrent of tension between the norm and the practice. Connubium remained confined largely to the Sikhs, and differences of caste and class were expected to be ignored. Gradually, compromises began to be made in favour of the traditional patterns. The increasing number of the Khalsa and the differences of class appearing among them with the advent of Khalsa Rāj also contributed to this development.

Religious life was open to Sikh women as much as to Sikh men. Women could go to the gurdwārā for congregational worship and commensality, participating actively in community life. Monogamy and mutual fidelity were ideally the bases of family life, and the Sikh widow was not allowed to burn herself on the funeral pyre of her husband. Female infanticide was normatively a sin worse than the killing of a cow or a Brahman, and called for excommunication. Besides the women from the Guru's household, some other women are known for their participation in public affairs during the eighteenth century. Thus, within the general patriarchal framework, there probably was reduction of gender inequalities, resulting in Sikh women gaining more space within and outside the home.

Sikh literature of the eighteenth century is generally seen as a source of Sikh history, but it is also a form of cultural expression. The institution of the Khalsa added several new features to the Sikh way of life, and concern with the propagation of these new features gave rise to a new literary form, the rahitnāmā. Since the institution of the Khalsa was seen as a momentous development in the time of the tenth Guru and in the history of the Sikh Panth, Guru Gobind Singh himself became a compelling subject of glorification, like Guru Nanak. However, the 'autobiographical' *Bachittar Nātak* and the biographical *Gur Sobhā* contained much that was based on contemporary evidence, and as a literary form the *Gurbilās* depicting the life of Guru Gobind Singh was more historical than the sākhī literature in which each sākhī (episode) was supposed to be an independent unit. During the eighteenth century, the Janamsākhīs of Guru Nanak became composite, combining sākhīs from different traditions developed earlier. The successors of Guru Nanak also became a subject for sākhīs. Thus, the scope of sākhī literature was expanded. The vār as a form was used for glorifying the Khalsa and its founder.

In this expanding scope of Sikh literature in the eighteenth century, we notice almost equal importance given to Guru Nanak and Guru Gobind Singh, seen respectively as founders of the Sikh Panth and the Khalsa Panth. If anything, contemporary Sikh literature dwells more on the Khalsa Panth, its way of life, and its affairs from the death of Guru Gobind Singh to the establishment of Khalsa Rāj. In this literature, eminent Sikhs of Guru Nanak are seen as Sikh bhagats and eminent Singhs of Guru Gobind Singh are admired as warriors and martyrs. While Banda Singh is presented as a great warrior, Bhai Mani Singh is presented as the prince of martyrs. The sarovar in Ramdaspur is praised as the most sacred place for pilgrimage, and a part of this sanctity is transferred to the city of Ramdaspur, which came to be known as Amritsar. A growing historical consciousness is evident in this literature, with keen interest in the Sikh past, concern for the present, and a vision of the future. Much of the eighteenth-century Sikh literature was quasi-religious and its basic purpose was not to please but to inform, to instruct, and to inspire.

Sikh cultural expression in the eighteenth century is partly visible in painting and architecture also. 'Sikh' painting started in the sixteenth century with illumination of scriptural manuscripts with geometric designs. This was replaced by floral designs in the time of Guru Gobind Singh. Illustrated Janamsākhīs appeared in the mid-seventeenth century, and contemporary portraits of Guru Tegh Bahadur and Guru Gobind Singh are still extant. Illuminated nishans and hukamnāmās have also survived. In the eighteenth century, scriptural manuscripts were illuminated, Janamsākhī manuscripts were illustrated, and portraits of all the ten Gurus were painted from imagination. In the last quarter of the eighteenth century, realistic portraits of some Sikh chiefs too were produced. This interest in painting was an important aspect of the cultural life of the Sikhs, leading also to a 'Sikh style' of painting.

Public architecture in the seventeenth century consisted of dharamsāls, the Guru's court, *dehurās* (structures built on spots of cremation), and the Lohgaṛh Fort built by Guru Hargobind. These forms of religious, secular, and domestic architecture were equally visible in Kiratpur and Anandpur, the two places associated with the Gurus in the foothills. All these, however, were relatively modest structures. In the eighteenth century, the gurdwaras built in different subregional styles at the places associated with the Gurus became larger and rather numerous. The forts, both old and new, with the chief's court and residence, also became numerous; the new forts built were larger than the Sikh forts of the seventeenth century. Many of the Mughal forts were renovated and used for residence as well. Domestic architecture of note was represented by havelīs of the chiefs and their jāgīrdārs. Similarly, samādhs were built for them over the spots of their cremation. Like the dehurā, shahīdganj at a place of martyrdom became sacred. The Harmandar, rebuilt in the late eighteenth century, provided a style of architecture that could be regarded as characteristically 'Sikh'. Sikh painting and architecture in the eighteenth century were patronized as much by local sangats and affluent individuals as by the Sikh chiefs and their jāgīrdārs.

A phrase used for the Khalsa in the Sikh literary works from the beginning to the end of the eighteenth century is 'tīsar panth', the third entity, distinct and different from the Muslim and the Hindu. Almost a hundred years earlier, Bhai Gurdas had underscored the distinct identity of the new Panth without using this phrase. This distinction was heightened after the institution of the Khalsa, which is graphically represented in some works as a source of great irritation for both Hindus and Muslims as if a particle of stone had entered their eyes. The 'Turks' (Muslims supporting the state) alone are presented as the enemy. It is not surprising, therefore, that in the period of Khalsa Rāj, there is no reference to the duty of destroying the 'Turks' or of fighting against them. The Singhs constituting the ruling class are exhorted to protect the cow and the Brahman; they should not denigrate any panth, for all panths in the world inculcate devotion to God.

Three components of the Sikh Panth are noticed by Sikh writers of the early eighteenth century: the reprobate groups called the Mīṇās, Dhir Mallias, Ram Raiyās, and the Masandias; the Sahajdhārīs who were a part of the Khalsa order but not yet initiated; and the Kesdhārī Khalsa who kept the hair unshorn, had the epithet 'Singh' added to their names, and bore arms. In late eighteenth-century works, the Khalsa stand equated with the Singh, and the Singh with the Sikh. In other words, the main line of division by this time is between the Kesdhārī Singhs and the rest. This is also the distinction that contemporary non-Sikh observers make, generally using the label 'Khulāsā' for the non-Singhs. The Kesdhārī Singhs stand distinguished not only due to their external appearance but also because of their own places and modes of worship, their sacred texts, their rites and ceremonies, and their dominance in numerical, social, and political terms. At the end of the century, at any rate, all other categories of Sikhs were overshadowed by the householder Singhs who were seen as representing the mainstream 'Nanak Panthīs'. The formula of 5Ks, which crisply defines the external markers of the Kesdhārī Singhs, had its origin in the eighteenth century itself.

The Singh Sabha reformers of the late nineteenth and early twentieth century tried, consciously and systematically and with better means of communication, to move forward from this position. They were working in the context of a fairly intense debate on Hindu–Sikh identity, which had emerged in the last two decades of the nineteenth century and in which two opposing positions came to be adopted—one, that Sikhism was a sect of Hinduism and Sikhs were an integral part of the Hindu social order; and the other, that Sikhism was an independent dispensation from the very beginning, and the Sikhs were distinct from Hindus as well as from other religious communities. There is a general impression among scholars that the question of Sikh identity arose during the colonial period. However, as we have seen, the consciousness of a distinct Sikh identity was explicitly expressed in the eighteenth century.

In fact, there could be no Singh Sabha movement without the eighteenth century in Sikh history. It served as a bridge between Sikh tradition of the sixteenth and seventeenth centuries and twentieth-century Sikhism, especially in terms of religious doctrines and institutions, political ideas and attitudes, social and ethical norms, rites and ceremonies, literary forms, and artistic conventions. All these developments of the eighteenth century converged on the crystallization and consciousness of a distinctive Sikh identity, which became a hallmark of the Sikh resurgence in colonial Punjab.

# Appendix

## The Goddess in Eighteenth-Century Sikh Literature

The problem of the Goddess in Sikh literature of the eighteenth century may be traced back to three compositions on the exploits of Durga or Chandi, which came to be included in the *Bachittar Nātak Granth* sometime in the late 1690s. The first two of these compositions, titled *Chandī Charitra Ukti Bilās* and *Chandī Charitra II*, are based on the *Markandeya Purana*, and are in Braj. The third, *Chandī dī Vār* based on the *Durga Saptaṣatī*, is in Punjabi. As noted already, the opening verses of the *Chandī dī Vār* are part of the Sikh prayer (ardās). It is absolutely certain that Guru Gobind Singh believed in no deity other than Akāl Purkh. However, Durga was 'recalled' for literary purpose at his court. All the three versions portray her heroic triumph over demons who are destroyed by the force of arms to protect gods. The tale was meant to inspire people to fight for a righteous cause.[1] Thus, a possibility was created for the later association of the Goddess with the institution of the Khalsa.

In the *Parchī* of Guru Gobind Singh, written soon after his death, Sewa Das Udāsī refers to the fire sacrifice (*hom*) performed by the Guru, but there is no reference to the Goddess. In fact, even hom is not the theme of the sākhī.[2] The reference to hom suggests, by implication, the presence of Brahmans in Anandpur, and the possibility of attributing a Brahmanical ritual to Guru Gobind Singh for the institution of the Khalsa.

It is not surprising that the episode of the Goddess in connection with the institution of the Khalsa is found in several major works of the eighteenth century, written nearly half a century after the event. One way of dealing with the problem of the Goddess in the literature of the period is to ignore her altogether, as has been done in the contributions to the *Encyclopaedia of Sikhism*.[3] We, however, propose to examine the role of the Goddess in the literary works in which she is made to appear.

The earliest known work of Sikh literature that introduces the Goddess in an account of the institution of the Khalsa is the rahitnāmā prepared by Gurbakhsh Singh Chhibber who was a collateral of Chaupa Singh (Chhibber). The Goddess appears in the narrative part (added sometime after 1740). Guru Gobind Singh was commissioned by God to create a panth for the propagation of true faith and destruction of the wicked. After the institution of the Khalsa and the removal of Masands in 1697, Guru Gobind Singh wanted to snatch power from the Turks (Mughals) and to give rāj to the newly created Khalsa Panth. Misar Kalika Das performed hom for the Guru at Naina Devi in 1699, and the Goddess was pleased with the sacrifice of Kalika Das's hands which were restored when a particular *istotar* (a hymn of praise) was recited. This was how the Khalsa were empowered to fight and establish their rule. The Khalsa Panth was made clearly distinct from Hindus and Muslims.[4] This story is further elaborated by Kesar Singh Chhibber, the son of Gurbakhsh Singh, in his *Bansāvalīnāmā*.

With reference to Koer Singh Kalal's treatment of the worship of Durga in his *Gurbilās Pātshāhī 10*, Gurtej Singh says that it was 'partly an expression of the dichotomy that prevailed in his mind'. He was unable to subscribe exclusively to 'Sikhism' or 'Hinduism'. He appears to rationalize the wielding of weapons by the lower castes through the tale of Durga puja. A popular tale was harnessed by Koer Singh to portray his theory that Mughal rule had lost its legitimacy by becoming unjust, particularly when Aurangzeb undertook to destroy Hinduism. Guru Gobind Singh decided to obtain the blessings of Durga to destroy 'Muslim rule'. Koer Singh presents Guru Gobind Singh as personally deciding to hold the ceremony and participating in its last phase. The gods and goddesses of the Brahmanical pantheon worship the Guru

after the devi appears. They offer weapons and other items, which
the Guru would later prescribe as mandatory symbols of the faith
of the Khalsa. An imaginary story was woven into the narrative for
the consumption of the Hindu masses. The Khalsa were destined
to succeed and they deserved wholehearted support of the Hindus
in the interest of preserving Hinduism. Gurtej Singh emphasizes
that this was the underlying purpose of Koer Singh's *Gurbilās*.[5]

Regarding it as the first mention of a tale that was to become
current in Sikh literature, Gurtej Singh says that the source of this
myth could be the Kashmiri Brahmans at whose request Guru
Tegh Bahadur had courted martyrdom.[6] We have seen, however,
that the episode of the Goddess figures in the rahitnāmā associated with Chaupa Singh. But there are differences of detail in the
episodes found in *The Chaupa Singh Rahit-Nama* and the *Gurbilās*.
It seems, therefore, that more than one version of the episode had
become current by about the mid-eighteenth century.

Gurtej Singh observes further that, shorn of its Brahmanical
features, Koer Singh's *Gurbilās* can provide 'a complete code of
conduct for the Khalsa'.[7] This observation carries the implication
that the episode of the Goddess does not impinge upon the beliefs
and practices of the Khalsa presented in this work. In other words,
this episode can be appreciated better in terms of its specific
function in the work as a whole.

Koer Singh places the episode of the Goddess after Guru Gobind
Singh's return to Makhowal-Anandpur from Paonta (after the
battle of Nadaun) and before the institution of the Khalsa. Unlike
the *Bachittar Nātak* and the *Gur Sobhā*, Koer Singh's *Gurbilās*
places all other battles after the institution of the Khalsa. He sets
out to narrate the appearance of Chandika (Bhavani, Ambika,
Kali, and Sharda Bhavani) to bless Guru Gobind Singh. She was
worshipped for three years but she did not appear. The Brahmans
told Guru Gobind Singh that the Goddess used to appear in one
year during the *Satyuga* (first cosmic age), in two years during
the *Tretāyuga* (second cosmic age), and in three years during the
*Duāparyuga* (third cosmic age), but in the Kaliyuga she took four
years. Therefore, they needed a secluded place to invoke her. Naina
Devi was chosen for this purpose. The Brahmans present the
Goddess as the Supreme Deity, the creator of Brahma, Vishnu, and

Mahesh. Her praises could bring political power (rāj), and Khalsa Panth could be made manifest to destroy the enemy. Destruction of the 'Turks' and the establishment of sovereign rule were two sides of the same political coin. Guru Gobind Singh participated in the worship. The gods were now afraid that the Guru might be empowered by the Goddess at their cost. Koer Singh goes on to say that the gods did not know that the Guru was doing all this for the sake of others (*par-upkār*). Millions of paradises and thousands of thrones were at his feet, and millions of boons from gods and goddesses were not equal to his feet. Only for the welfare of others did the Guru keep himself aloof and use the agency of the Goddess to institute the Khalsa. The successful invocation of the Goddess was his wondrous act (*kautak*).[8]

Many spirits are said to have tried to scare or lure the Guru when he was worshipping the Goddess without eating anything. However, they could not cross the line of 'satnām'. The Guru paid no attention to them. Those who had no faith in the Guru were sceptical about the whole project. When the time of her appearance was coming close, the officiant Brahman told Guru Gobind Singh that the Goddess required sacrifice of a brave person. The Guru told him that no one else was as brave as the Brahman himself. The Brahman ran away. Five Sikhs of the Guru offered themselves to be sacrificed. The Guru told them that he would call them if and when needed. They were 'the five beloved' (panj pyāre). The eight-armed Goddess appeared with weapons and other articles in all her hands. The Guru offered to make a sacrifice of 1,25,000 Sikhs. When the Goddess said, 'Ask for the boon', he asked for the creation of the Khalsa to destroy the mlechh. The Goddess said that like her son Shankar, the Guru would always remain detached (*nirbān*). Then she gave him the khaṇḍā with which she had killed the demons Sumbh and Nisumbh.[9]

Guru Gobind Singh praised the Goddess and he was praised by Brahma, Mahesh, and other gods. They offered whatever was in their power. Hanuwant gave *kachhehrā* (kachh), Vishnu gave kes, and the Goddess herself gave weapons. The Guru gave gifts to the Brahmans and they sang his praises. He was distinguished from everyone else in the world to have made the devi appear. Guru Gobind Singh now resolved to set his own house in order (*greh-sodh*) by removing the Masands. With one exception, they were all burnt. On the occasion of Baisākhī, the Sikhs came in large numbers as they had heard about the appearance of Kalika. The episode of the Guru and the Goddess, says Koer Singh, ends here.[10]

At the outset of his work, Koer Singh invokes the aid of Ād Purkh Kartar. He praises the True Guru. He seeks the aid also of Adi Shakti Mata, who made the Panth all powerful. At the time of Baisākhī, when Guru Gobind Singh asked for heads, some people said that the unbearable sight of Kali had an adverse effect on his mind; he had killed the Masands earlier and now he was out to kill the Sikhs. In his representation to Aurangzeb, Raja Bhim Chand states, among other things, that Guru Gobind Singh had the sight of Kalika after worship and received khandā from her, which made him very powerful. In connection with the arrival of Prince Mu'azzam in the Punjab (in 1696) for action against the rebels, Koer Singh mentions the worship of Kalika at the time of worshipping the weapons in Anandpur on the occasion of the Navrātā (Navrātra, the first nine days of the light half of the month of Asvin during which Goddess Durga is worshipped).[11] These are all the references to Kalika that we have in Koer Singh's Gurbilās in addition to the chapter in which the episode is narrated. It is not clear how the Khalsa were supposed to worship Kalika when they worshipped the weapons. In any case, the role of the Goddess remains restricted to the empowerment of the Khalsa, and Kalika remains peripheral and tangential to the belief system of the Khalsa. She finds no place in the Khalsa rahit.

Turning to Chhibber's *Bansāvalīnāmā*, we find that his chapter on Guru Gobind Singh is the longest. The treatment of the Goddess in this chapter is quite elaborate. After the martyrdom of Guru Tegh Bahadur, Guru Gobind Singh went into seclusion to perform austerities for the destruction of 'Turks'. A voice from above told him to grasp the khandā. He resumed his duties as the Guru. Pandit Devi Ditta used to recite and explain the Mahabharata to him. Guru Gobind Singh asked him how the Pandav Bhim Sen had become so powerful as to hurl elephants at the enemy. The Pandit replied, 'by performing *jagg-hom*'. Guru Gobind Singh expressed his wish to do so, and insisted that Bhavani should appear before him in person when hom was performed. Confessing his inability to make it happen, the Pandit suggested that Brahmans of Kashi and Kashmir might perform the hom successfully.[12]

Guru Gobind Singh tested a number of Brahmans to identify the true ones. They were invited to eat food. The cash award for eating meat was far larger than the one for vegetarian food. The award was steadily increased to tempt more and more Brahmans to eat meat. At the end, only three remained stuck to vegetarian food: Hari Das, Har Bhagwan, and Lachhi Ram. Even when threatened with death, they remained steadfast. Guru Gobind Singh appreciated their firmness, washed their feet, and took *charan-amrit*. Preparations for the hom were now made at Naina Devi. Two more Brahmans were specially invited: Vishanpal from Kashi and Shivbakar from Kashmir. The Guru insisted that the fire should arise from self-ignition and that the Goddess should appear in person. However, the Brahmans said that they were unable to do this. They told the Guru that Kalikadas was capable of making the Goddess appear anywhere.[13]

Kalikadas was invited from the south. He asked Guru Gobind Singh whether or not he would be prepared to undergo the hardship of the rite by remaining in the same posture for forty days. The Guru was prepared for the rite. Kalikadas then wanted to know why the Guru wanted to perform the rite. Guru Gobind Singh told him that he was ordained by God to destroy the wicked and the evil. Kalikadas suggested that this could be done by creating a panth that should destroy the wicked and the evil. The Guru decided to create a new panth for rāj. The sacred thread, the sacred mark, and dhoti should be replaced by new markers. Kalikadas argued that ruler-ship involved sin and the Guru should make room for sin in the panth. The Guru mentions four categories of Sikhs (dīdārī, mukte, murīd, and mayikī), and says that the last category was meant to accommodate sin.[14]

Guru Gobind Singh put on a new sacred thread and got ready for the rite. For forty days, hom was performed in the temple, and the praises of the Goddess were sung outside, along with kīrtan. On the fortieth day, the eight-armed Goddess appeared in all her splendour. Guru Gobind Singh could not open his eyes after the first glimpse. Kalikadas asked him to offer his head. When the

Guru said that Kalikadas should offer his head, he offered his
hands which were cut off by the khandā of the Goddess. Kalikadas
touched with his foot the Brahmans who had swooned and they
became conscious. Kalikadas asked them to recite a particular
prayer from the *Devi Strotar*. They did so and Kalikadas's hands
were restored. He told Guru Gobind Singh that his head would
have been restored in the same way if he had offered it to the
Goddess. Kalikadas could not offer his head because nobody
else knew how to revive him. Nevertheless, the hands offered by
Kalikadas pleased the Goddess and this went in Guru Gobind
Singh's favour. All the Brahmans were given generous *dakshinā*
(fee paid to a Brahman for performing a ritual) except Devi Das.
Guru Gobind Singh apologized for this omission and made him
happy with gifts and presents. In Chhibber's account, the Khalsa
Panth is created in several stages from 1693 to 1703.[15]

In the opening verse of the *Bansāvalīnāmā*, the writer invokes
Satgur Purkh, all the gods, Mata Gauri, Mata Sarsuti (Saraswati),
and Ganesh for aid in composing the work. In the body of his work,
Chhibber never misses the chance to minimize the difference
between the Sikh faith and the Brahmanical tradition. He saw no
contradiction between the belief in One God and in the devi at the
same time. Yet, in his own way, he mentions all the basic features
of the Khalsa rahit. He looks upon the Khalsa as clearly distinct
from Hindus and Muslims, as an entity which in fact was irritating
for both Hindus and Muslims. There are contradictions of this
kind in the work of Kesar Singh Chhibber and, consequently, his
treatment of the episode of the Goddess is rather diffused and
devoid of focus.[16]

Sākhī 17 in Sarup Das Bhalla's *Mahimā Prakāsh* relates to the
invocation of Chandi Mata for laying the foundation of the Khalsa
Panth through *kharag jagg*. Bhalla talks of a general situation in
which the Sikhs coming from all directions for the Guru's darshan
at Anandpur were ill-treated by Hindus and opposed by 'Turks',
resulting occasionally in armed fight. Due to the enmity of both
Hindus (hill Rajputs) and 'Turks', many Sikhs died on the way. The
Sikhs appealed to the Guru for protection.[17]

Bhalla says that Guru Gobind Singh did not wish to reveal his
spiritual attainments (*siddhī*) because it was against his dharam,

but nothing could be done without making use of siddhī. Therefore, he thought of creating brave Chhatrīs (Kshatriyas) through the medium (*ābāhan*) of Chandi. By performing kharag jagg, the dharam of Chhatrīs could be made manifest in order to destroy the mlechh. The temple at the top of the hill was chosen for this purpose and the materials required for hom were made available to the pandits. They assured the Guru that the Goddess would appear in person. They added that they would lose their senses on seeing the Goddess. Therefore, the Guru should make the offering prepared for her. For the sake of dharam, the Guru adopted the tradition of Kaliyuga and followed the *Atharva Veda*.[18]

The eight-armed Mata appeared on the proper recitation of mantras for hom. Guru Gobind Singh bowed to her, and offered food and his sword. The Goddess was pleased. She placed her khandā in the fire pit. Then the Guru awakened the pandits. The fire cooled down and the pit was cleared. The double-edged khandā was found there. The Guru took the khandā and gave generous charities to the pandits. The khandā was named 'Sri Sahib'. With the completion of kharag jagg the Guru acquired the means of victory over the enemy. He decided to propagate (*parchār*) the use of khandā to transform the whole sangat into the brave Khalsa bearing arms. The dharam-karam of the Kaliyuga were thus made manifest through the Khalsa.[19]

It may be noted that Sarup Das Bhalla invokes God and the True Guru for aid at the beginning of his work.[20] The Goddess does not figure anywhere in the work except in sākhī 17. She has no place in the rahit of the Khalsa. If sākhī 17 were to be dropped from the *Mahimā Prakāsh*, it would make no difference to the account of the Khalsa in the rest of this work. The mechanical imposition of the episode for the creation of the Khalsa is more evident in the *Mahimā Prakāsh* than in any other work.

Writing his Gurbilās towards the end of the eighteenth century, Sukha Singh devotes three chapters to the Goddess. These chapters follow the one on the battle of Nadaun and the expedition of the Khānzādā, and they precede the chapters on the killing of Masands and the manifestation of the Panth. The story goes that Guru Gobind Singh at Anandpur thought one day of instituting the Panth to fulfil the purpose for which he had been sent by God.

He invited Brahmans from different parts of the country, like Mathura, Kashi, Prayag, and Kashmir. All kinds of food were served to them. A *takā* (copper coin equal to two pice) was fixed as dakshinā for those who would eat vegetarian food, five *mohars* (gold coins) for those who would eat meat, and 500 *ashrafīs* (gold coins) for those who would drink alcohol too. In all, fourteen Brahmans did not eat meat (or drink alcohol). They were praised by the Guru as true Brahmans. They were told to worship the Goddess so that she appeared in person. They expressed their inability and named Datta Nand of Ujjain as the Brahman who could make the Goddess appear. Guru Gobind Singh was keen to have the blessings of the Goddess for creating the Khalsa Panth to destroy the 'Turks'. Through God's grace, the Brahman from Ujjain came to Anandpur. All the materials needed were made available to him. The Brahman suggested that the bank of the River Sutlej, which was as beautiful as the Ganges, was appropriate for the worship of Ādi Bhavani Chandi. All the necessary arrangements were made to perform the rite.[21]

For two and a half years, offerings of all kinds were made to the Goddess and her praises were sung, but she did not appear. Guru Gobind Singh called the Brahman to the court to know the reason for this delay. The Brahman said that he needed four years and a secluded place for the rite. Naina Devi was then chosen, and all the necessary arrangements were made.[22]

Sukha Singh then describes how Guru Gobind Singh participated in the rite. When the time for the appearance of the Goddess came close, he was warned that it was not easy to look at the Goddess. He remained steadfast. The Goddess asked Guru Gobind Singh to say what he wanted to have. He asked for the gift of the sword for his followers to be victorious and destroy the mlechh so that the sants and the whole world should remain in peace; no enemy should ever defeat them; deg, teg, and *bijay* (bounty, sword, and victory) should always be their lot. The Goddess gave the boon and vanished. There was all praise for the Guru. None else had seen the Goddess in person during the Kaliyuga. The Brahmans were generously rewarded by the Guru. The stage was set for the great event in the life of Guru Gobind Singh.[23]

Sukha Singh says in all modesty that he was no learned pandit; he related the episode as it was current in the world.[24] However, the episode given by Sukha Singh is rather close to what we find in Koer Singh's *Gurbilās*. Sukha Singh refers to Guru Nanak and Guru Gobind Singh as unique in the world for removing sin and ignorance. He refers to Ād Purkh Kartar, as the creator of the universe. Kalika, for Sukha Singh, is the power of God, as in the *Shastar Nām Mālā*.[25] In Sukha Singh's work too the Goddess has no relevance for the doctrines and conduct of the Khalsa.

On the whole, we have three versions: (*a*) presented in the rahitnāmā of Chaupa Singh and the *Bansāvalīnāmā* of Chhibber; (*b*) presented by Koer Singh and Sukha Singh; and (*c*) presented by Sarup Das Bhalla. It appears that the episode of the Goddess had become current in the oral tradition and Sikh writers incorporated the episode in their works for their own purposes. Paradoxically, the writers who tend to treat the Goddess as the supreme deity are also the writers who strongly support the Khalsa rahit in much detail from which the Goddess is absent. Thus, she plays a limited role, appearing only in one episode which does not integrate with any gurbilās or rahitnāmā as a whole.

## NOTES AND REFERENCES

1. *Bachittar Nātak*, in *Sri Dasam Granth Sāhib*, eds. Ratan Singh Jaggi and Gursharan Kaur Jaggi (New Delhi: Gobind Sadan, 1999), vol. 1, pp. 104–91. See also Robin Rinehart, 'The Guru, the Goddess: The Dasam Granth and Its Implications for Construction of Gender in Sikhism', in *Sikhism and Women: History, Texts, and Experience*, ed. Doris R. Jakobsh (New Delhi: Oxford University Press, 2010), pp. 40–59. Also, Rinehart, 'The Dasam Granth', in *The Oxford Handbook of Sikh Studies*, eds. Pashaura Singh and Louis E. Fenech (Oxford: Oxford University Press, 2014), p. 139.

2. Sewadas, *Episodes from Lives of the Gurus: Parchiān Sewādās*, trans. and eds. Kharak Singh and Gurtej Singh (Chandigarh: Institute of Sikh Studies, 1995), pp. 136–7.

3. Kesar Singh Chhibber, *Bansāvalīnāmā Dasān Pātshāhīān Kā*, ed. Ratan Singh Jaggi, text published in *Parkh*, vol. 2 (Chandigarh: Panjab University, 1972). K.S. Thapar, '*Gurbilās Pātshāhī Dasvin*' and Kirpal Singh, '*Mahimā Prakāsh*', in *The Encyclopaedia of Sikhism*, ed. Harbans

300 *Appendix*

Singh (Patiala: Punjabi University, 1992), vol. 1, pp. 279–80; vol. 2 (2001 [1996]), pp. 136–7; vol. 3 (1997), pp. 16–17, respectively.

4. W.H. McLeod, trans. and ed., *The Chaupa Singh Rahit-Nama* (Dunedin, New Zealand: University of Otago Press, 1987), pp. 86–92.

5. Gurtej Singh, 'Compromising the Khalsa Tradition: Koer Singh's *Gurbilas*', in *The Khalsa: Sikh and Non-Sikh Perspectives*, ed. J.S. Grewal (New Delhi: Manohar, 2004), pp. 49, 53–5.

6. Gurtej Singh, 'Compromising the Khalsa Tradition', pp. 54–6.

7. Gurtej Singh, 'Compromising the Khalsa Tradition', p. 56.

8. Koer Singh, *Gurbilās Pātshāhī 10*, ed. Shamsher Singh Ashok (Patiala: Punjabi University, 1968), pp. 110–16.

9. Koer Singh, *Gurbilās Pātshāhī 10*, pp. 116–21.

10. Koer Singh, *Gurbilās Pātshāhī 10*, pp. 121–6.

11. Koer Singh, *Gurbilās Pātshāhī 10*, pp. 17–18, 128, 143, 175.

12. Chhibber, *Bansāvalīnāmā*, pp. 100–2.

13. Chhibber, *Bansāvalīnāmā*, pp. 102–7.

14. Chhibber, *Bansāvalīnāmā*, pp. 107–12.

15. Chhibber, *Bansāvalīnāmā*, pp. 113–43.

16. J.S. Grewal, 'The Sikh Faith and the Khalsa Panth: Chhibber's *Bansāvalīnāmā*', in *Four Centuries of Sikh Tradition: History, Literature, and Identity* (New Delhi: Oxford University Press, 2013 [2011]), 227–52.

17. Sarup Das Bhalla, *Mahimā Prakāsh*, part II, eds. Gobind Singh Lamba and Khazan Singh (Patiala: Punjab Languages Department, Punjab, 1971), pp. 818–20.

18. Bhalla, *Mahimā Prakāsh*, part II, pp. 820–2. It may be added that the thrust of the *Atharva Veda* is on ritualism (*karam-kānd*).

19. Bhalla, *Mahimā Prakāsh*, part II, pp. 223–4.

20. Sarup Das Bhalla, *Mahimā Prakāsh*, part I, eds. Shamsher Singh Ashok and Gobind Singh Lamba (Patiala: Punjab Languages Department, 1970), p. 1.

21. Bhai Sukha Singh, *Gurbilās Pātsāhī 10*, ed. Gursharan Kaur Jaggi (Patiala: Punjab Languages Department, 1989), pp. 126–35.

22. Sukha Singh, *Gurbilās Pātsāhī 10*, pp. 136–40.

23. Sukha Singh, *Gurbilās Pātsāhī 10*, pp. 146–58.

24. Sukha Singh, *Gurbilās Pātsāhī 10*, p. 159.

25. Sukha Singh, *Gurbilās Pātsāhī 10*, pp. 1, 2.

# Glossary

Abchal Nagar (Abchalnagar): eternal city; used especially for Nander.

Ād Purkh: the primal being, an epithet for God.

Ādi Granth: the Sikh scripture, compiled by Guru Arjan in 1604 (containing the compositions of the first five Gurus and a number of *bhaktas*, *sants*, and *sūfīs*), and authenticated by Guru Gobind Singh with the compositions of Guru Tegh Bahadur. Now known as Guru Granth Sahib.

*āima*: grant of revenue-free land, also called *madad-i ma'āsh* or *dharmarth*.

Akāl Bungā: the structure raised over the platform (*takht*) built by Guru Hargobind adjacent to the Harmandar; now called Akāl Takht.

Akālī: a devotee of the Immortal, a staunch follower of Guru Gobind Singh.

*'ālam*: the world, the universe.

*'āmil*: an administrator; a revenue collector; interchangeable with *kārdār* as the administrator of a *ta'alluqa* under Sikh rule.

*amrit*: nectar, elixir of life; water prepared for initiation of the double-edged sword.

*amritsar*: literally the pool of nectar; the term originally used for the tank constructed by Guru Ram Das; the usage was extended to the town of Ramdaspur (Amritsar) by early nineteenth century.

*ardās*: a prayer; the formal and collective prayer of the Sikhs, noticed by the author of the *Dabistān-i Mazāhib* in the seventeenth century.

*ardāsiā*: one who performs ardās; a person employed for this purpose.

*ashnān (isnān)*: a bath.

*bādshāh*: a king, or king of kings.

*bai'nāma*: a deed of sale.

*bairāgī*: a renunciate, usually Vaishnavite.

*bakhshī*: an officer in charge of the army affairs in Mughal times; he was directly responsible to the emperor.

*bāṇī*: utterance; used for the utterance or the word of the Guru; generally
   equated with Gurbāṇī.

Banjārā: an itinerant trader, generally of grains.

*bāolī*: a well with steps for easy accessibility to water for several persons
   simultaneously; the well constructed by Guru Amar Das at Goindval,
   which came to be regarded as sacred.

*barat*: from *vrata* in Sanskrit for ritual fasting.

*begār*: forced labour.

*bhaddan (bhaddar)*: the rite of shaving the head, especially on the death
   of one's father.

*bhagautī*: used in Sikh literature generally for the sword, and not the
   Goddess 'Bhagavatī'.

bhang: hemp (*cannabis sativa*), its leaves and pistils; *hashish*.

Bhatt: a Brahman who kept records (*vahīs*) of genealogies or composed
   verses in praise of his patrons.

Bhattakharī: a special script used by Bhatts, different from both Gurmukhi
   and Devanagri.

*bhet*: an offering; an offering to a deity; an offering made to the Guru or
   Guru Granth Sahib; land given in charity.

*bhog*: conclusion of the reading of Guru Granth Sahib, followed generally
   by singing of hymns, ardās, and distribution of sacred food.

*bhujangī*: from *bhujang*, literally a reptile, used as a metaphor for the
   Khalsa warrior; a young Khalsa.

Bīr: used for a mythical being known for his bravery.

Bungā: a structure, a building; used for each of the many structures
   raised around the pool of nectar (amritsar) in Ramdaspur.

*chahārmī*: a holder of the *chahāram* (literally, one fourth; the fourth share
   generally of the produce, and sometimes of the revenues).

*chalīhā*: a kind of rite on the fortieth day after death; an offering for the
   Guru on this account.

Chandāl: one of the lowest categories of the outcastes; an untouchable.

*charan-pahul (charan-amrit)*: water of the foot; the initiatory rite of
   drinking the water in which the toes of the Sikhs have been dipped,
   symbolizing humility and dedication on the part of the initiate; also
   called *charan-amrit*.

*chaudharī*: the head of a group of villages for collecting revenues on behalf
   of the government; the office was generally hereditary.

*chaukā*: a square drawn on the ground and plastered with cow-dung
   generally by a Brahman for eating food, with the idea that all impurities
   would be kept out.

*chaukī-shabad*: kīrtan; kīrtan by turns for a fixed time called *chaukī* at the
   Harmandar Sahib.

*chaupaī*: a form of poetic composition consisting of units of four lines, with the rhyme scheme of a a, b b. The *Benatī Chaupaī* composed by Guru Gobind Singh is sometimes referred to as simply 'the *chaupaī*'.

Chhīpa: used for both a tailor and a calico-printer.

Dal Khalsa: a term used for the combined forces of Sikh leaders during the eighteenth century.

*dān*: charity; to give away something from one's honest earnings for the use of others.

*dargāh*: a holy place; the place of a pīr who is no longer alive, regarded as a place of pilgrimage.

*dārogha*: a superintendent or head of any organization.

*darshan*: the sight of a venerable person or place; used in the context of the Sikhs visiting the Guru as an act of merit.

*dasvandh*: one tenth; the share of annual income of a Sikh for the Guru's treasury, or expected to be spent for the welfare of others in the name of the Guru.

*deg*: literally, a cauldron, signifying bounty.

*derā*: a camp; a unit of soldiers; a religious establishment.

devi: a goddess or the Goddess as the Supreme Deity.

Devidwara: a temple dedicated to a goddess.

Devtā: a god.

*dhādī*: a singer who generally used a miniature drum (*dhad*) while singing of love or war for the entertainment of his patrons; used as a metaphor for the Guru as the singer of God's praises.

*dhādī darbār*: a gathering in which a minstrel (*dhādī*) sings heroic poems called *vārs*.

*dharam*: the appropriate moral and religious obligations attached to any particular group; duty, moral obligation; a righteous cause.

*dharmarth*: charitable grant; grant of revenue-free land; also called *madad-i ma'āsh* or *āima*.

*dharamsāl*: the place for earning merit; Sikh sacred space or the Sikh place of worship in early Sikh history, now generally called gurdwārā.

dharamsālā: a resting place for wayfarers, like a *sarai*.

*dharamsāliā*: one who looks after the Sikh sacred space called *dharamsāl*.

Dhir Mallia: a follower of Dhir Mal, the elder grandson of Guru Hargobind; a descendant of Dhir Mal.

*dīvān*: used for a religious gathering in Sikh literature as a synonym for sangat; also used for the keeper of a treasury; Dīvān as the head of the finance department and also a title.

Doāb: the land between two rivers; an interfluve.

*dohrā*: a rhyming couplet of a certain measure, popular in Punjabi poetry.

*du'ā*: a prayer.

fakir (*faqīr*): a pious person; a devotee of God; used generally for a mendicant.

*fateh*: victory.

Fateh Darshan: the slogan introduced by Banda Singh in place of '*Vāhegurūjī kā Khalsa, Vāhegurūjī kī fateh*'; used in his *hukamnāmā* of 1710, it appears to stand for the victory of a school or sect.

faujdār: one who keeps troops; a military officer under the Mughals whose duty in peace time was to maintain law and order and to assist civil authorities in a sarkār; the office survived into the early nineteenth century Punjab.

*gāyatrī*: a *mantra* of the Rig Veda, which is often recited by Brahmans as a prayer.

*gharī*: from the Sanskrit *ghati*, a duration of twenty-four minutes; the day is divided into eight *pahars* or sixty *gharīs*, which makes a pahar equal to seven and a half gharīs.

*ghee*: clarified butter, regarded as rich food.

Ghoriān: verses meant to be sung when the bridegroom mounts the mare at the time of wedding.

*ghumāon*: a measure of land consisting of eight kanals; also, equal to two *bighas* or about an acre; the actual size varied from region to region.

*girvīnāma*: a deed of mortgage.

*golak*: treasury; a box to receive cash offerings; money saved in a home to be carried to the Guru.

*gosht*: a discourse or debate, used for an episode in the *Miharbān Janamsākhī*.

granthī: a professional reader of Granth Sahib.

Gurbānī: an utterance of the Guru; compositions of the Gurus included in Guru Granth Sahib.

*Gurbilās*: a poetical work written in praise of a Guru.

Gurdwārā: 'the door of the Guru'; a Sikh place of worship, generally the centre of social activity too.

Gurmat: the Guru's instruction, the Guru's wisdom; Sikh ideology as a whole.

Gurmatā: decision of a general congregation of Sikhs, generally taken in the presence of Guru Granth Sahib.

Gurmukh: one who has turned to the Guru, a Sikh, a pious Sikh.

Gurpurab: celebration of an event associated with the Guru, like birth and death.

Gurtā: Guruship, the office of the Guru.

Guru: preceptor; religious teacher; an epithet used for the founder of Sikhism and each one of his nine successors, and also for the Granth Sahib and the Panth.

Guru Granth: the doctrine that the Sikh scripture authenticated by Guru Gobind Singh is the Guru, and not any individual other than the ten Gurus from Guru Nanak to Guru Gobind Singh.

Guru Panth or Guru Khalsa: the doctrine that the collective body of the Khalsa (Sikhs) is the Guru; the authority of this doctrine is next only to that of Guru Granth.

*guzarbān*: the official in charge of a ferry.

halāl: the traditional Muslim mode of slaughtering animals for meat; anything lawful, as opposed to harām (unlawful).

Harmandar: 'the temple of God'; the central Sikh Gurdwārā in Amritsar popularly called the Golden Temple.

*haumai*: the psyche of self-centredness, arising out of attributing to oneself what actually is due to God's will.

*havelī*: a large mansion for residence.

Holi: the festival of colours, sanctified by the belief in Lord Krishna's sportive practice.

*hom*: fire sacrifice.

*hukam*: an order; the divine order operative in the natural and the moral world as an expression of God's omnipotence.

*hukamnāmā*: 'a written order'; used generally for the letters of the Sikh Gurus to their followers.

*hukkā*: from the Arabic *huqqā*, a device for smoking tobacco.

*hundī*: a bill of exchange.

*huzūrī*: in the presence; in the presence of the Guru; used for Sikhs living in the Guru's presence; also for literary works prepared at the court of the Guru.

*jāgīr*: an assignment of land revenue in lieu of salary for performing service for the state.

*jāgīrdār*: the holder of a *jāgīr* who is entitled to collect revenues from a given piece of land in lieu of salary for service to the state.

*jāgīrdārī*: the system of paying the servants of the state by alienating land-revenue in their favour in lieu of cash salary.

*jamā 'atdār*: the head of a small unit of soldiers.

*Janamsākhī*: a collection of episodes associated with the life of Guru Nanak, meant primarily to depict his doctrines, ethics, and his spiritual status; several traditions of this genre developed in the seventeenth and eighteenth centuries.

*jantar*: a tool in general, an instrument or apparatus; a diagram of a mystical character.

*Japujī*: a composition of Guru Nanak used for the morning prayer; in Guru Granth Sahib, this composition includes a slok of Guru Angad at the end.

*jathā*: a band; a fighting band.

*jatī*: an occupational group placed within a larger category of caste, indicating its ritual status in the *varna* order.

Jhandā Bungā: the structure close to the Akāl Bungā or Akāl Takht, where standards and arms of the Khalsa were kept.

*jhatkā*: the mode of slaughtering an animal for meat with one stroke of the sword or some other weapon; the traditional mode of slaughtering animals in India. Unlike halāl, it carried no religious signification.

Jhīvar: a water carrier.

*jihād*: a religious war in the Islamic tradition.

*jogī* or *yogī*: one who practises yoga; a person belonging to any of the twelve orders of the followers of Gorakh Nāth.

*kachh (kachhehrā)*: drawers of a special kind meant to be worn by those Sikhs who are initiated through pahul of the double-edged sword.

*kalāl*: a vintner, a distiller of alcohol; a seller of alcoholic drinks; a person of the *jatī* called Kalāl.

Kaliyuga: the fourth and the last of the cosmic ages, traditionally regarded as the age of degeneration.

*kanpātā*: an order of the Gorakh Nathi jogīs who split the ear lobes for putting on large rings called *mundre* as a symbol of their spiritual status.

*kār*: offering to the Guru, probably as a share from profits or income.

*karāh parsād*: sacramental food distributed in gurdwaras to all persons present, generally prepared with equal quantities of wheat flour, sugar, and ghee.

*kard*: a short sword, a dagger.

*kārdār*: a functionary of the state, especially the person in-charge of the administration of a pargana, or a number of parganas, with wide powers to maintain law and order, to collect land revenue, and to perform judicial functions.

*kathā*: an exposition of the Guru's verses, generally in connection with the life of the Guru.

*katṛā*: a locality; enclosed market-cum-residential quarters.

*kes*: hair of the head, uncut hair.

Kesdhārī: an initiated Singh who maintained long unshorn hair.

Khalsa: the order instituted by Guru Gobind Singh; used for an individual as well as the collective body.

Khalsa Panth: the collectivity of the Khalsa.

*khandā*: a double-edged sword.

*khande kī pahul*: initiation of the double-edged sword introduced by Guru Gobind Singh as a rite for admission into the order of the Khalsa Singhs.

*khānqah*: a religious establishment under a Sūfī Pīr; a Sūfī hospice.

*kharīf:* the autumn harvest, sown in April–May before the commence-
ment of the rains and reaped in October–November.

*khidmatgār:* one who renders service; a servant; an attendant.

Khulāsā (Khalāsā): a term used for the Sikhs not initiated through pahul
of the double-edged sword and, consequently, not keeping unshorn
hair, and not bearing arms or the epithet 'Singh'; also called 'Khalāsā'.

kirpān: a sword.

*kīrtan:* the singing of hymns in praise of God, especially from the sacred
scriptures of the Sikhs; hence *kīrtan darbār* for an elaborate performance.

*kīryā (kīryā-karm):* performance of the traditional Brahmanical rituals on
the occasion of death.

langar: the kitchen attached to a gurdwārā from which food is served to all
regardless of caste or creed; a community meal.

*Lāvān:* the four verses of Guru Ram Das meant to be sung for the marriage
ceremony among Sikhs, called 'Anand' marriage because the *Ānand* of
Guru Amar Das was recited or sung at the end.

Mahant: the head of a religious establishment.

*mahāparsād:* used for cooked meat, but also for *karāh parsād.*

*makbara:* from *maqbarah,* a tomb.

*mannat:* an offering vowed for the fulfilment of a wish.

*mantar:* magical formulae; verses or words regarded as sacred.

*marhī:* a small structure raised on a spot of cremation, treated by some
people as an object of worship.

*māsā:* one twelfth of a *tolā;* a small quantity, roughly equal to a milligram.

Masand: a representative appointed by the Guru to look after the affairs
of a local congregation of Sikhs, or a number of such congregations.

Masandiā: the follower of a Masand.

*matth:* a religious establishment, a monastery; generally associated with
renunciates who remain celibate.

māyā: the material world and earthly attachments; treated in the Sikh
tradition as 'false' in contrast with the eternal truth of God.

*mazār:* a mausoleum; the tomb of a Sūfī Shaikh regarded as a place of
pilgrimage; the site of a *dargāh.*

Mazhabī: used for the outcaste Chuhṛā who accepts initiation of the
double-edged sword.

Mehra: a water carrier.

*melī:* an associate, a synonym for sahlang; a person initiated into the Sikh
faith by a Masand.

Mīṇā: a derogatory epithet used for Prithi Chand, the elder brother of
Guru Arjan, and also for the former's successors and their followers,
broadly meaning a cunning and perfidious pretender.

misal (*misl*): a small unit or group of soldiers; also used for a combination of Sikh leaders in the eighteenth century for the purpose of defence and occupation of territories.

misaldārī: generally but misleadingly refers to the system of polity established by Sikh leaders in the late eighteenth century.

*mlechh*: impure; a derogatory term used for an outcaste or a foreigner, both were regarded as outside the four-tier *varna* order.

*mukte*: generally refers to the forty Sikhs who had disowned the Guru at Anandpur, but later died fighting on his behalf near the present Muktsar, regarded as 'the redeemed'.

munshī: a writer or a scribe.

*murīd*: a disciple; also a devout Sikh.

*musaddī* (from *mutassadī*): a functionary of the government or an establishment.

Nāī: a barber.

*nām*: the Name, the name of God; the transcendent and immanent God; the whole creation; the Guru's *shabad*, Gurbāṇī.

*nām, dān, isnān*: the phrase used by Guru Nanak for the essential features of the Sikh way of life, that is, meditation on God, charity, and both physical and moral purity.

Nanak Panthīs: the followers of Guru Nanak equated with Sikhs in general.

Nāth: master; used for the jogī of an exalted status; one of the nine mythical Nāths.

*nāzim*: the governor of a province; an administrator.

Nihang: the militant followers of Guru Gobind Singh who regarded themselves as guardians of the faith.

*nirguṇ*: without qualities, without attributes; the primal state of God before creation.

Nirmalā: the ascetics and renunciates who propagated the Sikh faith.

*padārath*: a thing, a blessing; one of the four *padārath*s of observance of religious duties, material wealth, fulfilment of desires, and liberation (*dharma, artha, kāma,* and *moksh*).

Pādhā (Pāndhā): a Brahman officiant at social ceremonies; a teacher of arithmetic; an astrologer.

Pahāṛī style: any style of painting in the Punjab hills.

*pahul*: water used for initiating a person as a Sikh (*charan-pahul*) or a Singh (*khande kī pahul*).

*paisā*: a copper coin worth sixty-fourth part of a rupee.

*panch*: the five; one of the five; the member of a panchāyat; the headman of a village or one of its subdivisions; also of a locality or trade in urban areas.

Pandit: a learned Brahman; a learned person.

*panj pyāre*: the 'five beloved', so called for offering their heads to Guru Gobind Singh; they were the first to be initiated all afresh through pahul of the double-edged sword and authorized to initiate others, starting with Guru Gobind Singh himself.

Panth: literally a path; the people following a particular path; collectively the followers of the Gurus; the Sikh community.

pargana: a small unit of administration in a province under the Mughals; remained in use in the Punjab till the mid-nineteenth century and became synonymous with the *ta'alluqa*.

*parsād (prasād)*: sacred food; simply food.

*par-upkār*: something good done for others.

*pāṭh*: reading of Gurbāṇī or Guru Granth Sahib.

*pattal*: a tree leaf used as a plate.

*pattīdārī*: share-holding; a system by which a joint conquest was divided among partners, and each was authorized to collect revenues from his share in the conquered territory.

*pauṛī*: a stanza, a form of poetic composition.

*pind*: a ball of rice for feeding Brahmans as a part of mortuary rites.

*pīr* or Shaikh: among Muslim mystics the guide who leads on the path of union with God; believed to be a bestower of blessings after his death.

*pīrzādā*: literally, the son of a *pīr*; also used for a descendant.

*pothī*: a book, used interchangeably with *granth*.

Purkh/*purkh*: a person; used for God to clarify that God in the Sikh tradition is not an impersonal reality as in the Vedanta.

*purohit*: the Brahman who performs the priestly duties for a family, or a number of households.

Qur'ān: the scripture of Islam regarded as revealed by Allah to the prophet Muhammad through the angel Gabriel.

*qānūngo*: a hereditary keeper of the revenue records at the pargana or the *ta'alluqa* level.

*rabābī*: one who plays on the *rabāb*, a kind of violin with three strings.

*rāgī*: a singer, particularly of the hymns of the Sikh scripture.

*rahit*: a way of life, used especially for the Sikh way of life in accordance with the philosophic and ethical principles advocated by the Gurus.

*rahitnāmā*: a written code of belief and conduct; norms laid down for the Sikh way of life in accordance with the principles of Sikhism, including 'penance' for infringing those principles.

Rākhī: protection; payment made in cash or kind by cultivator to a Khalsa leader for protection against others.

Ranghretā: a Singh whose background is that of an untouchable Chuhṛā, also called Mazhabī.

*Sadd*: a form of poetic composition.

*sādh*: a religious and pious person.

*sahaj*: state of liberation-in-life.

Sahajdhārī: a Sikh who is not initiated as a Singh and does not adopt the Khalsa symbols; initially used for a non-Singh Khalsa, but later extended to all non-Singhs.

*sahaj-jog*: the path through which *sahaj* is pursued and attained; used for the path of Guru Nanak and his successors.

*sāhibzādā*: a son of the Master; used for the sons of Guru Gobind Singh.

*sahlang*: an associate; a person admitted to the Sikh faith by a representative of the Guru on his behalf.

*sākhī*: an eyewitness; testimony; an episode bearing witness to the spiritual status of a religious guide; a statement bearing witness to the truth of God; used generally for an episode in the life of a Guru.

*samādh*: a structure raised over a spot of cremation in honour of an important person, whether secular or religious; the counterpart of a mausoleum.

*sanad (dāstawīz)*: a voucher, document, note of hand or bond; a title deed; a written authority for holding land or an office.

*sandhyā*: a form of worship in the morning, at noon, and in the evening in the Brahmanical system.

*sangat*: association, an assembly, a religious congregation; a congregation of Sikhs; the collective body of Sikhs at one place.

Sānsī: a category of the outcastes.

sanyāsī: a renunciate, generally Shaivite.

sardār: a leader; a Sikh ruler.

*Sarkār*: the primary division of a province under the Mughals.

*sarkardā*: the leader of a number of small units under subordinate leaders; the head of number of small units of soldiers under *jamā 'atdārs*.

*sarovar*: a tank, a pool of water.

satī: the practice in which the wife burnt herself on the funeral pyre of her husband as a mark of her devotion and fidelity to him.

*Savvayyā*: a poem written in praise of God or a patron.

Sayyid: a descendant of Prophet Muhammad, especially one of his grandson, Husain, and held venerable by the rulers and people alike.

*sazāwal*: a special messenger, generally a horseman.

*sevā*: service; service of God; service of the Guru; service of the Sikhs; service of others.

*shabad*: the word; a hymn; a verse in Guru Granth Sahib.

shahīd: one who bears witness to his faith; a martyr, especially in Islam and Sikhism.

*shahīdganj*: a structure built in commemoration of a Sikh martyr or martyrs.

Shaikh: a leader; the head of a Sūfī order; a respectable Muslim.

*shaikhzādā*: the son of a guide on the Sūfī path, or his descendant.

sharī'at: Islamic law.

*shrāddh*: the rite by which the dead ancestors are supposed to be fed through the mediacy of Brahmans.

Siddh: a renunciate of great spiritual status; a mythical entity.

*siddhī*: possession of supernatural powers.

Sikh: a disciple; used generally for a follower of Guru Nanak and his successors.

*slok*: a unit of verse, generally rather short, like a *dohā* or a rhyming couplet.

Sohilā: a composition of Guru Nanak recited especially at the end of a ceremony.

*sūbedār*: the governor of a province.

sūfī: a mystic of Islam subscribing to devotional theism.

*sūtak*: the notion of pollution in certain situations, especially in relation to women during menstruation and childbirth.

*tabadār*: a subordinate; a servant.

*tabadārī*: a system in which the holder of the tenure served a Sikh chief as a retainer and received land revenue from a specified area of land for his services.

*takht*: a throne; one of the four or five Sikh religious centres of authority.

*tankhā*: ordinarily salary, but used by the compilers of the rahitnāmās (manuals for the Sikh way of life) for corrective penance prescribed for a Sikh who has infringed a particular norm.

Taksāl: a mint; used for a particular school of Gurmat.

Tarkhān: a carpenter.

*tarpan*: offering water in ritual worship.

*teg*: the sword, signifying physical force.

Thākurdwāra: a temple dedicated to Vishnu or one of his incarnations.

*thānā*: a place; a place where troops are posted for maintaining peace and order, and for assistance in the collection of revenues.

*thānādār*: the commandant of a garrison or a fort.

*tilak*: the sacred mark on the forehead, also called *tikkā*.

*tīrath*: a sacred place; a place of pilgrimage; one of the sixty-eight sacred places in India.

Udāsī: a renunciate belonging to an order tracing its origin to Guru Nanak through his son Sri Chand but not through Guru Angad and his successors.

*Vāhegurū*: praise be to the Guru; used for God.

*vakīl*: an agent or a deputy; an envoy; a representative.

*Vār*: a literary genre, generally used for heroic poetry; Guru Nanak used it for his religious compositions; the most famous vārs in Sikh literature were composed by Bhai Gurdas in the early seventeenth century for celebrating Sikh Gurus and the Sikh Panth.

varna: literally colour, used for any one of the ideal four-fold social order.

*varnāshrama*: the four-fold division of society into *varnas* or classes and of human life into *āshramas* or stages.

*vārtak*: a work in prose.

*wāguzār*: exempt; revenue-free.

wazīr: the first or the prime minister, next in authority and importance to the king; a minister.

zamīndār: literally the holder of land; applied alike to the intermediary who collected revenue on behalf of the state, to a vassal chief, and to a peasant proprietor.

# Select Bibliography

## CONTEMPORARY SOURCES

### Gurmukhi Sources

Ashok, Shamsher Singh, ed. *Gurū Khālse De Rahitnāme*. Amritsar: Sikh History Research Board, 1979.
——, ed. *Nishān Te Hukamnāme*. Amritsar: Shiromani Gurdwara Prabandhak Committee, 1967.
*Bachittar Nātak*. In Jaggi and Jaggi, *Sri Dasam Granth Sahib*. Vol. 1.
Bhai Sukha Singh. *Gurbilās Pātsāhī 10*. Edited by Gursharan Kaur Jaggi. Patiala: Punjab Languages Department, 1989.
Bhai Svarup Singh Kaushish. *Gurū Kiān Sākhiān*. Edited by Piara Singh Padam. Amritsar: Singh Brothers, 1999 [1986].
Bedi, Kala Singh, ed. *Vār Sri Bhagautī Kī (Chandī dī Vār)*. New Delhi: Punjab Book Store, 1965.
*Bibek Bardhi Granth*. MS 228. Dr Balbir Singh Sahitya Kendra, Dehradun.
Darshan Bhagat. *Vār Amritsar Ki*. In *Punjābī Vārān*, edited by Piara Singh Padam. Amritsar: Singh Brothers, 2008.
Gurdas (Singh). *Rāmkalī Vār Pātshāhī Dasven Kī*. In *Vārān Bhai Gurdas*, edited by Giani Hazara Singh. Amritsar: Khalsa Samachar, 1962 [1911].
Kankan Kavi. *Das Gur Kathā*. In Sarwan Singh, 'Amritsar in Medieval Punjabi Literature'.
Kaur, Joginder, ed. *Ram Sukh Rao's Sri Fateh Singh Partap Prabhākar: A History of Early Nineteenth Century Punjab*. Patiala: Published by the editor, 1980.
Kesar Singh Chhibber. *Bansāvalīnāmā Dasān Pātshāhiān Kā*. In Parkh, vol. 2, edited by Ratan Singh Jaggi. Chandigarh: Panjab University, 1972.

————. *Bansāvalīnāmā Dasān Pātshāhiān Kā.* Edited by Piara Singh Padam. Amritsar: Singh Brothers, 1997.

————. *Bansāvalīnāmā Dasān Pātshāhiān Kā.* Edited by Raijasbir Singh. Amritsar: Guru Nanak Dev University, 2001.

Koer Singh. *Gurbilās Pātshāhī 10.* Edited by Shamsher Singh Ashok. Patiala: Punjabi University, 1968.

McLeod, W.H., trans. and ed. *The B40 Janam-Sākhī.* Amritsar: Guru Nanak Dev University, 1980.

————, trans. and ed. *The Chaupa Singh Rahit-Nama.* Dunedin, New Zealand: University of Otago Press, 1987.

————, trans. *Prem Sumārag: The Testimony of a Sanatan Sikh.* New Delhi: Oxford University Press, 2006.

*Nasīhatnāmā.* MS No. 770. Guru Nanak Dev University, Amritsar.

Padam, Piara Singh, ed. *Rahitnāme.* Amritsar: Singh Brothers, 1995 (reprint).

Padam, S.S. *Sikhān dī Bhagatmālā.* Amritsar: Singh Brothers, 2013.

*Rahitnāmā.* In Ganda Singh, *Bhai Nand Lal Granthāvalī.*

*Rahitnāmā Bhai Daya Singh.* In Piara Singh Padam, *Rahitnāme.*

*Rahitnāmā Bhai Desa Singh.* In Piara Singh Padam, *Rahitnāme.*

*Rahitnāmā Bhai Prahilad Singh.* In Piara Singh Padam, *Rahitnāme.*

*Rahitnāmā Hazūrī, Bhai Chaupa Singh Chhibber.* In Piara Singh Padam, *Rahitnāme.*

Ram Sukh Rao. *Jassa Singh Binod.* MS, M/772. Punjab State Archives, Patiala.

————. *Sri Bhag Singh Chadaruday.* MS/573. Punjab State Archives, Patiala.

Ratan Singh Bhangu. *Prāchīn Panth Prakāsh.* Edited by Bhai Vir Singh. New Delhi: Bhai Vir Singh Sadan, 1993 [called 'new edition', but actually a reprint].

————. *Sri Gur Panth Prakāsh.* Edited by Balwant Singh Dhillon. *Amritsar:* Singh Brothers, 2004.

Sabar, Jasbir Singh, ed. *Giān Ratnāvalī: Janamsākhī Sri Guru Nanak Dev Jī.* Amritsar: Guru Nanak Dev University, 1993.

Sagar, Sabinderjit Singh, ed. *Hukamnāmās of Guru Tegh Bahadur: A Historical Study.* Amritsar: Guru Nanak Dev University, 2002.

Sainapat. *Shri Gur Sobhā.* Edited by Shamsher Singh Ashok. Amritsar: Shiromani Gurdwara Prabandhak Committee, 1967.

————. *Sri Gur Sobhā.* Edited by Ganda Singh. Patiala: Punjabi University, 1967.

*Sākhī Rahit Kī.* In Piara Singh Padam, *Rahitnāme.*

*Sākhī Rahit Pātisāhī 10.* In McLeod, *The Chaupa Singh Rahit-Nama.*

Sant Das Chhibber. '*Ustat Sri Amritsar Jī Kī*'. In Sarwan Singh, 'Sant Das Chhibber, *Ustat Sri Amritsar Jī Kī*'.

Sarup Das Bhalla. *Mahimā Prakāsh*. Edited by Shamsher Singh Ashok and Gobind Singh Lamba. Part I. Patiala: Punjab Languages Department, 1970.

———. *Mahimā Prakāsh*. Edited by Gobind Singh Lamba and Khazan Singh. Part II. Patiala: Punjab Languages Department, 1971.

Saundha Kavi. *Ustat Sri Amritsar Jī Kī*. In Sarwan Singh, 'Amritsar in Medieval Punjabi Literature'.

Sewadas. *Episodes from Lives of the Gurus: Parchian Sewadas*. Translated and edited by Kharak Singh and Gurtej Singh. Chandigarh: Institute of Sikh Studies, 1995.

Sewa Singh. *Shahīd Bilās* (Bhai Mani Singh). Edited by Giani Garja Singh. Ludhiana: Punjabi Sahit Akademi, 1961.

*Shabdārth Sri Guru Granth Sahib Jī*. 4 vols. Amritsar: Shiromani Gurdwara Prabandhak Committee (standard pagination).

Singh, Fauja, ed. *Hukamnāmās: Shri Guru Tegh Bahadur Sahib*. Patiala: Punjabi University, 1976.

Singh, Ganda, ed. *Bhai Nand Lal Granthāvalī*. Malacca (Malaysia): Sant Sohan Singh, 1968.

Singh, Ganda, ed. *Hukamnāme: Gurū Sāhibān, Mātā Sāhibān, Banda Singh Ate Khalsa Jī De*. Patiala: Punjabi University, 1967.

Singh, Piar, ed. *Janam Sākhī Sri Guru Nanak Dev Jī*. Amritsar: Guru Nanak Dev University, 1974.

Singh, Raijasbir, ed. *Guru Amar Das: Srot Pustak*. Amritsar: Guru Nanak Dev University, 1986.

Singh, Randhir, ed. *Prem Sumārag Granth Arthāt Khalsai Jīvan Jāch* (*Pātshāhī Dasvīn*). Jalandhar: New Book Company, 1953 [1965].

Jaggi, Ratan Singh and Gursharan Kaur Jaggi. *Sri Dasam Granth Sahib*. 5 vols. New Delhi: Gobind Sadan, 1999.

*Tankhānāmā*. In Ganda Singh, *Bhai Nand Lal Granthāvalī*.

*Vār Durgā Kī*. In *Punjābī Vārān*, edited by Piara Singh Padam. Amritsar: Singh Brothers, 2008.

*Zafarnāma*. In Jaggi and Jaggi, *Sri Dasam Granth Sahib*. Vol. 5.

## Persian Sources

*Ahkām-i 'Ālamgīrī* (1703–7). In J.S. Grewal and Habib, *Sikh History from Persian Sources*.

Anon. *Asrār-i Samadī*. Translated by Janak Singh. Patiala: Punjabi University, 1972.

Bhimsen. *Nuskha-i Dilkushā.* In J.S. Grewal and Habib, *Sikh History from Persian Sources.*

Ghulam Ali Khan. *Imādu's Sa'ādat.* In J.S. Grewal and Habib, *Sikh History from Persian Sources.*

Goswamy, B.N. and J.S Grewal, trans and eds. *The Mughals and the Jogis of Jakhbar: Some Madad-i-Ma'ash and Other Documents.* Simla: Indian Institute of Advanced Study, 1967.

————, trans and eds. *The Mughal and Sikh Rulers and the Vaishnavas of Pindori: A Historical Interpretation of 52 Persian Documents.* Simla: Indian Institute of Advanced Study, 2010 [1969].

Grewal, J.S., trans. and ed. *In the By-Lanes of History: Some Persian Documents from a Punjab Town* (belonging to the *Bhandari Collection,* Punjab State Archives, Patiala). Simla: Indian Institute of Advanced Study, 1975.

Grewal, J.S. and Indu Banga, trans and eds. *Early Nineteenth Century Punjab: From Ganesh Das's Chār Bāgh-i Panjāb.* Amritsar: Guru Nanak Dev University, 1975.

Grewal, J.S. and Irfan Habib, eds. *Sikh History from Persian Sources: Translations of Major Texts.* New Delhi: Tulika/Indian History Congress, 2001.

Khafi Khan. *Muntakhabu'l Lubāb.* In J.S. Grewal and Habib, *Sikh History from Persian Sources.*

Mirza Muhammad. '*Ibratnāma.* In J.S. Grewal and Habib, *Sikh History from Persian Sources.*

'Mobad'. *Dabistān-i Mazāhib.* In J.S. Grewal and Habib, *Sikh History from Persian Sources.*

Muhammad Hadi Kamwar Khan. *Tazkiratu's Salātīn Chaghatā.* In J.S. Grewal and Habib, Sikh History from Persian Sources.

Muhammad Qasim 'Ibrat'. '*Ibratnāma.* In J.S. Grewal and Habib, *Sikh History from Persian Sources.*

Muhammad Shafi 'Warid'. *Mir'āt-i Wāridāt.* In J.S. Grewal and Habib, *Sikh History from Persian Sources.*

Nath Mal. *Amarnāma,* translated and edited by Ganda Singh. Amritsar: Sikh History Society, 1953.

'News Reports from Bahadur Shah's Court, 1707–10'. In J.S. Grewal and Habib, *Sikh History from Persian Sources.*

'News Reports from Delhi, 1759–65'. In J.S. Grewal and Habib, *Sikh History from Persian Sources.*

Nur Muhammad, Qazi. *Jangnāma.* In J.S. Grewal and Habib, *Sikh History from Persian Sources.*

Rai Chaturman Saksena. *Chahār Gulshan.* In J.S. Grewal and Habib, *Sikh History from Persian Sources.*

Skinner, James. *Tashrīḥu'l Aqwām.* In J.S. Grewal and Habib, *Sikh History from Persian Sources.*

Sujan Rai Bhandari. *Khulāṣatu't Tawārīkh.* In J.S. Grewal and Habib, *Sikh History from Persian Sources.*

Tahmas Khan. *Qissa-i Tahmās-i Miskīn* or *Tahmās Nāma.* In J.S. Grewal and Habib, *Sikh History from Persian Sources.*

## Unpublished British Records at the National Archives of India, New Delhi

FOREIGN/POLITICAL CONSULTATION FILES

29 December 1849, No. 49A.
14 March 1851, Nos 113 E, F.
19 March 1852, Nos 67–8.

FOREIGN/POLITICAL PROCEEDINGS

31 December 1847, Nos 2192, 2200, 2204, 2443.
31 May 1850, No. 109.
23 August 1850, Nos 35A, 35C.
21 February 1851, Part I, Nos 142A, 218A.
14 March 1851, Nos 112, 114.
14 November 1851, No. 49.
12 March 1852, Nos 49, 78, 95.
16 April 1852, No. 49.
6–13 August 1852, No. 49.
15 October 1852, No. 117.
7 January 1853, Nos 213, 219–20, 222, 223, 225.
14 January 1853, Nos 213, 216, 219, 220, 223.
27 May 1853, Nos 196, 199, 202, 205, 208, 211.
3–10 June 1853, No. 119.
10 June 1853, Nos 217, 218, 219.
5–12 December 1853, No. 217.
23 June 1854, Nos 202, 205, 225.
1 May 1856, Nos 392–4.
4 July 1856, Nos 152–4.
4–11 July 1856, No. 162.
11 July 1856, No. 208.
29 August 1856, Nos 242, 249, 250, 252.
5 September 1856, Nos 110, 112.
26 September 1856, No. 238.

28 November 1856, Nos 112, 113, 125, 128, 135, 142.
5 December 1856, Nos 110, 217.
5–11 December 1856, Nos 210, 217, 227, 253.
9 January 1857, Nos 215–16.
6–13 February 1857, Nos 228, 283.
13 February 1857, Nos 288, 294, 295.
27 March 1857, Nos 240, 246.
1 May 1857, No. 419.
20 November 1857, No. 183.
27 May 1858, No. 1053.
4 June 1858, No. 148.
15 October 1858, Nos 372, 373, 379, 445.
31 December 1858, Nos 1069, 1677.
22 April 1859, No. 112.

## Other Contemporary and Near-Contemporary Sources in English

Browne, Major James. *History of the Origin and Progress of the Sikhs* [1788]. In Ganda Singh, *Early European Accounts of the Sikhs*.

[Captain Matthews], An Officer of Bengal Army. 'A Tour to Lahore in 1808'. In *The Panjab Past and Present* 1, nos 1–2 (1967 [1809]).

Francklin, William. 'The Sikhs and their Country' [1798]. In Ganda Singh, *Early European Accounts of the Sikhs*.

Forster, George. *A Journey from Bengal to England through the Northern Part of India, Kashmire, Afghanistan and Persia and into Russia by the Caspian Sea*. 2 vols. Patiala: Punjab Languages Department, 1970 [1798].

Griffin, Lepel, H. *Rajas of the Punjab*. Patiala: Punjab Languages Department, 1970 [1870].

Griffiths, John. 'A Memorandum on the Punjab and Kandhar' [1794]. In Ganda Singh, *Early European Accounts of the Sikhs*.

Madra, Amandeep Singh and Parmjit Singh, eds. *"Sicques, Tigers, or Thieves": Eyewitness Accounts of the Sikhs (1606–1809)*. New York: Palgrave Macmillan, 2004.

Malcolm, John. *Sketch of the Sikhs*. New Delhi: Asian Educational Services, 1986 [1812].

'Memoirs of an Irish Maharaja, 1803'. In Madra and Parmjit Singh, *"Sicques, Tigers, or Thieves"*.

'Of the Seikh's or Sikhan, c.1760'. In Madra and Parmjit Singh, *"Sicques, Tigers, or Thieves"*.

Polier, Colonel A.L.H. 'An Account of the Sikhs' [1787]. In Ganda Singh, *Early European Accounts of the Sikhs*.

————. 'The Sikhs'. Extract from a letter from Major Polier at Delhi to Colonel Ironside at Belgram, 22 May 1776. In Ganda Singh, *Early European Accounts of the Sikhs*.

Prinsep, Henry T. *Origin of the Sikh Power in the Punjab and Political Life of Maharaja Ranjit Singh with an Account of the Religion, Laws and Customs of the Sikhs*. Patiala: Punjab Languages Department, 1970 [1834].

Singh, Ganda, ed. *Early European Accounts of the Sikhs*. Calcutta: Indian Studies, Past & Present, 1962.

Surman, John and Edward Stephenson. 'Massacre of the Sikhs at Delhi in 1716'. In Ganda Singh, *Early European Accounts of the Sikhs*.

'Warren Hastings Memorandum on the Threat of the Sikhs, 1784'. In Madra and Parmjit Singh, *"Sicques, Tigers, or Thieves"*.

'Wendel's History of the Jats, Pathans, and Sikhs, 1768'. In Madra and Parmjit Singh, *"Sicques, Tigers, or Thieves"*.

Wilkins, Charles. 'The Sikhs and their College at Patna' [1788]. In Ganda Singh, *Early European Accounts of the Sikhs*.

'The Writings of Colonel Polier on the Sikhs, 1776–1802'. In Madra and Parmjit Singh, *"Sicques, Tigers, or Thieves"*.

## SECONDARY WORKS

### Books

Alam, Muzaffar. *The Crisis of Empire in Mughal North India: Awadh and the Punjab, 1707–48*. New Delhi: Oxford University Press, 2013 [1986].

Alavi, Seema, ed. *The Eighteenth Century India*. Delhi: Oxford University Press, 2002.

Arshi, P.S. *The Golden Temple: History, Art and Architecture*. New Delhi: Harman Publishing House, 1989.

Baagha, Ajit Singh. *Banur Had Orders: A Critical Study of an Hitherto Unknown 'Hukamnāmāh' of Guru Gobind Singh*. Delhi: Ranjit Printers and Publishers, 1980.

Bajwa, Kulwinder Singh, ed. *Mahimā Prakāsh (Vārtak)* (Punjabi). Amritsar: Singh Brothers, 2004.

Banga, Indu. *Agrarian System of the Sikhs: Late Eighteenth and Early Nineteenth Century*. New Delhi: Manohar, 1978.

Brown, Kerry, ed. *Sikh Art and Literature*. London: Routledge, 1999.

Chandra, Satish. *Parties and Politics at the Mughal Court, 1707–1740*. New Delhi: Oxford University Press, 2002 [1959].

Cole, W. Owen. *The Guru in Sikhism*. London: Darton, Longman & Todd, 1982.

Cunningham, Joseph Davey. *History of the Sikhs: From the Origin of the Nation to the Battles of the Sutlej*. New Delhi: Rupa & Co, 2003 [1849].

Daljeet. *The Sikh Heritage: A Search for Totality*. New Delhi: Prakash Book Depot, 2004.

Datta, V.N. *Amritsar: Past & Present*. Amritsar: The Municipal Committee, 1967.

Dhavan, Purnima. *When Sparrows Became Hawks: The Making of the Sikh Warrior Tradition, 1699–1799*. New York: Oxford University Press, 2014 [2011].

Fenech, Louis E. *The Darbar of the Sikh Gurus: The Court of God in the World of Men*. New Delhi: Oxford University Press, 2008.

———. *Martyrdom in the Sikh Tradition: Playing the "Game of Love"*. New Delhi: Oxford University Press, 2000.

———. *The Sikh Ẓafar-nāmah of Guru Gobind Singh: A Discursive Blade in the Heart of the Mughal Empire*. Oxford: Oxford University Press, 2013.

Goswamy, B.N. *Piety and Splendour: Sikh Heritage in Art*. New Delhi: National Museum, 2000.

Goswamy, B.N. and Caron Smith. *I See No Stranger: Early Sikh Art and Devotion*. New York and India: Rubin Museum of Art, in association with Mapin Publishing, 2006.

Grewal, J.S. *Contesting Interpretations of the Sikh Tradition*. New Delhi: Manohar Publications, 1998.

———. *Four Centuries of Sikh Tradition: History, Literature, and Identity*. New Delhi: Oxford University Press, 2013 [2011].

———. *Guru Nanak in History*. Chandigarh: Panjab University, 1998 [1969].

———. *Guru Nanak and Patriarchy*. Shimla: Indian Institute of Advanced Study, 1993.

———. *Historical Perspectives on Sikh Identity*. Patiala: Punjabi University, 1997.

———. *Historical Writings on the Sikhs (1784–2011): Western Enterprise and Indian Response*. New Delhi: Manohar, 2012.

———. ed. *The Khalsa: Sikh and Non-Sikh Perspectives*. New Delhi: Manohar, 2004.

———. *Lectures on History, Society and Culture of the Punjab*. Vol. 1. Patiala: Punjabi University, 2007.

———. *Recent Debates in Sikh Studies: An Assessment*. New Delhi: Manohar, 2011.

Grewal, J.S. *Sikh Ideology, Polity and Social Order: From Guru Nanak to Maharaja Ranjit Singh*. New Delhi: Manohar, 2007 [1996].

———. *The Sikhs: Ideology, Institutions and Identity*. New Delhi: Oxford University Press, 2009.

———. *The Sikhs of the Punjab*. The New Cambridge History of India, II.3. Cambridge: Cambridge University Press, 2014 [1990].

———. *A Study of Guru Granth Sahib: Doctrine, Social Content, History, Structure and Status*. Amritsar: Singh Brothers, 2009.

Grewal, J.S. and S.S. Bal. *Guru Gobind Singh: A Biographical Study*. Chandigarh: Panjab University, 1987 [1967].

Gupta, Hari Ram. *History of the Sikhs 1739–1768 (Evolution of the Sikh Confederacies)*. Calcutta: S.N. Sarkar, 1939.

———. *History of the Sikhs*. Vol. 1, *The Sikh Gurus, 1469–1708*. New Delhi: Munshiram Manoharlal, 2014 [1984].

———. *History of the Sikhs*. Vol. 2, *Evolution of the Sikh Confederacies (1708–69)*. New Delhi: Munshiram Manoharlal, 2014 [1939].

———. *History of the Sikhs*. Vol. 3, *Sikh Domination of the Mughal Empire (1764–1803)*. New Delhi: Munshiram Manoharlal, 2009 [1944].

———. *History of the Sikhs*. Vol. 4, *The Sikh Commonwealth or Rise and Fall of Sikh Misls*. New Delhi: Munshiram Manoharlal, 2007 [1982].

*Gurbilās Chhevīn Pātshāhī* (Punjabi). Patiala: Punjab Languages Department, 1970.

Habib, Irfan. *The Agrarian System of Mughal India 1556–1707*. New Delhi: Oxford University Press, 1999 [1963].

Hans, Surjit, ed. *B-40 Janamsākhī: Guru Baba Nanak Paintings*. Amritsar: Guru Nanak Dev University, 1987.

———. *A Reconstruction of Sikh History from Sikh Literature*. Patiala: Madaan Publications, 2005 [1987].

Herrli, Hans. *The Coins of the Sikhs*. New Delhi: Munshiram Manoharlal, 2004 [1993].

Jaggi, Ratan Singh. *Guru Granth Vishavkosh* (Punjabi). 2 parts. Patiala: Punjabi University, 2002.

Jakobsh, Doris R. *Relocating Gender in Sikh History: Transformation, Meaning and Identity*. Delhi: Oxford University Press, 2003.

———, ed. *Sikhism and Women: History, Texts, and Experience*. New Delhi: Oxford University Press, 2010.

Kaur, Madanjit. *The Golden Temple: Past and Present*. Amritsar: Guru Nanak Dev University, 1983.

Kohli, Surinder Singh. *Sikh Ethics*. New Delhi: Munshiram Manoharlal, 1975.

Malhotra, Anshu and Farina Mir, eds. *Punjab Reconsidered: History, Culture and Practice*. New Delhi: Oxford University Press, 2012.

Malhotra, Karamjit K., ed. *The Punjab Revisited: Social Order, Economic Life, Cultural Articulation, Politics, and Partition (18th–20th Centuries).* Patiala: Punjabi University, 2014.

Mann, Gurinder Singh. *The Goindval Pothis: The Earliest Extant Source of the Sikh Canon.* Cambridge, Massachusetts: Harvard University Press, 1996.

———. *The Making of the Sikh Scripture.* New Delhi: Oxford University Press, 2001.

Marshall, Peter, ed. *The Eighteenth Century in Indian History: Evolution or Revolution.* New Delhi: Oxford University Press, 2003.

McLeod, W.H. *Discovering the Sikhs: Autobiography of a Historian.* Delhi: Permanent Black, 2004.

———. *The Evolution of the Sikh Community.* Delhi: Oxford University Press, 1975.

———. *Popular Sikh Art.* Delhi: Oxford University Press, 1991.

———. *Sikhism.* London: Penguin Books, 1997.

———. *The Sikhs: History, Religion, and Society.* New York: Columbia University Press, 1989.

———. *Sikhs of the Khalsa: A History of Khalsa Rahit.* New Delhi: Oxford University Press, 2003.

———, trans. and ed. *Textual Sources for the Study of Sikhism.* Manchester: Manchester University Press, 1984.

Mitchell, G. Duncan, ed. *A Dictionary of Sociology.* London: Routledge, 1977 [1968].

Murphy, Anne. *The Materiality of the Past: History and Representation in Sikh Tradition.* New York: Oxford University Press, 2012.

Nabha, Bhai Kahan Singh. *Gurshabad Ratnākar Mahān Kosh* (Punjabi). Patiala: Punjab Languages Department, 1960 [1930].

Nayyar, Gurbachan Singh, ed. *Gur Ratan Māl: Sau Sākhī* (Punjabi). Patiala: Punjabi University, 1995.

Nijhawan, Michael. *Dhadi Darbar: Religion, Violence, and the Performance of Sikh History.* New Delhi: Oxford University Press, 2006.

Oberoi, Harjot. *The Construction of Religious Boundaries: Culture, Identity and Diversity in Sikh Tradition.* New Delhi: Oxford University Press, 1994.

Padam, Piara Singh. *Sri Guru Gobind Singh Jī De Darbārī Ratan* (Punjabi). Jalandhar: Hamdard Printing Press, 1994 [1974].

———, ed. *Parchiān Sau Sākhī* (Punjabi). Amritsar: Singh Brothers, 1997.

Pandey, Raj Bali. *Hindu Samskaras: Socio-Religious Study of the Hindu Sacraments,* 2nd rev. ed. Delhi: Motilal Banarsidass, 1969.

Qaiser, Iqbal. *Historical Sikh Shrines in Pakistan.* Lahore: Punjabi History Board, 1998.

Sachdeva, Veena. *Polity and Economy of the Punjab: During the Late Eighteenth Century.* New Delhi: Manohar, 1993.

Sekhon, Sant Singh and Kartar Singh Duggal. *A History of Punjabi Literature.* New Delhi: Sahitya Akademi, 1992.

Singh, Avtar. *Ethics of the Sikhs.* Patiala: Punjabi University, 1996 [1970].

Singh, Bhagat. *Sikh Polity in the Eighteenth and Nineteenth Centuries.* New Delhi: Oriental Publishers and Distributors, 1978.

Singh, Bhayee Sikander and Roopinder Singh. *Sikh Heritage: Ethos and Relics.* New Delhi: Rupa Publications, 2012.

Singh, Chetan. *Region and Empire: Punjab in the Seventeenth Century.* Delhi: Oxford University Press, 1991.

Singh, G.B. *Sri Guru Granth Sahib Dian Prachin Biran* (Punjabi). London: International Supreme Council of Sikhs, 2004 [1944].

Singh, Ganda. *Ahmad Shah Durrani: Father of Modern Afghanistan.* Bombay: Asia Publishing House, 1959.

———. *Guru Gobind Singh's Death at Nanded: An Examination of Succession Theories.* Patiala: Punjabi University, 2008 [1972].

———. *Life of Banda Singh Bahadur.* Patiala: Punjabi University, 2006 [1935].

———. *Sardar Jassa Singh Ahluwalia.* Patiala: Punjabi University, 1969 (Punjabi); 1990 (English).

Singh, Gurmukh, ed. *Gurbilās Pātshāhī 6* (Punjabi). Patiala: Punjabi University, 1997.

Singh, Harbans. *Guru Tegh Bahadur.* New Delhi: Sterling Publishers, 1982.

Singh, Harbans and N. Gerald Barrier, eds. *Panjab Past and Present: Essays in Honour of Dr Ganda Singh.* Patiala: Punjabi University, 1976.

Singh, Nikky-Guninder Kaur. *The Feminine Principle in the Sikh Vision of the Transcendent.* Cambridge: Cambridge University Press, 1994.

Singh, Nripinder. *The Sikh Moral Tradition: Ethical Perceptions of the Sikhs in the Late Nineteenth/Early Twentieth Century.* Columbia Missouri: South Asia Publications, 1990.

Singh, Pashaura and Louis E. Fenech, eds. *The Oxford Handbook of Sikh Studies.* Oxford: Oxford University Press, 2014.

Singh, Surinder. *Sikh Coinage: Symbol of Sikh Sovereignty.* New Delhi: Manohar, 2004.

Singh, Teja and Ganda Singh. *A Short History of the Sikhs (1465–1765).* Patiala: Punjabi University, 1999 [1950].

Singh, Trilochan and Anurag Singh. *A Brief Account of Life and Works of Guru Gobind Singh.* Amritsar: Bhai Chattar Singh, Jiwan Singh, 2002.

Sinha, Narendra Krishna. *Rise of the Sikh Power.* Calcutta: A. Mukherjee & Co., 1963 [1936].

## Articles in Edited Volumes

Banga, Indu. 'Alha Singh: The Founder of Patiala State'. In Harbans Singh and Barrier, *Panjab Past and Present: Essays in Honour of Dr Ganda Singh.*

———. 'Formation of the Sikh State, 1765–1845'. In *Five Punjabi Centuries: Polity, Economy, Society, Culture, c.1500–1990*, edited by Indu Banga. New Delhi: Manohar, 2000 [1997].

———. 'Gender Relations in Medieval India'. In *The State and Society in Medieval India*, vol. 7, part 1 of *History of Science, Philosophy and Culture in Indian Civilization*, edited by J.S. Grewal. New Delhi: Oxford University Press, 2005.

Banga, Indu and J.S. Grewal. 'The Study of Regional History'. In *Different Types of History*, vol. 14, part 4 of *History of Science, Philosophy and Culture in Indian Civilization*, edited by Bharati Ray. Delhi: Pearson Education, 2009.

Bhatti, S.S. 'The Golden Temple: A Spiritual Marvel in Architecture'. In *Golden Temple*, edited by Parm Bakhshish Singh, Devinder Kumar Verma, R. K. Ghai, and Gursharan Singh. Patiala: Punjabi University, 1999.

Bonta, Robert J. Del. 'An Illustrated Life: Guru Nanak in Narrative Art'. In Brown, *Sikh Art and Literature.*

Deol, Jeevan Singh. 'Eighteenth Century Khalsa Identity: Discourse, Praxis, and Narrative'. In *Sikh Religion, Culture, and Ehtnicity*, edited by Christopher Shackle, Gurharpal Singh, and Arvind-Pal Singh. Mandair, Surrey: Curzon, 2000.

———. 'Illustration and Illumination in Sikh Scriptural Manuscripts'. In *New Insights into Sikh Art*, edited by Kavita Singh. Mumbai: Marg Publications, 2003.

Fenech, Louis E. 'The History of *Zafarnamah* of Guru Gobind Singh'. In A. Malhotra and Mir, *Punjab Reconsidered.*

Grewal, J.S. 'The *B40 Janamsakhi*'. In J.S. Grewal, *Lectures on History, Society and Culture of the Punjab.*

———. '*Bachittar Nātak*: Proclamation of a Mission'. In J.S. Grewal, *Sikh Ideology, Polity and Social Order.*

———. 'The Basic Significance of the *Mahima Prakash (Vartak)*'. In K.K. Malhotra, *The Punjab Revisited.*

———. 'Caste and the Sikh Social Order'. In J.S. Grewal, *The Sikhs: Ideology, Institutions and Identity.*

———. 'Celebrating Freedom: The *Vār* of Gurdas'. In J.S. Grewal, *Sikh Ideology, Polity and Social Order.*

Grewal, J.S. 'Cleavage in the Panth'. In J.S. Grewal, *Sikh Ideology, Polity and Social Order*.

———. 'Declaration of "Righteous War": The *Bachittar Nāṭak*'. In J.S. Grewal, *History, Literature, and Identity*.

———. 'In Defence of the Freedom of Conscience'. In J.S. Grewal, *Sikh Ideology, Polity and Social Order*.

———. 'An Early Eighteenth Century Janamsākhī'. In J.S. Grewal, *The Sikhs: Ideology, Institutions and Identity*.

———. '"Frighten No One and Be Afraid of None": Guru Tegh Bahadur'. In J.S. Grewal, *History, Literature, and Identity*.

———. 'The Gurdwara'. In *Religious Movements and Institutions in Medieval India*, vol. 7, part 2 of *History of Indian Science, Philosophy and Culture in Indian Civilization*, edited by J.S. Grewal. New Delhi: Oxford University Press, 2006.

———. 'The Guru-Khalsa: Sainapat's *Sri Gur Sobhā*'. In J.S. Grewal, *History, Literature, and Identity*.

———. '*Gursobhā*: In Praise of the Khalsa'. In J.S. Grewal, *Sikh Ideology, Polity and Social Order*.

———. 'Insistence on Justice'. In J.S. Grewal, *Sikh Ideology, Polity and Social Order*.

———. 'The Prem Sumarag: A Theory of Sikh Social Order'. In Harbans Singh and Barrier, *Panjab Past and Present*.

———. 'The *Prem Sumārag*: A Sant Khalsa Vision of the Sikh Panth'. In J.S. Grewal, *The Sikhs: Ideology, Institutions and Identity*.

———. 'The Sikh Faith and the Khalsa Panth: Chhibber's *Bansāvlīnāma*'. In J.S. Grewal, *History, Literature, and Identity*.

———. 'Sikhism and Gender'. In J.S. Grewal, *The Sikhs: Ideology, Institutions and Identity*.

———. 'The Singh Way of Life: The *Rahitnāmas*'. In J.S. Grewal, *History, Literature, and Identity*.

———. 'Social History in Sikh Literature'. In *Studies in Sikhism and Comparative Religion*, vol. 8. New Delhi: Guru Nanak Foundation, 1989.

———. 'Study of Sikhism, Sikh History and Sikh Literature'. In *Approaches to History: Essays in Indian Historiography*, edited by Sabyasachi Bhattacharya. Delhi: Indian Council of Historical Research in association with Primus Books, 2011.

———. 'Valorizing The Tradition: Bhangu's *Guru Panth Prakash*'. In J.S. Grewal, *The Khalsa*.

———. '*Zafarnāma*: Declaration of Moral Victory'. In J.S. Grewal, *Sikh Ideology, Polity and Social Order*.

Kaur, Anurupita. 'Sikhs in the Early Census Reports'. In *Five Centuries of Sikh Tradition: Ideology, Society, Politics and Culture (Essays for Indu Banga)*, edited by R. Grewal and Sheena Pall. New Delhi: Manohar, 2005.

Kaur, Madanjit. 'Koer Singh's *Gurbilas Patshahi 10:* An Eighteenth Century Sikh Literature'. In *Sikhism*, edited by Jasbir Singh Mann and Kharak Singh. Patiala: Punjabi University, 1992.

Malhotra, Karamjit K., 'The Earliest Manual on the Sikh Way of Life'. In R. Grewal and Pall, *Five Centuries of Sikh Tradition*.

———. 'Religious Beliefs and Practices of the Eighteenth-Century Sikhs'. In K.K. Malhotra, *The Punjab Revisited*.

Mann, Gurinder Singh. 'Five Hundred Years of Sikh Educational Heritage'. In R. Grewal and Pall, *Five Centuries of Sikh Tradition*.

———. 'Gender and the Sikh Panth'. In *Essays in Sikh History, Tradition, and Society*. New Delhi: Oxford University Press, 2007.

Murphy, Anne. 'An Idea of Religion: Identity, Difference, and Comparison in the *Gurbilas*'. In A. Malhotra and Mir, *Punjab Reconsidered*.

Rai, Gurmeet and Kavita Singh. 'Brick by Sacred Brick: Architectural Projects of Guru Arjan and Guru Hargobind'. In Kavita Singh, *New Insights into Sikh Art*.

Rinehart, Robin. 'The Dasam Granth'. In Pashaura Singh and Fenech, *The Oxford Handbook of Sikh Studies*.

Singh, Gurtej. 'Compromising the Khalsa Tradition: Koer Singh's *Gurbilas*'. In J.S. Grewal, *The Khalsa*.

Singh, Kirpal. 'Mahimā Prakāsh'. In *The Encyclopaedia of Sikhism*, vol. 3, edited by Harbans Singh. Patiala: Punjabi University, 1997.

Thapar, K.S. 'Gurbilās Pātshāhī Dasvin'. In *The Encyclopaedia of Sikhism*, vol. 1, edited by Harbans Singh. Patiala: Punjabi University, 1992.

## Journal Articles

Banga, Indu. 'Raj-Khalsa: Ideology and Praxis'. *Journal of Punjab Studies* (Special Issue on Guru Gobind Singh) 15, nos 1 and 2 (Spring–Fall, 2008): 33–64.

Cohn, Bernard. 'Political Systems in Eighteenth Century India: The Banaras Region'. *Journal of American Oriental Society* 82, no. 3 (1962).

Dosanj, S.S. and Rao Uttam Singh. 'A Dated Janam Sakhi of Guru Nanak'. In *Roop Lekha* 39, no. 1.

Grewal, J.S. 'To Update Guru Gobind Singh: New Dimensions of Historical Scholarship'. *Journal of Regional History* 13–14 (2007–8): 39–74.

———. 'Guru Gobind Singh: Life and Mission'. *Journal of Punjab Studies* (Special Issue on Guru Gobind Singh) 15, nos 1 and 2 (Spring–Fall 2008): 3–31.

Grewal, J.S. and Indu Banga, 'The Sikh Prayer (*Ardas*)'. *Punjab Journal of Sikh Studies* 1 (2011): 9–23.

Grewal, Reeta. 'Anandpur: The City of Guru Gobind Singh'. *Journal of Punjab Studies* (Special Issue on Guru Gobind Singh) 15, nos 1 and 2 (Spring–Fall 2008): 65–93.

Malhotra, Karamjit K. 'Banda Singh Bahadur in the *Mahima Prakash*'. *Journal of Sikh Studies* 36 (2012): 99–110.

———. 'Banda Singh in Chhibber's *Bansavalinama* : Image, Idea and Reality'. *Panjab Journal of Sikh Studies* 2 (2012): 111–22.

———. 'Contemporary Evidence on Sikh Rites and Rituals in the Eighteenth Century'. *Journal of Punjab Studies* 16, no. 2 (Fall 2009): 179–97.

———. 'Expanding Scope of Sikh Studies on the Eighteenth Century'. *Panjab Journal of Sikh Studies* 3 (2013): 33–71.

———. 'Goddess in Sikh Literature of the Eighteenth Century'. *The Panjab Past and Present* 39, no. 2 (October 2010): 6–14.

———. '*Guru Granth Sahib* in the Eighteenth Century'. *The Panjab Past and Present* 43, no. 1 (2012): 11–20.

———. 'History, Literature and Ideology: A Historiographical Perspective on the Rahitnāmās'. *Journal of Regional History* 13–14 (2007–8): 75–96.

———. 'Issues of Gender among the Sikhs: Eighteenth-Century Literature'. *Journal of Punjab Studies* 20, nos 1 and 2 (Spring–Fall 2013): 53–76.

———. 'Situating Banda Singh in His Historical Context'. *The Calcutta Historical Journal* 30, nos 1, 2 (2014): 47–66.

———. 'On the Study of Sikh Ethics'. *Panjab Journal of Sikh Studies* 1 (2011): 70–1.

Mann, Gurinder Singh. 'Sources for the Study of Guru Gobind Singh's Life and Times'. *Journal of Punjab Studies* (Special Issue on Guru Gobind Singh) 15, nos 1 and 2 (Spring–Fall 2008): 229–84.

McLeod, W.H. 'Reflections on Prem Sumarag'. Review article. *Journal of Punjab Studies* 14, no. 1 (Spring 2007): 123–32.

Murphy, Anne. 'History in the Sikh Past'. *History and Theory* 46, no. 2 (October 2007): 345–65.

Randhawa, M.S. 'Paintings of the Sikh Gurus in the Collection of Mahant of Gurdwara Ram Rai, Dehradun'. *Roopa Lekha* 39, no. 1.

## Proceedings of History Conferences

Banga, Indu. 'Ahmad Shah Abdali's Designs over the Punjab'. *Proceedings Indian History Congress*, 67th Session. Patiala, 1968.

Grewal, J.S. 'Gender Relations in the *Mahimā Prakāsh (Vārtak)*'. Forty-Fourth Session, *Proceedings Punjab History Conference*. Patiala: Punjabi University, 2013.

Malhotra, Karamjit K. 'Equality and Caste among Eighteenth-Century Sikhs'. *Proceedings Indian History Congress*, 72nd Session. Patiala, 2012.

———. 'In Search of Early Sikh Art'. *Proceedings Indian History Congress*, 71st Session. Malda, 2011.

Singh, Fauja. 'A Study of the Paintings of Guru Nanak'. *Proceedings Punjab History Conference*. Patiala: Punjabi University, 1970.

Singh, Gurtej. 'Bhai Mani Singh: In Historical Perspective'. *Proceedings Punjab History Conference*. Patiala: Punjabi University, 1968.


## Dissertations

Singh, Sarwan, 'Amritsar in Medieval Punjabi Literature: An Historical Analysis'. PhD diss., Guru Nanak Dev University, Amritsar, 1994.

———. 'Sant Das Chhibber, *Ustat Sri Amritsar Ji Ki*'. M. Phil diss., Guru Nanak Dev University, Amritsar, 1988.

# Index

Abchal Nagar (Abchalnagar) 7, 118,
119, 247, 248
Abdul Ahad Khan 49
Abdul Rahman 263, 264
Abd-us-Samad Khan 29, 30–2
Ād Purkh 102, 294, 299
Ādi Granth 106–7, 126, 128–30,
137, 158, 197–8, 241
Adina Beg Khan 39, 41, 43, 122
Afghanistan 49, 50, 52
Agra 25, 248
Ahmad Shah Abdali (Durrani) 13,
19, 20, 39–48, 51–2, 60, 64,
74–9, 92, 12–3, 125, 249, 272
Ahmad Shah of Batala 56, 59, 74,
75, 88, 91
Ajit Singh 196, 198, 241
Ajita Randhawa 263
Ajmer 28
Akāl Bungā 34, 37, 46, 63, 68–70,
74, 77, 80, 85, 88, 90–2, 120–1,
134, 249, 250, 271–3, 282
Akāl Purkh 77, 102–4, 109, 111,
115–17, 130, 146, 149, 156–7, 161,
171, 174, 180, 199, 206, 208, 213,
243, 247, 283, 290
Akāl Purkhiā 33
Akāl Sāhāi 40, 77, 81, 83, 87, 91,
282

Akāl Takht 20, 271, 272
Akāl Ustat 104, 130, 254
Akālī 63–4, 68, 74–6, 85, 88, 90,
119, 158–9, 197–8, 269, 285
Ala Singh 32, 55, 68, 72, 78–9, 92,
94, 218
Alāhniān 143, 150, 162, 165
Alam Chand (Raj) 252, 259, 260,
261, 263, 270
Alam Singh of Akhnur 48
Alamganj 111
Ali Singh 27
Aligarh 49
Amar Singh 80, 82, 83
Amar Singh Bagga 97
Amar Singh Kingra 97
Amar Singh of Patiala 49, 79
Ambala 27, 49, 72
amrit 23, 109, 119, 147, 153, 155–7,
162, 176, 215, 247
amritsar (amrit sarovar) 33, 76,
121–2, 125, 157, 236, 249, 250
Amritsar 3, 5, 8, 26, 34, 41, 46–7,
57, 61, 63–4, 68–9, 73, 75–8,
80, 85, 87–8, 92, 101, 118–19,
125, 129, 130–2, 134, 140, 159,
192, 194, 197, 216, 247–50, 254,
257, 259, 271, 276, 281–2, 284,
287

*Ānand* 115, 143, 146, 149, 153, 156–7, 159, 162, 165, 211, 244, 254, 284

Anand Ram Mukhlis 38

Anandpur 6, 7, 22–5, 74, 111, 118–19, 130, 134, 147, 155, 202, 207–8, 216–17, 226, 241, 245, 247–8, 258, 272, 276, 284, 288, 290, 292, 294, 296–8

*Ānandpur Bīṛ* 217, 257

*Āratī Sohilā (Sohilā)* 111, 116, 130, 143, 160, 162, 164

*ardās* 39, 57, 77, 110, 112, 114–16, 130, 132, 144, 146, 148–53, 155–7, 160, 162–3, 166, 171, 211, 235, 238, 244, 284, 290

*ardāsiā* 119, 121

*ashnān (isnān)* 78, 116, 125, 130

Attock 273

Aurangabad 19, 28

Aurangzeb 21, 22, 24, 25, 60, 111, 125, 195, 291, 294

Awadh 47, 50, 78

Baba Deep Singh 120

Baba Gurditta 20, 111

Baba Sunder 143, 159, 165

Badbhag Singh (Sodhi) 43, 83

*bādshāh* 74, 91, 245

Baghel Singh (Karoṛasinghia) 49, 70, 97, 259

Bahadur Shah (Muʻazzam) 22, 25, 28, 29, 148, 195, 294

Bahlolpur 27

Baisākhī 23, 39, 46, 65, 69, 77–8, 92, 119, 120, 125, 131, 155, 192, 199, 207, 216, 236, 248, 294

Baj Singh 27

Bakala 21

Bakht Mal 40

Bal Nath 267

Banda Singh (Banda, 'Banda Sahib', Bairagi Banda, Banda Bahadur) 1, 19, 25–32, 46, 51, 53–4, 62–3, 70, 92, 111, 120, 123, 147–8, 186, 192–3, 196, 198–9, 203, 216, 219, 236, 241, 250, 272, 282, 287

Bandaī 120, 198

*bāṇī (bāṇī-shabad)* 104–5, 115–17, 124, 130, 146, 178, 237, 247

Barnala 44, 218

Basohli 48

Batala 28–9, 43 48, 59, 74, 86, 88, 91, 93

Bebe Gulabo 216

Begam Samru 50

Benares (Kashi) 111, 147, 199, 218, 248, 257, 295, 298

Bengal 30, 193, 220, 268

Bhadarwah 48

Bhadaur 49

*bhaddan (bhaddar)* 146, 162 185

*bhaddanī* 159

Bhadson 248, 253

Bhag Singh 83–4, 98, 270

Bhag Singh Ahluwalia 84, 269

Bhag Singh Chiniot 98

Bhag Singh Kalalwala 84

Bhag Singh of Jind 72, 98

*bhagautī* 147, 235

*bhagtī* 116

*bhagtī-bhāo* 241

Bhagwant Rai 27

Bhai Alam Singh 32, 48, 218

Bhai Bālā (Bālā) 234, 259, 266

Bhai Bhagat Singh 11

Bhai Binta 218

Bhai Daya Singh (Daya Singh) 5, 13, 103, 105, 109, 113, 115, 117, 118, 119, 122, 139, 157, 159, 180, 201, 209, 215, 242, 247, 255

Bhai Daya Singh (Daya Singh, one of the *panj pyaras*) 153–6

Bhai Des Raj 74, 121

Bhai Desa Singh (Desa Singh) 5, 13, 103, 105–6, 108, 113–14, 136, 156, 159, 181–2, 201, 209, 215, 242, 246, 254

Bhai Gurdas 8, 20, 108, 110, 126–7, 144–5, 166, 234, 237, 248, 288

Bhai Mani Singh 8, 34, 35–6, 69, 237, 240, 248–9, 275, 287

Bhai Nand Lal 5, 7, 23, 102, 104, 199, 242–4, 247

Bhai Nand Lal Goya 6

Bhai Pheru 86

Bhai Prahilad Singh (Prahilad Singh, Prahilad Rai, Prihlad Singh) 5, 7, 12, 103–4, 108, 116, 180, 242–3

Bhai Qandhara Singh 274

Bhai Rama (Rama) 27, 32, 217–18, 257

Bhai Rupa 257

Bhai Sahib Singh 9

Bhai Sangu Mal 252

Bhai Sangu Shah 270

Bhai Santokh Das 86

Bhai Surat Singh 8

Bhai Svarup Singh Kaushish 248, 253

Bhai Tara Singh 35, 36

Bhai Taru Singh 38, 275

Bhai Tiloka 27, 257

bhang 114, 173, 182, 185, 188

Bhangani 22

Bharatpur 47, 206

Bharog 73

Bhatinda 194

Bhatt 7

Bhatt Bhikha 248

Bhatt Chhajju Singh of Bhadson 248, 253

Bhattakharī 7, 248, 253

*bhet* 77, 82, 176, 243, 244

Bhim Chand 21–3, 294

Bhimbar 48, 198

Bhimsen 192

*bhog* 114–15

*bhog-path* 150, 152

*bhujangī* 70

Bhup Prakash 28

Bianpur 82

Bidar 153, 155

Bidhi Chand 257

Bilaspur 21, 267

Bina 111

Binod Singh 27

Binod Singh Bhalla 34

Bir Singh (Ramgharia) 270

Bir Singh 98

Bir Singh Ranghretā 34

Bota Singh 37, 38

Brij Raj Dev 48

Browne, Major James 62, 79, 124, 157, 186

Buddh Singh Singhpuria 72

Burhanpur 248

Buria 27, 49

Chain Singh 72–3

*chalīhā* 77, 155

Chamba 48, 269

Chamiari 85

Chamkaur 24, 201, 208

*Chandī Charitra* 151, 290

*charan-pahul* (*charan-amrit*, *pag-pahul*) 144–5, 162, 295

Charhat Singh 98

Charhat Singh Sukarchakiya 40, 44, 48, 78, 84, 86, 126, 274–5

Chaudhari Phul 32

Chaudhari Sahib Rai 35
*chaukā* 172, 183, 206, 221
*chaukī- shabad* 159
Chaupa Singh Chhibber (Bhai
  Chaupa Rai) 6, 12–13, 103–5,
  108, 149–152, 155, 175, 207, 242,
  245–6, 291–2, 299
*Chaupaī* 156–7, 254
Chhachhrauli 49
Chhat 25, 27
*chhotā ghallūghārā* 44, 56
Chilaundi 49
Chuhaṛ Kana 275
Collins, Lieutenant Colonel J. 50
Cunningham, J.D. 59, 66, 67, 68,
  89, 193, 194

Dal Khalsa 20, 62, 71, 88, 90, 94,
  282
Dalla 248
Damdama (Talwandi Sabo) 134,
  216
Dara Shukoh 21
Darbār Sāhib (Harmandar Sāhib,
  Harmandar, Harmandir) 3, 20,
  33–4, 37, 69, 71, 74, 76–7, 85,
  91, 101, 118–22, 125, 132, 134, 139,
  216, 221, 249–50, 254, 271–3,
  277, 288
Darbara Singh 33
Darshan Bhagat 236
*Darshanī Deorhī* 121, 273
*Dasam (Dasven) Pātshāh kā
  Granth* 107, 158
*Dasam Granth* 2, 53, 106–7, 126,
  137, 162, 239, 251, 253, 283–4,
  299
Dasaundha Singh 34, 98
*dasvandh* 77, 116, 121, 155, 184, 244
Dattaji Sindhia 43
Dattatreya 267

Daya Ram Abrol 252
Deep Singh 34
*deg* 6, 26, 32, 46, 54, 80, 92, 148,
  215, 282, 298
Dehradun 21, 277
Delhi 21, 28, 30, 32, 36, 43–6, 49,
  50, 56, 84, 88, 94–5, 111, 119,
  120, 123, 125, 186, 196, 198, 205,
  208, 216, 218–19, 240, 248,
  257, 281
Desa Singh of Kaithal 49
*dhādī* 85, 115, 234, 236, 252
*dhādī darbār* 236
Dhadi Nath Mal (Nath Mal) 235,
  252
Dhaka 111
*dharam* 23, 116–18, 173, 177, 179,
  185, 188, 208–9, 214, 296–7
*dharam dī kirt* 175, 206, 207
*dharam niān* 218
Dharam Singh (one of the *panj
  pyaras*) 153, 155
*dharamsāl* 101, 110–16, 119, 128,
  130–1, 133–4, 214, 221, 245, 247,
  271, 273–4, 276, 284, 287
*dharamsāliā* 112
*dharmarth* 59, 82, 90, 93, 221
Dhianpur 83
Dhir Mal 20, 21, 74, 196, 202
Dhir Malliā 146, 154, 156, 158, 178,
  180, 185, 198, 200, 285, 288
Dina Nath 267
Divān Mani Ram 155
Diwali (Kattakī) 34, 39, 65, 67, 69,
  78, 92, 119, 120, 125–6, 131, 216,
  218
Dulcha Singh 49
Dulla Bhatti 251
Durga (Bhavani, Chandi, Kali,
  Kalika) 102, 127, 156, 235, 251,
  290, 291, 292, 294, 296, 297

Dusehra 78, 92, 125, 126
Dwarka 153, 155

Eminabad 38, 46

Faridkot 49
Farrukh Siyar 29, 196
*fateh* 26, 32–3, 46, 54, 80, 282
Fateh Darshan 198
Fateh Singh 25, 27
Fateh Singh Ahluwalia 72, 121
Fateh Singh Kanhiya 84
Fateh Singh Shahid 98
Fatehabad 72
Fatehgaṛh 50, 272
Forster, George 60, 61, 95, 124, 157, 197, 204
Francklin, William 125, 186

Ganda Singh Bhangi 139
Ganesh Das 59, 75, 76, 77, 91, 273, 274
Gaṛhwal 22
Garja Singh Ranghretā 38
Gaura Singh 82
Ghazipur 217
*Ghoṛiān* 143, 162
Ghulam Ali Khan 123, 193, 196, 204
Giani Surat Singh 237
Goindval 134
*golak* 116, 178, 244
Gorakh Nath 263–4
Granthī (*granthī*) 34, 85, 86, 121, 221
Griffiths, John 124, 157, 204
Gujjar Singh Bhangi 46, 48, 76, 78, 84, 91
Gujranwala 85, 274, 275
Gujrat 19, 47, 75, 76, 84, 194, 273, 274

Guler 266–7, 269
Gurbakhsh Singh (Chhibber) 33, 119, 246, 291
Gurbakhsh Singh (Kanhiya) 80, 81, 84, 269, 270
Gurbakhsh Singh Nihang 46, 71
Gurbakhsh Singh Waraich 77
Gurbāṇī 10, 103, 108, 110, 112, 115–16, 122–3, 131–2, 144, 179, 214, 237, 243, 284
Gurbhāī 180, 185
*Gurbilās (gurbilās)* 7, 10, 11, 13, 105, 109, 114, 118, 145, 151, 170, 188, 215, 217, 222, 234, 239–41, 250, 286, 291–2, 294, 297, 299
Gurdas (Singh) 9, 10, 103, 126, 200, 235
Gurdas Nangal 29, 55
Gurdwara (*gurdwārā*) 3, 68, 72, 85, 101, 110, 115, 119–20, 134, 217, 221, 260, 272–7, 283–6, 288
*guṛhtī* 148
Gurmatā 20, 45, 61–5, 67, 69, 70, 75, 78, 87, 90, 93, 107, 109, 121, 137, 216, 282
Gurpurab 111, 130, 211
Guru Amar Das 34, 85, 110, 143, 156, 165, 242, 248, 254
Guru Angad (Lehna) 34, 85, 108, 110, 144, 248, 261, 26–5, 268
Guru Arjan 20, 37, 105, 110, 129, 132, 143–5, 151, 164, 183, 192, 195, 248, 256–7, 269, 271
Guru Gobind Singh 2, 6–11, 13, 15, 19, 21, 23–6, 32, 34–5, 46, 51, 54, 63–4, 67–8, 70–1, 79–80, 86, 88, 90, 92, 101, 103–9, 111, 113, 115, 118–19, 123–4, 127–9, 131–4, 143–5, 147–8, 150–6, 158–60, 162, 176, 180, 181, 183, 185, 195–203, 205–9, 214–17, 234–55,

257–8, 261, 265, 269, 272, 276, 278, 281–4, 286, 287, 290–9
Guru Granth Sāhib (Granth Sāhib, Guru Granth) 2, 3, 25, 45, 51, 69, 90, 101–2, 105–7, 109–10, 112, 124, 130–1, 133, 136, 144, 148, 150, 152–3, 161–2, 184–5, 188, 200, 214, 224, 234, 238, 240, 245, 248, 283–4
Guru Har Krishan 21, 111, 238
Guru Har Rai 21, 238, 257, 274
Guru Hargobind 20, 21, 37, 51–52, 85, 111, 127, 195, 199, 238, 248, 257–8, 268–9, 271, 274–6, 287
Guru Harsahai 202, 226
Guru Nanak 5, 26, 64, 67, 71–2, 79, 80, 85, 92, 105, 108, 110, 113, 117, 123–8, 131–3, 142–4, 152, 156, 159, 161, 164, 170, 176–8, 185, 192, 194–8, 200–4, 224, 234, 236–9, 241–2, 248, 250, 254, 259, 260–8, 274, 285–6, 299
Guru Panth (Guru Khalsa) 2, 3, 69, 77, 90–1, 101, 105, 107–10, 130–1, 133, 136, 152, 182, 200, 209, 224, 248, 281, 285
Guru Ram Das 37, 39, 71, 85, 104, 108, 115, 122, 133, 143, 145, 164–6, 248, 268–9
Guru Tegh Bahadur 15, 21, 51, 85, 110–11, 125, 129, 132, 199, 205, 208, 217, 236, 238, 240, 249, 257–8, 268, 271, 275, 281, 287, 292, 294
Gwalior 20

Hakikat Rai 251
Hakikat Singh Kanhiya 84
*halāl* 133, 187, 188
*hanne hanne mīr* 90
*hanne hanne pātshāhī* 7, 90

Hansi 220
Haṛappa 85
Harbakhsh Singh 80, 82
Hari Singh 8, 40, 84, 152
Hari Singh Bhangi 76, 91, 139
Haryana 25, 193, 204, 220
Hasan Abdal 45
Hastinapur 153, 155
Himmat Singh (one of the *panj pyaras*) 153
Hindur 20
Holgaṛh 272
Holi (*holkā*) 78, 92, 125
Hoshiarpur 28, 72
*hukamnāmā* 4, 25–6, 32, 54, 59, 77, 86, 91, 109, 111, 120, 138, 147, 152, 199, 202, 217–19, 222, 252, 257, 258, 275, 277, 282, 287
*hukkā* 131, 183
Hukumat Singh 40, 42, 56, 80, 81, 82, 84
Hyderabad 196

Jagannath 118, 153, 155
Jagat Singh 29
*jagg pavit* 156
Jagrup Singh 269
Jahan Khan (Wazir) 42–3, 72, 126
Jahandar Shah 29, 30
Jahangir 20, 81
Jai Singh Kanhiya 39, 40, 48, 56, 80, 84, 86, 269–70
Jai Singh Sodhi of Anandpur 74
Jaimal-Fatta 251
Jakhbaṛ 83
Jalandhar 28, 41, 72, 77, 194
Jammu 22, 29, 48, 220
*Janamsākhī* 110, 234, 236–7, 250, 252, 259, 263–4, 266, 268, 270, 276, 278, 286–7
*Jāp* 113, 115–16, 130, 243, 254

*Japujī* 113, 115–16, 130, 142, 153, 156–7, 162, 252, 254
Jaspat Rai 38
Jassa Singh Ahluwalia (Kalal) 39, 40, 44–5, 48, 71–4, 76, 78–9, 84, 90–2, 94, 121, 254, 270
Jassa Singh Ramgaṛhia (Thoka) 39, 40–1, 48, 78, 84, 269–70
Jaswan 48, 269
Jaswant Singh of Nabha 72
*jathā* 27, 34
Jattowal 82
Jhandā Bungā 272
Jhanda Singh Bhangi 40, 48, 84, 139
*jhatkā* 182, 187–8
Jind 27, 49, 72, 79, 80, 98, 274
Jiwan Singh 77, 273
Jiwan Singh Ranghretā 208
Jodh Singh 98
Jodh Singh Ramgaṛhia 97, 270
Jodh Singh Saurianwala 98
Jodh Singh Waraich (Wazirabadia) 77, 97
Jogi Subuddh Nath 83
Jujhar (Singh) 217
Jujhar Singh 22

Ka'ba 262
Kabir 127, 261, 263–4
Kabul 49, 50, 193
*kachh (kachhehrā)* 112, 130, 146, 150, 153, 156–7, 181, 293
Kahan Singh Kalal 120
Kahan Singh Trehan 34, 208
Kahlur 21, 23, 24
Kahnuwan 29, 38, 40, 42, 81–2
Kaithal 49, 79, 80, 84
Kalāl (kalāl) 71, 79, 120, 206–7, 209, 210, 291
Kalanaur 28, 29, 31

Kalijpur 82
Kalsia 49
Kangra 48, 71, 262, 269, 270, 273
Kapur Singh 33–4, 36, 39, 70
Kapurthala 71, 94, 98
*kār* 77, 243
*kaṛāh parsād* 103, 113–14, 130, 132, 144, 149, 152, 156–7, 160, 162–3, 166, 211, 238, 244, 246–7, 284
Karam Singh 34, 70, 98
Karam Singh Chheena 97
Karam Singh Nirmala (Shahabadia) 72
Karoṛa Singh 40, 49, 70
Kartarpur (Dera Baba Nanak) 128, 132, 134
Kartarpur 21, 43, 74, 196, 202, 226
Kashmir 48, 64, 193, 248, 295, 298
Kasur 72, 109
*kathā* 114, 150, 155, 159, 239, 240
*katṛa* 76, 121, 273
Kauṛa Mal 39, 40, 197
Kavi Kankan 122, 249
Kavi Sant Das 122, 249
Kavi Saundha 249
*kes* 23, 31, 35, 112, 130, 146–8, 150–6, 162, 200–1, 238, 243, 245, 293
*kesān dī pahul* 151
Kesar Singh Chhibber 32–3, 35, 103, 105–7, 121, 131, 154, 184, 201, 215, 236, 241, 272, 291, 296
Kesdhārī 146, 148, 152, 154, 186, 197–8, 200–3, 223, 243, 245–6, 285, 288–9
Kesgaṛh 118, 119, 155, 248, 272
*keskī* 154, 238
Khadur 134
Khafi Khan 30, 203, 219
Khalsa Panth 33, 77, 91, 153, 200–1, 221, 240, 243, 245, 281–3, 287, 291, 293, 296, 298

Khalsa Rāj 20, 52, 76, 90, 92–3, 240, 282, 286–8

*khandā* 23, 148, 162–3, 211, 235, 293–4, 296–7

*khande kī pahul* 23, 144, 146–9, 154–6, 162–3, 199, 201, 210–11, 284

*khandedhār* 200

Khara Bhai Mangat 85, 86

*kharag jagg* 296–7

Kharkhauda 25

Khidrana 24

Khulāsā (Khalāsā) 153, 168, 196–8, 200, 203, 285, 289

Khurja 49

Kiratpur 20, 21, 134, 288

Kiri Pathan 29

*kirpā* 102

Kirpa Ram 153

*kirpān* 112, 146

*kīrtan* 111–12, 114–16, 130, 143, 150, 152, 155, 159, 212, 238, 295

Koer Singh 11, 13, 103–6, 109, 114–15, 118, 151, 153, 183, 201, 207, 215, 239–41, 291–4, 299

Kot Buddha 34

Kulu 48

Kunjpura 46

*kurahatiā* 178

Kurukshetra 120, 268

Ladwa 49

Lahore 19, 20, 27–30, 32, 35–52, 56, 60–1, 64, 66, 76, 78–80, 84–5, 88, 90–2, 94, 120, 153, 193–4, 248–9, 273, 275, 282

Lakhpat Rai 34, 38–9

Lalo 268

*langar* 35, 101, 103, 110, 113–14, 147–8, 156, 162, 208, 218–19, 246–7, 271

*Lāvān* 143, 149, 162, 165–6

Lehna Singh 46, 84

Lohgaṛh 27–9, 272, 287

Lucknow 248

Ludhiana 12, 26–7, 69, 194, 257

Machhiwara 27, 201

Mahadji Sindhia 49–50

Mahan Singh Sukarchakia 48–9, 84, 91, 251, 274, 275

*mahāparsād* 166, 172

Maharajpura 82

Makhowal (Chak Nanaki) 21–2, 271, 272, 292

Malcolm, John 59, 62–4, 88, 107, 126–30, 136–7, 158, 186–7, 193, 197–8, 205, 220

Mandi 48, 278

Mandiali 37

Mani Majra 72

Mankot 267

*mannat* 155, 171, 243

Mardana 236, 259, 262, 265–6

*marjīvaṛe* 155

Masand 106, 111, 133, 146–8, 150, 152–5, 178, 184–5, 195, 199–203, 214, 257, 291, 294, 297

Masandiā 71, 146, 156, 158, 178, 180, 185, 202, 243, 288

Mastan Singh 70

Mata Gujri 24, 111, 214–16

Mata Jito 215, 217

Mata Sahib Devi 32–33, 111, 119, 147, 153, 196, 199, 215–19, 241, 250

Mata Sundari 32, 111, 119, 147, 196, 199, 215, 217–19, 250

Mathura 196, 298

Matthews, Captain 159–60, 220

Mazhabī 208

Mecca 46, 262, 264–5

Meerut 49
Mehtab Singh 37
Mehtab Singh Ramgaṛhia 98
*melī* 194
Mian Mitha 264
Mihrbān (Miharbān) 21, 195, 234
Milkha Singh 77, 98
Miṇā 20, 146, 153–5, 158, 166, 178, 180, 184–5, 195, 198, 200, 238, 243, 285, 288
Mir Mannu 39, 40–1, 122, 197
Mir Nasir Khan 46
Mirza Muhammad 27, 30, 123, 151, 195
Misal (*misl*) 20, 65–8, 70–1, 74–6, 88–91, 94, 282
Misaldār 66, 89, 94
Misaldārī (*misaldārī*) 2, 64, 66, 89, 94, 282
Misar Kalika Das (Kalikadas) 291, 295–6
*mlechh* 117, 178, 185, 209, 293, 297–8
Mohar Singh Atariwala 77, 273
Mohar Singh Shahid 98
Momin Khan 36
Muhammad Amin Khan 28–30
Muhammad Hadi Kamwar Khan 55, 192, 203
Muhammad Qasim Lahauri 125, 151, 195
Muhammad Shafi 'Warid' 193, 196, 203, 204
Muhammad Shah 19, 87
Mukhlispur 27
*mukte* 118, 245–6, 295
*muktī* 156
Muktsar 24, 139, 248
Multan 19, 31, 36, 40, 48, 80, 85, 91–2, 94, 193, 198

Mungher 111
*murīd* 246, 295
Murray, Captain 12, 64, 69
Murshidabad 268, 276

Nabha 27, 49, 72, 79, 80, 144, 257, 274
Nadaun 22, 240, 292, 297
Nadir Shah 19, 36–7, 39, 44, 56, 64, 251
Nahan 21, 28
Nainsukh 266, 269
Najibuddaula 49, 78
Nalagaṛh 20
*nām, dān, isnān* 116, 130
Nanak-Panthī 31, 123, 194–6, 289
Nandeṛ 8, 25, 27, 105, 115, 118, 130, 134, 217, 235, 241, 248, 284
Narain Singh 269
Narla 70
Natha Singh Shahid 72, 77, 84, 273, 275
Naushehra Pannuan 111, 218
Naushera 35, 121
Nibahu Singh Ranghretā 38
Nihang 34, 46, 65, 71–2, 119, 285
Nihchal Singh (Mohkam Chand, one of the *panj pyaras*) 153
Nirmalā 72, 86, 197–8, 285
*nishān* 256–8, 275, 287
*nit-nem* 164–5
Nurmahal 85
Nurpur 48

Padhana 37–8
*pahul* 23, 25, 70–2, 107, 111, 121, 129–30, 145–9, 151–5, 157–8, 160, 163, 182, 200, 202, 209, 212, 214, 241
*pahuliā* 215
Pail 27

Pakpattan (Pattan Sheikh Farid,
    Pattan Farid, Pattan) 77, 111, 119,
    138, 199, 218, 275
panch kakār 154, 238
Panipat 26
panj pyāre 23, 154–5, 293
panj-mel 200
Paonta 22, 272, 292
par-upkār (parsuārth) 112, 175, 178,
    187, 293
Pasrur 19, 28, 32, 217
Pathankot 48
Patiala 27, 49, 64, 72–3, 78, 79,
    92, 94, 205, 218, 257, 259,
    274
Patna 111, 118, 124, 130, 134, 199,
    217–18, 241, 247–48, 254, 256,
    284
Patti 35, 41, 148
pattīdār 66, 89, 221
pattīdārī 66, 89
Persia 49, 50
Peshawar 36
Phaphre 199
Pindori 40, 42, 59, 81–3
Polier, Colonel Antione Henry 60,
    61, 95, 157, 186, 204
Poola 38
Pragas Chand 269
Prayag 298
Prinsep, Henry T. 59, 64–6, 88–9
Pritam Das 86
Prithi Chand (Pirthia) 20, 195,
    196, 202, 238, 285
Purkhu 269

Qazi Mir Muhammad 86–7
Qazi Muhammadi 86–7
Qazi Nur Muhammad 46, 57, 123,
    125, 186, 196, 272

rabābī 85, 115
Rafi us Shan 28
Raghunath Rao 43
rāgī 85, 221
Rahirās 115–16, 130, 243
rahit 2, 6, 9, 25–6, 69, 104, 106,
    112, 117, 129, 131, 145–8, 153, 155,
    171, 177–8, 180–5, 188, 200–1,
    209–10, 235, 242, 245–7,
    249–50, 254, 283, 294, 296–7,
    299
Rahit Maryādā 164
Rahitnāmā (rahitnāmā) 4–7, 12–13,
    23, 53, 103–5, 108–9, 111, 113, 116,
    130–2, 135–6, 145–7, 149, 151–2,
    156, 170–1, 175, 177–8, 180–2,
    187–9, 200–2, 207, 210, 214–15,
    221–2, 234, 242
rahitvant 114
Rahon 26, 27
Rai Anand Singh Bhandari 87
Rai Chaturman Saksena 123, 196
rāj karegā khālsā 19, 23, 32, 37, 42,
    51, 53, 90, 92, 244, 281
Raj Singh 269
Rajasthan 271
Rākhī 20, 41–2, 61–2, 88, 90, 94,
    282
Ram Rai 21, 158, 202, 238, 257,
    285
Ram Raiyās 146, 154, 156, 178, 180,
    185, 200, 285, 288
Ram Rauni 39, 40–1, 272
Ram Sukh Rao 59, 71–3, 90, 121
Ramdas Ugar Sain (Masand) 257
Ramdaspur (Chak Guru) 20, 21,
    26, 32–4, 37, 39, 40–2, 45–6,
    52, 76, 78, 119, 120, 122, 125–6,
    134, 148, 157, 236, 249, 257,
    271–3, 276, 281, 287

Ramgaṛh 41, 272
Ranghretā 34, 38, 71, 205, 208
Ranjit Dev of Jammu 48
Ranjit Singh (Maharaja) 2, 5, 6, 10, 49–51, 64, 68, 71–2, 74, 76, 84, 91, 273–5, 277
Ratan Singh Bhangu 12, 33–8, 44–6, 59, 69, 70–1, 90, 109, 120, 251
*rauṇī* 39
Rawalpindi 77
Rohilkhand 47, 50
Rohtas 49, 273
Ropar 27, 29
Rukn ud-Din (Shaikh) 263
Rustam Dil Khan 28–9
Rustam Khan Bangash 44

Sa'adat Khan 44
Sabharwal 248
*sach āchār* 170
*sachchā sāhib* 103
Sada Kaur 80–4, 86–7
*Sadd* 143, 159, 162
Sadhaura 25, 27–9, 272
*sādh-sangat* 110–12, 116, 146, 165, 201
Sadiq Khan 44
Sahaj Singh Trehan 119
Sahajdhārī 152–3, 162, 168, 200, 202, 245–6, 285, 288
Saharanpur 27, 45, 78
Sahib Singh (one of the *panj pyaras*) 153
Sahib Singh 77, 80–2, 273–4
Sahib Singh Bedi 202, 274
Sahib Singh Bhangi (Gujratia) 48, 84
Sahib Singh of Patiala 72, 79
*sāhībzādā* 214, 216–17

*sahlang* 194, 199, 202
Saidpur 262
Sainapat 11, 102, 104–5, 107, 110, 114, 139, 147, 150, 183, 200, 207, 239
*sākhī* 7–10, 15, 54, 104, 117, 122, 216, 219, 234, 236–9, 241, 248, 250, 259–0, 263–5, 267, 286–7, 290, 296–7
Salabat Khan 39
Samana 25, 27
*sangat* 3, 21, 25, 69, 91, 101, 106, 108–11, 114–15, 118, 130, 133, 147, 177, 179, 183, 185, 199–201, 214–15, 217–19, 237, 240, 244, 246, 248, 252, 257, 270, 284–5, 288, 297
*sanjog* 211
Sansar Chand 269
Sant Khalsa 199, 244
Sarbat Khalsa (*sarbat*) 33–4, 65, 67, 89, 136, 138, 178, 206, 246, 287
Sardār (*sardār*) 65–6, 68, 70–7, 81–2, 84, 89, 91, 93, 121, 146, 196, 216, 251, 259, 273
Sardar Ata Khan (Ata Khan) 42–3
Sarhind 24, 25–9, 32, 43, 45, 57, 66, 68, 73, 121, 192–3, 248
Sarup Das Bhalla 9, 103–6, 119, 122, 154, 159, 201, 208, 216, 236, 241, 296–7, 299
Sat Srī Akāl 39, 77, 109
*satī* 112, 143, 153, 161, 163, 215, 220, 222
*sat-sangat* 114
Saurian 85
*Savvayyā* 115–16, 151, 156–7, 246, 248, 254

*sevā (tehal)* 181, 217, 243
Sewa Das Udasi ('Udas') 7, 9, 12,
    229, 236–7, 252, 290
Sewa Singh 236, 248
*shabad* 104, 105, 114–17, 124, 132,
    147, 150, 155, 210, 237, 243
*shabad-bāṇī* 101, 104–5, 116–17, 147,
    150, 210–11, 214
Shabad-Guru 105, 132
Shah Jahan 20–1
Shah Nawaz Khan 39
Shah Zaman 48–9, 50–1
Shahabad 27–8, 49
Shahīd 34, 65, 68, 71–2, 77, 84,
    98, 197–8, 273, 275
*Shahīd Bilās* 234, 236, 248
*shahīdganj* 46, 85, 120, 246,
    273–6, 288
*shahīdī* 36
Shaikh Ibrahim 263
Shaikh Kamāl 264
Shaikh Sharaf 264–5
Shams Khan 27–8
Sheikhupura 85, 275
Shiam Singh 70–1
*shrādh* 143, 283
Shujauddaula 78
Sialkot 19, 44, 72, 77, 85, 155, 217,
    273–5
Siba 48, 269
*Siddh-Gosht* 252
Sikandara 49
Sikhṇī  Gursikhṇī) 120, 147, 210,
    214
Sirmur 21–2
Skinner, James 187, 197, 204
Sobha Singh 46, 84, 98
Sobha Singh Dodea 98
Sohan Kavi 11
Sohan Lal Suri 40
Sri Akāl Purkhjī kā Khālsā 147

Sri Hargobindpur 271
Stephenson, Edward 30, 186
Stuart, Lieutenant Colonel Robert
    50
Subeg Singh 33
Sucha Nand 26
Sujan Rai Bhandari 123, 195
Suket 48
Sukha Singh 7, 13, 37–8, 40, 70,
    103–5, 109, 118, 155–6, 159,
    185, 201, 208, 217, 240–1,
    297–9
*Sukhmaṇī* 35, 144
Sultanpur 248
Sunam 194
Sur Singh 257
Surman, John 30, 186
*sūtak* 142

Tahmas Khan 40–4, 125, 196, 272
Taimur Shah 41–2, 48
Takht (*takht*) 33, 118
*tankhā* 13, 33, 151, 183, 213, 242,
    246, 254
*tankhāiyā* 214
Tara Singh 84
Tara Singh Chainpuria 84
Tara Singh Dallewalia 72
Tara Singh Gheba 269–70
Tara Singh Kathgaṛhia 98
Tara Singh Pathankotia 84
Tara Singh Ramgaṛhia 98
Tarn Taran 82, 85, 271
*teg* 6, 26, 32, 46, 54, 80, 92, 148,
    282, 298
Thanesar 27, 49, 248, 253
Thatte Kheṛa 271
Thomas, George 47, 50, 193, 204,
    220
Tiloka 27, 257
*tīsar panth* 154, 156, 200, 288

Udāsī 8, 15, 86, 98, 121, 153, 195,
202, 23–7, 252, 267, 285, 290
Ujjain 298
Ustat 234, 249

*vaddhā ghallūghārā* 44, 56, 70
*Vāhegurū (Vāhgurū)* 102–4, 111, 113,
115, 130, 149, 151, 155–6, 177, 183,
199, 207, 214, 218, 283
*Vāhegurūjī dā Khālsā* 147
*Vāhegurūjī kā Khālsā Vāhegurūjī
kī fateh* 130, 132, 145, 152, 157,
158–9, 198
*Vāhegurūjī kī fateh* 33, 131, 147
Valla 85
Van 35
*Vār (vār)* 9, 10, 108, 110, 126, 144,
234, 235–6, 237, 248, 250–1, 287

*varna (baran)* 156, 182, 185, 188,
206–9, 212
*Vidyā vichārī tān par-upkārī*
178

Wade, Captain 64
Wazir Khan 24–7, 193, 204
Wazirabad 77, 274–5
Wendel, Francis Xavier 60
Wilkins, Charles 124, 157

Yahiya Khan 38

Zain Khan 45
Zainuddin Ahmad 29
Zakariya Khan 30, 32, 33–8, 40,
56, 249, 251
Zorawar (Singh) 217

# About the Author

**Karamjit K. Malhotra** is Assistant Professor in the Department of Punjab Historical Studies, Punjabi University, Patiala, India. She has edited a book titled *The Punjab Revisited: Social Order, Economic Life, Cultural Articulation, Politics, and Partition (18th–20th Centuries)*, and published over a dozen research papers on Sikh history in national and international journals. Currently, she is working on a historical analysis of the Sikh literature of the eighteenth century.